THE BETRAYERS

Books by *Hubert Cole*

THE
BETRAYERS

Joachim and Caroline Murat

HUBERT COLE

Saturday Review Press · New York

Library of Congress Catalog Card Number: 72-79048
ISBN 0-8415-0179-3

Saturday Review Press
230 Park Avenue
New York, New York 10017

The author and publisher are grateful to the Mansell Collection for plates 3, 4, 5,
6, 7, 8, 9, 10, 11, 12, 13, 14, 15, 17.

PRINTED IN THE UNITED STATES OF AMERICA

To the guest
of the Ile St-Louis

Contents

List of Illustrations

(Illustration section follows page 64)

PART I

A Brilliant Young Couple
1781–1805

I

Nunziata was less than three years old when her father died, leaving the guardianship of his large family to her great-uncle Luciano, Archdeacon of Ajaccio, a careful and venerable man, who had been once her father's guardian too. Advanced age and rheumaticky knees kept him confined to his bedroom on the ground floor of the house in the rue St-Charles, tended by his almost equally ricketty sister-in-law, Maria-Severia. On the next floor the newly-widowed Letizia Buonaparte coped with the four younger children who were still at home. Above them, embattled and unevictable, because the apartment had come to them as a dowry, lived members of the Pozzo di Borgo clan, related to the Buonapartes by marriage, divided from them by politics.

The house, flat-faced and grey-complexioned, was sparsely furnished, with one completely empty room for the children to play in and scribble on the walls. Opposite, on the other side of a square of sand, uneven cobbles, and dispirited acacias, stood the Pietra Santa house, where Nunziata's *minanna* Maria-Angela lived. Indoors there was the shrill, elderly maid-of-all-work whom they called *mammucia* Caterina. Behind Caterina, silent, severe and short-tempered, stood their mother, a handsome woman in her formidable fashion, pale-cheeked and dark-eyed, a redoubtable disciplinarian, dispensing sharp words and slaps and thumps with a promptness that impressed even her austere neighbours in this harsh, unsmiling, joylessly conniving, proud, penurious country. They spoke admiringly of the time when, on a steep path where she had forbidden one of the children to follow her, she turned round, waited for him to catch up with her, paused just long enough to administer a resounding box on the ears and continued on her way without tarrying to see if the blow merely felled him to the ground or lifted him over the edge.

Carlo Buonaparte, the father who was less than a memory to Nunziata, had been a patriot and loyal follower of Paoli in the struggle for independence from the Genoese Republic; but he deserted the cause of freedom when the French assumed control of the island in 1768. He inserted the aristocratic particle *de* in his name, shrugged off the reproaches of his former comrades, and spent most of what remained of his life in Paris and Versailles, soliciting smart-money in the form of favours for himself, free education for his children, small concessions that might set him a little above his neighbours. He was a handsome, cheerful man with tastes beyond his pocket and an optimism unjustified by experience. When he died in Montpellier in 1785, a month before his thirty-ninth birthday, his wife Letizia, whom he married when he was eighteen and she fourteen, had borne him twelve children of whom five sons and three daughters were still living.[1] Widowhood brought her no deep sorrow but much worry. Her family, the Ramolinos, like the Buonapartes, had lived in Corsica for two centuries or more and, in common with most of their neighbours, claimed to be of noble and even royal and imperial descent. There was a stone escutcheon above the front door, but the ancestral estates were small and scattered and some of them disputed at law.

Nunziata was four-and-a-half in September 1786 when Napoleone marched into her life, a grown-up brother from a story book, smart in his blue uniform with red facings and yellow buttons, friendly but preoccupied, his mind engrossed with resentment of his fellow-officers who were better bred than he, who had been born rich and French, who expected as a right what he and his father had been forced to crawl for as a charity. Here in Corsica, where the Buonapartes had held minor office and French was a despised language, Napoleone was able to relax a little, swagger a little, get on with his project of establishing himself as the head of the family, leaping on to the shoulders of his elder brother Giuseppe and of his great-uncle Luciano. Peacetime service in the army of the King of France was not onerous. Nunziata saw a great deal of Napoleone during the next six years.[2] She also made the acquaintance of Giuseppe, who came home in the spring of 1788 from studying law in Pisa and brought with him a Tuscan maid-of-all-work to replace *mammucia* Caterina – forty years old, willing to do plain cooking, sewing and ironing for three or four francs a month – as Letizia had stipulated.

The revolution of 1789 set Corsica seething with factions. Luciano, the third son, returned in 1790. His poor health and myopia had prompted the family to withdraw him from the military school and send him to a seminary at Aix. But he now joined Giuseppe in the political mêlée, the two brothers elbowing their way towards the prizes that so suddenly appeared within their grasp. In September 1791, Napoleone was home again, and in the following month great-uncle Luciano died. Napoleone sharpened his challenge to Giuseppe's position as head of the family.

The Buonaparte brothers established themselves as party-leaders in Ajaccio and instigators of violence and mob rule. They acclaimed the return from exile of Paoli, the great patriot, but were soon working against his dream of independence for Corsica. They saw more profit to be won from subservience to France.

Nunziata was almost ten. There were whispers of promotion for Napoleone from lieutenant to *adjudant-major* in the National Guard, but the jubilation which followed his nomination for the post was almost immediately dispelled by news that all regular soldiers below the rank of lieutenant-colonel had been ordered back to their units. If he was to remain on the island, Napoleone must aim higher; and this time it was a matter not of soliciting an appointment but of winning an election, since all posts except those of adjutant and regimental sergeant-major were filled by vote. The house became full of strange visitors; Letizia provided free meals, free lodging and small bribes for those who promised to vote for Napoleone. Of the three commissioners who were to preside over the election, she entertained one in her own home and lodged another with the Pietra Santas; while the third – who had gone to stay with a rival candidate – was abducted at gun-point by Napoleone's men. There were protests and scuffles but the superior Buonaparte organization prevailed. Napoleone was elected *lieutenant-colonel en second* in the 2nd battalion of the Corsican Volunteers.

The unsuccessful parties – among them members of the Pozzo clan – took their grievances into the streets, where they were joined by many who distrusted the volunteers and wanted them to leave the town. Napoleone, who had been strolling in the Grande Rue, took refuge from the rioting in his home until some of his officers arrived to provide him with an escort. Letizia, waiting at the foot of the stairs with Paola and Nunziata, threw her arms around him, begging him to remain until the excitement had died down. Responding to the drama of the situation, he kissed the foreheads of his wide-eyed sisters and addressed them gravely: 'Honour summons me to the barracks and I go. I do not compound with honour. A man may not escape his destiny. If I am to perish out there, it is better that you should weep over my dead body than for my shame.'[3]

Sporadic firing continued that night and during the next three days. As a result of an inquiry by the departmental government, the Ajaccio National Guard was split in two, one portion being sent to Bonifacio, under the senior lieutenant-colonel, and the other to Corte under Napoleone. He was coldly received by Paoli, who refused to recognize his command. His excursion into the National Guard having led him into a blind alley, Napoleone returned to France in May 1792. The war department recommissioned him in July as a captain, but instead of going to fight on the eastern battlefront he collected his sister Anna from her school at Saint-Cyr and took her back to Ajaccio.

The outbreaks of terrifying mob fury in Paris, the deposition of the king and the increasing influence of the Jacobins, had crystallized the conflicting interests in Corsica: peasants against townsmen; churchgoers of the old order against adherents of the new and partisans of none; secessionists against Francophiles and even a faction that wanted union with Spain. These, in varying degrees and combinations, kept the island twitching with intrigue. Paoli, rallying both royalists and secessionists, was soon in open conflict with the Jacobin Buonapartes: Giuseppe, for whom he had obtained a seat in the departmental council, Luciano whom he had been employing as his secretary, and Napoleone who, failing to capture Paolist citadel of Ajaccio by a ruse at the end of April 1793, took refuge with Giuseppe in Bastia.

It was the early summer of 1793. Since the Archdeacon Luciano died, leaving his savings to Letizia and the children, life had become easier in the rue St-Charles. But now the Paolist patriots planned to strike back at the Buonapartes. Men came to the house again, this time by night, urgent, stealthy, low-voiced and smelling of fear. Nunziata and Girolamo, she eleven and he not yet nine, were taken across the square to stay with *minanna* Angela-Maria in the Pietra Santa house. Letizia left secretly with Anna and Paola, and only her half-brother Giuseppe Fesch[4] and the fourteen-year-old Luigi as escort. Their home was pillaged and set on fire by the Paolists. It was almost a fortnight before Nunziata was reunited with her mother – in the port of Calvi.

They stayed in Calvi for ten days, until Napoleone found a boat to take them to Toulon, fugitives from their native land, unwittingly leaping from the frying pan into the fire. Less than a month after finding rooms in the suburb of La Valette, Letizia was fleeing again, this time from the royalist rising on July 12. In constant peril as the mother of known Jacobin sympathizers, she flitted with the younger children through a succession of lodgings each more ramshackle than the last; Le Beausset, Mionac, Bandol; Marseilles, when the Revolutionary Army recaptured it at the end of August, in a fourth floor apartment in the dingy rue Pavillon in the old Port, then lofty but neglected quarters in the requisitioned Hôtel de Cypières in the rue du Faubourg de Rome from which its aristocratic owner had long since fled.

Here, thanks to the help of the representatives on mission from the National Convention, Barras, Fréron and a Corsican friend, Solicetti, Letizia was able to maintain a household that 'if not sumptuous, was at least decent.[5]' The younger children went to the private school kept by the citoyenne Dandou when money was available; when it was not they stayed at home, cleaned the house, learned to knit, spin and cook. Their passports described them – and their mother – as dressmakers, but they made more money as laundresses. Letizia, helped by Nunziata, did the washing; Anna and Paola collected and delivered. Here Nunziata fell ill and came near to dying; here Paola fell in love with the witty, debauched Fréron, twenty-six years her senior, and, since she was illiterate, called in Anna to help compose her love letters.

As the Reign of Terror tightened its bloody grip on France, so Napoleone's fortunes flourished. When it ended he was arrested as a Jacobin and friend of the Robespierre family.

Fortunately Letizia had other means of support: Giuseppe had met and was shortly to marry Julie Clary, the daughter of a rich Marseilles shipowner. Anna was engaged by the Clary's as governess and Paola as companion. Napoleone talked his way out of his difficulties and was given command of the Army of Italy early in 1796.

Letizia was comfortably off now. There was an opportunity for more gracious living: 'a salon, receptions . . . plays performed by candlelight in front of a couple of screens'.[6] Giuseppe's marriage brought the security of rich relations. Luigi, whom Napoleone had managed to place in the military school at Châlons, was almost immediately out again with a post on Napoleone's staff. Even Luciano, who had disgraced himself by carrying his egalitarian principles to the point of marrying an innkeeper's daughter, was provided with a job as commissioner to the army in Germany.

Marriage was a problem for the Buonapartes. Giuseppe's rich conquest more than compensated for Luciano's misalliance; but Desirée, the pretty, sharp-tongued sister of Julie Clary, whom Letizia favoured as a second daughter-in-law, somehow frightened off Napoleone, who, between the summer of 1795 and March 1796, met, wooed and married a widow six years his senior and a great deal higher in the social scale. Paola, though not entirely weaned from her affection for Fréron, was casting eyes at the town-major, young Colonel Leclerc; she was only in her mid-teens, but it was apparent that she was a girl who should be married as soon as possible. Anna was showing an interest in Pasquale Baciocchi, a serious-minded fellow-Corsican with respectable connections in Ajaccio and a sympathetic touch on the violin. To Madame Buonaparte he seemed an eligible suitor, but Giuseppe considered he should have more money, Luciano disliked his royalist past, and Napoleone was looking for brothers-in-law of more distinction and influence, while all of them resented his former attachment to the Pozzo di Borgo faction. It was a relief that for the moment nobody had to worry about the matrimonial plans of Girolamo or Nunziata.

Girolamo, in the early summer of 1796, was away at the fashionable, newly-reopened Oratorian school at Juilly. Nunziata, now fourteen years old, was quiet, rather overshadowed, lacking Anna's intellectual pretentions and Paola's importunate good looks. The terrors and uncertainties of the past three years had perhaps affected her more than the others. She had inherited her father's rounded features, unlike the rest of the family, who took after their mother; it was only in semi-profile that she showed a hint of their sombre, avian appearance, more owlish than aquiline.

The family had begun to modify its Italian ways, refining its heavy Italian accent, translating its Italian names: Giuseppe became Joseph, Luciano Lucien, Luigi Louis, Girolamo Jérôme. Napoleone had long lost the final e of his forename, and now dropped the u from Buonaparte. Anna was known as Elisa, the name she had had at school. Paola became Pauline, and Nunziata Caroline.[7]

At the beginning of May 1796, they were visited by Napoleon's first aide-de-camp, Colonel Murat, returning from Paris where he had taken news of Bonaparte's victories over the Austrians. Murat, ruddy-faced, full-lipped and flashing-eyed, a Gascon with a warm enthusiastic nature and a great way of charming the ladies, received a favourable response from Madame Letizia, who noticed that he had the same height, the same 'martial air and gallant bearing',[8] as her late husband. On Caroline he made a deeper impression; she fell head over heels in love with him. It turned out that they shared the same birthday, March 25, and that he was exactly fifteen years older. But there was no indication that the handsome colonel saw in the thin, shy girl anything more interesting than his commanding officer's young sister.

2

Joachim Murat was born at La Bastide-Fortunière,[1] a village in the heart of the bleak limestone plateaus in the ancient province of Guyenne. He was the eleventh[2] and last child of Pierre and Jeanne Murat; of his two surviving brothers and three sisters, the eldest, Pierre, was almost nineteen years his senior. The Murats supported their large family on the proceeds from a smallholding, worked by the father, and the village inn and posting station, where the children tended the horses while their mother waited on the travellers.

Jeanne Murat was forty-five when her youngest boy was born on March 25, 1767. It was her dearest ambition that he should become a priest. When he was ten, his father obtained a bursary for him at the Collège Saint-Michel in Cahors, through the influence of the Talleyrand family. From Cahors, with help from another local family of aristocrats, the de Corns, and money from his eldest brother Pierre, he went to a seminary of the Lazarist order at Toulouse. A month before his twentieth birthday, a light cavalry regiment, the Chasseurs des Ardennes, spent the night in Toulouse, on its way to Carcassonne. The uniforms, the horses, the glamour of military life were irresistible to the young priest-to-be.

His education and enthusiasm – and the emigration of many officers when the Revolution began – brought him steady promotion, though his outspoken advocacy of republican principles got him into several scrapes. By October 1792 he was a second-lieutenant. France had been at war since June. 'My family will realize that I had no great leaning towards the priesthood,' he wrote to a friend, 'I hope to prove before long in a more positive way that I was not wrong in wanting to be a soldier. I shall make my way, if God and the bullets permit.'[3] By the end of the month he was a full lieutenant.

His commanding officer, Colonel Joseph d'Urré de Molans, was promoted brigadier in February 1793 and appointed Joachim as his aide-de-camp. In April he was promoted captain. In May he was transferred to the 16th Chasseurs as a major. He was on very active service now, defending the northern frontiers against the advancing Austrians.

After the fall of the Jacobins he returned with his regiment to Paris, a city on the verge of insurrection because of the shortage of food. Police action against civilians did not appeal to him. He looked back longingly to his spell as aide-de-camp to Brigadier Molans, and told an acquaintance on the general staff that he felt he was in a dead end: In a regiment 'you are lost in the masses, and if you succeed in distinguishing yourself, jealousy prevents anybody from mentioning it'.[4] The ambitious young officer feared that the war was coming to an end and his chances of promotion with it.

The National Convention, purged and debilitated after the upheavals of the past year, tottered towards dissolution. In October 1795, hoping to give it a final push, a strange alliance of optimistic royalists, disaffected National Guardsmen and disillusioned simple citizens began to riot in the streets. Bonaparte, hanging about Paris in the hope of a profitable appointment, was ordered to take command of the artillery protecting the Convention. His guns, he discovered, were at Sablons, guarded by only a score of men. If the insurgents captured them there would be no hope of preserving order in the city. Bonaparte called for a cavalry officer; Murat appeared. It was their first meeting.

'Take two hundred horsemen,' said Bonaparte. 'Go to the plaine des Sablons immediately; bring back the forty pieces of artillery . . . Use your sabres if you have to, but bring them here . . .'[5] It was one o'clock in the morning of October 5 (13 Vendémiaire). When Murat reached the artillery park he saw a column of men from the Le Pelletier section of Paris advancing on the guns. He formed his men into line and the insurgents fled. At six o'clock in the morning he galloped into the Tuileries gardens with the guns. That afternoon Bonaparte fired his 'Whiff of Grapeshot', saved the Convention, and founded his fortune.

He did not forget the enterprising young cavalryman who had made his success possible. When, three days after his marriage to Joséphine Beauharnais on March 9, 1796, he left Paris to assume the command of the Army of Italy, he took Murat with him as his first aide-de-camp, with the rank of colonel. The night of 13 Vendémiaire had impressed him with Murat's efficiency; he now had the opportunity to observe his amazing courage. Wherever there was fighting, Murat was itching to take part. He drove the Austrians out of Dego at the head of two squadrons of dragoons and a week later, at Mondovi, when General Stengel was mortally wounded and his cavalry put to flight, it was Colonel Murat who rallied them, led them back into battle, and chased the enemy from the field. Bonaparte sent him to Cherasco to negotiate an armistice with the beaten Piedmontese, and then to Paris with the treaty signed by the defeated king of Sardinia. It was on his way back from this mission of honour that Murat made his first acquaintance with the Bonaparte family in Marseilles.

Awaiting him in Italy was promotion to brigadier[6] and more action. The Sardinians had quit the fight but the Austrians were as determined as ever to throw the French out of Italy. He remained attached to Bonaparte's staff, but moved from one division to another. At the end of June 1796, he led a sudden raid on Leghorn, occupying it without resistance. In mid-July he just failed to achieve the same surprise at Mantua; two days later he exchanged his cavalry brigade for a thousand grenadiers; a week afterwards he came down with a bout of malaria. He went to recuperate in Brescia, where he won the affections of the beautiful Madame Ruga, the wife of a local lawyer. He returned to duty in mid-August. While trying to storm through the suburbs of Mantua he was wounded by a sabre cut on his arm. 'That madman Murat!', his future brother-in-law Leclerc said to a friend: 'While the enemy was firing down on us from the walls of Gradisca with artillery as well as muskets, what does he do but go and rap on the town gates with the pommel of his sword and call on . . . the *"pekins"* to open them to him.'

His speed, as well as his courage commended him to Bonaparte. Murat, hurtling at the head of his cavalry through darkness and across rivers was the perfect spearhead. He had another quality that made him invaluable as the commander of an advance guard: 'On catching sight of a column, an army in the act of deploying, a division of any kind, he could estimate its strength with astonishing accuracy.'[7]

By April 1797 the Austrians had been driven back to Leoben and forced to ask for an armistice.[8] Within a fortnight in May, Venice was attacked and overrun. By June, Murat was back in Brescia with Madame Ruga, and Bonaparte was at the castle of Mombello near Milan preparing to impress his family with the splendour in which a victorious general could live.

3

It was a tense meeting for Letizia and the girls. Genoa, where they landed from Marseilles, was still in political turmoil; and their cavalry escort to Milan was clearly not simply a flattering gesture. Trouble of a different kind probably awaited them at their destination, for they knew that Napoleon was annoyed with them for having permitted Elisa to marry Baciocchi, when he had intended her for his chief-of-staff, Berthier. Yet he was unruffled when he greeted them at the Serbelloni Palace in Milan and then took them on to Mombello where they met for the first time the cause of *their* resentment – his wife Joséphine.

From Napoleon's lack of interest in women they had hopefully concluded that he might never marry. Now they beheld him tied to a widow with children of her own to be supported (the boy older than Caroline, the girl older than Jérôme), a woman of expensive tastes and a fashionable background in which they would be at a disadvantage. The fact that she treated them with infinite grace and charm and kindliness only compounded her offence. Letizia sat bolt upright and mute, determined not to expose to possible ridicule her inadequate knowledge of French and her thick Corsican-Italian accent. Pauline, who was to marry Leclerc had preceded them with Uncle Fesch. She was already almost at open war with her sister-in-law, derisively sticking out her tongue whenever Joséphine's back was turned. Elisa, anxious not to lose a potential ally until her marriage to Baciocchi had been forgiven, was reserved but polite. Jérôme, delighted to be on holiday, romped with his school-fellow[1] Eugène de Beauharnais, three years his senior and just appointed aide-de-camp to Bonaparte. And Caroline, suddenly blossoming into a beautiful young girl, had eyes for nobody but the brilliant General Murat, a magnificent peacock in his gaudily-braided jacket and skin-tight cavalry breeches. But his visit was brief; as soon as his military duties were completed he returned to Brescia and Madame Ruga.

Caroline spent the autumn in Rome, where Joseph had been appointed ambassador with the mission of stirring up sufficient trouble to provide the French with an excuse to overthrow the Papal government and set up an independent republic. This he did in December; and she was taken to Paris to join Letizia at Joseph's house in the rue des Errancis,[2] before going off to Madame Campan's academy at St-Germain-en-Laye.

Madame Campan had in her youth been a reader to Louis XV's daughters, and subsequently a member of Marie-Antoinette's household. She survived the Terror with her head intact but her purse empty. Having received what, for a woman of the time, was an extensive education (though shaky in spelling and grammar), she decided to provide for herself and her invalid husband by founding the Institution National de St-Germain for the daughters of whatever gentlefolk or would-be gentlefolk still existed in July

1795. Among her earlier pupils was Joséphine's daughter, Hortense de Beauharnais. When General Bonaparte, shortly after his marriage, came to inspect the school, he was favourably impressed. With the result that Madame Campan eventually found herself presiding over the most exclusive and prestigious school for young ladies in the whole of France.

The pupils were taught in four classes, distinguished, as at St-Cyr, by the colour of their hats, scarves and ribbons, from green for the youngest, through saffron and blue to the orange-red of the seniors. Geography, natural history, grammar and spelling were the province of the abbé Bertrand. Madame Campan inculcated those polite accomplishments which had been so lacking in society in recent years. The discipline was gentle yet firm. The severest punishment was to be condemned to eat one's meals at the Wooden Table, with no cloth and a slate suspended over one's head, proclaiming the nature of the offence. Madame drew her pupils into the more gracious days of yesteryear on a carpet of anecdotes, never impressing on them the importance of curtseying whenever somebody sneezed without mentioning the occasions when their martyred majesties Louis XVI and Marie-Antoinette had bad head colds and the ladies of the royal circle would be constantly dipping and rising in salutation; never completing instruction on the use of fingerbowls without the amusing story of the ill-nurtured member of the Assembly of Notables 'who, after spending a fortnight at court, complained that his health was suffering because every time he finished a meal the servants gave him a great bowl of lukewarm water to drink'.[3]

'I warn you that she knows absolutely nothing,' Bonaparte said to Madame Campan. 'Try to make her as clever as our dear Hortense.'[4] She seemed never able to escape these comparisons with Hortense – who was herself embarrassed by them, or so she claimed. 'It was the general's fault – he was too often setting me up as an example to his sister. . . . I made the most of what she did know. I retouched her sketches so that she could win a prize, but I never gained her affection. Her aversion for me even led her to make unjust complaints. To the general, she accused me of always shining at her expense and of being the cause of the minor humiliations that our fellow-pupils made her suffer.'[5]

Hortense finally taxed Caroline with having misjudged her.

Caroline, always more forthright than the rest of the family, responded at once to this approach. 'Her frankness disarmed me. She admitted she was wrong and confided to me that she loved Colonel Murat and that she had used every device to get back to Paris.'[6] By the time Hortense wrote her memoirs their rôles had changed; it was she who had long been jealous of Caroline: which may explain the unwitting demotion to colonel of Murat who had been a general for more than eighteen months. For that matter, a return to Paris from St-Germain would have been no use to Caroline: Murat was in Genoa lodged in a handsomely furnished mansion in the piazza della Fontane Marose and so reduced in pocket by his adventures with Madame Ruga and another mistress, the Countess Gerardi, that he had to borrow 12,000 francs from a friend to equip himself for the expedition that Bonaparte was about to lead to Egypt.

4

The campaign began badly for Murat, who was in the section of the convoy that had set out from Genoa. Never content to be merely one of a crowd, he was irked by shipboard life, by the lack of opportunity to distinguish himself. He wrote home to his father, saying he was not well. (In times of stress he often developed a bilious fever.) To Barras, now one of the Directors, he was more explicit.

'Bad health compels me to write to General Bonaparte today to offer my regrets at not being able to accompany him in his path of conquest. I can see his friendship for me diminishing every day . . . I do not think Berthier will ever forgive me for having spoken home truths about him. I have reason to believe it is he who is trying to turn the general against me . . . Be good enough, therefore, my dear Barras, to get me a posting somewhere else.'[1]

These moods of petulance and dejection seldom lasted long. A brilliant charge at the battle of the Pyramids, on July 21, 1798, his appointment as governor of the province of Kélioub, north of Cairo, the knowledge that the annihilation of the French fleet in Aboukir Bay on August 1 had cut them off from France for a long period – all this gave him occupation and stability. Early in 1799 he accompanied Bonaparte on the abortive expedition to Syria. After his failure to reduce Acre by siege, Bonaparte led the remnants of his men, depleted by at least a third, back to Cairo in June 1799. Three weeks later news came of the landing of 18,000 Turks, convoyed by the English fleet, evidently intending to join forces with the Mamelukes under Murad Bey; Bonaparte set off to meet them. Murat commanded the advance guard, composed of four battalions of infantry and all the cavalry with the exception of two squadrons. He found the Turks advancing westward along the Aboukir peninsula in the direction of Alexandria. At the approach of the French, the Turkish commander, Mustapha Pasha, formed his troops into two lines diagonally across the peninsula. The French attacked on the flanks. Murat, perceiving that Mustapha had withdrawn troops from his centre to meet the pressure, brought his cavalry through the gap and, as the Turks began to fall back on their second line, Murat's horsemen wheeled left and right, cutting them down or driving them into the sea.

The first line was totally destroyed. The second was based on the village and fort of Aboukir. Bonaparte opened artillery fire on the enemy left flank, to drive the defenders in on their centre. Murat, at the head of three regiments of dragoons, swept forward. But this time the Turks were ready; the French cavalry were caught in artillery crossfire from the land and from the warships cruising off shore. Though they were severely mauled and in danger of destruction, Murat rallied the men and, while the infantry stormed the central redoubt and captured the enemy batteries, he charged on into the heart of the Turkish camp. There he found Mustapha Pasha outside his tent, fighting on with his guard of two hundred janissaries.

Murat called on the Turkish commander to surrender. Mustapha replied by raising his pistol and shooting Murat in the face. Murat slashed downwards with his sword, severing two fingers from the Turk's hand. Two hussars dismounted and seized him.

The battle was over. A messenger took the news to Bonaparte that Murat had been wounded by a bullet that had pierced both cheeks.

'Is his tongue injured?' asked Bonaparte.

'No. He had his mouth open at the time.'

'It's the first time he's opened it to good purpose,' he said.[2] But in his report to the Directory he was fulsome. 'The success of this battle, which will so much enhance the glory of the Republic, is principally due to General Murat; I ask you to promote him lieutenant-general; his cavalry brigade has performed the impossible.'[3]

From his bed, where he was kept invalid for several days with a bandaged face, Murat wrote to his father: 'A Turk has had the kindness to pierce my jaw with a pistol-shot ... It is certainly a rare and extremely lucky wound, for the bullet, which went in on one side, beside my ear, came straight out on the other, without injuring my jaw or my tongue, or breaking a tooth. So they assure me there will be no disfigurement.'[4]

Bonaparte was delighted with the battle. 'It was one of the most beautiful I have ever seen,' he wrote. 'Of all the army that the enemy landed, not a man escaped.'[5] But this time he had a special reason to be pleased. On the previous night he had told Murat: 'This battle will decide the future of the world.'[6] He had left France a year before because he did not wish to be implicated in the misfortunes which threatened the Directory. His request for a seat in the government had been refused; he had rejected suggestions that he should attempt to seize power because he did not believe that the time was right. But recently he had heard from his brothers of the growing dissatisfaction at home and the series of defeats that French arms had suffered in Europe. It was time for him to return. He needed one dazzling victory as a springboard. Murat had provided it.

He waited for an opportunity to slip past the British ships. On August 22, having learned that the British fleet had sailed towards Cyprus to take on fresh water, Bonaparte left in the frigate *La Muiron*. Accompanying him in the *Carrère* were Murat, his wound almost healed, Lannes and Marront. On October 9 they landed in France – Bonaparte at Fréjus, Murat at Toulon. Bonaparte was on his way to Paris within six hours. Murat followed him. Good news awaited him in Paris – the Directory had confirmed his promotion to lieutenant-general.

ſ

In his scheme to seize power, Bonaparte relied on Murat to win the support of the cavalry stationed near Paris. One of the regiments was the 21st, formerly the 16th Chasseurs, in which he had served as a young officer, the other two were the 8th and 9th Dragoons, who had fought in the Army of Italy.

Faced with growing rumours of a *coup*, but uncertain from what quarter, the Council of Seniors, in accordance with a provision of the constitution, tried to assure their protection by appointing a general as military governor of Paris and commander of the army of the Interior. Guided by the conspirators, they chose Bonaparte. On November 9 he went to the debating chamber in the Tuileries and formally accepted the command, but avoided taking the oath of allegiance which should have been administered to him. The Council of Seniors and the lower chamber, the Council of Five Hundred, transferred their deliberations from the menacing environment of Paris to what they believed to be the security of St-Cloud.

Before dawn on November 10, 1799 (18 Brunaere), Bonaparte left the house in the rue de la Victoire, marshalled his troops in the Tuileries Gardens and rode with them to St-Cloud. With him went Murat who had the day before been appointed commander of the cavalry of the Paris garrison. Bonaparte went first to the Council of Seniors, who were assembled in the gallery and were for the most part opposed to the Directory. His task was to announce the dissolution of the government and the establishment of a consulate, and to give his assurance that liberty and the ideals of the revolution would be preserved. He blundered, faltered, hit the wrong note and left them antagonistic. In the Council of Five Hundred, which met in the Orangery, he had the advantage that Lucien was that day in the presidential chair, the disadvantage that the majority of the members distrusted him. Here his performance was even more pitiful. Greeted with shouts of 'traitor' and 'outlaw him', he flinched, almost fainted, and was whisked outside to safety by Murat. Lucien, determined not to lose the day by default, hurried out, leaped on a horse, ordered a drummer to beat a roll and harangued the troops drawn up in the gardens: 'Conspirators with daggers in their hands have violated the proceedings of the Council. The Council is dissolved!'[1]

Murat drew his sword. 'President!' he shouted, 'It shall be done!'[2] He turned to the grenadiers of the Legislative Corps Guard. 'Grenadiers, forward![3] Throw them all out!'[4] He led them at the double into the Orangery. The councillors fled through the windows.

Late that night there was a thunderous knocking on the doors of the Institution Nationale de St-Germain. Four grenadiers brought the news from General Murat to Citizeness Bonaparte that the Directory no longer existed and that General Bonaparte had been appointed one of the three consuls who would take temporary charge of the government.

'Madame Campan was severely critical of this military way of delivering information,' noted Hortense. But Caroline saw it only 'as a proof of gallantry and love',[5] for Murat had been very attentive to her since his return from Egypt.

Caroline had no cause to worry about Madame Campan's displeasure. Two days later she and Hortense left the school and did not return. She was to live with her brother and Josephine again – but this time in the Palace of the Petit Luxembourg.

Laure Permon, daughter of an old family friend, accused Caroline of having no conversation, and no interest outside her jewel-box, which, as she enviously confessed, 'was very remarkable for a young person'.[6] The one thing on which she had set her heart was marriage to Murat.

Napoleon was firmly opposed. 'She is behaving like a scatterbrain, with no thought for my position,' he complained to Madame Campan. 'There'll come a time when sovereigns might vie for her hand. She is marrying a brave man, but in my circumstances that is not enough.'[7] He browbeat the girl, reminding her at one moment that 'Murat had no intelligence even if he had a little learning; he had been raised as a priest',[8] and at the next that 'he had not even received primary education'.[9]

'One day you'll learn what it is to go to bed with a man who cannot control himself,' he shouted. 'Find yourself alone with him, without your chemise, and the man naked.'[10] The threat was not of a kind to make any of his sisters quail.

On December 24, 1799, under the new constitution that he had introduced twelve days before, Napoleon became First Consul and the most powerful man in the land. But he was still not head of the Bonaparte family. If Joseph approved Caroline's marriage – as he did – there was little that Napoleon could do about it. He sulked, was with difficulty persuaded to add his signature to the marriage contract[11] on January 18, 1800, and flatly refused to go down to Joseph's estate at Morfontaine for the wedding two days later. Once it was done he decided to make the best of it. He took the other two consuls with him to the ball that Lucien gave in honour of Caroline and Murat at the Ministry of the Interior, he established them in an apartment on the ground floor of the Hôtel de Brionne on the north side of the cour des Tuileries. He arranged for his brother-in-law to join the rest of the family at the top of the subscription list for shares in the recently-founded Banque de France.

They made a handsome couple, idyllically happy. 'Tomorrow I shall be the happiest of men,' Murat wrote to his brother André on the eve of his wedding. 'Tomorrow I shall possess the most adorable of women.'[12] The enchantment lasted. 'Isn't my wife pretty?'[13] he said to Roustam when the mameluke called at the Hôtel de Brionne one day; and Roustam found her indeed very pretty and very amiable, though she had a marked will of her own. 'The contrast of the rather childish grace of her face with the decisiveness of her character made her an extremely engaging person,' said Madame Récamier's niece, Madame Lenormand;[14] while Madame de Chastenay grew sentimental at the sight of 'the tall Murat, with sunburnt face and black hair, holding the gloves and fan of the slim, white little creature dancing in front of him'.[15] She took her husband out to St-Germain to show him off proudly to her old school-fellows, 'her carriage full of sugared almonds'.[16]

The honeymoon lasted six weeks. Then Bonaparte, needing another military victory to consolidate his position, appointed Murat commander of the cavalry of the Army of Reserve, and sent him to Dijon to prepare for an attack on the Austrians in Italy, where Masséna was besieged in Genoa. On May 9, 1800, Napoleon joined the army on the shores of Lake Geneva. Lannes, in command of the advance guard, crossed the Great Saint

Bernard in falling snow on May 16. By May 26 Bonaparte was at Ivrea, conferring with Murat who, now that they were emerging from the mountains, could at last bring his cavalry into action. Bonaparte decided not to continue southward to rescue Masséna but to strike west.

He unleashed Murat on the Piedmontese plains. By May 29 Murat had driven the enemy from Vercelli and was at Novara. On May 31, fighting from dawn until after nightfall, he was across the Ticino and in Turbigo. He had cut the way open to Milan. He entered the capital of the Cisalpine Republic at the head of six regiments of cavalry at 4 p.m. on June 2. There followed twelve days of confusion in which Bonaparte and the Austrian general, Melas, vied with each other in the mismanagement of their forces and the misinterpretation of each other's moves. In the afternoon of June 14, Bonaparte was saved from seemingly certain defeat at Marengo by the arrival of Desaix. Shattered by this incredible turn of events, Melas next day begged for a suspension of hostilities and agreed to withdraw all Austrian troops beyond the Mincio. Murat was back in Paris by the beginning of July, 1800. While he was in Italy the contract had been signed for the purchase of a small country house[17] in the village of Villiers, whose grounds extended to the Seine opposite the Ile de la Grande Jatte.

He and Caroline continued to live in the Hôtel de Brionne for a few weeks, 'she as pretty as an angel, he superb in stature, vigour, looks . . . It would have been difficult to be more unaffected than Murat, more natural than this future queen.'[18] Entertaining a friend to breakfast they produced at the end of the meal a coarse earthenware pot containing fruit preserved in grape juice. 'It is a treat in my part of the country,' Murat explained. 'My mother made it and sent it to me.'[19] Early in August he wrote to her. 'My good Caroline, who loves you very much, sends you her kisses. She is soon to make me the happiest of fathers, as she has already made me the happiest of husbands.'[20]

It was a happiness that they would gladly have shared with Hortense. Discovering at this time that she and General Duroc were falling in love, Joachim took Duroc on one side and offered him advice which no doubt came from Caroline. 'She is a romantic young thing,' he said. 'You will have to court her a long time before you win her. But you must declare your feelings – let her know that she is loved.'[21] Duroc slipped a letter into a book that Hortense left lying in the salon at Malmaison. She, with a priggishness that never quite left her, handed it to Caroline to pass to Murat and so back to Duroc. 'I do not know what fate holds for me,' she said, 'but I shall never have to reproach myself for having read a love letter from any man other than he who is to be my husband.'[22]

At the beginning of August, Joachim was appointed to form a special division of grenadiers and scouts drawn from existing regiments, but he did not spend a great deal of time with his new command at Amiens, leaving the day-to-day administration to his two subordinate generals. Caroline was still active socially – she went with Josephine and Hortense to the magnificent ball given by Madame Berthier on October 30, the day on which the contract of marriage was drawn up for her friend Laure Permon and Napoleon's former aide-de-camp, General Junot. Some weeks later she took Laure with her to inspect the alterations that were being made at Villiers and, to Laure's astonishment, managed to consume 'ten or twelve large bunches of grapes and two rolls' on the way.[23]

On November 8, Murat was given command of the Corps d'Observation du Midi composed of the division for which he was responsible at Amiens and additional grenadiers and carabineers already assembled at Dijon. He left for Dijon on November 23, but was soon writing anxiously to Bonaparte begging not to be put under the orders of General Brune – for he had learned that his corps was to operate in Italy where Brune was commander-in-chief. The tetchy pride that was at the root of his continual complaints, his bilious fevers and his dazzling courage would permit him to serve under Bonaparte but under nobody else. His suspicions were increased when the minister of War, Alexandre Berthier, ordered him to send one of his divisions from Switzerland into the Val d'Aosta and put it at Brune's disposal.

The solicitous Josephine assured him that, 'If there is fighting, Bonaparte will come and join you.' She told him that 'we talk of you every day with Caroline who, although very brave, cannot hide her tears when your name is mentioned. She still has her big stomach, which she is carrying very well; you can rely, . . . on my not leaving her for an instant from the moment she feels her pains. . . .' I have taken her to my heart as a daughter.'[24]

Caroline was indeed being cared for like a daughter by Joséphine and a sister by Hortense – though her relationship was that of sister-in-law and step-aunt. A little before 8 p.m. on the third day of Nivôse in the Year Nine (which would have been Christmas Eve 1800, in the old calendar) she was in the main salon of the Tuileries waiting to go with them to what promised to be the musical event of the winter – a performance of Haydn's *Creation* in the Theatre of the Republic and the Arts. Bonaparte led the way with his duty aide-de-camp and two other officers and Joséphine was about to follow him down the stairs when the young Colonel Rapp, who was to accompany the ladies, pointed out that her shawl was disarrayed. She let Rapp set it straight while Caroline, anxious not to upset her brother, who had not wanted to go out that evening, said, 'Hurry, Sister, Bonaparte is leaving already.'[25]

They hastened down the stairs and into their carriage, Joséphine and Caroline at the back with Hortense and Rapp facing them. Bonaparte's coachman was mildly drunk and driving faster than usual, so that the First Consul's coach and escort were out of sight by the time that Joséphine's carriage turned left and then right into the rue Nicaise.

As they entered the narrow street they felt the blast of a violent explosion. The horses reared, shattered glass from the windows fell on the passengers, the air filled with the smell of gunpowder. Joséphine screamed that it was an attempt on Bonaparte's life. Rapp leaped out of the carriage to investigate. Hortense looked down at her wrist, saw that it had been cut by the falling glass and wrapped her handkerchief round it. Caroline, completely cool, tried to calm Josephine, telling her that she had seen flames – a house must have fallen down – it could not have been intended to harm her brother. But none of this comforted Joséphine, even after a trooper of the escort returned to tell her that a barrel of gunpowder had been detonated in the street but that the First Consul was unhurt.

When the three women joined Bonaparte in his box at the theatre, Joséphine was white and terrified. Hortense was on the verge of tears. Only Caroline preserved an outward calm.

6

News of the attempt reached Murat on the last day of the year. He asked Bonaparte for permission to return, following up his request with the accusation that Brune 'has completely lost his head, he thinks he is going to be poisoned at every moment'.[1] Still determined not to take orders from anybody but Bonaparte, he pleaded unceasingly to be given the rank of *général en chef*, frequently wrote directly to the First Consul instead of to the minister of War, and constantly threatened to throw up his command rather than compromise his dignity. But Napoleon was not impressed. He told him he must stay where he was and, bitter blow, that 'the Corps of Observation forms part of the Army of Italy. You must therefore correspond with the commander-in-chief and account to him for all your operations.'[2] Caroline had moved back to the Hôtel de Brionne for the birth of her child. Other members of the family joined her in assuring Murat that she was perfectly well and that he must not rashly give up his post. Fesch who had dined with her and spent the evening playing *bouillotte*, reported that she was 'gay and happy'.[3]

While Brune held off the Austrians along the Mincio, it was Murat's task to try to re-establish the control that France had previously exercised over the rest of Italy down to the Kingdom of Naples, and to squeeze whatever concessions he could out of Naples itself, whose king had marched his armies into the Papal States. He made his headquarters in Florence[4] and it was here that he learned that his son had been born in Paris on January 21, 1801. Caroline wrote to her mother-in-law the same day. 'Dear Mama, I write to tell you of my successful confinement; I have brought a beautiful boy into the world. I know how much pleasure this news will give you, on my own account and that of dear Murat, whom he resembles. I beg you, dear and good mama,[5] to believe in the feelings of most tender friendship that your affectionate and loving daughter has for you. Murat, née Bonaparte.'[6] A few days later Hortense sent a friendly coy note to Italy: 'I am charged by Caroline to write to Murat – a task that I fulfil with great pleasure. I have many things to impart to him:

first, that his little child is in marvellous health and will be as pretty as an angel. Buonaparte [*sic*] who yesterday chose me to be the newborn's godmother, has named him Achille. Caroline, as always happens, has milk-fever, but they claim that this will be over in a few days. She sends you a lock of Achille's hair; there is very little of it but at his age it is difficult to have more. . . .'[7]

The news aggravated his desire to go home, to get on, to do something. Taking an active part in an active campaign – fighting, pursuing, celebrating success with friend or enemy – these were the elements of soldiering that delighted him. He was too much of a romantic to enjoy passing on the drab threats of military diplomacy, and too easily moved by the aftermath of military brutality. 'Here in Tuscany I am surrounded by ruins,' he wrote to Bonaparte on January 24, 1801, 'Tears flow from every eye and complaints from all quarters. Turn and turn about, from French, Austrians, Neapolitans and English, the Tuscan people have been the target for all the horrors of war and internal strife. Exorbitant levies have been imposed . . . Tuscany, which was so beautiful and fertile when you last saw it, is today penniless – Florence is deserted.'[8]

He went across to Ancona to demand the Neapolitan evacuation of the Papal States and acceptance of France's other terms – and thought up a new argument for being given the title of général-en-chef. 'You yourself authorized it by instructing me to tell the Neapolitan general that I should march against him with my *army* if he did not evacuate Roman territory,'[9] he wrote to the minister of War. 'I beg you will let me know by return of courier what decision the Government has taken in this respect.'[10] He was rather taken by this line of reasoning and on February 18, after concluding an armistice at Foligno, he wrote to Talleyrand telling him he had signed as *général-en-chef* and was now worried lest the Neapolitans later used this as a pretext for declaring the agreement void. 'Could you not, my dear minister, as a precaution and to guard against any results of my rashness, have me confirmed in the rank of *général-en-chef* which I gave myself in anticipation?'[11] Very pleased with himself he went off to Rome, where he was flatteringly received by the pope and made a great impression on the secretary of State, Cardinal Consalvi, who declared that, 'It would be impossible for me to describe all his virtues . . . honourable conduct

and moderation, and justice and candour, and respectful atten-
tiveness.'[12]

Bonaparte had in fact already decided to reinforce Murat's
corps, to rename it the Army of Observation of the South, and to
give its commander the rank he was clamouring for. But the order,
signed on February 13, 1801, did not reach Italy until March 1.
Caroline was growing daily more anxious lest Murat should throw
up his command in a fit of pique. Fesch joined his avuncular
reproofs to her wifely pleas: 'The Consul is paying no attention
to your eternal complaints,' he wrote. '. . . You cannot doubt how
pleased Caroline would be to see you, but she trembles at the voice
of her brother, who gets irritable, grumbles and swears if anybody
seems to oppose or anticipate his decisions.'[13]

Shortly afterwards, Fesch called on Caroline and found her in
tears. Joachim had written accusing her of not wanting to join
him in Italy, and of gadding about Paris and neglecting the baby.
He had written at the same time to Napoleon, urging him to
'scold Caroline, she is going to all the balls, she will fall ill, I shall
lose my dearest Caroline and your Achille his little mother'.[14]

Fesch replied indignantly that Caroline could not avoid
attending festivities in celebration of the peace. 'It would be
ridiculous to claim that she should refuse invitations from her
brothers, her sisters, her mother, all the family. And what would
she do with herself, all alone, when the others are in company?
Her child is in her arms all day; he goes to sleep in the evening;
surely you do not wish her to stay all night staring at him? . . . If
it were not for fear of his health – he was vaccinated only 5 days
ago – she would be leaving for Italy in three days' time; but she
promises that by the 15th or 20th germinal[15] either she will be on
the way with her child, or she will see that you are sent an order to
return.'[16]

On April 24 Bonaparte added as a postscript to an official letter:
'I have authorized your wife to proceed to Florence.'[17] Caroline
left Paris on April 30 and arrived on May 6. It was a passionate
reunion. 'I am the happiest of men,' he wrote to his mother,
sending her a portrait of the pope and two rosaries that he had
blessed. 'I have with me my Caroline and my pretty Achille.'[18]
They went to Pisa for a week at the end of May, to take the waters
at the near-by Bagni di San Giuliono. In August he was given

command of all French troops in Italy. After mounting a splendid parade in Florence in honour of the short-lived Kingdom of Etruria, formed from the Grand Duchy of Tuscany, with Louis, duke of Parma, he transferred his headquarters to Milan, a capital seething with political intrigue.

By October Caroline was certain that she would be having another child in the spring. If the baby was to be born in Paris, as she wished, she must leave almost immediately, before winter made the roads too treacherous. Joachim applied to Bonaparte for permission to accompany her, promising to return to Italy after a week in Paris. He received no direct reply, though Joseph wrote: 'When it is possible for you to come here, the Consul will arrange it,'[19] and Bourrienne, Bonaparte's secretary and former school-mate, explained: 'The First Consul considers your presence in the Cisalpine essential for the organization of the government that will be given it under the new constitution.'[20]

Caroline arrived in Paris on October 24. Napoleon received her pleasantly, told her to invest another 10,000 francs in the Bank of France, but said nothing about Joachim's return. 'Why the devil does not Bonaparte want me to come home?' Murat wrote to his steward, Aymé. 'My enemies must be kicking up the devil of a fuss to keep me away, pretending my presence is necessary here. I do not care, I shall leave on the 10th [of Grumaire, i.e. November] unless I get an order to the contrary from Bonaparte in person.'[21] But Bonaparte had already given instructions – this time through Talleyrand – that Murat was to remain where he was.

Floods descended on Milan and gloom on the Hôtel de Brionne. 'Yesterday we learned that you will be staying another month in Italy. I have never seen Caroline in such a miserable temper,' Louis wrote to Murat, 'and I got my share of it when I went to the trouble of paying my respects to her.'[22] She visited Letizia, stayed to dinner and poured out her troubles. It was not until December 30 that Murat got away from Milan, accompanying the Cisalpine delegates to Lyons, where Bonaparte confronted them with his new constitution for their republic, with himself as president, and a new title – the Italian Republic – as a sop to their nationalist aspirations.

He went straight on to Paris for the wedding of Hortense to Louis, a strengthening of the links between the two families that pleased Napoleon but not his brothers and sisters, nor either of the bridal pair. After a melancholy civil ceremony at the Tuileries, on January 4 ,1802, the newly married couple went back to the bride's old home in the rue de la Victoire for a benediction from the Papal Legate, Cardinal Caprara. When he had finished, Joachim asked him for a similar blessing for himself and Caroline. There was no doubting that they, at least, were still supremely happy.

Four days later Joachim was in Lyons with the First Consul for negotiations with the Cisalpine deputies, and then went on to Milan, where he declared the creation of the Italian Republic on February 14. He returned to Paris at the end of March. The alterations and additions at Villiers had been completed: he and Caroline entertained the family there on April 6, but almost immediately he was off again on missions to Rome and Naples to arrange the withdrawal of French troops to northern Italy in accordance with the Treaty of Amiens. Once more, he was away when their second child arrived on April 26, 1802. The baby, Marie-Letitia-Joséphine-Annunziade, was plump and large: large eyes, large mouth and a head so large that it would not fit into the bonnet that had served for Achille. Achille, who was just beginning to walk, sulked, refused to kiss his sister, and did not want her anywhere near him.

The Treaty of Amiens, bringing peace between France and Britain, was signed on March 27. At the beginning of June the Army of Observation of the South, was officially disbanded, a week after Murat's return to Paris, where, for the next five months he had time to occupy himself with his family affairs and his properties though he still remained in nominal command of the Army of Italy. Bonaparte encouraged his generals to make the most of the victorious soldier's opportunities for looting. He set the example and his subordinates were not slow to follow. Murat, who had been forced to borrow money to equip himself for the Egyptian campaign, was said to have accepted from Naples, at the signing of the Treaty of Foligno, the customary 'sweetener' to the negotiator on the winning side; a sum variously estimated at 'five hundred thousand francs in cash'[23] and 'fifteen hundred thousand livres'.[24]

Certainly, during the past year, Joachim had spent a great deal of money. In addition to the expensive alterations to the house at

Villiers, he had bought more land there, an estate at La Motte-Sainte-Héraye in the Deux-Sèvres, and the Hôtel Thélusson in Paris – the last two purchases alone amounting to a million francs. His obligations, both public and private, were increasing. He undertook the education of his brother André's son, Pierre-Gaetan, and daughter, Clotilde-Jeanne, and his niece Marie-Antoinette, daughter of Pierre who died in October 1792. He acted as host to the military on occasions such as July 14 – entertaining two hundred guests the following week to a magnificent dinner in a tent at Villiers, with a firework display in the park afterwards. A royalist spy reported from Paris on July 28, 1802, that, 'General Murat... displays the most revolting luxury at his house at Villiers; he is having the appartments parqueted in mahogany and putting lace flouces on the curtains worth thirty louis each.'[25]

In October he left for Italy to resume his command of the French troops and to supervise the establishment of the army of the new Italian Republic, taking Caroline, who was again pregnant with him. It was a delicate situation: the Italians, already suspecting that their hopes of independence were futile, resented Murat as the representative and brother-in-law of the man who had fooled them; he, warmhearted, eager to please, was unsure of his status and temperamentally prickly. He fell foul of the vice-president, Melzi, on his arrival in Milan and developed an attack of jaundice. On November 20, 1802, he complained to Bonaparte that Melzi 'has not yet received Caroline, nor invited me to take a glass of water with him'.[26] He subdued his pride and had Melzi to dinner.

'I am sorry if you are having difficulties,' Bonaparte told Joachim, 'but everything that is happening in Milan is making a good many for me. I have enough to occupy me at the moment and I insist that you do everything possible to get on well with Melzi.'[27] In a postscript, added in his own hand, he suggested that Melzi should be invited to stand as godfather to the new baby. So the child, a boy born on May 16, was named Lucien-Napoléon his two Bonaparte uncles, Charles for his Bonaparte grandfather, and François for Melzi. In mid-June Achille had the first attack of the epilepsy which was to cloud his early life: the result, it was supposed, of Caroline's ordeal in the rue Nicaise. They decided to send him to Paris for treatment. The new baby went with him but Caroline was not well enough to follow them until the end of July. Murat joined her in Paris a month later.

7

The atmosphere in the Tuileries was tense for reasons other than the First Consul's proposed attack on Britain. He was displeased with Pauline, who, widowed in November 1802, had found and married a second husband, Prince Borghese, in August, thus flouting Napoleon's injunction to stay a widow for at least a year. In October Lucien similarly defied his brother by marrying his mistress, Madame Jouberthon, whose husband also had died in St-Domingue of yellow fever. Napoleon ordered Pauline to keep her first marriage to Borghese secret and go through another one in public in November. It took place at Joseph's estate. Napoleon, by accident or design, was inspecting his invasion troops at Boulogne and unable to attend – and he gave explicit instructions that Lucien was not to be invited. It was a merry family occasion, despite the absence of two brothers, and of Joachim who had gone to Cahors to preside over the electoral college of the department of the Lot. Caroline and Hortense, gay young matrons of twenty-one and twenty, organized a game of prisoner's base, which their gentlemen partners entered into with such zest that one of them dislocated his shoulder.

At La Bastide the villagers erected a triumphal arch for Joachim. He picked up his mother, now nearly eighty, set her on his knee and proudly recounted his many successes, honours and responsibilities – and she delighted him by commenting, 'They're you are: they're putting such a load on the donkey, they'll break his back.'[1]

In the First Consul's absence his brothers began to assert themselves. Louis maintained that Joseph, as the eldest son, was the only one who could decide whether the family should recognize Lucien's marriage. When Napoleon returned on November 18, 1803, he discovered that Joseph, Louis, Hortense and Caroline had not only received their new sister-in-law but had also returned her calls. Finding Caroline and Hortense in the salon at Malmaison one morning, he burst into an angry tirade, accusing them of conduct unworthy of themselves as well as of him. 'I am trying to restore moral values, and a woman like that is brought into my family. I am the leader of a nation to whom I must account not only for my actions but also for the example that I set . . . The French are a moral people. Their leaders must be the same. I have duties and I shall fulfill them. I shall be inexorable. By heaven, I'm sorry I wasn't born a bastard. I might well be, for nobody understands me.'[2]

It was a tempestuous period for everybody. Napoleon often gave way to the strong sadistic element in his character, tugging the hair of his aides-de-camp, pinching women's cheeks and nipping children's ears, all in a pretence of friendly fun. He one day gave the three-year-old Achille such a vicious tweak that the child cried out in pain. Delighted with this reaction, Napoleon repeated the pinching with more force. Achille, stamping his feet and clenching his fist, shouted at him: 'You're a nasty, nasty, wicked, wicked . . .'[3] Whereupon Napoleon boxed his ears. Caroline fainted, and Napoleon strode out of the room, slamming the door and saying that Caroline had always been a stuck-up creature and that was how parents spoilt their children. The breach between uncle and nephew was never fully healed.

About this time Napoleon decided to adopt Hortense's son, Napoléon-Charles. This revived the suspicions Lucien had implanted in Louis's mind that Napoleon had been Hortense's lover and was the child's father. It produced a strong protest from Joseph, who would be deprived of his position as Napoleon's heir; and Louis refused permission, threatening to leave France and take the child with him. Napoleon did not give up the idea. One day, when most of the family was present, Napoleon took the boy on his lap and said: 'Little bambino, do you know you're in danger of becoming a king one day?' 'What about Achille?' asked Murat. 'Oh, Achille will make a good soldier,' said Napoleon – then, pleased to see that Caroline was furious at her son being publicly subordinated to Hortense's, he added, 'If you want to go on living, my poor child, I advise you not to accept any meals from your cousins.'[4]

Murat had been recalled to Paris because Bonaparte intended to use him in the assault on England. But now he found more urgent employment for him. For months past, royalist agents had been entering France in preparation for the *Coup Essential* – the kidnapping and possibly the murder of the First Consul, followed by the seizure of the capital and the government. The police were aware of the plot's existence but had failed to lay their hands on the ring-leaders. The *coup* was expected at any moment. On January 15, 1804, Murat was appointed Governor of Paris with command of the garrison, the National Guard, and the troops of the first military division.

At the end of January an arrested royalist revealed the scope of the plot and the fact that the dreaded Georges Cadoudal, the Breton resistance leader, was already in Paris, awaiting the opportunity to strike. In mid-February it was learned that Bonaparte's old military rival, Moreau, was implicated in the plot. At the end of February, General Pichegru, who had secretly entered France from England, was tracked down and arrested. But still Cadoudal remained at large.

Murat ordered the gates to the city to be closed each night from 7 p.m. to 6 a.m. Sentries were stationed all round the outside of the walls, each within sight of the next, supported by detachments of cavalry from the Consular Guard. Sailors set up guard floats in midstream opposite the barrière de la Rapée and the barrière de Passy. By day, all vehicles were searched and any persons whose papers were not in order were sent to the Prefecture of Police. Paris, in fact, was put in a state of blockade.

On March 9, after a running battle through the streets, Cadoudal was captured in the place de l'Odéon. Two days later, on Palm Sunday, his remaining accomplices fell into the hands of the police, the barriers were opened, life in the city returned to normal. And at Malmaison Bonaparte, badly shaken by his weeks of fear, put the finishing touches to a murder of revenge.

Had the *Coup Essentiel* succeeded, temporary control of the government of France was to have been exercised by the comte d'Artois, or his son the duc de Berri, as regent for Artois's elder brother, the comte de Provence. Among the conspirators' papers there were references to the prince whose arrival was awaited, but no identification of who this prince might be. On flimsy and inaccurate evidence, Bonaparte chose to believe that the unnamed prince was the duc d'Enghien, grandson of prince de Condé.

Certainty on this point was of little importance to him: reared in the tradition of the *vendetta* he was prepared to take revenge on any member of a family that attacked him, whether the attack was successful or not. Enghien was living at Ettenheim in Baden, only about ten miles over the border. On March 10, 1804, Bonaparte signed an order to the Minister of War, instructing General Ordener to travel under an assumed name to Strasbourg, where he would take command of a raiding party. 'The purpose of his mission is to proceed to Ettenheim, to seal the town, to carry off the duc d'Enghien . . . and any other person who may be with them.'[5]

Murat did not hear of the kidnapping until March 19, when he was summoned to Malmaison. Bonaparte told him that the duke was being taken under escort to Vincennes and that Murat would be charged with appointing a court-martial to try him. He returned to Paris, spent the night weighing Bonaparte's argument that he was justified in taking revenge in order to frighten the Bourbons and protect the legacy of the Revolution, and decided that honour would not permit him to take part in the affair.

Next morning, between 10 and 11 a.m., he received a dispatch from the Minister of War, enclosing a written order from Bonaparte for Enghien to be taken before 'a court-martial, composed of seven members nominated by the General Governor of Paris, which will assemble at Vincennes'.[6] Turning to his private secretary, Agar, he burst out: 'Bonaparte is trying to bespatter my coat but he will not succeed.'[7] He hurriedly dressed and then went to confront his brother-in-law. It was a violent interview. Bonaparte, 'his cheeks sunken and livid, his eyes hard, his complexion pale and blotchy, his appearance saturnine and frightening',[8] eventually brought it to an abrupt end: 'If you don't carry out my orders, I'll send you back to your mountains in the Quercy,'[9] he said, and dismissed him.

Returning to the Hôtel Thélusson, Murat found his chief-of-staff, César Berthier, brother of the Minister of War, waiting for instructions to notify the members of the court. Murat told him sharply that if he had wanted him to do anything he would have informed him. Who *had* informed him? 'My brother,' said Berthier. 'So that no time should be lost in such an urgent affair.'[10]

Murat boiled over. 'Well, you can go and tell your brother that

I've just seen the First Consul, that I've told him I do not wish to nominate the members of the court-martial, and that I will not nominate them.'[11] Alexandre Berthier shortly arrived in person and urged Murat to change his mind. Murat replied over and over again, 'No I will not appoint the military commission: if Bonaparte wants it, let him appoint it.'[12]

The minister of War left. There was silence throughout the afternoon. Some time between six and seven General Savary, commander of Bonaparte's shock-police, the *gendarmerie d'élite*, came with a letter from the First Consul, ordering Murat to appoint General Hullin and six colonels whom he named, as members of the court-martial, and to send forty of the *gendarmes d'élite* and sixty men of the Paris garrison to Vincennes, 'to carry out the sentence. Let it be known to the members of the commission that the trial must be completed tonight, and order the verdict – if, as I cannot doubt, it involves the death sentence – to be carried out on the spot and the condemned man buried in one of the courtyards of the fort. I have ordered Savary to come to you. He will himself designate the officers and men of his legion who are to make up the two detachments and he will see to everything.'[13]

Murat had developed one of his fevers during the day. He regarded Savary as his enemy. Now, flushing at this direct invitation to murder, he looked up from the letter and said contemptuously: 'You have your orders from the First Consul, you have no need of mine. I have nothing to say to you.'[14]

Soon after Savary left, César Berthier returned with the order appointing the commission. Berthier urged Murat to sign it, pointing out that Bonaparte had in fact named the members of the court, as Murat had asked – there was no point in refusing his signature as governor of Paris. Murat took the pen and signed. About 8 p.m. a messenger arrived from Savary – he had forgotten to ask Murat for the written order that he needed for himself and his forty gendarmes to pass through the city barriers at night.

That evening, Hortense and Louis, who called on the Murats almost every day, found Caroline deeply distressed. In the morning two of Murat's staff officers brought news that the duc d'Enghien had been tried, shot and his body thrown into the grave dug ready for it inside the walls of the château de Vincennes. Murat and

Caroline were still in bed. The officers delivered their message and saw tears come to the eyes of them both. During the previous day Murat had sent an informal message to his former aide-de-camp, now Colonel August Colbert, warning him to leave his quarters, not to return until morning, and not to say where he could be found. He had saved Colbert from the obloquy of serving on the court-martial – but, because of his weakness in signing the order that Berthier presented to him, he had not himself escaped being bespattered by the blood from Bonaparte's crime.

A few days later he learned that the *gendarmerie d'élite* were whispering that he had gone personally to Vincennes to demand the death sentence on Enghien. He sent Bonaparte his resignation as governor, ending: 'I will go back to my mountains of Quercy; then they can freely spread the story that Madame Bonaparte threw herself at your feet to ask for mercy for the duc d'Enghien, and that it was I who wanted him dead.'[15] Bonaparte, belatedly aware of the tide of resentment and disgust that swept through Europe, meekly accepted Murat's outburst and talked him out of his threat to resign. This was not a moment when he could afford to lose him. Shortly afterwards he produced an event of greater interest to occupy the world's attention. He had the Senate offer him the title of emperor.

8

Rumours had been in the air for some days before the official decision of the Senate was read to the Bonaparte family on May 14, 1804. And what the rumours said and implied did not at all please Caroline and Murat – in particular, that Joseph was to be appointed Grand Elector and Louis Constable of France, each with the title of Prince Imperial. If Napoleon had no male children, theirs would succeed to the throne.

On May 18 the members of the imperial family dined together at St-Cloud. The weather was heavy and thundery. When Caroline heard Hortense, in her quality as Louis's wife, addressed as *Your Highness*, she burst into tears, gulped several large glasses of water, but could not regain her composure. Bonaparte, now Napoleon, emperor of the French republic, amused himself by constantly repeating the new titles. At dinner the following day Elisa and Caroline openly expostulated. 'To listen to you, my sisters,' he sneered, 'one would think I had cheated you of your heritage from the late king, our father!'[1]

But the protest brought results. On May 19 Murat was appointed a *Maréchal d'Empire*. Next day's *Moniteur* carried the announcement: 'The French princes and princesses are given the title of Imperial Highness. The emperor's sisters will bear the same title.'[2]

Caroline was taking things easily, suspecting that she was pregnant for the fourth time. Her newly appointed *première dame pour accompagner*, Armande Saint-Cyr, was surprised and disappointed to discover that Caroline was 'very stay-at-home and does not care for society, so that except for a few close friends, she does not entertain. However, she had decided on an At Home Day: it will be Mondays.'[3] Meanwhile Madame Saint-Cyr found little to write about to her daughters in Italy.[4] There were the new bonnets – 'It is only the two princesses, Louis and Murat, Madame Bernadotte[5] and I who have them at the moment. The hair must be flat at the back . . . the bonnet set on one side . . . the ribbon brought up and tied on the top of the head.'[6] There was a tendency for waists to get lower, an absolute necessity for the *très grande negligée* to be completed with a cambric or lilac crêpe hat, very large, with a spray of bell-shaped flowers of the same colour. A spray of flowers was, indeed, of the utmost importance on both bonnet and hat. Apart from these items of news there was nothing to note except the steady rain outside and the wind whistling everywhere.

In March 1804, the Murats bought the adjoining property up-river from Villiers, the château de Neuilly, a long, single-storied building with terraces leading down to the Seine. Caroline went there in August with Madame Saint-Cyr, who reported that 'the weather continues to be detestable. It makes me ill, it gets on my nerves. We live very quietly. Some of the aides-de-camp stay behind in the evening and we play parlour games. We go to bed at eleven or midnight.'[7]

On August 15 there was the excitement of a visit to Notre

Dame for the *Te Deum* in honour of the emperor's birthday. But although the spectacle was impressive and the music very fine, it all went on too long and they drove back exhausted through the incessant rain: back to the daily round for Madame Saint-Cyr of two hours in the morning with the princess, dealing with correspondence and household affairs, rest until four, when it was time to dress for a return to duty at five and the prospect of another long evening of reading and polite conversation. 'I could not be more pleased with Madame Murat,' she assured her daughter. 'She is very kind and perfectly considerate – as is the marshal.'[8] But the fact remained that life in the imperial princely circle provided little excitement beyond waist lengths (which turned out to be staying very high after all), the princess's *déshabillés* (short, in embroidered and laced muslin), her flounced evening gowns, and her shoes ('they have the same fault as yours. They are too covered-in and too pointed. And her legs and feet are not as pretty and perfectly formed as her arms and hands.'[9])

Hortense, like Caroline, was expecting another child. This time the father was almost certainly Louis, though she had now fallen in love with Talleyrand's illegitimate son, Charles de Flahault. Charles, still only nineteen, was one of Joachim's aides-de-camp. Caroline, perhaps out of loyalty to Louis and perhaps from resentment at Hortense's poaching on what she might regard as her own preserves, publicly twitted the young man on his interest in her sister-in-law and, according to Hortense, told him in private that, although kind and gentle, she was too frigid ever to respond to his attentions.

Flahault avoided Hortense for a time. One evening in September, she went to visit Caroline at Villiers. Madame la Maréchale was on the island in the river. When she returned to the mainland, she was, Hortense noticed in the moonlight, leaning on the arm of M. de Flahault. 'All the blood in my body rushed to my heart . . .' Hortense recorded. 'The more he sought to speak with me, the more I avoided him; but the effort that I exerted on myself the strength of the emotion that I experienced told me the plain truth. I was in love.'[10] A month later she gave birth to her second son, Napoléon-Louis. Napoleon, who returned from his eastern tour on October 12, 1804, paraded all the available members of the Imperial Family in her salon on October 24 for the ceremony of signing the birth certificate. This was the first Bonaparte to be born a prince.

Letizia, still in Rome, where she had gone to visit Fesch in March, gave no sign of returning to Paris. She was offended because as a reprisal for her having stayed with Lucien at Frascati, Napoleon at first refused to give her a title. It looked as though she was unwilling to attend her son's coronation. She would not be the only absentee. Jérôme had joined Lucien in disgrace by marrying the American Elizabeth Patterson. Her other sons and daughters were complaining openly about Napoleon's preference for the Beauharnais family and the fact that Josephine was to be set so ostentatiously above them by being crowned with Napoleon.

He in his turn could not forgive his brother Joseph for being his senior and therefore the rightful head of the family. He accused him of stirring up all the trouble. 'They're jealous of my wife, of Eugène, of Hortense, of everybody around me ... Joseph's daughters don't even know yet that I'm called Emperor – they call me Consul ... Whereas little Napoléon [Hortense's eldest child, Napoléon-Charles], when he goes past the grenadiers in the garden, shouts to them "Long live Nonon the soldier!" I love Hortense. ... If Hortense asked to see me when I was in council, I would go out to her. If Madame Murat asked for me, I would not. With her I always have to take up positions for a pitched battle; to make a young woman of my own family understand my point of view I have to make speeches as long as I would to the Senate or the Council of State. They say my wife is untrustworthy and her children's attentions insincere. Well, I like them; they treat me like an old uncle; that sweetens my life; I'm growing old, I'm thirty-six; I want some peace and quiet.'[11]

He was not to have it. A few days later, his sisters rebelled against carrying the train of Josephine's mantle, again led by Joseph on behalf of his wife Julie.[12] Napoleon shouted that if they wouldn't carry it they could not come. There was a great deal of sulking on both sides until the princesses gave way ten days later. Caroline and Joachim moved to the Paris house in order to carry out their formal functions leaving the children with their governess, Madame de Roquemont at Villiers. Achille in particular was in need of quiet surroundings, for his epileptic fits had begun to recur.

The coronation was on Sunday, December 2; on the day before Napoleon managed to set the family in another uproar by having the Senate declare the status of Emperor hereditary in the legitimate issue of Napoleon or, failing any male children by him, in the male issue of Joseph and Louis. This was unacceptable to Joseph, who had only daughters and in any case claimed that he was the rightful successor, as head of the family. It enraged Louis, who had already refused Napoleon's demand to be allowed to adopt Napoléon-Charles on the surly grounds that he did not intend to play second fiddle to his own son, and alternatively found in the offer fresh proof that not he but Napoleon was the child's father. It increased Caroline's discontent at her own children being outdistanced by Hortense's. It gave the family an interest in persuading Napoleon to agree to the only solution that would meet the approval of all of them – to divorce Josephine and marry a woman capable of giving him sons of his own.

Resentment was momentarily forgotten in the excitement and fatigue of the celebrations into which they were dragooned by the new emperor. He had provided his family and officials with large allowances – Caroline received 240,000 francs a year – and he intended they should spend them in his glorification. Murat was seldom out of his uniform by day nor Caroline from a succession of lavish ball-gowns by night: the swearing by senior officers of an oath of personal loyalty to the emperor; the distribution of the Eagles on the Champ de Mars; the review of detachments of National Guardsmen from every part of the Empire; the opening session of the Corps Législatif, followed by the unveiling, by Murat and Masséna of a statue of the Emperor in white marble; the reception for foreign princes; the ball given for the emperor by the minister of War, by the minister of Marine, by Caroline (at all of which the emperor forbade the princesses to take part in the waltz, though Madame Saint-Martin, one of Caroline's four *dames pour accompagner*, did so, and disgraced herself by falling flat on her back while reversing, dragging her partner down on top of her, so inextricably entangled that neither could get up without help); the dinner given by the marshals to the princes and the great dignitaries of the Empire; the presentation of the members of the princely households to the empress; the empress's *cercle* on New Year's Day attended by nine hundred persons; the ball given by the marshals of Empire for the empress; the festival staged by the Paris municipal council for the emperor, who personally set off the firework display along the left bank of the Seine depicting his legendary[13] feat of leading his army across the St-Bernard pass.

There was joy at the beginning of February when Napoleon rewarded Joachim with a new title and a new dignity. 'You can be very sure of the pleasure I have in my heart, my dear granny,' Caroline wrote to her mother-in-law, 'in being the first to tell you that the Emperor has given Murat the title of Prince and has named him Lord High Admiral . . . I count on telling you in a month's time of the birth of a grandson. My other children are marvellously well and my own health is keeping up despite my pregnancy. Adieu, my dear granny, it is always a renewed pleasure for me to tell you once more how much I love you.'[14]

Napoleon enjoyed dispensing honey with one hand and vinegar with the other. On the same day that he honoured Joachim he also created Eugène arch-chancellor of the State of the Empire, with the rank and title of prince. In the official notification to the Senate he made it clear that his intention was not only to recognize Murat's service to France and the emperor 'but also to render what is due to the lustre and dignity of our crown, in elevating to the rank of Prince a person who is so closely linked to us by ties of blood'.[15] This insistence that Murat was being rewarded not on his merits but as Caroline's husband was likely to cause trouble between the two, and it may well be that Napoleon was hoping to widen a gap that he suspected to exist already. It was about this time that Hortense had a long earnest conversation with Caroline on the subject of loving and being loved. 'Her passion for her husband, hitherto so strong, seemed to have abated.'[16] Hortense assumed this was because Caroline was falling in love with Flahault. Certainly Joachim had renewed acquaintance with his old flame, Madame Ruga. On March 21[17] Caroline gave birth to her fourth child and second daughter, Louise-Julie-Caroline.

The child arrived opportunely, for Napoleon had arranged that the pope should baptize Hortense's son, Napoléon-Louis, at St-Cloud on Sunday afternoon, March 24. Murat promptly requested that his daughter be baptized at the same time. The Emperor's reply came as a slap in the face: 'Sunday's ceremony would be much too long if two baptisms had to be done; and there would have to be two quite different ceremonies, since the ceremonial for the one and the other are entirely different.'[18] So Hortense's child was important enough to be baptized by the pope; Caroline's was not. The snubs were coming thick and fast. A few days earlier Napoleon had been offered, and had accepted, the crown of Italy from his puppet Lombard deputies; and it was well known that he intended to confer it on Hortense's elder boy if ever Louis agreed to let him be adopted. The day after becoming King of Italy, he created his eldest sister Princess of Piombino so Elisa's children now were heirs to princely estates and titles. Hortense reported that Caroline 'with a forced laugh, said to us: "Well, here's Elisa a sovereign princess! She'll have an army of four men and a corporal. There's a fine thing!"'[19]

There was no melancholy in the note that Caroline sent to her mother-in-law to tell her of the birth of Louise. 'After having suffered a good deal to give you a great big healthy granddaughter,' she wrote, 'I am as well as could be wished, apart from a little tiredness. My daughter looks very like her father, and I believe will be as tall as he, to judge by her length when she came into the world. I beg you, dear granny, to accept these few pieces of material which are in fashion at the moment. Would you be kind enough to share them out among my sisters-in-law and nieces? I am adding some shawls and ribbons – none of which will have any merit except that of being given by you. I hope, dear granny, that if you have need of anything for yourself or for Murat's relations, you will let me know.'[20] 'My Caroline has just given me a pretty little girl,' Joachim had written to his mother the previous day. 'She looks very much like you; may she have your lovable qualities and your virtues!'[21] The old woman was becoming very frail. From Vienna later in the year he wrote to André telling him that he wished her to be buried on one of his estates and asking his brother to have her embalmed when the time came.

Napoleon left St-Cloud on the last day of March for his coronation in Milan and a leisurely tour of his new kingdom. The Murat household settled down to a period of peace and quiet. Had it not been for his duties as Governor of Paris, Murat would have expected to accompany Napoleon to Italy. He had served there with distinction; in recent times he had become familiar with the problems of its government and grown to admire its people. Instead, Eugène had been sent in January with a detachment of the Imperial Guard to take command of the entire Italian Guard – and in June came the shattering news that he had been appointed viceroy of Italy. Caroline took to her bed.

However, Napoleon was now trying to patch up some of his family quarrels. In Italy he had browbeaten Jérôme into agreeing to part from his wife; he came to Paris to call on his mother, who returned in December 1804, after the coronation, with the title of Madame Mère and on the last Saturday in July he attended Pauline's party at the Little Trianon in honour of her husband's birthday. Caroline was still not well enough to attend, but Murat went – and a week later Napoleon invited them to join him at Boulogne, where he was inspecting the army that he intended to launch against England.

PART II

The Emperor's Lieutenant
1805–1808

I

On August 25, 1805, Napoleon told Murat that he was to go on a secret mission. He had decided to call off the invasion of England. Instead he would strike against Austria, which, alarmed by the threat implicit in his assumption of the crown of Italy, had joined the coalition of Britain, Russia and Sweden. Murat was to leave immediately. Travelling by post-chaise under the name of Colonel Beaumont he was to reconnoitre the routes through Frankfurt, Würzburg, Bamburg, Nürnberg and Ratisbon, as far as the junction of the Danube and the Inn at Passau, and return via Munich and Ulm. Three days after his departure Napoleon announced his appointment as the Emperor's Lieutenant, with command of the Grande Armée in his absence. He was given the specific command of the Cavalry Reserve, the spearhead of the Grand Armée, an advance guard rather than a reserve: eight regiments of cuirassiers and two of carabineers, eighteen regiments of mounted dragoons and four dismounted, and four regiments of light cavalry.[1]

'See that your couriers are warned to deliver my letters to Neuilly, even when I am at St-Cloud.' Caroline wrote to him on September 20, 'since it is disagreeable for me to receive them in the Emperor's presence. Take good care not to leave lying around any letter that you do not wish to be seen, for you will be kept under observation. You know the Emperor likes to know what is happening with everybody, even down to the smallest details.'[2] It was a warning that most wives would not have found necessary to give their husbands in the Napoleonic police state, but she distrusted Joachim's carefree nature. She repeated her request to Agar, Murat's man of business who was accompanying him on the campaign, to ensure that letters were sent only by reliable messengers and delivered only to Neuilly. 'Take good care of Murat,' she told him, 'make sure he does not overtire himself; I recommend him to you and rely on your attachment to him.'[3]

The weather was depressing at Neuilly, she added, but the children were well. Achille, who she feared might be having a recurrence of his fits, turned out to be merely cutting a tooth.

Murat was at his headquarters at Kork, just across the Rhine from Strasbourg, where the emperor arrived in the evening of September 26. Somewhere to the east an Austrian army of 70,000 men under General Mack had begun to advance against France's allies, Bavaria, Würtemberg and Baden, without waiting for the troops that Tsar Alexander was sending from Russia. Napoleon, ordering Murat to move forward to Offenburg and send heavy patrols into the Black Forest as if intending to attack along the Danube, marched the main body of his force of 200,000 men northward. At Rastatt the French swung eastward, keeping the Swabian Juras between themselves and the Austrians.

The pace was hot; the cavalry were not fully recovered from their forced march across France from Boulogne. Many of his fellow generals resented Murat's appointment as Lieutenant of the emperor. Tempers frayed under the continuous rain. Murat in turn snapped and snarled at the emperor through Berthier, the chief-of-staff. 'You tell me to occupy Göppingen on the 11th and Geislingen on the 12th, and send one division only to Heidenheim, and remain in person at Göppingen,' he wrote to him on October 2, 1805, 'whereas in the last paragraph of your letter you express yourself thus: "The position at Heidenheim being a very important post for the enemy, it is necessary that M. le maréchal Murat should arrive there in force . . ." With the best will in the world it is impossible in the circumstances to carry out His Majesty's orders satisfactorily. I cannot be personally at Göppingen when you order me to arrive in force at Heidenheim, and I cannot arrive in force at Heidenheim when you tell me to send only a single division there . . .'[4]

Five days later he was well beyond the mountains and in sight of the enemy. With the prospect of action his spirits rose. The Austrians had established patrols along the south bank of the Danube. Murat found the bridge at Donauwörth blown up. He sent cavalry across higher up the stream, took possession of the opposite bank, chased the Austrians across the Lech, and pivoted to face southwestwards towards Ulm, where Mack with the main Austrian army was now virtually cut off from his base. Mack sent out a reconnaissance corps of nine infantry battalions and four squadrons of cavalry which took its duties so lightly, or was so unprepared for the speed of Murat's movements, that its officers were still at breakfast when French hussars drove in their advance posts in front of the town of Wertingen. Murat sent one of his aides, Exelmans, with two squadrons of Klein's dragoons to turn their flank. Following up with Beaumont's dragoons and Oudinot's grenadiers, he broke the Austrian squares and sent them flying for shelter in the woods. 'Your Majestys' troops have encountered the enemy and completely defeated him,' he wrote jubilantly, '2,000 prisoners, six cannon and six standards taken from the Austrians – that is the result of the first success of our arms in this campaign.'[5]

Two-thirds of the Austrian forces were herded back within the walls of Ulm and besieged there. The remaining third, under the Archduke Ferdinand and General Werneck, escaped in the direction of Bohemia. Napoleon told Murat to pursue them. In five days of hard riding, fighting pitched battles, throwing out encircling forces to right and left, leading cavalry charges in person, Murat captured Werneck and 15,000 of his men, 11 standards, 128 guns. The Archduke Ferdinand, deceiving Klein by pretending to open negotiations, escaped into Bohemia with scarcely 2,000 men. On October 19, Napoleon received Mack's surrender at Ulm. Making his way gently on to Munich he was joined there on October 26 by Murat whom he ordered to take command of the advance guard in the drive on Vienna. The Russians under Kutusov, who had reached the Inn when they received news of Mack's surrender, were retiring, picking up Austrian reinforcements as they went.

Murat, cantering through the frosted, snow-draped forests of oak and pine with his scouts, came suddenly upon an open space where eight Austrian and Hungarian regiments were drawn up in waiting. 'Murat had very few men with him, yet he had the audacity to attack them.'[6] The Austrians withstood the charge and counterattacked, driving the French back into the narrow forest road. Murat had his horse shot under him and was on the point of being killed or captured when a young artillery officer brought two guns into position. 'The grape shot ... bowled over the whole of the head of the enemy column ... The shock brought

down on us the masses of snow in the trees . . . the enemy squadrons disappeared in a cloud of smoke and a dense hail of snow,
some of which, fell from a height of more than a hundred feet,
clattering on the helmets of the fugitives . . . A sudden panic
seized the Austrians and set them in flight. Murat saw this, immediately returned to the charge, gave chase to the enemy, and
we slept that night twenty miles farther on.'[7] On the heights of
Amstetten he caught up with the Russians and, himself leading a
bayonet charge of Oudinot's grenadiers, drove them back into
flight again. By November 7 he was at Melk, recently evacuated
by the Austrian Kaiser, and his advance troops were at St Pölten,
thirty miles from Vienna.

Napoleon had sent an army corps under Mortier along the left
bank of the Danube with orders to maintain the distance of a day's
march between each division. Learning of this, the Russian
commander passed his troops over the Danube at Krems, burned
the bridge behind him and left an Austrian corps under Kienmayer
to distract Murat. While Murat overwhelmed the Austrians and
brought his headquarters to within four miles of Vienna, Kutusov
was badly mauling Mortier's leading troops at Diernstein. Unable
to blame Mortier, who had merely followed instructions, Napoleon
sent a furious dispatch to Murat: 'My cousin I cannot approve of
the way you march. You proceed like a scatterbrain and do not
weigh up the orders I give you . . . You have thought of nothing
but the vainglory of entering Vienna . . . There is no glory except
where there is danger; there is none in entering an undefended
city.'[8]

The waspish and largely undeserved reproof stung Murat to
reply that he was 'grieved and dumbfounded' and 'did not merit
this cruel treatment'.[9] Napoleon instructed him to stay where he
was for one day, then released him on Vienna. The main bridge
across the Danube was mined and guarded by Austrian troops,
supported by 7,000 men under General Auersberg, and covered
by artillery. Murat's advance guard of hussars and dragoons
rushed the bridge, but halted when they saw that the Austrians
were about to blow it up. Murat rode up with a division of
grenadiers, concealed them among the trees on the near bank and
went forward with Lannes to talk with the Austrians. While
Lannes assured them that their commander-in-chief had asked for

an armistice, Murat filtered his grenadiers across the bridge. By the time the Austrians realized they had been fooled, it was too late – the French cavalry had joined their infantry and disarmed the Austrian artillerymen.[10]

Kutusov had last been heard of at Krems. He might be heading northwest for the safety of Bohemia, or he might have gone north by east towards Moravia, risking the chance of being intercepted by the French in order to join forces with the second Russian army under Buxhoewden. Murat headed for Znojmo, sending out light cavalry to left and right, sweeping the area to east and west. At Höllabrunn he made contact with the advance guard of a Russian corps commanded by Prince Bagration.

Murat, playing for time to bring up his infantry, suggested a temporary truce. Bagration agreed to talk, and Murat was surprised and impressed to see that they were joined by Count Wintzingerode, one of the tsar's aides-de-camp. The discussion was detailed and important, the final proposal being that in return for an armistice the Russians would renounce their alliance with the Austrians and withdraw their forces from Austrian territory. Wintzingerode went back for confirmation of the terms by his superiors and Murat sent a report of the negotiations to Napoleon who was resting at Schöenbrunn.

The emperor's reply came early next morning. 'It is impossible for me to find words to express my displeasure. You are only commanding my advance-gaurd and you have no right to make an armistice without my orders. You are losing me the fruits of a campaign. Break the armistice immediately and march on the enemy . . . I cannot conceive how you allowed yourself to be tricked to this extent.'[11] Murat discovered that Kutusov had passed his main forces behind the screen of Bagration's corps and was making at full speed towards Brünn. He attacked Bagration, who had meanwhile strengthened his main position at Schöngraben.

The bitter fighting over broken ground lasted until eleven o'clock that night, by which time Murat had captured 1,800 prisoners and 12 guns, but had failed to prevent Bagration from retiring in reasonably good order. He pursued him along the road to Znojmo where he was in turn overtaken by Napoleon, whose rage had been increased by the news he received that morning of the catastrophic French defeat at Trafalgar.[12] After a stormy interview,

Murat resumed the pursuit, driving the Russians out of Brünn and chasing them along the road to Olmütz. But by now the table was turning. Kutusov had made contact with the second Russian army under Buxhoewden. Reinforced by Prince Liechtenstein's Austrian corps, he halted and faced the French. For a week the two armies confronted each other, making no move other than sporadic cavalry forays.

The Austrian kaiser was now with his troops, and so, unfortunately for Kutusov, was Tsar Alexander, flushed with his success at having got the king ? of Prussia's agreement to join the Allies if Napoleon failed to comply with an ultimatum to cease hostilities and evacuate Piedmont, Switzerland and Holland within a month. While Napoleon surveyed the ground and decided on the battle-field to which he intended to lure his opponents, Alexander convinced himself that the French leader, far from his base and with his forces dispersed, was facing certain defeat. Against the advice of Kutusov, who wished to wait for more Austrian reinforcements under the Archduke Charles, Alexander ordered the advance. At dawn on December 2, cannon and musketry fire boomed and rattled through a thick mist. A little before eight o'clock the sun broke through: the red Sun of Austerlitz. Within three hours the Russian centre had been shattered. By mid-afternoon they were in full retreat. As they fled across the frozen Lake Satschen, Napoleon ordered his artillery to break the ice with cannonballs. He claimed to have drowned 20,000 men in this way; the true total is probably not more than 2,000.

Napoleon returned to Schoenbrunn and, in the palace of the last rulers of the Holy Roman Empire, dreamed of the day when he would dominate first Europe, then Asia, then ... He planned to surround his empire with new kingdoms that would serve as buffer states and springboards for fresh wars of expansion. As rulers of these kingdoms he would promote existing princes who had served him as allies, or appoint members of his own family. The scope of his scheme was not yet apparent, but rumours were widespread. Joseph told the Prussian ambassador in Paris in November that Napoleon was forming a Polish Legion with a view to re-establishing the kingdom of Poland (which had been partitioned between Russia, Austria and Prussia in 1795), and giving the crown to Murat. A month later Hauterive, Talleyrand's righthand man at the ministry of Foreign Affairs, passed on the same story, adding, 'Prince Murat seems Polish enough: he is gallant, brilliant, bold, spendthrift, and Gascon.'[13]

2

Caroline had been having trouble since the autumn with an injury to her knee which prevented her from accompanying Josephine to Strasbourg. She kept closely in touch with events in Germany and Austria, forwarding requests for employment, news of the children[1] and of Murat's relations, enclosing aiguillettes for his aides-de-camp, urging him to write to her and to others of their friends. She had been worried because her letters were frequently not reaching Joachim and she was receiving few from him. She suspected that they were being intercepted and shown to Napoleon.

Early in December 1805 she persuaded Pauline to go into Germany with her, to spend the winter with Murat and Borghese. On December 11 they learned of the victory at Austerlitz and that the war was over. Pauline, never in a great hurry to join her husband, decided to remain in Paris, but Caroline set off on December 17, taking with her three ladies of her household: Mesdames Claude de Beauharnais, Lambert and La Grange. They whiled away the tedious and uncomfortable journey by playing on the fears of Madame de Beauharnais, who was terrified of heights and, whenever they approached a hilly stretch of road, was convinced that they would all tumble over a precipice. About five miles beyond Augsburg they were met by Exelmans, whom Joachim had sent to escort them. He paid his respects, turned his carriage round and led the way towards Munich. Less than a quarter of an hour later, Caroline's carriage suddenly slid off the road and tipped over in a ditch full of icy water.

'Madame Lambert and Madame La Grange finally managed to get out,' Caroline wrote to Hortense two days later; 'they broke the door window and slid out along the ground. Madame de Beauharnais, with her legs in the air, remained buried under the cushions with me; she grabbed at everything she could find, and unhappily I was the closest to hand. I can assure you that she did not spare me; her hands, elbows and knees pummelled me all over, and I saw myself on the point of being suffocated by my own dame d'honneur.'[2] Madame de Beauharnais finally saw a chink of light through the broken door and crawled out, followed by the much bruised Caroline, who had received such a blow on the shoulder that she had to carry her arm in a sling the following day.

On Christmas Eve she wrote again to Hortense, a gossipy letter from the Birkenfeld Palace in Munich which had been put at her disposal by Duke William of Bavaria. 'The Electress,' she told her, 'is tall and thin: she has a large goitre on the left side of her neck, but despite all that she is gracious and pleasing . . . Princess Charlotte, aged fourteen, is excessively ugly, as ugly as possible in every way, but she is full of intelligence . . . The Electoral Prince amuses me a great deal; we sometimes talk together for two hours on end . . . You will be surprised to learn that he is deaf and stammers, and when I talk to him everybody stares at me because I have to shout . . . Yesterday at the concert, seeing me take snuff and thinking that nobody could hear him, he said to me: "The most beautiful princess in the world ought not to take snuff." Now you will think he is blind . . .'[3]

Hortense had evidently suggested ways in which Caroline could get on better with Josephine, for Caroline told her that 'she is very well disposed to me, but I must say that I have been charming and have followed your advice'.[4] It was equally evident that Josephine, who knew all about the secret negotiations to marry the Elector's daughter Augusta to Eugéne, had not taken Caroline into her confidence. For Caroline's description of Augusta to her future sister-in-law was characteristically outspoken. 'She has a very pretty complexion, very pretty bust, horrible very red arms. Her head is a bit big, she has charming eyes, the same colour as mine, heavy eyebrows more than an inch thick, a straight nose, baggy cheeks, a very large mouth and very thick lips, much more pronounced than mine. Her teeth are not very beautiful, rather discoloured, though not decayed. Her mouth gives her an extremely friendly look, gay, very childish, and I do not think she is very intelligent. I am perhaps being a little severe, but I tell you exactly what I see. The Empress told me yesterday that they are going to marry her to Prince Charles of Baden. The marriage was arranged about a year ago.'[5]

Two days later she learned the truth. 'My dear Hortense,' she wrote at once, 'I hasten to let you have the news that you have possibly not yet received. The Elector of Bavaria has just consented to the marriage of his elder daughter, Princess Augusta, to Prince Eugène. Marshal Duroc was charged with making the proposal; he has just left me after giving me the official announcement. It is generally thought here that the Emperor will be back in a few days and we shall return with him to Paris, where the wedding ceremony will take place. So get ready, my dear Hortense, for fêtes and balls . . .'[6]

But Napoleon decided that the marriage should take place in Munich. He arrived from Schoenbrunn on the last day of the year, accompanied by Joachim, and on January 1, 1806, the obedient Elector's reward was proclaimed in the streets: henceforward Maximilien Joseph would bear the title of king of Bavaria, and his realm would be increased by the inclusion of the Tyrol, taken from Austria. On January 11, Caroline wrote to Hortense again, dictating the letter as she sat at her toilet and chiding her for not having written: 'Prince Eugène arrived yesterday morning; he is in wonderful health and now that he has seen his future wife I am sure he must be congratulating himself on the choice the Emperor had made for him. Princess Augusta is charming and I am convinced in advance that you will like her very much.'[7]

The marriage took place on January 13. Caroline and Joachim left Munich on January 18. Hortense stated in her memoirs that when Caroline called on her in Paris 'she spoke frankly to me and confessed that in Munich she had advised her brother to get a divorce and marry Princess Augusta himself'.[8] This is clearly untrue, for Caroline had written quite differently in her letters and, in any event, did not see Napoleon until several days after the marriage was announced; but she must have been distressed at this fresh advancement of the Beauharnais. When the emperor told Murat of the alliance – and that he was officially adopting Eugène as his son – Joachim made no attempt to conceal his resentment.

He was incensed that Eugène, who had remained comparatively safe in Italy during the campaign, should be singled out for such honour and advancement, and he was genuinely shocked at realizing that Napoleon desired to link himself with the old aristocracy and royalty of Europe. 'When France raised you to the throne,' he told him, 'she believed she had found a popular leader, a plebeian leader, and gave him a title that would set him above all the sovereigns of Europe; she did not intend to renew the monarchy of Louis XIV, with all the abuses and all the pretentions of the old courts. Yet you surround yourself with the former nobility. You have filled the salons of the Tuileries with them . . . They look on all your companions-in-arms, and you as well perhaps, as parvenus, intruders, usurpers. Today you claim the right to ally yourself with the royal house of Bavaria through Eugène's marriage; and you are doing it to show Europe how much store you set upon something that we all lack: distinction of birth. You pay homage to titles to authority which are not yours, which are opposed to ours; you make it plain to France and the sovereigns of Europe that you want to be the continuation of an ancient dynasty; and yours, make no mistake, will always be new in the eyes of the sovereigns.'[9]

Napoleon, twitching with anger, replied: 'I appreciate your courage and I shall always be glad to see you at the head of my cavalry, but this is not a military operation, it is a political act and I have carefully considered it. This marriage displeases you. Well, it pleases me, and I regard it as a great success – a success equal to the victory at Austerlitz.'[10]

'I hope,' said Murat bitterly, 'that it will not turn out to be as harmful for you as Austerlitz was useful and glorious.'[11]

In March Napoleon adopted yet another Beauharnais – Stephanie – as his daughter, and married her to the Grand Duke of Baden who had until a few months before been intended for Augusta. There was no more talk of Joachim's kingdom in Poland, but on March 30, 1806 Joseph was given the crown of Naples which French troops had recently taken from the Bourbon Ferdinand IV. The final disappointment was to come in June, when the Batavian Republic was transformed into the kingdom of Holland, with Louis as its king and Hortense as its queen.

The thought once more occurred to Caroline and Joachim that if all these favours were to be showered on others, and particularly on the emperor's stepchildren and adopted children, it would be better to persuade him to have children of his own. He had been

4. Hortense de Beauharnais, by J. B. Tegnault

5. Jérôme presents his bride to Napoleon and Josephine. Louis, Eugène and Joseph stand behind Elisa, Hortense, Pauline and Julie. Madame Mère is seated at Napoleon's left hand, then Stephanie de Beauharnais (Princess of Baden), Augusta (wife of Eugène) and Caroline. Behind them are Augusta (wife of Eugène) and Caroline. Behind them are Felix Bacciochi, Camille Borghèse and Joachim. In the corner, the Prince of Baden and Cardinal Fesch

6. Insurrection in Madrid, by Goya

7. The attractive Austrian ambassador,
Count Metternich

8. Joachim directs the attack on Capri, a painting by Eduardo Fischietti

9. Caroline with Louise, Achille, Lucien and Letitia—and Vesuvius in the background

indulging in brief amours during the past two or three years, but they knew that his attachment to Josephine, and lack of confidence in his own sexual potency, made him regard divorce and remarriage as a pointless disturbance of his domestic life.

During the winter of 1804–5 he had begun an affair with Madame Duchatel, one of Josephine's *dames du palais*. Joachim and Caroline were suspected by Hortense of encouraging the short-lived liaison, which was all the more galling to the Beauharnais because Eugène was a rival for the lady's affections. Napoleon made no secret of his interest in the young woman – a blue-eyed blonde in her early twenties – and on evenings when Josephine entertained in her own apartments he would make up a party of whist at the opposite end with Caroline, Claire de Rémusat and Madame Duchatel. Sometimes he visited her in her home and sometimes, if Hortense is to be believed, in the Murat's home at Neuilly. At Lyons in April 1805 he had met Madame Pellapra, who became his mistress probably in 1806. And in the spring of this year Josephine claimed to have surprised him in the arms of his sister Pauline.[12] Caroline and Joachim now set about proving to him there was a sound reason for obtaining a divorce – that he was capable of fathering a child of his own.

For their purpose they had at hand an attractive young woman whom Caroline had befriended the year before – Eléonore Denuelle de la Plaigne. Eléonore, one of Madame Campan's pupils, had been married at the age of seventeen to an army captain named Revel who turned out to be a thorough rogue. Caroline, whom Madame Campan asked for help, paid for Eléonore to stay in a pension at Chantilly until she could obtain a divorce. Now, however, she brought her to Neuilly, set her up in a little pavillion in the grounds and, on the next occasion that Napoleon visited her, introduced her as one of her *dames d'annonce*. Napoleon was subject to brief spasms of lust. One of them occurred at this time.

In March a scrap had been thrown to the Murats from the imperial table: the duchies of Cleves and Berg. With the formation of the Confederation of the Rhine on July 12, 1806, they were given more territory,[13] and the combined duchies were erected into the Grand Duchy of Berg and Cleves. Joachim spent most of March and April at his capital city, Düsseldorf, and returned there on July 19.[14] Caroline evidently intended joining him, for she told Hortense: 'I count on leaving the day after the emperor's festival. ... I hope you will want to come and be bored at Düsseldorf with me, for no court has been formed yet – but we shall see each other and, for my part, I confess that is worth any amount of festivities.'[15]

Napoleon wanted Joachim in position to marshal the advance troops for the war on Prussia. He was more than eager to begin. Prussian troops remained obstinately in garrison in parts of the Grand Duchy recently allotted to him and he prepared to turn them out by force. 'Your decision ... is sheer folly,' Napoleon wrote to him on August 2. 'It will then be you who are insulting Prussia, and that is very contrary to my intentions. . . .'[16] He knew that the losses and indignities he had inflicted after Austerlitz, together with the increasing influence of the Prussian war party encouraged by the queen, would soon force the king into action. 'You don't know what I am doing,' he insisted. 'Remain calm. With a power such as Prussia, one can never go too gently. . . . I cannot express the anxiety I feel in reading your letters. You are hopelessly rash!'[17]

'Your Majesty says ... that I do not know what you are doing,' Joachim replied. 'Oh! I know it only too well, and that is what makes me despair ... I am here in deadly idleness while another's arm will accomplish what your genius may yet conceive.'[18] (He had lived close enough to Napoleon to know there was no limit to the flattery and effusive language that he would accept.) 'Send me to the army, it is only there, serving Your Majesty, that I can prove that you have no more devoted, more dutiful subject, and no relation who better appreciates the honour of his connection with you. Maintain your friendship for me, and do what you will with my life.'[19] In a more matter-of-fact vein, he wrote to Talleyrand: 'Try to calm the Emperor, he seems a little cross with me.'[20]

Despite the irritation of the sabre-rattling across the border, where Prussian officers had taken to sharpening their swords on the doorstep of the French embassy in Berlin, he was enjoying his sovereign role. There was a letter from Prince Anton of Hohenzollern-Sigmaringen asking for the hand in marriage of Joachim's niece, Antoinette, for his son, Prince Charles. There was the designing of an escutcheon: the arms of Cleves and Berg and the imperial eagle, the double anchor of Lord High Admiral, the marshal's baton and collar of the Legion of Honour, a ducal mantle and an elector's cap, and above it a banderole with the brave device: FOR GOD, GLORY AND THE LADIES. There was the pleasure of notifying the sovereigns of Europe that, 'Divine Providence having called us to the government of the Principalities of the Duchies of Cleves and Berg ... in virtue of the Confederation of the Rhine the title of Grand Duke has been conferred on us with the rights, honours and prerogatives attached to the royal dignity, to remain in succession in our family.'[21] Each letter was addressed to 'My Brother,' a greeting that the king of Prussia took so amiss that he could not bring himself to acknowledge it.

Napoleon arrived at Mainz on September 28, and on September 30 decided to make a direct thrust through the Frankenwald in the direction of Leipzig and Berlin, turning the Prussian left flank. On October 7 he was with the main army at Bamberg. The Prussians that day demanded that he should remove his troops from German soil. Napoleon claimed this to be an affront to France and ordered a general advance.

Joachim led the cavalry on reconnaissance ahead of the main body, which marched in three columns. At Jena on October 14, Napoleon with 100,000 men encountered a Prussian corps of 35,000 under Prince Hohenlohe and put them to flight. 'The cuirassiers fell upon the enemy cavalry and overthrew them at the first impact; then they turned on the infantry squares and sabred them; they captured the artillery parks and carried confusion wherever they went; in short, that avalanche of men and horses, directed by Murat, gave us complete victory.'[22] On the same day, fifteen miles to the north at Auerstedt, Davout with only his 3rd corps attacked the main Prussian army. It outnumbered him two to one and was commanded by the Duke of Brunswick in the presence of the King of Prussia. With great skill and bravery Davout forced them back and won himself the title of duke of Averstadt. In retreating they became entangled with Hohenlohe's beaten men, each demoralizing the other.

Murat led the pursuit from Jena, encircling the town of Weimar and rounding up thousands of prisoners. By nightfall the next day he had received the surrender of the city of Erfurt, with 14,000 men and 120 guns. On October 16 Klein's division of dragoons, which Murat had sent northeast, cut the road between Erfurt and Sonderhausen along which Blücher was escaping with the king of Prussia. Blücher gave his word of honour that an armistice had been concluded and Klein let him pass. This brought down abuse on his head from Napoleon, who was heading with Davout's corps towards Berlin and maintaining a familiar patter of contradictory orders and disapprobation. Murat concentrated on preventing Hohenlohe, with the largest remaining group of the Prussian army, from moving eastward to Berlin or across the lower Oder.

Hohenlohe, headed off from Berlin, made for Stettin. At Oranienburg Murat picked up the trail. His two advance brigades under Lasalle and Milhaud, met and routed the Prussian Black Hussars and Queen's Dragoons at Zedenick and the King's Gendarmes at Boitzenburg, Hohenlohe marched his men day and night, intending to pause for breath within the fortifications of Prenzlau, but he found Lasalle's hussars had entered the outskirts before him. While he hesitated, Murat swooped on him with nine regiments of cavalry. 'Sire,' Joachim reported from Prenzlau on October 28, 1806, 'Your Majesty's orders have been carried out: Prince von Hohenlohe is in my power with his army corps . . . 16,000 infrantrymen, six cavalry regiments, sixty pieces of artillery, sixty standards, Prince August Ferdinand.'[23] At Pasewalk, Milhaud's two regiments defeated six of the enemy and two battalions of infantry. Lasalle moved on to Stettin and, by nothing more than threats, obtained its surrender.

Napoleon was in Berlin. His sunny mood was reflected in his dispatch of October 31 to Murat: 'I compliment you on the capture of Stettin. If your light cavalry takes fortified towns like this, I shall have to disband the engineers and melt down my heavy artillery.'[24]

The king of Prussia had escaped across the Oder and was on his way to refuge with the Russians. Blücher remained at large with more than 20,000 men, probably making for Stralsund, where he could transport them by sea to East Pomerania. Murat resumed the chase, blocked Blücher's northward route at Jarmen and Demmin, and herded him in the direction of Schwerin. On

November 4, Blücher was outside the free town of Lübeck and Bernadotte with 1st Corps had joined Murat. Next day, Blücher broke into the city but the French also broke in after him. He made for the Danish frontier. Murat headed him off for the last time. 'Sire,' he wrote to Napoleon on November 7, 'the combat has ended for lack of combatants.'[25]

It was the end of 'one of the most extraordinary pursuits recorded in history, and sufficient in itself to class Murat among the first of cavalry generals'.[26] He was often criticized for driving his men and horses too fast and too far. But without these almost superhuman pursuits many a battle and campaign would have fallen short of total victory. 'If Murat had halted, if he had feared tiring his horses, if he had had but one moment of indecision, the Prussians would have reached Stettin, which would have been defended, and Napoleon's armies would perhaps have been obliged to halt on the Oder, whereas he could now move them without hindrance up to the Vistula.'[27]

3

Two days before he entered Berlin, Napoleon proclaimed to his troops: 'Soldiers, the Russians boast that they are coming against us; we shall go to meet them.'[1] He advanced the 3rd, 5th and 7th corps under Davout, Lannes and Augereau, to the line of the Oder, supported by a newly formed corps of Würtembergers and Bavarians under Jérôme. The units which had taken part in the great pursuit of the Prussians were rested in the second line at Berlin, but Murat was sent to take command of the forward troops, which had now reached Posen. With Beaumont's dragoons from the cavalry reserve, and the light cavalry of Davout's 3rd corps, he rode eastward. At his approach the advance guard of the Russian general Bennigsen's 90,000 men fell back to the right bank of the Vistula. Three weeks' march to the east, a second Russian army of 40,000 men was approaching under Buxhoeden.

Through swamps and dismal forests of firs, along roads that were little more than tracks on which the summer's dust had turned to winter mud, the French marched on Warsaw, once the capital of an independent Poland, now a neglected provincial town at the eastern edge of the Prussian domain. Murat rode in at the head of the 1st Chasseurs on November 28, 1806. It was raining, but the streets – irregular and lined with a jumble of hovels and decaying palaces, an almost welcome contrast after the rectilinear symmetry of Berlin – were crowded with delirious patriots, convinced that the arrival of the French army marked the restitution of Polish independence, and spontaneously recognizing as their new ruler the tall, muscular, strikingly handsome, surprisingly amiable marshal-grand-duke who led the liberators, a figure of theatrical improbability from the white plume in his hat and his jet black curls, to the white silk breeches, jewelled sabre, gold spurs and bridle, and the sprawled tiger-skin beneath his saddle – 'a young prince who threw himself into the midst of enemy batteries as if into a ballroom'.[2] It was a triumphant entry, a royal welcome.

While his troops feasted in the drizzle at tables loaded with food and wine that the citizens had set out in the streets, Murat established himself in the untenanted Roczynski Palace; but neglect had gone too far: as soon as fires were lit the clogged chimneys filled the building with smoke. He moved to the home of the Countess Potocka, a disdainful hostess who retired to the upper floor and, in her memoirs, made no secret of her contempt for this upstart. 'It was easy to see that his manners were put on for the occasion, and would be quite different at other times. He did not express himself badly, for he kept a close watch on himself; but his Gascon accent and some over-soldierly expressions rather gave the lie to "the Prince" . . . Murat had already contracted princely habits: he did not chat, he spoke, flattering himself that he was listened to, if not with pleasure, at least with respectful deference.'[3] Barante, who called on him about this time, formed quite a different opinion: 'He was talkative, without any princely airs, and politely familiar.'[4]

'The Poles,' the countess brought herself to admit, 'charmed by such valour,'[5] would readily have placed a crown on Murat's head. Duroc, Grand Marshal of the Palace and one of the emperor's closest companions, told Junot: 'This nation wants a king from us. King Murat would please them greatly, with his panaches and his brilliant uniforms, but above all because of his bravery.'[6]

The bulletin announcing Joachim's entry into Warsaw had said: 'Will the throne of Poland be re-established? . . . Only God, who holds in his hands the combination of all events, can be the arbiter of this great political problem.'[7] Napoleon was keeping the world – and his family – in suspense.

'Everybody in Paris says you are to be King of Poland,' Paulette wrote to Joachim. 'For myself I wish it if it will please you, but I shall be cross because it will keep me so far from you.'[8] 'I rejoice in all your successes as much as you do,' wrote Fouché. 'I am eager to see them crowned with the happiest conclusion and to learn of the re-establishment of the king of Poland.'[9] And shortly afterwards: 'May we soon see Poland restored to the status of a nation. It is not for your personal happiness that I desire to see you at the head of this new nation, but for the welfare and tranquillity of our empire.'[10]

A delegation of notables called at the Potocka palace and asked him to forward a petition to Napoleon. It was a request that the emperor should proclaim the independence of Poland and give the nation a king chosen from among his own family. Joachim did as he was asked, and waited. The courier returned with Napoleon's reply: 'Let them know that I have not come to beg a throne for one of my relations. I have no lack of thrones to give my family.'[11]

It was like a bucket of icy water, and, combined with the fatigues of the past month in miserable weather, brought on the usual bout of fever. Murat took to his bed, leaving command of the reconnaissance forces to Nansouty. Napoleon arrived in Warsaw on December 19 and forbade him to resume command of his troop until he was fully recovered, but when the army moved forward on December 23 he was back in the saddle again. 'My day's ride has done me a lot of good,' he wrote to Napoleon on Christmas Day. 'And I feel much better than I did this morning.'[12] His next night's lodging was in a stable at Golymin, shared with Augereau.

The emperor had taken personal command. They went northward across the Vistula and the Bug. The rain fell in torrents, bogging down the artillery, halving the pace of the infantry, slowing the cavalry to a walk. Napoleon had no idea where the enemy forces were concentrated. His scattered army corps stumbled on them haphazard, gave battle, lost touch. He went back to Warsaw by way of Pultusk where, on the last day of the year, a message reached him that Eléonore de la Plaigne had given birth to a boy who greatly resembled him.[13]

On New Year's Day, 1807, at a posting house between Pultusk and Warsaw, Napoleon caught sight of the young Countess Walewska. Using Polish independence as a bait and Duroc as his pimp, he made her his mistress later in the month. On January 28, learning that Bennigsen had moved east to attack Bernadotte's 1st Corps, he ordered an advance northward. On February 1 a dispatch from Berthier giving Napoleon's plans in detail fell into the hands of Bennigsen's Cossack patrols. Bennigsen swung away. Murat, seeking the enemy in the forests south of Freymarckt, came upon them between Sienken and Hof: a force of a dozen battalions of infantry supported by cavalry and artillery under Barclay de Tolly, entrenched on the far side of a marshy stream. The only means of crossing the stream was a bridge just wide enough to take four horsemen abreast.

His critics said of Murat that as a general he knew only two words of command: one was 'Forward!' and the other was 'Charge!' He gave the first one now. Under heavy fire, from the infantry on their left and artillery on their right, the 3rd Hussars and 10th Chasseurs of 6 Corps galloped across the bridge, faltered and were flung back. Reinforced by two regiments of dragoons from Klein's division, they returned to the attack, captured four guns, but were again driven back. The 1st Cuirassiers and the remaining two regiments of Klein's dragoons were now over the bridge. They made a third attack, and this too was repulsed. Murat rode to the centre of Hautpoul's division of Cuirassiers: 'his tunic covered with embroidery, white breeches, half boots, a marten-fur busby with a red crown and black ostrich plumes, an antique sword slung on a baldric across his chest, its jewelled hilt sparkling in the sunlight.'[14] Thus signalling himself as the main target for the enemy fire, he raised his riding crop and thundered out his second order: 'Charge!' The line of horsemen leaped forward, irresistibly pounding upon the Russian infantry, overturning their cavalry, flooding about the guns. 'Sire,' Murat, wrote from the captured village of Hoff at ten o'clock that night. 'Your Majesty's cavalry has today deserved the praise that you have so often lavished on it ... The day has ended with the capture of 9 pieces of artillery, 4 standards, 700 to 800 prisoners, and 1,000 to 1,500 dead on the field of battle.'[15]

Next day he stormed the plateau of Ziegelhof, still hard on the heels of the Russians, and then drove them out of the village of Preussisch-Eylau, where Napoleon joined him that evening. It looked as though the enemy was turning to fight a pitched battle, and Napoleon had once again dispersed his forces too far. He sent urgent dispatches for Ney and Davout to converge on him. But when the Russians – 80,000 men with 400 guns – opened artillery fire at dawn, he still had only Murat's cavalry, the three infantry divisions of Soult's 4th Corps, with 150 guns, and the 10,000 men of Augereau's 7th Corps in reserve. Throughout the morning the two armies faced each other, exchanging artillery fire in which the French were at a grave disadvantage. At midday Davout arrived and was ordered to attack the Russian left wing. Bennigsen committed some of his reserves and Napoleon thought he saw a chance to pierce the Russian centre. He threw Augereau's force into a gathering snowstorm. Blinded by the snow, they swung left and marched unaware on to a massed Russian battery of 72 guns. 7th Corps lost 5,000 men in a few minutes. The Russian cavalry hurled back the remaining men. The Russian infantry advanced in line behind them.

Soult's corps had half its men out of action. Augereau's no longer existed as a fighting entity. Davout's was desperately engaged on the right. Murat brought up the whole of his cavalry, eighty squadrons. At the head of Grouchy's dragoons, he trotted them across the exposed French front, and then, forming each squadron to the right, galloped them in line after line upon the Russian infantry. Grouchy's dragoons, followed by Hautpoul's cuirassiers, followed by Klein's dragoons, and on the flanks Lasalle's hussars, Milhaud's chasseurs. The shock and fury were so great that the first two lines of the Russians were bowled completely over, and the French found themselves halted by the third and last line. They regrouped, but were now faced by the uninjured men who had turned about. They were caught between two fires, with not enough room to gather momentum to burst their way out. But Bessières charged with the mounted grenadiers and chasseurs of the Guard and, reopening the breach made by Murat's horsemen, drove right through the remaining Russian line.

Napoleon had only to throw in his infantry to complete the destruction of the Russians, wedging Bennigsen's wings apart. He had available the eight battalions of his personal guard but he refused to commit them. While he hesitated, fresh troops arrived on the battlefield. They were not Ney's 6th Corps, as he had hoped, but Prussians, 7,000 men who had not been engaged in the Jena campaign. Napoleon had lost the initiative; he decided to withdraw under cover of darkness. The army would begin its retreat at 10 p.m.

When the brief grey day was ending, Ney had covered some twenty miles with 6th Corps and was marching on a bearing that would take him wide of the battlefield. A soldier running down from a ridge reported that a great battle was in progress. The marshal rode to the top of the slope and saw the smoke and flashing of gunfire whose noise he had not heard because the wind was blowing away from him. It was seven o'clock before his troops took up position. Though they could not know it in the dark, they had come in on the enemy's right flank, threatening his communications.

On the right of the French line Davout was preparing to give the order for his exhausted 3rd Corps to begin withdrawal. An officer from a forward post came to his bivouac and reported that there was a great deal of noise in the enemy lines. Davout put his ear to the ground. The noise was clear and recognizable – the heavy rumble of guns and caissons. And it was receding.

Napoleon cancelled his orders, found shelter in a farm a mile or two at the rear and went into an uneasy sleep, surrounded by his Guard. In the morning one of Davout's officers brought confirmation of the Russian retreat. Each side had lost more than 20,000 men. Napoleon ordered that the official account should show the French casualties at 15,000 killed and 4,300 wounded and that the battle had been won at 4.30 in the afternoon. He withdrew to winter quarters in the Ordensschloss at Osterode until the end of March, then moved to the castle of Finkenstein, where he was joined by Maria Walewska. He passed his days riding or walking in the garden with Joachim, parading troops in the grounds, and planning the great blockade of Britain, which he had decreed in Berlin on November 21.

In June the sodden soil of Poland had dried out. Bennigsen,

striking southwest at 1st, 4th and 6th Corps, forced the latter back from Guttstedt on to Soult's Corps at Deppen. Murat's cavalry swam the Alle and drove the enemy out of Guttstedt on to fortified positions they had prepared at Heilsberg. Anxious to come to grips but suspecting that Bennigsen would retreat if he tried to outflank him, Napoleon ordered a direct attack by Murat with his cavalry, 4th Corps and Lannes's Reserve Corps.[16] These were to engage and hold the enemy while the remaining four corps passed through. It was a dangerous manoeuvre, for the road up the Alle passed through a defile dominated by Russian artillery while the wooded country on the right gave protection for their infantry.

'To get at the enemy we had to traverse an almost impassable ravine, filing in twos and fours, and take up our formation under the enemy's fire at 200 paces from his front line.'[17] But it was an order, and Murat executed it at the gallop. 'Caring little for the lives of his cavalrymen, and even less for his own,'[18] he sped along the ranks, 'leaning over his horse's whithers, and hurled at General Espagne[19] as he moved very quickly in front of him, the simple word "*Charge*!"'[20] They were thrown back, and charged again. Murat had two horses killed under him and lost his left boot. On the first occasion, saved by one of Espagne's men, Serjeant Clarinet who fought off the Russian officer and four men who were charging down on him, he took refuge in a square of the 26th Infantry, shouting: 'I come in here as if it were a fortress.'[21] He returned to the attack, was surrounded by Russian cavalry, saved by Lasalle, commanding the light cavalry division of 3rd Corps and a few minutes later led a charge that freed Lasalle in his turn. By sheer fury they drove the Russians back. At last the enemy were in full retreat, and Colonel Davenay of the 6th Cuirassiers rode up, flourishing his sabre dripping with blood. 'Prince,' he said, 'you may inspect the whole of my regiment and not find a single cuirassier whose sabre is not like mine.'[22]

The victory of Heilsberg had been won at a dreadful price. The troops were shocked by the slaughter – 10,000 or more Russians killed and wounded; 7,000 French. Napoleon, sensing this, let it be known that 'he had not intended the Russians should be attacked so determinedly'[23] in the battle which he himself ordered.

The idea that Murat was a brutalized butcher was fostered by his rival generals as well as by Napoleon. Josephine said of him, 'He smells of gunpowder half a league off and would put his Creator to the sword.'[24] Yet Agar, who knew him perhaps better than any other man, put it on record that away from the field of battle the sight of blood made him shudder. After the Italian and Egyptian campaigns 'he never carried a sabre, or even a fighting sword; only the very small, very short Roman sword which was of no use either in defence or attack . . . Hundreds of times when talking privately with me he has said: "When I look back on my military career, my liveliest satisfaction is never to have seen a man fall killed by my own hand. It is possible, of course, that in firing a pistol shot at an enemy who was attacking me or whom I was over-taking, I may have wounded one, perhaps mortally; but I did not know it. If a man had died before my eyes, beneath my blows, the vision would never have left me; it would have followed me to my grave."'[25] To a fellow-general who boasted that he had never known fear, he replied: 'I congratulate you – I am always afraid, but I always go forward.'[26] Napoleon, talking to Molé one day about contrasts in character, said: 'Who is there who doesn't know of Murat's wild courage, and who would not believe that a warrior like that has a soul of steel, an indomitable character? Well, there is not a softer, more gentle creature in private life, even more weak at times. In camp, if he receives a letter from his wife he cries like a child. But at the sound of cannon his head is up, he rushes out and throws himself into the fray – on the battle-field, that Achilles has twenty elbows.'[27]

In the morning Napoleon did not resume the battle, but began moving in a northerly direction, sending Murat ahead to capture Königsberg. Bennigsen, learning of this, marched his army along the right bank of the Alle on a roughly parallel course. At Friedland he came in contact with Lannes's Corps, which was screening the right flank of the French advance. Bennigsen foolishly transferred most of his men to the left bank and attacked; Lannes held him until he was joined first by Mortier and then by Ney, Victor and the Imperial Guard. The tables were now turned on Bennigsen, who lost ten thousand men before he could get back to the other side of the river.

Murat, summoned from Königsberg, took up the pursuit of the Russians escaping towards the Niemen. On June 19, 1807, just short of Tilsit, he received requests for an armistice. Conversations between the emperor and the tsar began on June 25 and continued until July 9. Each professing respect and affection for the other, they split Europe between them at the expense of the tsar's ally, the king of Prussia, who lost all his possessions west of the Elbe and the provinces he had gained in the last two partitions of Poland. For the Poles there was no change except of masters. A few were transferred to Russia; the remainder, converted into a nominal grand duchy, were handed over to the Elector of Saxony, now promoted king.

Murat's outgoing disposition made him very popular with the Russians, in particular the Grand Duke Constantine. On most days the emperor and the tsar went riding.[28] 'Frederick William, [King of Prussia] wearing a sort of cap that had nothing royal about it and gave a final clumsy touch to a long thin body without grace or dignity, almost always followed on alone after the two emperors, who scarcely paid any attention to him. Constantine and Murat, one a Grand Duke by birth, the other a reigning Grand Duke, made up the third rank, usually laughing like madmen.'[29] Constantine had his tailor make up a pair of baggy Cossack trousers for the Prince.[30] Murat wore them for the first time at the dinner given by Napoleon for the other two sovereigns on July 6. Napoleon made a great show of eyebrow-raising and scoffing until Murat silenced him with, 'I received these trousers from the Grand Duke Constantine.'[31] Napoleon said no more until the guests had left, but then broke into a tirade of abuse that could be heard by Alexander's aides-de-camp in the anteroom. 'The Emperor,' said Murat to the queen of Prussia, still weeping over her husband's loss of half his kingdom, and the humiliation to which Napoleon had subjected her in the French press, 'is a cad.'[32]

On July 9, after the ceremonies of signing the peace treaty, Napoleon set off for Paris. On his way he sent instructions to Talleyrand to threaten Portugal with war unless she ceased all trade with Britain. He also learned from Savary the latest scandal in Paris; that Caroline was said to be having a love affair with Junot.

4

It had been a long ten months for Caroline. From October to December 1806 there was the anxiety of the Polish campaign, and in February the brief flare-up of Eylau. But then came the protracted peace in spring and early summer, with no worries about Joachim, not even about the children: only the restlessness of a young woman, pretty, temporarily husbandless, much admired and – by order of the emperor who always wanted revelry at home while he was expending lives and limbs abroad – constantly entertaining or being entertained.

She had agreed with Pauline, whose influence was certainly not calculated to restrain, to share their evening receptions on alternate Mondays.[1] 'For the past month my life has been a constant turmoil,' she wrote to Hortense on the last day of February 1807. 'I dance at night, sleep part of the day, and spend the rest attending to my correspondence, receiving visits and then impatiently waiting for the dispatches. They do not come and I am worried; they do come and I wonder why I worry still: For the news is never satisfactory and today's only makes me fear a new affair tomorrow. . . . Why are you not here, my dear Hortense? You would have enjoyed our dances so much! The latest was given by the arch-treasurer [Lebrun, once Third Consul], it was gay and brilliant. I danced a lot, as at all the others, despite my good intentions when I leave home not to tire myself. It seems the agitation of one's legs soothes that of one's mind, and how can one be calm at a time like this? . . . I go to the empress's nearly every evening, we talk about you, always with renewed pleasure; she misses you, and that gives us another thing in common. She also talks about little Napoléon a great deal – how much she loves him!'[2]

The little Napoléon whom Josephine loved so much was not the emperor but Hortense's eldest son, now four-and-a-half years old and, since Joseph still had only daughters, third in succession to the throne. According to Laure Junot, Josephine doubted whether the boy's claims would be accepted in the event of Napoleon's death, because of the dangers of a regency. She therefore tried to win the support of Junot, as Governor of Paris, for Eugène's candidature for the throne; whereupon Caroline, still according to Laure's thesis, seduced Junot in order to get him to favour Murat. There are two difficulties in accepting this – one is that Junot did not have the necessary influence to impose Murat in defiance of the constitution. The other is that while the campaigning was in progress Murat was a great deal more likely to be killed than Napoleon. And in any case neither Josephine's grandson nor her son had any claim while Joseph and Louis were alive.

The truth appears to be much less complex, and is provided by Laure herself. 'During the winter of 1807 all the Ministers gave *fêtes*. The Grand Duchess was the Queen of them all because of the absence of Queen Hortense, and the age of the Empress, who no longer danced [Josephine was forty-three], left the field open for her. . . . She dressed very elegantly, opened all the balls with the Governor of Paris, played whist with the Governor of Paris, rose on horseback with the Governor of Paris, received the Governor of Paris alone in preference to all other persons.'[3] Caroline was lonely, adventurous and fond of displaying her power over men – particularly over her friends' husbands or lovers. Junot was handsome and a confirmed woman-chaser. Propinquity did the rest, though Caroline maintained that the affair did not go beyond a very serious flirtation.

But if it was not deeply felt it was publicly displayed. On March 19, St Joseph's day, Caroline and Pauline arranged an entertainment for Josephine at Malmaison – including a sketch with music by Spontini and words by Caroline's *secrétaire des commandements*, Longchamps. When Longchamps' piece was performed, it at once became clear that he had written it very much for the occasion and for the two leading players – Caroline and Junot. Poor Laure, whose small role allowed her plenty of time to observe the performances of the stars, was caustic in her memoirs:

'The Grand Duchess of Berg was very pretty that day, though very ill-behaved; she wore a peasant's dress, white with a golden cross attached to a black velvet ribbon. The velvet enhanced the whiteness of her shoulders and bosom; she also benefited from the fact that her very commonplace height and figure, a drawback in a sovereign, would pass unnoticed in a peasant; it is even appropriate. But what was not so in any manner was that she should have been set to sing with the duke of Abrantès.[4] They were in love with each other in this piece and, from beginning to end, to the great amusement of everybody there, they exchanged every possible caress. They had been born on the same day;[5] they were called Charles and Caroline; there was no end to the sentimental refinements ...! It was highly comical to see and hear. M. d'Abrantès had a very true voice but he had never cultivated it; it was powerful and deep enough for the part of Basile in *The Barber*. One can imagine the effect of this bass voice trying to be tender with the soprano of Princess Caroline, shrill, harsh and off-key to the last degree. One would have got up and run away, had one not laughed so much.'[6]

There was little enough for Laure to laugh about that day. She was edgy, in the early days of a pregnancy which she desperately hoped would provide Junot with a son (after five daughters). When they were ready to leave, Caroline insisted they should all go in her carriage. They got to Paris at three o'clock in the morning. Junot escorted Caroline into the Elysèe Palace, leaving Laure outside. She waited and waited. Junot did not return. She ordered the coachman to drive her to her own house in the rue des Champs-Elysées.[7]

According to Laure, the affair between Caroline and Junot continued until August, when he left Paris to take command of the Army of Observation of the Gironde which threatened Spain and Portugal and on the night before his departure he received a note in Caroline's hand, begging him to keep one last rendezvous with her. 'Come the usual way. Everything will be open. *But above all do not fail to come armed, well armed.* You know why.' Junot showed the letter to Laure. Caroline, he said, planned to have him confront and kill Murat. He kept the assignation but his ardour was cooled by her murderous intentions. 'She employed every art of seduction to revive the waning flicker of love. But the blindfold had been loosened, the glamour had fled, and Alexandre[8] told me that when he saw that woman exhausting herself in unavailing lascivious efforts, playing the part of a prostitute, the only effect she had on him was to render him impotent.' It is quite unthinkable that Caroline would wish to widow herself, even more so that she would send such a note written in her own hand. Yet this was the sort of story that Laure was spreading about her, and which many people were only too delighted to repeat.[9]

Caroline was twenty-five-years old the week after Josephine's saint's day. 'All the members of my little society, which is restricted to three or four persons, have made verses to celebrate my birthday,' she wrote to Joachim next day, 'And I hasten to send them to you.[10] I do not want to reproach you, but you doubtless forgot the 25th of March, for you do not mention it in your letters. The children came with flowers to recite their verses. . . . The youngest . . . presented me with a bouquet. I asked her, "Who is Mama's little Plain Jane?" She answered, "Me!" "And who is Papa's little Plain Jane?" "Mama!" We could not help laughing. Fortunately for me, you do not share your daughter's opinion . . . Goodbye, you are unjust, you see that I write to you as often as possible and you are always complaining of not receiving letters from me. Goodbye again. Despite your injustice I embrace you very tenderly.'[11]

She wrote to Hortense too, quoting the verses that the second boy, Lucien, had recited to her. 'Tell me about your children and in as much detail as I tell you of mine; you know how much I love them and you cannot doubt my great pleasure in knowing they are well . . . Believe in my tender and constant love, my dear Hortense, and accept many kisses from your affectionate Caroline.'[12]

This was not insincere. With hindsight many of her contemporaries accused her of cold ambition – having 'the head of Cromwell on the shoulders of a pretty woman',[13] as Talleyrand said – but her heart was warm and impulsive. In May, when she heard that the little Napoléon had died suddenly of croup on May 5, 1807, she left Paris at 10 o'clock at night to drive to the Hague to comfort the heartbroken Hortense. With two former school friends, Adèle Aiguié and her sister, Madame Ney, she took Hortense to Laeken, where Josephine joined them. The news reached Finkenstein on May 14, and Joachim wrote immediately to Louis and to Josephine to offer his sympathy. Napoleon wrote to Hortense too, but soon lost patience with her protracted grief and snapped: 'You are unreasonable. However legitimate your sorrow may be, it must have some limits . . .'[14] Josephine and Caroline brought her back to Paris on May 19.

'We shall beat the enemy and I shall return to place the laurels I have gathered in Poland on the prettiest head in the world,'[15] Joachim had written to his daughter Letitia from Finkenstein. They were, in fact, worn on the less pretty heads of the emperor's postillions when Murat returned with him to St-Cloud on July 27. Napoleon (once more according to Laure) sent for Junot and upbraided him for compromising Caroline. Murat, who went straight on to the Elysée palace, seems to have been undisturbed by the rumours[16] and in any case was now sharing with Caroline a fresh grievance against the emperor.

Not only had Tilsit resulted in a new kingdom of Westphalia, bordering on Murat's grand duchy and given to Jérôme, but Napoleon had taken away Murat's only strongly fortified place, Wesel (though he had also during the Prussian campaign rewarded him with some extra territory).[17] And not only had Jérôme leapfrogged over Murat's head in the roll of royal precedence, but the insignificant though charming Prince Borghese was now established as Joachim's senior too. The occasion was Jérôme's marriage to Catherine of Würtemberg, daughter of the man whom Napoleon had promoted from duke to king after Austerlitz. When Murat discovered that he had been placed after Camille Borghese in the order of precedence, he sent notes to Ségur, the Grand Master of Ceremonies and to Napoleon, pointing out that he had been given equality with the sovereigns of Europe by the terms of the Confederation of the Rhine, and that Borghese was only a minor prince. He received replies from both of them on the same day. Ségur briefly stated that he had referred the matter to the emperor 'who has told me that he persists in his decision that, within the family, Monseigneur Prince Borghese takes the rank of the Princess his wife, and that I should therefore place him before Your Highness'.[18]

Napoleon answered at greater length: 'Your rank in my palace is determined by the rank you have in my family, and your rank in my family is determined by my sister's rank; her elders must precede her. . . . If you were treated as a grand duke you would lose by it, since I have decided that the custom observed in France throughout the ages shall be followed and that the Brothers and Sisters of the Emperor shall precede Grand Dukes and Grand Duchesses. Any other decision would be contrary to the prerogatives of France and the dignity of my Crown. . . . You are too devoted to the glory of my family not to appreciate how shocking it would be for the people of France to see the Grand Duchess of Hesse-Darmstadt, the Grand Duke of Würzburg, the Margraf of Baden take precedence over my family in Paris . . .'[19] His father, the late king, could not have delivered the snub more regally.

The civil marriage took place in the galerie de Diane at the Tuileries on August 22, and the religious ceremony in the chapel on Sunday, August 23. The court progressed to St-Cloud, back to the Tuileries, then down to Rambouillet, where, despite the miserable rainy weather that had succeeded several days of swelter-ing heat, the emperor had them out every day for stag hunting, which began at two in the afternoon and went on until eight or nine at night. The party broke up, snuffling, on Tuesday, Septem-ber 15. Caroline returned to Paris and called for Catherine at the Tuileries on the Thursday to show her round the Neuilly estate, and on Sunday gave a fête in her honour at the Elysée, attended by the emperor and empress. Catherine, still suffering from a cold in the head, arrived in a mood of resignation, but after an after-noon and evening of Caroline's warmhearted affection, left in a state of happiness that was close to tears.

'The fête given by the Grand Duchess of Berg last Sunday was charming,' she wrote to her father. 'It would be impossible to combine more taste, more magnificence and at the same time more kindness, finer, more delicate attention. She had questioned me several times about my garden at Ludwigsburg; and I had told her about it in detail. But imagine my surprise when, walking that evening into the garden, which was lit by coloured lanterns and set out like a German village, I saw in the distance a model of my own little house. . . . I scarcely had the strength to hold back my tears. It is such a sweet sensation to find oneself at home, even if only for a few moments.'[20] It momentarily resigned her to the eight weeks of regimentation that awaited her at Fontainebleau where the imperial family again assembled.

Though Caroline and Joachim had taken great pains to ease life for the newest member, they were still resentful at their treatment by Napoleon. In addition to demanding the cession of Wesel to France and three towns to Holland, he decreed that half the navigation dues collected by the Grand Duchy on vessels passing along the Rhine should be paid to the French treasury. When Joachim protested, Napoleon told him to send a minister to Fontainebleau. Joachim appointed Agar, who was received by Napoleon in person. The emperor quickly dispelled any fiction of negotiation and dismissed Agar with the warning: 'Remember that I wish to be obeyed; my orders must be carried out without argument and without delay.'[21]

When Agar reported this Murat flew into a rage. 'What!' he cried. 'The emperor wants me to be a sovereign so as to obey, to receive orders? It is impossible; it is a contradiction. Why didn't he leave me as a colonel or a brigadier? Then I would not degrade myself if I obeyed.'[22] He talked for a moment of shutting himself up with his army in Wesel and defying Napoleon to turn him out, but the fit of temper passed. He was beginning to learn that Napoleon created sovereigns only to use them as deputies. It was a bitter realization for, like Louis of Holland, he had made a favourable impression on his subjects, despite the comparatively short periods that he had spent among them. 'He showed himself to be intelligent and well-intentioned,' wrote Beugnot, who was certainly not one of his keenest admirers. 'His military glory served as a pedestal for him. During the Prussian campaign, when the bulletins continually spoke of the Grand Duke of Berg and his prowess, his new subjects were immensely proud; newspapers were read out in public places, and there was serious concern for the life of this intrepid prince.'[23]

There was a rumour in Paris, at the end of September 1807, that under a secret clause in the treaty of Tilsit a new kingdom of Dalmatia was to be formed from Austrian and Turkish provinces and given to Murat. And another that the crown of Portugal, with whom war was evidently imminent, was destined for him. War was certainly in the air. Napoleon was tidying up Europe in order to lock all its doors in the Continental Blockade which he hoped would bankrupt Britain. The people of France, dazzled by the glory of possessing an empire and an army that made Europe tremble, were still delighted with their emperor. But there were some who began to wonder where they were going; and among them was Letizia, Madame Mère. Caroline called on her one evening at the Hôtel de Brienne which she had bought from Lucien in 1806 and found her in her principal salon, a gloomy room draped in bluish green, playing piquet with an old Corsican friend, General Casabianca. A companion was seated close to her, trying to read a book by the faint light of two candles on the chimney-piece and another two on the card table.

'You are not very well lit, Mama,' said Caroline, after kissing her and chatting for a few moments, 'you really *are* very thrifty!'

'Very thrifty!' Madame Mère replied without looking up from her cards, 'you think I'm very thrifty! Do you realize that one day I shall perhaps have five or six kings or queens on my hands? How shall I support them? They won't reproach me for being thrifty then, my daughter!'[24] Caroline repeated this and it became a great joke in the family. Her mother continued to practise her economies, converting her spare cash into diamonds, which she had sewn into the petticoats of her small, ugly *femme de chambre*, the faithful Saveria.[25]

On October 27, Napoleon concluded a secret treaty with Spain at Fontainebleau, agreeing to a joint attack on Portugal. Junot marched his men through Spain to Ciudad Rodrigo and across the Portugese frontier: by November 30 he was in Lisbon.[26]

5

The emperor ordered his sisters to give a ball once a week: Caroline on Fridays, and Pauline on Wednesdays. Hortense, who escaped from Holland and her husband as often as she could, had Mondays; and Laure Junot decided to set an example by giving lavish children's parties, 'being the mother of the eldest of the emperor's god-children'.[1] On January 6, 1808, she entertained about 130 children with ices, cream-cakes, General Jacquot the learned ape, Oliver the juggler, Fitzjames the ventriloquist and a highly-educated team of pistol-shooting canaries. Among the liveliest of the guests was Achille Murat; 'a very fine young prince but a mischievous little imp, whose rowdiness provided a striking contrast with those of his cousins, the Princes Louis and Napoléon'.[2] Caroline was occupied with preparations for the marriage arranged eighteen months before between Murat's niece Antoinette and Prince Charles of Hohenzollern-Sigmaringen.

Antoinette was created a Princess of France on January 28 and married on February 4 – an honour that was, as usual, balanced by the fact that three days earlier Hortense's kinswoman, Stephanie Tascher de la Pagerie, had been married at the Tuileries in the presence of the emperor to Prince von Arenberg.

But at least the quadrille which Caroline arranged to celebrate Antoinette's wedding was admitted even by Laure to be 'really the first one which deserved the name: for those introduced at the marriage of the Princess of Baden had none of the characteristics of a quadrille, except that of being danced by four couples, dressed in red, green and blue'.[3] This time Caroline had decided that all the dancers should be women, dressed as Tyrolean peasants in red silk stockings and black slippers, short red skirts trimmed with dark blue and embroidered with flowers in coloured wools and gold lace. Scarlet and gold braces were worn over white pleated muslin blouses with long wide sleeves caught in at the wrist. On their heads were muslin caps which covered their hair and which Laure considered 'too heavy. Had we not known that Princess Caroline was habitually badly dressed, particularly from the point of view of her own appearance, we should have been astonished that, with a head much too large for her height and her body in general, she chose a coiffure which increased the size of her head still more: but she never failed to have something which disturbed the harmony of her toilet.'[4]

The dancers assembled in Laure's house in the Champs-Elysées,[5] where they were joined by Camille Borghese, giggling drunk, wearing a similar costume to theirs, facetiously padded, and a mask, and determined to kill all the ladies. On arrival at the Elysée palace about 11 p.m. they were bustled about by 'a little mask in blue',[6] Napoleon, who frequently amused himself by abusing the female guests verbally and physically while somebody else impersonated him.[7] At the end of the quadrille, arranged by Despréaux, director of the court ballet, the ladies changed out of their Tyrolean dresses and reappeared in gowns and dominoes – with the exception of Caroline, who put on a ginger wig, a mask, and a postman's uniform.

'At this time she had a way of walking that could be distinguished from a thousand others,' said Laure, adding rather inconsequently, 'I recognized her before she took a single step.

She had letters in her postman's bag and she distributed them to those whose names were on them. . . . Count ————, of the resident diplomatic corps in Paris . . . received one of these. . . . It was in fact probably nothing, yet it gave rise to a lot of gossip.'[8] And, in this instance, a lot of jealousy: Laure was having an affair with the brilliant young Metternich, the Austrian ambassador, and she suspected that Caroline was trying to steal him.

Caroline had invited Hortense to arrange a second quadrille. Hortense chose the currently popular theme of the Vestal Virgin, and decided to appear in it herself – thus, as Laure remarked, 'making it all the more comical and carnival, since the Vestal was eight months pregnant; which made the punishment to which she was being taken less unjust'.[9]

It was the witty M. de Longchamps's idea that the Virgins should be marshalled and led by a young woman representing Folly. Hortense had no difficulty in finding a suitable candidate for the part, the beautiful eighteen-year-old Mlle Guillebeau, who was a talented dancer. She had also, though Hortense feigned at the time to be ignorant of this, been mistress of Murat, Junot and other notabilities. Caroline, at least, was well aware of it, and on seeing her enter the ballroom she promptly ordered her out. Hortense protested that the young woman was an invited member of her party, and should be allowed to remain for the rest of the evening, even if she were banned ever after.

Caroline repeated her request that she should leave. Mlle Guillebeau was led away, sobbing impressively: Hortense, tight-lipped, proceeded with her quadrille. The evening's jollity returned and was eventually rounded off towards dawn with the grand-père, a country dance in which as many as forty couples had been known to take part at the Elysée, prancing and promenading from one floor to another.

On the morning of Saturday, February 20, 1808, Murat was at the Tuileries. He spoke briefly with Napoleon. There had been rumours for some time of moves, concerted with the tsar, to attack Turkey and draw British pressure off Europe by threatening India. It might have included the old project of a Dalmatian crown or a kingdom to be won even farther to the east. But Napoleon said nothing. That evening, completely out of the blue, came an order from Clarke who had succeeded Berthier as minister of War in

August 1807, to take command of all French troops in Spain. Once again Joachim was to be Lieutenant-General of the Emperor. His orders were that he should be in Bayonne on February 26 or February 27 at the latest.

He was in Bayonne on February 25. There he waited for fresh instructions, an indication of the emperor's intentions. He met Michel, the banker, who was returning from Madrid and talks with Godoy. He led the contredance at a fête given in his honour in the Bayonne theatre – and found himself almost immediately alone, the other six dancers having disappeared into the pit when the temporary ballroom floor collapsed, while Murat, who had grabbed his partner round the waist, hung suspended by his other hand from the ledge of one of the boxes.

He checked the disposition of the army that awaited him beyond the Pyrenees. Dupont was at Valladolid, Moncey at Burgos, controlling between them the former kingdoms of Leon and Old Castille; to the east an army corps under Duhesme kept watch on Aragon and Catalonia; behind them lay a division in Navarre, guarding the road from Bayonne. Murat's orders in the letter of February 20 were to seize the fortress at Pampeluna and others lying between Valladolid and the French border using force if necessary. But he found that this had all been done before he arrived at Bayonne.

For what purpose had he been sent to Spain? Officially he was merely the commander of the friendly forces of an allied power. He knew enough of his brother-in-law's methods to realize that he was now in a situation where he could count on small credit and possibly much blame. 'I thought I deserved a little confidence of Your Majesty,' he wrote to the emperor on March 2, 1808, 'and I did not expect to find myself here not knowing to some extent what preparations I have to make for military action in which I may have to take part.'[10] He waited until the night of March 8-9 before crossing the frontier. He stopped at Vitoria on March 10 and then at Burgos, from where he wrote to Napoleon on March 13, telling him of 'demonstrations of enthusiasm', and his welcome by the bishop and magistrates. 'Your Majesty is everywhere awaited with an impatience bordering on delirium.'[11]

6

The French were greeted at first, and as so often before, as liberators. Charles IV's eldest son, the Prince of the Asturias, with whom Napoleon had been secretly in communication through Josephine's brother-in-law, François de Beauharnais, the French ambassador, was the nation's hope for relief from mis-government by the queen and her favourite, Godoy. During the night of March 17–18, Godoy was wounded and taken prisoner in an insurrection; Charles IV abdicated on March 19 in favour of the Prince, who came to the throne as Ferdinand VII. That day Murat crossed the Sierra de Guadarrama, and on March 23 he entered Madrid, acclaimed by the crowds as the ally of their liberator Ferdinand.

He had been told not to take any political decisions. The upheaval in the government made this well-nigh impossible. He was face to face with the threat of civil war: 'I foresee that blood will flow and Europe will not fail to say that France ordained it . . .[1] What distresses me most is that all these disorders are commited to cries of *Vive l'Empereur! Vive l'ambassadeur de France!* . . . It is my duty, for the honour of the French name, to end such horrors . . .[2] If Your Majesty would or could grant me more confidence, even a single word about your real plans . . .'[3] If those plans were to establish a French king, then, with Joseph, Louis and Jérôme already crowned and Lucien in deeper disgrace than ever, surely this rich prize must be intended for him? But the only answer he got was, 'I see nothing in your fears . . . Say you know nothing and are waiting for me.'[4]

He avoided recognizing Ferdinand as king, but he had already made contact with Godoy and Charles, trying to secure the release from prison of the one and offering refuge to the other. 'If [Ferdinand] comes to my headquarters I will send him to Your Majesty,' he wrote to Napoleon, 'and then Spain will truly be without a king, since the father will have abdicated and you will be at liberty not to recognize the son, who can be regarded as a usurper.'[5] He had hit upon the plan which Napoleon intended to follow. Or, more probably, this letter put it into the emperor's mind: for Joachim's swift appreciation of a situation was not confined to the battlefield, even though Napoleon chose to describe him as 'an idiot, totally lacking in judgement'.[6]

Joachim repeated that he needed instructions on how to deal with the royal family. Ferdinand had entered Madrid on March 24 and appointed a government, but was still unrecognized by France. Charles and the queen were virtual prisoners under a French guard in the royal palace of Aranjuez, some thirty miles south of the capital. Napoleon repeated: 'You say you have no instructions; I never stop giving you them, every time I tell you to keep your troops rested, replenish your stocks, do not prejudice matters in any way. It does not seem to me that you need to know anything else.'[7]

But the iron was hot, and he knew that it was the moment to strike. On the day before he entered Madrid he sent General Monthion to Aranjuez with the draft of a letter which he invited Charles IV to sign in return for the promise of protection. It was a renunciation of his abdication of March 19 in favour of his son Ferdinand, and what could well be construed as a second abdication in favour of Napoleon. 'Filled with confidence in the magnanimity of the great man who has always shown himself to be my friend,' the king committed to the Emperor's hands 'my fate, that of the Queen, and that of the Prince de la Paix'.[8] The letter was returned next day, copied in his own handwriting by the king, and antedated to March 21 to make it appear that he had acted without pressure from the French.

Murat set about improving relations between his troops and the Spaniards. He ordered Moncey to check drunkenness among his officers and to forbid them to make irregular demands on the civilians with whom they were billeted. He made a show of power by holding military reviews every Sunday, but was also punctilious in attending mass[9] beforehand at the church of Santa-Maria de Atocha with his staff. 'In all the streets I passed through,' he wrote to Napoleon at midnight on his first Sunday in Madrid, 'I was greeted with cries of *Viva*! and there was general enthusiasm when the troops marched past . . . I am very anxious to know if we are to stay long in Madrid; it is essential that I should begin treating the troops for scabies.'[10] He was deceiving himself. He may well have been popular personally for a time, but the general enthusiasm for his troops was fast waning.

He begged, hinted, fished for information. 'I am very eager to receive your orders . . . we have news of the 22nd that the affairs of Spain are being dealt with and will soon be concluded.'[11] '. . . It is widely believed that your Majesty wishes to put one of his brothers on the throne . . .[12] I am very anxious to see you arrive. I am very uneasy here, I have never known a more difficult moment. I should much prefer to be fighting.'[13] Fouché's police bulletin that day reported that in Paris, 'They say His Majesty is on the point of leaving for Spain, that its monarchy has been dissolved, that the provinces of Biscay, Navarre, Aragon and Catalonia will be united to the French empire, and the remainder will form a kingdom for the grand duke of Berg.'[14]

He had taken up residence in Godoy's palace, guarded by marines, as a Lord High Admiral should be, and by a company of Basques recruited at his request by the Prefect of the Lower Pyrenees. Ferdinand, disquieted at Joachim's refusal to recognize him as king, worked hard to rouse popular indignation against the French presence and was believed to be supplying the peasants with arms and ammunition. To avoid hurting Spanish suscepti-bilities, Joachim left the policing of Madrid to Spanish troops, putting the French into camp outside the town, but he retained four squadrons of cavalry and two battalions of the Imperial Guard in barracks at the rear of his palace. Charles IV returned to the Escurial from Aranjuez on April 9 and from time to time reviewed the French division under General Mouton that stood guard over him: a largish, graceless, rheumaticky seventy-year-old, his chest crowded with medals and decorations, closely followed by 'the stiff little Queen Maria-Luisa, straight as a ramrod, hair piled high, never leaving the king and ruling him entirely'.[15]

From Napoleon all that Murat could get was, 'Announce my arrival. . . .[16] Affairs in general have forced me to delay my de-parture. Russia has declared war on Sweden . . . and my army at Copenhagen will link with the Russian army outside Stock-holm. . . .[17] Announce that the Swedish expedition and affairs of the North will detain me a few more days, but that I have no wish to delay coming.'[18] So on April 1, in an order of the day, Murat published the news that the emperor had been delayed by the situation in Sweden but would be arriving shortly. From Napoleon came a furious denunciation: 'I do not approve of your order. What have the Swedes and the Russians to do with my army? Why announce that I am going to Spain? I did not authorize you to do so. I have never said that I was going to Spain. You could say it, but not write it. The less you write the better.'[19]

On April 3 he received a letter from Napoleon, written on March 27, telling him not to recognize Ferdinand as king. Fortunately he had long ago resolved on this course, but it was clear that nothing but confusion could result from this situation in which Napoleon's decisions, taken on information a week old, were delayed for a further week before they reached his lieutenant. Napoleon moved down towards Bayonne, writing to Murat from Bordeaux on April 5; 'As for the new king, you tell me that he will be coming to Bayonne. I think this can only be useful,'[20] – a sufficiently grudging admission that he was coming round to acceptance of Murat's plan. Meanwhile Beauharnais reported a suspected movement towards insurrection in Madrid. 'If it happens, you will put it down with gunfire,' the emperor wrote to Murat, 'and you will deal out severe justice. You will remember the circumstances in which, under my command, you have made war in large towns. You do not come to grips in the streets, you occupy the houses at the end of the streets and establish strong batteries.'[21]

With the help of Savary, who arrived with messages from Napoleon on April 7, Murat successfully persuaded Ferdinand that he must plead for the emperor's support in person, and Charles that he must do the same. Ferdinand left for Bayonne on April 10, escorted by Savary. Murat obtained Godoy's release on April 21, and sent him likewise to Bayonne. He was followed next day by Charles and the queen. On April 23 Murat reported that public opinion was 'entirely in our favour. Castilian amour-propre has been affronted by the Prince of the Asturias's having crossed the frontier to meet Your Majesty.' He quoted Spanish criticism that 'The Prince of the Asturias has made himself unworthy of the Spanish nation; he did not deserve the esteem and sympathy we had for him. Since he is out of Spain, and his father and mother are on their way to Bayonne, since therefore we are without a sovereign, let the emperor give us one, but let him not make us wait for a long time,'[22] and from among those who gathered at the booksellers for the special editions of the gazette, he quoted an even more pertinent anonymous suggestion: 'Let us run to the grand duke's palace; let us take him for our king: that way we shall *not* have long to wait.'[23]

The latest speculation in Paris was, that 'The emperor has given the kingdom of Spain to the king of Naples, the kingdom of Naples to the king of Holland, the kingdom of Holland to the grand duke of Berg, the kingdom of Portugal to Senator Lucien.'[24] It was not far from what Napoleon wished to do: but he was meeting with difficulties in the family. Joseph wanted to remain in Naples, very sensibly realizing that he had neither the flair nor the character nor the courage to govern so proud and determined a people as the Spaniards. Napoleon therefore offered the throne of Spain to Louis but Louis preferring to stay with the Dutch people whom he considered it his duty to serve and to protect, replied: 'There is no promotion for kings.'[25] Jérôme also did not want to move. Joseph, in order that the richer throne (Spain still controlled a large part of the Americas) should not go to Murat, accepted. And to keep Murat out of Naples, he strongly urged that Lucien should be granted that kingdom. But Napoleon would give nothing to his disobedient brother, to whom he had already offered Portugal if he would agree to a divorce.

Some of this filtered through to Madrid. 'There is much talk of the kings of Naples and Holland for king,' Joachim wrote on May 1. 'Others speak of the king of Westphalia, because he is a sailor.'[26] But he had been in position for six weeks; it really seemed unlikely that Napoleon would make changes now; the Spaniards must almost regard him as their king already.

He had a rude awakening the following day. Many Spaniards had reached the extreme of disillusion. Handwritten pamphlets sent by Ferdinand from Bayonne warned that the French had kidnapped the royal family; and when word went round at dawn on May 2 that the Queen of Etruria and her brother, Don Francisco, youngest son of Charles IV, were being taken away from the royal palace, the storm broke. A shouting mob fell upon Major Lagrange, one of Murat's staff officers, who had come to see the travellers off. He was rescued from being lynched by some of the Spanish officers of the queen's escort and they were saved in turn by the fire of the French troops on guard at the palace.

The fighting became general. Unarmed French soldiers were hacked down in the streets. The bulk of the French troops, stationed in different camps two or three miles out of the town, arrived at midday. For two or three hours the bloodshed, massacre and reprisal, was continuous. Shots were fired from a monastery; the French stormed it and killed every living thing inside. In the French military hospital the Spanish attendants slaughtered their patients. By mid-afternoon the streets were empty and the French in complete control.[27]

Murat seized the opportunity to tighten his grip. 'Tomorrow I shall take command of the Spanish troops,' he wrote to Napoleon early in the morning of March 4.[28] At the same time he sent a message to the Junta appointed by Ferdinand to rule in his absence, telling them he was assuming the presidency of the council. He thus had direct control of the government and all military forces. 'Since I find myself very badly housed here,' he wrote that afternoon in a second letter to Napoleon, 'I shall perhaps decide to go and occupy the Prince of the Asturias's apartment which adjoins Your Majesty's in the Royal Palace. I think it is a politic step; it will leave no further hope of a return of the Bourbons; it will certainly be regarded as taking possession on behalf of a prince of your dynasty.'[29]

At 4 p.m. on May 5, Murat's courier arrived in Bayonne bringing his report on the uprising in Madrid. Napoleon threw himself into one of his synthetic rages, shouting at his Spanish guests that his patience was exhausted. Charles, terrified of what might happen to him, put all the blame on Ferdinand and threatened to hit him with his stick, while the queen unexpectedly screamed that her son was a bastard. Napoleon threatened him with execution as a rebel if he did not recognize his father as the legal king of Spain. The comedy was concluded. Ferdinand VII of Spain abdicated in favour of his father, Charles IV; and Charles IV surrendered his rights to the crown of Spain to Napoleon, emperor of the French.

Meanwhile, Murat had received a dispatch that Napoleon wrote at 11 o'clock in the evening of May 2: 'I intend the king of Naples to rule Spain. I wish to give you the kingdom of Naples or

Portugal. Send me your thoughts on this immediately, for it must be done within a day. You will for the time being remain lieutenant-general of the kingdom. . . .'[30]

It was not what he had hoped for. Nor what he believed he deserved. But he must try to put the best face on his disappointment. He wrote to Junot next day: 'I hope the king of Naples, so generally esteemed in Europe, will reign over the Spaniards.'[31] He went through the royal ceremonials, receiving the court officials, generals and officers of the household and garrison. 'Today's session has been what they call a day of hand-kissing, but I thought it was my duty to dispense with the ceremony,' he reported a little wistfully. 'I shall have them follow the Tuileries etiquette here.'[33] He dropped hints that Joseph was to be king and found no resistance to the idea: 'They've swallowed the pill.'[33]

Two things he insisted on – that Napoleon should win the support of the public servants, who had not been paid for six months or more, by granting a loan to the Spanish Treasury, and that he should name the new king immediately. 'I will continue to repeat: I believe it is very urgent that Your Majesty should make him known, and that he should arrive here. . . .'[34] I cannot avoid repeating to Your Majesty that, even if the new king is not to come at once, it is nevertheless of the utmost importance that he should be made known immediately.'[35] And on the other topic, two separate letters in one day pleaded: 'Your Majesty has so much money; I have often heard you say you did not know what to do with it; you could never put it to better use. . . .'[36] I must repeat to Your Majesty my request to come to the help of Spain by lending her a few millions.'[37] Napoleon was horrified at the suggestion. 'The fact is that Spain is a country lacking in order. . . . There is money in the ports and towns, you will easily find a few millions to provide for expenses.'[38]

Early in April a new French Ambassador, La Forest, took over from Beauharnais, who was recalled because of his bias in favour of Ferdinand. He wrote to the Foreign Minister, setting out his opinion that Joseph would not be as acceptable to the Spanish people as Murat. Napoleon told Talleyrand's successor, Champagny to reprimand La Forest: 'There is not a single voice in favour of the Grand Duke.'[39]

There had been more than enough frustration during the past

six weeks to bring on an attack of Murat's nervous fever, and he now collapsed with colic. With an obvious reference to the harsh phrasing of the letter to La Forest, Joachim wrote on May 23, 'I shall never cease to tell you that it is imperative to name the new king; and do not believe, Sire, that I am speaking for myself.'[40] It was not until May 28 that he was able to write again. 'It is reported to me that tranquillity reigns in every province of the kingdom. The few minor indications of discontent that appeared in Malaga and Valencia have been entirely dispersed.'[41]

Unfortunately, the minor indications were the precursors of major ones. Napoleon's shilly-shallying had offended Spanish pride and given time for patriotic resentment against the French to grow. Murat's illness, as La Forest remarked, was deplorable and untimely. 'He was constantly watchful,' despite the Emperor's accusations of over-confidence, and, 'anticipated or smothered every incident'.[42] 'I am still not very well,' Joachim wrote to Napoleon on May 31, 'and there are fears that my convalescence may be long. If this condition continues, Your Majesty will no doubt feel the need to send somebody here[43] or to address your orders directly to your ambassador . . . I venture to repeat to Your Majesty: every day's delay in the nomination of the king of Spain provides fresh resources to the enemies of the new policy; I hope that this important business is by now concluded.'[44]

It was not. 'The conflagration is spreading rapidly,' Murat wrote at midnight on June 2. 'Seville and Badajoz have risen again. Lieutenant-General comte de la Torré has been killed at Badajoz, and one of the principal municipal officials at Seville. I hope that General Dupont, who will arrive at Cordoba tomorrow will restore everything to order in Andalusia, and that one example will be enough to enforce it in the rest of Spain . . . I hope that, in another direction, Marshal Moncey's march, and a proclamation that I am having made, will impose it in Saragossa and Valencia. Sire, this is no longer a time for delay. In the opinion of all right-minded Spaniards here, Your Majesty should have the new king proclaimed at once, and attach to the proclamation the draft constitution that you sent us.'[45]

On June 4 he told Napoleon that he counted on returning to Madrid next day, 'to let the inhabitants see that I am neither dead nor on the point of dying'.[46] He did so, and at last received permission from Napoleon to announce that Joseph had accepted the throne. But after only two nights at the royal palace his condition deteriorated so much that he left again, this time for the duke del Infantado's estate at Chamartin, two or three miles outside the city. On June 12 he wrote to Napoleon that he could no longer remain in Spain without danger to his health, and repeated two days later that 'I still can neither walk nor attend to affairs. However, I will not leave Spain until I have received Your Majesty's authorization, and until all is peaceful; although the physicians continue to say that I cannot recover except in France. The heat is excessive; it greatly prejudices my convalescence.'[47]

On June 16, Savary returned, sent by the emperor to act as Murat's lieutenant. Joachim revived a little, but had another relapse on June 22. The country was sliding rapidly into insurrection. Savary ordered government departments to be moved to El Retiro, overlooking the city. In the provinces the rebels controlled even the main roads. One of Berthier's aides-de-camp, Captain Montgardé, who arrived with dispatches on June 29, found Madrid outwardly peaceful 'but it was not prudent to go out alone and unarmed at night, nor to stray far'.[48]

Montgardé had brought permission for Murat to leave. He was to hand over the government to the Junta and command of the army to Savary. He left that evening, too weak to ride, in a litter escorted by his Basque chasseurs. He arrived in Bayonne to find Caroline waiting for him.

7

She had gone through an exciting, trying and finally triumphant time since he left her. The round of receptions, balls and attendances at court functions at St-Cloud ended early in April when Napoleon went south. Hortense's third son, Charles-Louis-Napoléon was born later that month. And Laure Junot moved to Elisa Baciocchi's house at the entrance to the Bois de Boulogne on the other side of the road from the Murat property.

One of Laure's reasons for taking the Folie Sainte-James was that the attractive Austrian ambassador, Count Metternich had a

small house in the village of Boulogne, on the south side of the
Bois – and was soon in possession of the key to the garden of the
Folie. One afternoon he confessed that he was being pursued by
Caroline, but added that 'she disgusts me physically'.[1] Leaving this
yeasty item to work on Laure's competitive nature, the artful
ambassador retired. That evening, when she was walking in the
part of the garden where the late baron de Sainte-James had
built a grotto concealing a luxurious bathroom, Laure was,
according to her own account, startled to see Metternich suddenly
appear in front of her, drop to his knees, and exclaim: 'I am
determined to end my days if you will not give me the final proof
that you love me.' Laure burst into tears. 'He rose to support me;
his mouth encountered mine . . . I do not know what became of
me, but he carried me in his arms into the grotto which was just
one pace away from us, and, when I returned to my senses, I had
committed an error that I was destined to expiate with tears of
blood.'[2]

Despite Laure's well-established claim, Caroline invited
Metternich to lunch one day. He returned to the Folie Sainte-
James afterwards and told Laure that 'after a lunch which she had
arranged like a supper for libertines in a bawdyhouse, she made
him go into a small boudoir whose floor was covered with rose
petals, had him sit beside her, took his hands and, looking at him
with shameful boldness, asked if he did not find this a charming
spot. He replied with considerable coldness that he considered
that a woman's boudoir should suggest something other *than just
one thing*.'[3]

A few days later, Caroline asked Laure to call on her. She said
she had heard that Laure had accused her of being jealous –
'Even over M. de Metternich . . . If I wished to give myself the
trouble I could take him away from you with no difficulty at all.'[4]
If there is any grain of truth in Laure's story it undoubtedly lies
in that last sentence. Flahault from Hortense, Junot and Metternich from Laure – Caroline delighted in exercising power. How
far she went is another matter: for another set of critics alleged
that Metternich was so little disgusted with her that he fell under
her spell to the extent of sacrificing Austria's interests to her a few
years later.

Laure said Caroline's accession to the throne 'must have sent her mad with joy'.[5] Other close observers, such as Beugnot, believed that she was grievously disappointed at not having that of Spain.[6] Disappointed or not, with Joachim ill, Caroline set about her change of home and station with brisk efficiency. 'It is decided that we are to leave Düsseldorf,' she wrote to Agar on June 17, 'and it is urgent that you should raise as much capital as possible, for since we are going to a poor country where there will be many expenses, it would be inadvisable to begin the reign by imposing new taxes. . . . The grand Duke has not had time to study all the details and, since his illness, he will not have been able to write to you . . . Send all my furniture, a chest of music. Madame Agar can remain at Düsseldorf for the birth of her baby, for, as you will probably remain two or three months, waiting for our successor to take possession, she will have time to recover: I will be godmother to her child, if it is a boy you will name him Joachim-Charles; if a girl Caroline.'[7]

She went down to Bayonne, where Napoleon had leased the Lauga estate for her on the banks of the Nive.[8] Joachim joined her just over a week later, on July 3. Joseph left for Spain on July 9, without having been to visit his brother-in-law. Napoleon called at Lauga the following morning. After a long talk, Joachim drove off in a carriage for Pau, and from there continued to Barèges in search of treatment for the fever that he could not shake off. He delegated powers to the marchese di Gallo, the Neapolitan Foreign Minister who had accompanied Joseph to Bayonne, and who now remained behind with Caroline to arrange the terms for taking over the kingdom.

The Spanish experience had seriously affected Joachim's health. Barère, who saw him at Barèges, thought it unlikely that he would live long. 'He was thin, yellow and hollow-eyed; he suffered from shortness of breath.'[9] But Joachim was encouraged to find that Lannes and Ney, who were already taking the cure, 'are twenty years younger; this is truly the Fountain of Youth'.[10] On July 18 he received details of the conditions under which the emperor was giving him the throne of Naples. In addition to surrendering the grand duchy of Berg, he was to make over to the emperor all his property in France, valued at ten million francs. In return he was to receive half of the annual revenue of 1,000,000 francs which Napoleon had attributed to himself in March 1806 when Naples was taken over by French troops, and the Farnese properties in Rome. He was also to accept the existing liability to set aside estates large enough to support six duchies each with an income of 60,000. In the event of war, he was to maintain, pay and set at Napoleon's disposal 16,000 infantry, 2,500 cavalry and 20 pieces of horse artillery; two 80-gun ships of the line, four 74's, six frigates and six brigs. He was also to maintain and pay all French troops on Neapolitan territory.

On his elevation to royal rank, Murat qualified for a further honour: he was now to be known as Joachim-Napoléon. And to underline the source of all his blessings, Article Three of the Treaty signed by Gallo and the French foreign secretary at Bayonne on July 15, 1808, stated: 'If her Imperial and Royal Highness the Princess Caroline survives her august spouse, she shall remain queen of the Two Sicilies, enjoying alone and fully exercising, the title and powers of Royalty. This unique exception is made to a fundamental principle [the Salic Law] because the Princess who now places her family upon the throne and in whose favour this cession is particularly made must always occupy a rank superior to that of her children.'[11] It made the point with painful clarity that Murat was to sit on the throne not because of any virtues or exertions of his own, but simply because he was his wife's husband, brother-in-law of the great man whose name he must now take. Joachim-Napoléon went off to Cauterets, to try the waters there, and then on to the château de Bouillas [12] where he stayed with Lannes.

Caroline went straight back to Paris, where Joachim joined her on August 5. He had officially succeeded to the Neapolitan throne on August 1, but thought it advisable to remain in Paris for a few more days until the emperor's return, so that he could settle the difficulties that were already arising about the surrender of the Grand Duchy, where the emperor's representative, Beugnot, had accused Agar of selling or sending to Naples property which now belonged to Napoleon. 'Your agents are packing and sending everything across the river,' Napoleon complained in a letter of June 30. 'Your stallions and blood-mares are filing in one long line across the Tyrol. Is it worth while to be so eager about trifles?'[13] It was the pot reproaching the kettle. Napoleon returned to St-Cloud on August 14. It was the eve of his thirty-ninth birthday and he was still in a furious temper over the news of the surrender of Dupont's army at Baylen and a dispatch from Joseph in which the new king of Spain announced that he had quit Madrid and thought he would be forced to abdicate. The surrender of 20,000 troops at Baylen struck the first blow at the legend of the invincibility of Napoleon's armies. Joseph's panic served to underline the double madness of embarking on the Spanish venture without a plan, procrastinating and then failing to give Murat the throne.

Napoleon did not easily forgive others for his mistakes. When Murat saw him that evening he raged on about the horses he had taken from the Spanish stables for his carriages and from Mecklenburg for his stud. Murat resentfully stayed away from the birthday celebrations next day, sending instead a note of indignant protest. 'I am incapable of doing what Your Majesty accused me of yesterday evening. . . . I have asked Caroline to offer my excuses for not coming this morning to add my wishes to those of all your subjects, but I am not able to, first because my uniforms have gone and I have only that of the carabineers which I wore yesterday evening, and then because I do not seek to prove my attachment to Your Majesty by words.'[14]

Two days later he sent Napoleon a list of questions on how he should conduct himself when he got to Naples. On August 21 he went to the ball at the Hôtel de Ville in honour of the emperor; and the following day he left for Italy, travelling slowly for fear of a relapse. On September, at four o'clock in the afternoon, he entered his kingdom at Portella. He spent the night at Gaëta and next day made his ceremonial entry into the capital.

PART III

Their Majesties
1808–1815

I

In 1735 Don Carlos of Spain brought the kingdoms of Naples and Sicily under one rule. The crown remained in Spanish Bourbon hands until 1798, when its sovereign, Ferdinand IV, joined the alliance of Britain, Russia, Austria, Turkey and Portugal against France, and opened the campaign by sending his troops under the Austrian general Mack in an attempt to overthrow the Roman Republic and restore the pope. In the subsequent riposte by France, Ferdinand was forced to take refuge in Sicily, and Southern Italy emerged as the Parthenopean Republic. The new state existed for only a few months. Ferdinand returned; egged on by his unlovely queen, Mary Caroline,[1] and shamefully supported by Nelson and the British fleet, he took a terrifying revenge on those of his subjects who had supported the republic. After Austerlitz Napoleon declared Ferdinand's rule ended and sent a French army to occupy the southern half of the Italian peninsula. In March 1806, he appointed Joseph to the throne of the Two Sicilies – though Sicily itself was still safely in the hands of Ferdinand and guarded by British men-of-war.

Joseph ascended the throne with the approval of the surviving Neapolitan liberals who admired the vigour of the French empire and the ideals of the French republic. The majority of his new subjects were apathetic, miserable souls, weighed down by feudal iniquities, brutalized by poverty, battened on by a great menagerie of priests often scarcely better endowed with money or education than themselves. His frontier with the Papal States ran from the Mediterranean between Terracina and Gaëta, to the Adriatic between Ancona and Pescara: the whole leg of Italy from the Abruzzi in the north to the bony toe of Reggio in the south. In Calabria, the poorest and most backward area of the kingdom, guerilla warfare broke out soon after his arrival, and was still unabated when he moved on to Spain.

A quiet man with a bent for lust, accidie and greed, Joseph

preferred to leave the conduct of affairs to others. Gratitude for his reforms – he lit the streets of Naples, forbade the castration of boys for church choirs, drafted a constitution – was effaced by resentment at the extortion of his tax-gatherers, the severity of his troops, the ubiquity of his secret police. Yet this was a country that could have brought a tolerable standard of prosperity and happiness to its people. In the long plain of Puglia, in the land northwest of Naples and in many of the mountain valleys, the soil was fertile enough to produce two or even three crops a year under the Mediterranean sun; around the long coastline the sea was rich in fish, though the activities of the British Navy impeded the fishermen, particularly since the British capture and occupation of Capri, partially blockading Naples.

The new king Joachim had a character and style that won him immediate affection in the streets. The notorious *lazzaroni*, the Neapolitan beggars whose children 'screamed like young tigers and roused painful and terrifying emotions'[2] in the hearts of French generals, were impressed by Joachim's looks, his swagger, the prospect that a more vigorous ruler might bring them a more bearable life. They compared him with Renaldo, one of their legendary heroes. 'His affability and charm have seduced them in no time', the French ambassador, Aubusson, reported after ten days. 'When he appears in the streets . . . the *lazzaroni* run after him in crowds to applaud him. He salutes them and they go away enchanted . . . "He is a fine Fellow!" they say "He can go on his own wherever he likes, nothing will happen to him."'[3]

He worked hard and did not for a time bother with formal court functions. Caroline, overcome by the heat, wrote to Ségur on October 2 that 'the country is superb, but I have hardly left my room'.[4] When she did it was usually to supervise the furnishing of new apartments for herself. 'I am lodged up in heaven,' she told her Uncle Fesch. 'I have to climb two hundred and sixteen steps to reach my rooms. You see I can get a lot of exercise without going out . . .'[5]

Sending Hortense some sketches of Naples and its surroundings that she had specially engraved for her, she told her: 'My room is like a warehouse: hats, jewels, cases, all jumbled together. My writing desk was broken on the way here. When I need something, everything has to be turned upside down.' But she was delighted with what she had seen of her new kingdom – Portici, Capo di Monte, the Chiaia promenade the palace at Caserta, 'which cannot be described, it is more beautiful than anything one could imagine. Versailles is nothing compared with it. I will give you an idea: only one small wing is inhabited, and in this little block of buildings you can lodge five thousand people. ... The queen's apartment has fifty salons, her library alone is composed of six rooms furnished with bookcases, but not a single book. ... The apartment that is being prepared for me will be superb, not because of the beauty of its furniture but because of its situation. I will make a little sketch and send it to you. ... I have not written to you in my own hand, because I am cross with you ... I left Paris more than a month ago and you have not written me a word. ... She is not kind, the queen of Holland. But I prefer to believe that her letters have gone astray.' She signed it, 'I kiss you and love you, Caroline.'[6] In one short sentence halfway through her letter she had revealed the secret of Joachim's inaccessibility: 'Capri had just capitulated.'[7]

Before leaving Paris, Joachim discussed with Napoleon the possibility of dislodging the British troops from the island opposite Naples (which Joseph had twice failed to do). Immediately on arrival he sent officers out in fishing boats to inspect the British defences and the possible landing places. On the side facing the mainland lay a narrow harbour and a patch of beach where troops might get a footing; but both were well watched, and covered by artillery. Beyond this comparatively low-lying part of the island rose Anacapri, precipitous, guarded by rocky shores where landings could be made safely only in calm weather. Joachim knew that Colonel Lowe, the future governor of St Helena, had a garrison of 600 Corsican Rangers; his spies failed to discover that the British Commander in Sicily, Sir John Stuart, on learning that Joseph had been replaced by the energetic Murat, had sent the 700 men of the Maltese Regiment to reinforce them. Assembling a small flotilla at Salerno and a larger one in Naples, Joachim sent off 3,000 men under the command of General Lamarque on the night of October 3. In the morning, while the larger flotilla made a feint attack on Capri, Lamarque led a thousand of his men to the rocks of Anacapri, guarded by the Maltese. These failed to see the arrival of the advance party, which scaled high enough up the cliffs to give covering fire to the remainder. That night, after picking off the Maltese defenders on the cliff tops outlined by the light of the moon, Lamarque's men stormed up the rest of the way. Next day Joachim sent them light artillery and provisions, which they hauled up to the top of the cliff. Descending to the lower half of the island they laid siege to the town of Capri. A change in the weather prevented Lowe from receiving supplies and reinforcements from Sicily; on October 16 he surrendered the fort, arms and all supplies to Lamarque, on condition that his troops were allowed to return to Sicily.

Joachim was at once eager to pass on to a new triumph. 'The signals from Capri, and Your Majesty's banners and mine floating from its towers, announce that the enemy has capitulated . . .,' he wrote to Napoleon. 'They say that [the reinforcements arriving too late in British vessels] are all the troops that there were in Sicily and that there is practically nothing left in that island. Sire, . . . this is the moment to attempt the expedition; I ask only eight thousand men from Your Majesty and I will guarantee success; it is impossible for the enemy to prevent me from landing – he is sending everything he has to Spain.'[8]

In celebration of the capture of Capri he issued an amnesty for political exiles, released their property from sequestration, established welfare committees and free dispensaries for the poor, set up a small-pox vaccination service, founded a botanical garden and a library named after Achille, gave 1,200 ducats to the Royal Society of Science, Letters and Arts, and cancelled the ban on night-fishing in the bay of Naples. To the long-unpaid, marauding soldiers he gave a month's wages in August and paid them regularly thenceforward, promising to settle the arrears as soon as the national budget would permit.

Napoleon's reaction to all this was shattering to Joachim's pride. He got no credit for having taken Capri, only a snub for having communicated the news by a personal letter. 'This is ridiculous,' the emperor wrote to him. 'Capri having been taken by my troops, I ought to have learned of the event from my Minister of War to whom you should have reported it.'[9] In addition he nagged at him for his leniency to the political exiles, for his reforms, even for offering medals to the soldiers who had served in Capri, without first obtaining permission.

On November 25, from the palace at Portici, Joachim sent an indignant reply: 'Your Majesty's letters to me have long ceased to be those of a benefactor. . . . To you I am now merely a man who is unwillingly tolerated, who has become suspect. . . . At that price, Sire, I cannot reign any longer; I would prefer to lose the crown and retain your friendship and kindness rather than keep it and become estranged from Your Majesty.'[10] It was the first – but very far from the last – time that he threatened to hand back the crown if he could not be king.

Immediately after the fall of Capri he began passing his forces south for the invasion of Sicily, and made no secret of his intention. Napoleon showed interest but could not be brought to give permission. Joachim assured him that the British had withdrawn their troops to provide reinforcements in Spain, but Napoleon was counting on the invasion scare to draw them back again. He sent instructions to Fouché to publicize the threat as widely as possible.

'I have this moment received a letter from Your Majesty's Minister of War,' Joachim wrote to Napoleon on December 3, 'which orders me to send back four regiments to [the Kingdom of] Italy and to continue my preparations for the Sicilian expedition. Sire, these two orders scarcely tally with each other; however, I shall carry them out punctually. . . . I begin to suspect that the moment [for the start of the expedition] is not so near.'[11]

On top of this came information that Napoleon was having secret inquiries made in Naples to check whether Joachim was allowing breaches in the blockade against Britain. The accusation was, at this time, completely unjustified. 'I am informed that somebody has dared to report to Your Majesty that I have authorized the introduction of English merchandise: and that you have ordered an investigation. I am dumbfounded and I have nothing to say, except that I am neither a rebel, nor an ingrate, nor a fool, and that I should be fit to be sent to the madhouse and worthy of contempt, if I were capable of such conduct. Sire, cease being suspicious of me, or you will make the most unhappy of men he who is the most devoted to you.'[12]

2

The misunderstanding and recrimination were aggravated by postal delays. From Spain to Paris it had been a week or ten days; from Spain, where Napoleon remained until January 1809, to Naples it was a fortnight or more. Napoleon was not accustomed to getting letters couched in the terms that the indignant Joachim used. Joachim suggested that modifications should be made to the sections providing for divorce in the *Code Napoléon* when it was introduced in Naples in the new year. 'I would prefer Naples to pass to the former king of Sicily rather than allow the *Code Napoléon* be castrated,'[1] the emperor threatened. Joachim, either from stubbornness or because the latter was slow in reaching him, insisted: 'It was a good policy in France, where Your Majesty had different subjects of different religions, but here we have only one, and it is the Catholic religion.'[2] The answer was a curt order to put the Code into operation without alteration.

In January 1809, Napoleon's suspicions deepened. At Astorga he received letters from Paris which told him of meetings between Talleyrand and Fouché, hitherto enemies, and sent him hurrying back to the capital. The rumour was that the two men, one Grand Chamberlain and the other minister of Police, had agreed upon a successor to the throne. As Fouché had made plain to the emperor, none of his brothers would be acceptable: the choice lay between Eugène Beauharnais, who had a specious claim as the emperor's adopted son, and Murat, who could count on more support in the army. Talleyrand and Fouché decided that Murat was the best candidate, and one whom they would be able to manipulate.[4] They then, it was said, sent a letter to Murat offering their services. It was at this point that Napoleon was alerted.

His informant is usually thought to have been Lavalette, the director of Posts, who was married to Josephine's niece, Emilie. But according to Agar, a warning was sent by Madame Mère, who was told of a conversation in which Fouché said of the emperor: 'He is a madman who sets fire to everything; he is stirring up the whole of Europe and he'll end by capsizing France. We must put an end to it.'[3] Agar believed that Murat never had any inkling of the plot, whatever it may have been. Corroborative evidence was said to have been provided by the letter, intercepted by Eugène, from the two conspirators in Paris to Murat, though it seems highly unlikely that they would have put their proposals in writing. Poor Josephine, a prey to every sort of anxiety, was told that Murat had boasted that he would run Eugène through with his sword if he stood in his way to the throne. Napoleon's impression, when he raged back to Paris on January 23, was evidently that the plot was to dispose of him. He showered filthy abuse on Talleyrand and deprived him of his office, but he could not yet spare Fouché, who eventually found an opportunity to explain that the plan had been to find somebody not to supplant him but to succeed him.

Napoleon was probably aware by now that this was merely another skirmish in the continuing battle of the Bonapartes and the Beauharnais, and a temporary alliance of both against Murat,[4] but he was riled by Joachim's lack of complete obedience, and the doubt had been planted.

As Agar noted: 'From that time Napoleon's distrust of Murat continually increased, often showing itself in outbursts that were very offensive to the King of Naples. The latter, whose pride was easily touched and who did not know the real cause of the criticisms that the emperor seemed to delight in showering on him, supposed that this was part of a set plan against him, and that the emperor was only looking for a pretext to take away his crown.'[5]

The bad feeling upset Caroline, who got noticeably thin with worry. She had been living very quietly, receiving fifteen or twenty people – including Aubusson – for cards in the evening, but spending most of the day alone with the ladies of her household. 'In all her conduct, even it appears towards the king, she shows a circumspection that is very remarkable in so young a princess,' Aubusson reported. 'One can imagine that the strong claims she had to take part in the government as heir-presumptive to the crown might arouse some shadow of distrust in the mind of a prince who is jealous of his authority, but . . . she is so reserved and prudent in her behaviour that the intriguers who might hope to profit from minor misunderstandings . . . seem baffled.'[6] As for Joachim, 'The king seems to believe that there is an attempt to distort everything he has so far tried to do to repair the evils of the past and the extreme disorder that prevailed in every branch of the administration . . . and in fact it is my duty to state, with the greatest regret, that it was time a change was made.'7

At the beginning of February the emperor ordered him to dismiss his newly appointed Prefect of Police, Maghella, because he was a Frenchman and had not obtained permission to leave France. He threatened to recall other Frenchmen who had taken service in Naples without permission. 'All the notes that have reached me will be acted upon,' Joachim replied resignedly. 'It might perhaps have been desirable if Your Majesty could have shown a more kindly attitude in your demands, and the formalities had been better observed.'8 In the middle of February he received news from his ambassador in Paris that Napoleon had refused to accept the Order of the Two Sicilies, because his brothers had received theirs first. Joachim protested that he had told his ambassador to ask for permission to take the insignia to Spain, but Napoleon had never replied. And in any case the honours had been offered by Joseph not by him.

'In refusing, Your Majesty humiliates nobody but the Neapolitan nation. I will see to it that this refusal has no effect on the feelings of gratitude and love that it owes you . . . Although it has seemed for some time that every effort is being made to sicken and disgust me, I will remain none the less faithful to Your Majesty . . . The queen's health is not good, she grows noticeably weaker every day. It is one more worry for me in the unhappy position in which I find myself.'9 Sending Hortense a copy of a song, 'the tune seemed pretty to me – think of me when you sing it', Caroline confessed that, 'I am sad, I am moody, I have gloom in my heart that prevents me from enjoying myself much. They say you are having very pretty little dances and that the emperor goes to them; I would give everything in the world to spend an hour there, not for the ball but to chat with the emperor. I believe an hour's talk with him would dispel all my troubles.'10

Napoleon had Berthier send Joachim some advice: 'The Emperor loves you greatly, he loves his sister, he has said a thousand kind things on the subject, and I do not speak to you as a courtier. Here is what you must do, Sire: be a king to your subjects; be a Vice-Roy to the emperor. Be a Frenchman, not a Neapolitan. Consult His Imperial Majesty about everything . . . it is for us to follow and obey his designs and his ideas without seeking to plumb their depths. . . . Submit to all the emperor's wishes, consult him on everything, obey his desires – thus you will work towards the happiness of your realm and of yourself.'[11]

It was not an argument that appealed to Joachim. 'As a soldier,' he said to Agar, 'I have always been ready to obey and I always shall be; when I command the Emperor's troops, nobody will execute his orders more faithfully; but in my kingdom I am king, I must be independent. When it is a question of my kingdom, I must negotiate with him, not submit to his decree. . . . That would be treachery to my subjects, who have the right to find in me a protector and a father, and can only give me their confidence and love on that basis. If he wanted to dispose of them at his own pleasure . . . why did he not give them a prefect instead of giving them a king? That title imposes on me duties towards them and towards myself which I intend to fulfil. He can take it away from me, because he is the stronger, but he cannot force me to besmirch it.'[12]

From Aymé,[13] his Chamberlain, whom Napoleon would not permit to leave Paris, he heard of the allegation that there was 'a deep misunderstanding between the King and the Queen, that the Queen was not happy; there was much emphasis on this last point, in the hope that these stories would come to the ears of the emperor, who, being very fond of his sister, would be more inclined to form further unfavourable impressions of the king. This has always been regarded as a reliable weapon. . . . The king of Naples has no real enemies except in the imperial family, and this hostility is quite simple and natural in the case of the brothers, who did not wish the throne of Naples to pass out of the direct line, and in the case of the empress it is known that the king of Naples has on occasions openly spoken in favour of the emperor's divorce.'[14]

Napoleon was not the only one to have heard of the rumoured differences between the king and the queen. A little later in the month Madame Mère wrote to her *carrissimo figlio* Joachim that, 'I have waited some time for an opportunity such as the present one to speak of something that grieves my heart and which I have not wished to confide to the post – I refer to the disunity which prevails in your family, as I hear from common gossip. I am deeply distressed by it.'[15]

Caroline denied that there was any trouble. A few days before she had written to her mother, 'I have just this moment received a letter in which you tell me I am coming to Paris. I am very surprised by it . . . The emperor has not asked for me and I have no plans to go there. So write to me, dear mama, what I should think of all this. I have been in bed for ten days with a rather bad fever; I got up today for the first time but I hope soon to be completely well. So do not worry yourself. The king is now in marvellous health; my children are all well.'[16] And on the 20th she had her secretary, Janvier, chide Aymé about the bulletin which Joachim had shown her. 'How, my dear Aymé,' he wrote, 'can you who know the household better than anybody repeat the stupid gossip of the capital about what happens or is said here and what may be said in certain palaces in Paris? You know that people often attach much more importance than it deserves to this sort of nonsense.'[17]

But the seed of misunderstanding was there, and in the next two or three months it grew. At the back of Joachim's mind was the clause in the Bayonne treaty emphasizing Caroline's claim to the throne. Was Napoleon planning to hand it over to her? Did she know? Was she conniving? He had copied the Tuileries procedure with the diplomatic corps, receiving them with a cool formality on ceremonial occasions, avoiding them the rest of the time; but Caroline's apartments were open to them. He knew Aubusson's principal duty was to send secret reports on him as it was the duty of the First Secretary at the French embassy, Grosbois, to send secret reports on Aubusson. Caroline received Aubusson; one of her ladies-in-waiting, was thought to be having an affair with another of the family ambassadors, Louis's representative, Dedem; and Dedem was suspected of conveying information to Caroline. It was all talk, speculation, malicious chatter. But beneath it was the reality of his position as an outsider in this jealous Corsican fraternity – and his own hot-headed Gascon mistrust. For the moment there was no outward sign of disunity at court. The king inspected the fortifications of Capri and reviewed the two regiments of Velites that he was training as the nucleus of a *corps d'élite*; the queen went to see a new crater on Vesuvius.

She was carried up in a litter, then got out and walked across a brittle bridge of recently cooled lava to peer down into the frothing cauldron. 'But they made me leave that spot,' she wrote to Ségur, 'and I had scarcely moved away when it was covered with a shower of burning stones . . . Two minutes after I crossed the lava bridge that the fire ran under, the crust exploded noisily over a wide area and was no longer passable.'[18] She was accompanied by Dedem, who confirmed that 'she showed great courage. We could see the lava flowing below the cooled-off scoria on which we were walking.'[19]

The royal couple celebrated their joint birthday on March 25, when the king laid the first stone of the Foro Murat, the great square (now the piazza del Plebiscito) that he had decided to construct between the royal palace and the church of San Francesco Paola. The following day, 12,000 soldiers, damp from a deluge that caught them early in the morning, were reviewed by the king, and the newly-raised provincial legions received regimental colours from the queen, who had embroidered them with the help of her ladies. The king took his place beside the queen on an open-air throne in the Strada di Chiaja, flanked by their four children, Achille wearing the uniform of the Velites. After the colours had been blessed the troops marched past to a long row of tables in the Villa Reale gardens, where chicken, cold ham, pastries, fruit and a bottle of wine for each man awaited them. When Joachim and Caroline drove past on their way back to the palace 'glasses, plates and forks were waved in the air as a sign of merriment'.[20] That evening the city was illuminated and soldiers were admitted to the theatre free. It was Saturday and the festivities spread over into Sunday.

Joachim was delighted with the enthusiasm. 'Public opinion has resumed its sway over intrigue and the works of malevolence . . . The fear of war has been replaced by the desire to spring to arms in defence of the state,'[21] he wrote to Napoleon. He was mistaken – as he was also in believing that the Neapolitans were as enthusiastic 'as on the day of my entry into the kingdom'.[22] Violent but not bellicose, too recently emerged from a degrading feudalism to have yet shaken off old habits of servility and suspicion, they were beginning to see in their dashing Reinaldo the relentless recruiting sergeant and the Jacobin anti-christ whom the pope refused to recognize. Four days after the birthday celebrations the Royal Guard gave a banquet to the officers of the new legions at which the king and queen appeared before going to Caserta for the weekend, and at which meat was served, though it was in High Lent, the Wednesday before Easter. 'The people are not satisfied with these proceedings,' the lawyer Nicola recorded, adding that their trip to Caserta 'seems to have been made expressly so as not to perform the duties of Holy Week'.[23]

For the war in Spain, Napoleon had drawn upon some of the Neapolitan regular soldiers and some of the French army of occupation. Now, for the war against Austria, he needed more. At the end of February he grumbled at Joachim for not having enough men available and told him to introduce conscription: a measure which he had previously forbidden because he did not wish to strengthen Joachim's hand against Sicily. 'Before I left [France] I asked Your Majesty if I should form new regiments,' Joachim answered, 'and the reply was that I must pay what I owed to the existing troops before I raised new ones. For three months past I have continually asked Your Majesty to establish conscription, and it was not until yesterday that it was authorized. Sire, I should be at fault were I not to tell you that such a measure may not be without certain drawbacks in present circumstances; I will therefore defer its execution for another few days and I hope to obtain the same results by the means I have recently adopted.'[24]

The means he was using was that of voluntary enlistment; the most evident of the certain drawbacks that he foresaw was the unwillingness of the Neapolitans to finding themselves marched off to some foreign battlefield to face Napoleon's enemy's guns. But Napoleon was not to be denied.[25] He repeated the order. 'I make bold to advance the opinion,' snapped Joachim, 'that if I had received permission three months ago, there would be 20,000 more men under arms today to give Your Majesty, in the event of war, the opportunity to draw upon my kingdom for resources which it might be dangerous to withdraw from it today.'[26] On

March 26 he made the point quite clear: 'I am almost certain that I am on the point of being invaded.'[27]

Dangerous or not, Napoleon intended to have them. Joachim's kingdom was threatened from the south; he had to stand by and watch while his troops marched north: the 23rd and 62nd regiments, a battalion of La Tour d'Auvergne and an artillery company from the French forces, one regiment each of infantry and cavalry from the Neapolitan.

3

Melancholy closed in on the palace that had been so smiling six months before. Caroline, unhappy now in her own private life, wrote to Hortense, increasingly estranged from Louis, to thank her for her birthday greetings. 'Though I laughed at what you said to me about the pleasures and tranquillity that we can look forward to at fifty, I think you may well be speaking the truth, which is not the kind of thought that cheers one up very much.'[1]

Agar reported to the king that the collection of taxes, and even the transport of those that had been collected, was hindered in almost every province 'by the absence of any military force that one can employ on the one hand to compel those who defer payment and on the other to protect public vehicles'.[2] On April 15 Austria declared war. Eugène, in command of the Army of Italy was defeated by the southern Austrian army under Archduke John and forced back to the Adige. 'Desertion among the Velites and the new conscripts is immense,'[3] recorded Nicola. The deserters, pursued by the police, joined the brigand *comitive* that were ravaging the provinces. In Sicily, General Stuart hesitated between sending 12,000 men across the straits of Messina to attack Murat, or landing half that number in Tuscany where they would be of more immediate assistance to Archduke John.

Murat could not resist crowing over Eugène when he next wrote to Napoleon. 'Your Majesty's troops have retreated before an enemy so often before defeated! And in which theatre of war? – that of your own glory ...!' He begged to be allowed to drive the

Austrians out again. 'Sire, put my courage to the test once more, and the enemy will see that I am worthy of your favour. Your Majesty will say that I can serve you here. But no – here it is my own interest that I serve, here I fight for myself and nobody will believe that I fight for Your Majesty.'[4]

He wrote at midnight on April 28. At that moment Napoleon was already on Austrian soil, a week of victories behind him and an almost empty road to Vienna ahead. The welcome news arrived at Naples. Joachim, accompanied by Caroline and the children, held a review at Bagnoli. His cannon thundered the triumphs of Eckmühl, and Ratisbon from Scilla and Reggio. Across the straits of Messina, Stuart had been having trouble with his officers, who believed him 'incompetent for the command of an army on active service'.[5] He decided the best way to distract them was to send them all off on an expedition, and threaten Naples by seizing the island of Ischia, which lies off the northern tip of the Bay of Naples as Capri lies off the southern.

'We are very quiet here,' Caroline wrote to Hortense on May 20, 'especially since we heard of the emperor's great successes.[6] Still, we have had a visit from two English men-of-war which entered the port up to cannon range. The King would very much like them to make a landing so that, by beating them, he could console himself a little for not going to war.'[7] They did not land. Joachim received orders from Napoleon to take command of all troops in the Papal States and to declare Rome and its dependencies annexed to the French empire. It was not the best moment to be absent. The malcontents were becoming more active; the priests were developing the attack that Joachim had foreseen on the divorce provisions in the new civil code; more families were being affected by the call-up of young men in the army.

Taking over a state that was in no condition to put up a fight was not work that appealed to Joachim. He learned that Napoleon had received a damaging check beyond Vienna. He believed more than ever that Napoleon needed him.[8] 'The king appears to be excessively bored and seeks every opportunity to escape from the inactivity which wearies him to death,' reported Aubusson. 'The queen would doubtless be happier if the king could be occupied in some more agreeable way.'[9]

On June 11, Stuart's invasion force set out from Milazzo, 14,000 strong, under the nominal command of Mary Caroline's favourite son, Prince Leopold. Less than 4,000 British troops remained in Sicily, but Stuart calculated that when Partouneaux, the French commander in Calabria, saw that the ships were sailing north, he would withdraw his army on Naples. 1,200 men under Lt-Col. Haviland Smith were detached from the convoy soon after sailing and sent to the northern end of the Straits of Messina to capture the fort at Scilla. By June 14 Naples was stirring with rumours of landings, nobody knew where, and misgivings because Napoleon had issued no more bulletins from the Grande Armée. On June 15 Nicola recorded 'Alarm is growing; they say the king is leaving tonight. The Civil Guard have taken over garrison duties in the city. . . . The telegraph is said to have announced a squadron of a hundred sail – some say a hundred and fifty – both men-of-war and transports, coming from the direction of Eboli.'[10] The following day: 'There is said to be a landing in the Gulf of Policastro . . . the force embarked in Sicily is believed to amount to about fifteen thousand men.'[11]

Stuart's armada was almost becalmed. Joachim cancelled his journey to Rome, paraded his guards and told them that within two days he would lead them to throw the enemy back into the sea. Enthusiasm among the conscripts for this line of conduct was not great. In May and June one regiment lost a hundred men by desertion. There was a general and reasonable fear that those not killed in defence of the French régime might at any moment find themselves deserted by it and exposed to the brutality and vengeance of Ferdinand and Mary Caroline. On June 18 it was freely stated that the queen's household had been warned to be in readiness to accompany her to Rome; the king was said to have been seen taking the road to Salerno but the wiseacres claimed that all the troops sent in that direction were in fact turning off to Nola and from there doubling back north to Capua.

Stuart's convoy appeared off Ischia on June 24, and the following morning he sent in two battalions of light infantry under supporting fire from the warships. The garrison retreated to the castle, offering little resistance. On the smaller island of Procida, between Ischia and Naples, the garrison, 'formed out of foreign deserters and prisoners of war, Russians, Sclavonians, and what-not',[12] mutinied. By the time that the British troops landed, they had broken open the stores, got at the brandy, and were threatening to cut the throats of their own officers.

Joachim, despite the strain of panic around him and an inadequate staff, reacted very coolly to the threat from Stuart. He ordered his local commanders, strung out along the four hundred miles of the Tyrrhenian coast, not to move until it was clear where the main enemy blow would fall. He called in the troops from Apulia and warned Miollis that he might need those in the Papal States. Despite the feint attack by Prince Leopold in the Gulf of Policastro, he did not fall into the trap of committing any of his forces.

He had collected a flotilla of gun-boats, half of which he stationed at Naples and the remainder up the coast at Gaëta. Immediately he learned of the attack on Ischia, he ordered the thirty-four boats at Gaëta to return during the night, keeping well inshore to avoid detection by the British ships.

At 3 a.m. on June 26, Colonel Bunbury, Stuart's Quarter-master-General, was woken by a Neapolitan boatman who brought news that the Gaëta gun-boats were moving. The calm which usually accompanies the dawn along that coast prevented the British men-of-war from intercepting them, but six British gun-boats pulled after them and attacked. They were now nearing Cape Miseno and counted on getting protective fire from the land batteries and also those of Procida, which they did not know had surrendered. Shortly afterwards a sufficient breeze sprang up for two of the lighter British ships to get among them. Twenty-four of the Neapolitan boats were captured, five destroyed, and only five managed to limp into port at Baïa. Four days later the fort at Ischia surrendered and both islands were completely under Stuart's control.

'Do not worry,' Joachim wrote to Elisa, now Grand Duchess of Tuscany, when the British first began their attack, 'the English expedition is not against you; it has just dropped anchor in the Procida channel; it has designs on my islands and then, apparently, on my kingdom; I shall do my best to give it a warm welcome and dispute both. I hope you will not be jealous of the preference these gentlemen have shown me and that you will wish me well. The sight of the enemy has only doubled the zeal, enthusiasm and devotion of my subjects.'[13] It was a kindly reassurance, but far from true. Outbreaks of lawlessness moved in from the wilder parts of the provinces to the towns. In Naples itself the army and civil guard manned street barricades and sent out patrols by day as well as by night. As Bunbury said: 'Always in active exertion, encouraging his soldiery, daunting the disaffected by a display of his own intrepidity, and longing impatiently for the landing of the English army, still Murat must have felt his position very embarrassing while the great war remained undecided in Austria.'[14]

Elisa answered. 'I have not the slightest doubt of your success, yet you ought to send the queen and your children to Tuscany . . . If you do not want it to seem that you are making them leave because of the war, they can come and take the waters at Pisa or Lucca.'[15] Joachim had already suggested this, but Caroline refused saying that the children could go but she would not. 'The Queen shows truly admirable courage,' he wrote to Napoleon, 'she insists on staying, and my family will not leave until the last extremity. Her presence produces an extraordinary effect and seems to endear her to the nation.'[16] But he failed to communicate his admiration to Caroline. Aubusson, asked by Champagny whether his criticisms of the king's conduct were made with the queen's knowledge, replied with a clear implication that they were. He added next day that Murat was counting too much on the loyalty of the Neapolitans. 'No doubt his reputation inspires it . . . but what is happening in Germany is really the barometer of our tranquillity and perhaps of the action the English will take . . . Your Excellency has no idea how much what they call the stagnation of affairs in Austria disturbs some and helps others.'[17]

Aubusson took everything in this family a little too much at its face value – Caroline's resentment at not being consulted by Joachim, and Joachim's belief in the loyalty of his subjects. Their relationship was never a crude struggle for power one against the other, though it has often been represented as such. Each appreciated the other's qualities – his energy and courage, her charm and shrewd levelheadedness. But his pride would not accept her interference; her consciousness of her own abilities would not let her stay out of the game.

At Schoenbrunn, His Imperial and Royal Majesty was about to

end the stagnation of affairs in Austria. New troops had arrived to replace those slaughtered at Aspern-Essling.

The pope had excommunicated both Napoleon and Joachim on June 10. On Napoleon's orders he was arrested in the Quirinal Palace at 4 a.m. on July 6 and bundled off in a carriage to France.[18] The News reached Naples on July 8 but failed to produce any popular reaction, though it increased the rate of desertion, the troops having been told that if they continued to serve Murat the pope would turn them blind. Next day it was learned that Partouneaux, who had withdrawn from Scilla when Colonel Smith invaded, had returned and driven the British back across the straits. Throughout the crisis, Joachim had bolstered public morale by frequently driving through the streets with Caroline and the children; on July 15, Caroline having gone with him to dine at Portici, they determined to defy the British blockade by returning to Naples by sea, a decision that was not received with great enthusiasm at their table. 'It was 10 o'clock in the evening. The night was dark and the sea misty. Finally, by dint of begging, we prevailed on Their Majesties not to wait for the boats but to return by land,'[19] reported Aubusson, the only person outside the royal household who had attended the dinner.

Stuart, meanwhile, was facing problems on Ischia. He had not enough men to attack Naples, but too many to remain where he was. 'There we were,' said Bunbury, 'with 13,000 or 14,000 eating men (including officers and followers) and some 1,500 horses and mules, upon a small island, extremely beautiful, but yielding none of the supplies which an army requires excepting wine. Even of good water there was a scarcity. In a few days the inconvenience was increased by the arrival of Prince Leopold with his part of the expedition.'[20] Bunbury urged an attack higher up the coast, at Civita Vecchia or Leghorn; or, if not an attack, then a feint that might draw troops away from Austria. Sir John was still in his customary state of indecision when three items of news made up his mind for him; the report of the failure of Colonel Smith's expedition in Calabria and the consequent danger of a Neapolitan counter-invasion of Sicily; a dispatch from Lord Collingwood, commanding the Mediterranean fleet, warning that the French fleet at Toulon might in bad weather be able to slip past him and cut Stuart's forces off from Palermo; the information, sent by Joachim from the mainland, of Napoleon's defeat of the Austrians at Wagram. Sir John put his troops back into their transports and sailed for Messina.

Joachim had a *Te Deum* sung in the Royal Chapel. But he had little reason for rejoicing. The brigands were now 'more in the ascendant than they have been before'.[21] They were gaining the upper hand not only in Calabria but beyond the Gran Sasso in the province of Teramo. During 1809 there were 33,000 reported acts of brigandage. The worst outbreaks were in the province of Cilento, and there the king sent Colonel Manhes, his former aide-de-camp, to restore order.[22]

4

At sunset on August 14, a salvo from beflagged gun-boats in the harbour announced the eve of the emperor's feast day. At the palace, the king and queen attended the play, a ball and supper. At dawn next morning the salvo was repeated but turned out to be from three British frigates, a corvette and eleven gun-boats which were engaging the shore batteries. Joachim, instead of driving to the Academy and then to the Mercatello, where he had instituted an annual trade fair to be held during the fortnight following the emperor's birthday, leaped on his horse and went first to the Castel dell'Ovo to direct the return fire and then to the Chiaja promenade where he reviewed the Guard of Honour in defiance of the enemy, while Caroline called for her carriage and drove around the city. That evening the theatres were open free, with a grand cantata at the theatre of San Carlo, adjoining the palace. On August 20 there were renewed festivities for Joachim's own name day.[1] The British squadron did not reappear. Aubusson returned to France on August 22, leaving his French secretary, Hué de Grosbois as Chargé d'Affaires, and the relationship between Caroline and Joachim – which the ambassador had certainly painted too darkly and perhaps aggravated – began to improve.

Joachim's principal preoccupation was with the weakness of the country's finances, from which so many other problems flowed.

Napoleon's Continental System was strangling trade and impeding production by increasing discontent. On September 8 the diarist Nicola noted that a bandit in the province of Basilicata was marching at the head of a thousand men with drums beating and banners flying. Agar reported that in eight months only 100,000 ducats had been collected of the annual 800,000 in taxes. Joachim ordered renewed efforts by the provincial intendants and closer cooperation with military detachments. He sent one of his aides-de-camp to Schoenbrunn with a plea that he should be allowed to open his ports to the Americans (three of their vessels were under arrest and another sixteen expected). 'The trade of my kingdom is absolutely nil; granaries, warehouses and stores are crammed with our produce; the land lies uncultivated, even the harvest has not been fully brought in, and in consequence the taxes cannot be collected; in a word, I am in an unimaginable difficulty; I no longer know how to pay the troops and carry on the government.'[2] Treading softly, for he knew that the emperor's most sensitive spot was his self-defeating trade war with Britain: 'May I dare beg Your Majesty to let me know whether I can permit the export of oil to neutrals for countries friendly to, or at peace with, Your Majesty? The vessels would be compelled to come in ballast to collect it; with that precaution no foreign merchandise can be fraudulently imported into my realm and I shall receive sufficient currency to operate all the services.'[3]

The emperor's reply was: 'French cloth is paying duty, issue a decree exempting French merchandise and cloth in particular.'[4] Joachim passed it to Agar asking for a detailed report on its effect. He also told him to draft a letter 'in which you will show that if the emperor persisted with this project it would be impossible for me to pay his troops ... and the manufactures at present being established in my kingdom would be stifled at birth'.[5] He had paid considerable attention to the cloth industry. He had ordered a thousand merino sheep from Spain to improve the native breed; he had advanced money to local manufacturers and granted them sites for factories; he had issued instructions for his troops to be dressed in nothing but Neapolitan materials. Agar reported that, 'On the day when products of French manufacture are admitted without paying any tax, we shall have to give up all manufacture in the kingdom . . . In the province of Naples alone, 60,000 individuals will be exposed to the most abject poverty . . . The revenue from customs, which may currently be assessed at 400,000 francs a month, will be reduced by two thirds.'[6]

Joachim was in the dilemma that he had foreseen and that was shortly to compel Louis to renounce his throne. Was he to obey the emperor or to defend the welfare of his subjects? It was clear that as long as Napoleon persisted in his Continental System, and tried to protect France from its consequences, the two duties were incompatible. Eventually Joachim would have to break faith with one or the other. For a few months more his decision hung in the balance. He asked Napoleon to take him with when he returned to Spain. He asked for permission to go to Paris for talks, accompanied by Caroline. He saw the need for confrontation, but he seemed to be speaking to a deaf man.

Misery and uneasiness began to descend on the royal household again. Caroline spent two days in September at the Real Casa Carolina, her girls' school at Aversa; she went to Pompeii to watch new excavations and stayed during most of October at Portici, reading and doing needlework. 'I have the most pleasant and at the same time the most magnificent view in the universe,' she wrote to Hortense, sending her a tea-set decorated with pictures of the royal palaces and villas. 'From my bed I can see that famous Capri; on the left the shores of Sorrento, farther off Ischia and Procida, and on my right Naples rising like an amphitheatre on the edge of the bay.'[7] But the view was no compensation for the life she led. 'I hope you are sorry for me, five hundred leagues away from you and unable to enjoy your delightful talk – for here they do not even know how to play hot cockles. . . . If I did not have a good library I believe I should die of boredom.'[8]

In the third week of November, Joachim received a letter from the emperor giving him permission to go to Paris for consultations. He set off on November 20. Caroline followed him next day at a slower pace. It was cold and wet, the Volturno had broken its banks in Capua, the roads into France were already covered in snow. In Naples the word went round that Joachim had gone to beg Napoleon not to take his kingdom from him, and Caroline to ask for it to be left to her.

There were many great events imminent when he reached Paris on November 30: the celebration of the fifth anniversary of the coronation, receptions for the sovereigns of Europe who came as vassals to attend it, and above all the divorce which the emperor had at last made up his mind to impose on Josephine. Caroline joined Joachim on December 4 in the lodgings provided for them in the Pavillon de Flore. Both attended the reception and ball at the hôtel de Ville that night, he in Laure Junot's words, 'very handsome, wearing the uniform of his guards, a white tunic with amaranthine facings, the gold brandenburgs making a sort of golden cuirass across his chest, on which gleamed the diamonds of many orders, in the middle of which one saw the sparkle of the Legion of Honour; he went to each woman and repeated the homage that he rendered them when he was still no more than General Murat, and did it with a good nature that deprived the action of any appearance of the ridiculous.'9 To her rival Caroline, Laure was less lenient. She accused her of starchiness and coldness and 'a sneering laugh that was odious and provoking to the last degree. . . . Since she had little intelligence there was nothing to compensate for her loss of beauty, which was already deserting her in 1809 and 1810. In any event she had never had anything more than freshness and a beautiful skin; once that freshness was lost there was nothing left but very ordinary woman, had she not been a queen.'10

On December 9 Joachim had a long talk with Napoleon at which they temporarily settled their differences. The following day, not trusting to his brother-in-law's memory, Joachim sent him a letter confirming the points of their conversation, including Napoleon's agreement to abolish the French general staff headquarters in Naples, and to let Murat have licences for the export of oil. To Agar he wrote a letter full of reproaches for the Neapolitan Council of State which had urged trade with America and Britain. 'No doubt it is of essential importance to the nation . . . but it will be injurious to the Emperor's plans.'11 He entrusted the letter to the ordinary courier with the sure knowledge that it would be intercepted and a copy sent to Napoleon.

On December 14 the imperial family gathered at the Tuileries for the dissolution of the Emperor's marriage. Pauline was credited with having given the final push to her hesitant brother by supplying him during the past month with one of her *dames d'honneur* as his mistress, but all on the Bonaparte side had played their part and savoured their victory in this greatest of all battles with the Beauharnais. Napoleon, rightly apprehensive of divorce from his gentle Lady of Victories, was 'in a filthy temper'[12] for a week or more afterwards, fuming at his inability to justify himself and the impertinence of Louis, who had chosen this moment to ask for a separation from Hortense.

With the departure of the king of Saxony from Paris, Joachim and Caroline were able to move from the Pavillon de Flore to their old home at the Elysée. When she left Naples Caroline had told her household that she would return in five or six weeks, but in mid-December she wrote to Agar that 'our stay here may be prolonged until the end of January'.[13] The letter crossed one from Agar to Joachim telling him that 'only the hope that Your Majesty will soon return to your kingdom sustains the administration. If your absence should continue for long, all our efforts will be powerless to combat the effects of a lassitude which can already be felt and which will degenerate into a sort of general prostration.'[14] Two days before Christmas, Salicetti, the powerful and experienced minister of Police, died suddenly. There was a new scare that an English force had retaken Ponza and was to make an attack on Naples. 'King Joachim absent, Salicetti dead, few and insufficient troops, widespread discontent,' noted Nicola. 'God preserve us from disaster.'[15]

The harmony between king and emperor was short-lived. Joachim soon found himself at odds with Napoleon over the revenue of the six duchies which the emperor had established in the Two Sicilies. Napoleon claimed 480,000 francs: Joachim countered, quite correctly, that he was entitled to only half that amount, and offered to send a special messenger to Naples to check the claims. Napoleon tried a flanking movement. 'Inform the Neapolitan ambassador,' he told Champagny, 'that the amount owing to the French Treasury has been established beyond question, and there is no need to verify it . . . steps must be taken for an immediate settlement, or I shall give my generals orders to obtain payment for me.'[16] Joachim still denied that he was liable for more than half the sum. He also asked permission to return to his kingdom. He received no reply.

5

In addition to the continuing argument about money with Napoleon, Joachim was called upon in the Imperial Family Council to give his opinion on the choice of a new wife for the emperor: the daughter of the king of Saxony, the Austrian archduchess Marie-Louise, or the Tsar's sister. The discussion was a formality, though Joachim did not know this. Napoleon considered a Saxon princess not important enough, and had sufficient indication that Alexander would not agree to his sister marrying beneath her. He had already suggested to most of those present what he wished their answer to be. Joachim dashed in with his usual impetuosity and denounced the folly of expecting any benefit from marriage with Austria. The embers of his old revolutionary fervour glowed red at the thought of the ruler of France marrying the grandniece of *La Louve Autrichienne*, Marie-Antoinette. His fears for his own kingdom were heightened at the prospect of Mary Caroline's granddaughter[1] becoming empress. But his arguments against an Austrian alliance were based on sounder considerations than past passions or present selfishness.

'You have chased her out of Italy; you have deprived her of rich provinces; you have torn the German empire from her!' he said. 'If she offers you an archduchess, do not regard that proposal as either proof of friendship or a guarantee of peace ... She imagines that she will recover what she has lost in battle through the influence of the Empress on you and your court; ... and if she is not successful during your reign, she can become all-powerful during that of your successor; she can dominate France during a minority. You well know that Austrian Princesses never cease to be Austrian ... Far from becoming attached to you by such a marriage, Austria will hate you the more, because of the sacrifice she will think she had made to you ... Do not think that she will be restrained by the interests of the Princess you will have married, or of the children she may have given you; one of the maxims of that family is *Sovereigns have no relations*.'[2]

He gave his vote for the daughter of the King of Saxony. If, however, the emperor would not accept a Saxon marriage, Joachim was in favour of an alliance with Russia. 'Since that country has no point of contact with France, the policies of the two Empires can easily agree; each is equally in competition with England and Austria. If they were united they would dominate Europe. Consequently I prefer a grand duchess to an arch-duchess.'[3] Lavalette, who was no admirer of Murat, found the argument 'full of sense, but . . . of no avail against a resolve which had already been made'.[4] Pressing his point, Joachim continued: 'We shall have war with the power that we do not marry, and I would prefer war against the Austrians to war against the Russians.'

As the other members of the council gave their opinions – all of them in favour of an Austrian marriage[5] – Joachim grew more and more indignant, until he eventually burst out at Napoleon: 'Since you had already made your decision, why was I the only one from whom it was kept secret? Why ask me when my honest reply could have no other effect than to set against me the House of Austria which is to become our ally, and the archduchess who will soon be empress?'[6] He knew that the secrecy of the council chamber would not long stand against gossip and ill-will. 'My enemies will not fail to remind her repeatedly that I tried to keep her from the throne on which you are going to place her.'[7] He was in such a temper that he accused Napoleon to his face, and in front of the others, of deliberately leading him into a trap. 'You can have been in no doubt of my opinions since Eugène's marriage – of how little I am in favour of alliances between your family and the old dynasties. In my eyes, Saxony is a new dynasty, since she owes her royalty to you.'[8]

The outburst had an unexpected effect on Napoleon. Impressed despite himself by Joachim's sincerity, he answered that neither he nor the new empress would listen to criticisms of him. He admitted the validity of the arguments about the money owed by Naples and wrote to Champagny: 'It seems to be a fact that there are only four Neapolitan duchies, and that the other two are Sicilian. It also appears correct that the amount of the endowment is in each case sixty and not eighty thousand francs.' This was precisely what Joachim had maintained: that the amount due was not 480,000 francs but 240,000. He also gave Joachim permission to return to his kingdom, and twenty-four licences for export of Neapolitan oil, silk, corn and liquorice. Joachim set off for Naples on January 30, reasonably pleased with the result of his journey. He had taken the first step towards breaching the blockade that was strangling his kingdom, and he believed that he had persuaded Napoleon to give full backing to his long post-poned invasion of Sicily. On the other hand he was more than ever suspicious of Napoleon's real intentions towards him.

'I am miserable indeed at your leaving,' Caroline wrote to him on February 3. 'I am at the Pavillon de Flore, my move here has tired me a little. The emperor still treats me very kindly, and has already asked me several times if I have news of you. Send me some soon. . . . Hug the children for me, and remember that there is somebody at the Pavillon de Flore who is devoted to you and who thinks of you often.'[9] And two days later: 'I am very impatient to receive your news; it seems to me that you are in no hurry to send any. The king of Bavaria said to me yesterday that if he had the good fortune to be in the king of Naples's shoes and to be my husband, he would write to me all the time, night and morning. . . . You must have passed Turin by now. Think of me often and write to me. [P.S.] I am numbering my letters, to make sure that you receive them all.'[10] And next day: 'M. Rochambeau is leaving and I am giving him a little letter for you. . . . There is nothing new about the marriage. . . . I am very bored, very sad. . . . If you go into the provinces be on your guard against those evil Cala-brese. Goodbye again. My God, how miserable I am!'[11]

Two more days went by without news. 'I will begin by telling you that I am very annoyed with you,' she wrote. 'Not a single line from you! That has never happened with you before! We went to a ball at Princess Pauline's yesterday, and hunting today. It was very wet and the emperor said to me: *"Well! The Lazzarone has forgotten you; he doesn't think of you any longer! He is going to be very upset because I am marrying an Austrian."* But he was laughing all the time. . . .'[12] She asked him to have Lechat his major-domo, 'send me the hundred thousand francs that you owe me, for I need a lot of money here, bills are raining on me from all sides.

. . . There is nothing new. . . . I see nobody, and I get bored in my obscure little room. I hope you will come back for the marriage and that you will take me back to Naples, never to leave you again. Hug the children for me and do not spoil Letitia and Achille too much. . . . Do as I do; I often deprive myself of the pleasure of seeing them for fear of spoiling them. Farewell Naples – I miss you Naples, and my beautiful terrace.'[13]

She had stayed behind to woo more concessions, such as that for the trade under licence with America; but there was another reason for her delay in returning to Naples: Napoleon needed a hostess to replace Josephine and to receive his new bride. Hortense would have been his choice but it was scarcely fitting to use her in the present circumstances. Pauline was unsuitable in any event. Elisa was busy ruling her principality. Caroline undoubtedly knew that she would be ordered to remain in Paris until the new empress had settled in, but she concealed this from Joachim for fear of upsetting him.

On February 11, thanking him for a letter he had written from Turin, she gave the first hint. 'I hope to see you in March, for that is when the wedding will be. The emperor is always asking me for news of you and treats me with kindness. All the family will be coming for the wedding, for you know that he is marrying an Austrian.'[14] That was the worry: because he was marrying an Austrian, was it possible that Joachim would refuse to come? Next day she told him the rest of the news. 'I am very miserable. There is a question of my making a long journey. The emperor wishes me to go as far as Braunau to fetch the new empress. We should have to go and come back by short stages – imagine how pleasant that will be! . . . Hug my children for me, send me news of them often, and of you. . . . Do not let Letitia go out too much, it will upset Achille and Lucien.'[15]

Her misery was not as great as she made out. She enjoyed the distinction of going to meet the new Empress, and the opportunity to establish a hold on her. She advised on the choice of women to attend Marie-Louise and it was with great reluctance she refused Napoleon's offer to make her superintendent of the empress's household. The position, he assured her, would be unique, never to be passed on to any successor, not inferior in rank to that of any queen. Indeed, 'I should take precedence over the queens of

Spain and Holland,'[16] – a very tempting proposition. But he insisted that she should remain in the post for at least two years and she was not willing to leave Joachim and the children for so long.

6

Joachim arrived in Naples on February 14, the fourth anniversary of the entry of French troops under Joseph. The streets and the balconies were decorated in his honour, the *lazzaroni* shouted *Long live the King!* ('under the guidance of a policeman',[1] remarked the unenthusiastic Nicola) and on February 15 a fountain outside the palace, representing Napoleon as Jove, Caroline as Diana and Joachim as an identified figure on Pegasus, flowed with free wine, using up 740 casks during the course of the afternoon. The third day's rejoicing was over-clouded by demonstrations against the rising price of flour, a high wind which blew down the decorations and illuminations, and an earth tremor.

Conscious of the implications of the Austrian marriage, and wary of a possible Trojan Horse within his frontiers, Joachim set about some urgent readjustments. From the minister of War, Daure, he asked for a list of all French officers in Neapolitan employment. It was his intention, he said, 'to restore all the different branches of the administration of my kingdom to Neapolitan subjects and in future to entrust the command of my troops and my provinces only to generals in my service. All artillery and engineer commands should similarly be given to Neapolitans; so that French generals and all French heads of services and employees should in future be charged only with the service of French troops.'[2] The training of Neapolitans for these posts would take time; meanwhile there were Frenchmen in offices of power whom he must watch. Reynier, the Minister of Posts, for example, whom he had begun to suspect of dubious allegiance, as he had the even more powerful Salicetti before his recent death. 'At the time, when the English occupied the islands,' he wrote to Reynier, 'orders were given to the Post Office to keep watch on the correspondence of individuals notified by the police as suspects. I judged it proper to continue that surveillance during my absence; but now that order has been restored . . . I direct that this surveillance ceases . . . No letter may be opened under any pretext whatsoever.'[3]

His desire to set his army on an all-Neapolitan footing was prompted by considerations of economy as well as of security. For a long time he had been paying Neapolitan troops on service in Spain; both paying and maintaining those in the north of Italy; and feeding and paying the French units quartered in the Kingdom of Naples. 'The Viceroy warns me that, by Your Majesty's order, 5,300 men are to return to the kingdom,' he wrote to Napoleon. 'These, added to those already arrived from Rome, make a total of about eleven thousand men. If these troops are destined to make the expedition into Sicily, I thank Your Majesty very much; but if they are to remain at my charge in my kingdom, I cannot conceal my embarrassment from you. I have already had the honour of telling you in Paris that it is impossible for me to pay them.'[4]

He was on the point of going to Calabria to lead a drive against the brigands when he received Napoleon's summons to be in Paris by March 20 for his wedding with Marie-Louise on March 29. Next day, Andral, Caroline's doctor, arrived with a confidential letter from her on all the outstanding matters that she had been waiting to tell him about: 'There are so few safe opportunities, and it is not worth writing at all if one does it by post or the estafette, since one cannot say anything.'[5]

She began by grumbling about the people to whom he was awarding the Order of the Two Sicilies. 'You are giving it to everybody and many people are making jokes about it.'[6] With that off her mind she passed to the principal business of the letter: the members of her household whom she wished sent to attend her at the wedding. 'The emperor desires that I shall have at least four Neapolitan ladies, beautiful and with good figures, and they must be chosen from the richest and greatest names.'[7] She gave him a list, adding with the briskness of a woman who sees a wedding approaching and intends to enjoy it: 'You will see that they are given 15,000 francs for the journey and a carriage from my stables, and they can make their own arrangements about their maids. I do not want to hear any more about this. If you do not want the expense of it I will pay it out of my own purse, for the emperor wishes me to have an attractive court.'[8]

She knew he had gone off with the suspicion that Napoleon, now that the intervening Papal States had been annexed to France might be planning to simplify the Italian scene by adding Naples as well. 'The emperor is very well disposed towards you, and from what he says, I can see that he will never have any intention of taking over Naples.'[9] She repeated her injunction that he should make every effort to get to the wedding, 'because otherwise the emperor will be very displeased. If, however, you have very strong objections which prevent you from making this journey, write them to me in secret and write a charming letter to the emperor to excuse yourself. But . . . I regard your coming here for the marriage as something very useful to our interests.'[10]

She wrote again two days later, worried by news of an earthquake and a report that the tremors were still continuing. 'I was very pleased to hear that you are to go hunting at Mondragone. . . . I would so much like to be with you and our poor children, although I am very happy here and the Emperor overwhelms me and, without meaning to reproach you, they spoil me a great deal more here than you do in Naples, and sometimes they say they are very glad to see me. I do not want to complain about you, but I hope that on my return you will spoil me so much that I will never again want to come back to Paris. Do not be vexed by this little joke . . . I am so happy at the thought of seeing you soon.'[11]

Joachim received Napoleon's invitation on March 9. Despite Caroline's fears,[12] he seems not to have hesitated about going to Paris, though he made it clear in his acknowledgement, written an hour before he left on March 12, that he hoped not to be kept hanging around as he had been on the last occasion. 'My departure will certainly create a bad effect, which will be especially felt in Calabria; the brigands will become bold again, as well as the English and the court at Palermo; but my Guard and my transport are proceeding to Monteleone as well as other troops; and preparations for the expedition continue; and finally, to calm anxiety, I have promised to be back before the end of April.'[13] He reached Compiègne on March 22, 1810.

7

Caroline was already in Munich, recovering from the bruises inflicted by the 'detestable' south German highways. 'The thawing of the snow has flooded the roads to such an extent that the horses swim while the wheels stay stuck in the ruts,'[1] she told Hortense. She lodged with the king and queen of Bavaria for five days, leaving on March 14. The meeting at Braunau on March 16 was saddened by the young bride's having to leave behind her Austrian retainers and her pet dog, Napoleon having decided to follow in the minutest detail the protocol observed at the reception of Marie-Antoinette in 1770. But the queen and the empress took to each other almost at first sight. Caroline admiring Marie-Louise's 'charming figure, dignified bearing, very fresh complexion (perhaps too much so), charming blonde hair, hands and feet that left nothing to be desired, and cultivated mind',[2] while Marie-Louise after a moment of hesitation on the first day – 'I do not entirely trust her'[3] – was soon captivated by Caroline's warmth and sympathy.

It was an exhausting journey for both of them. Back in Munich on March 18 Caroline told Hortense that 'I am very tired, for they are driving me as if I were in the army.'[4] Berthier frequently had them up at 5 a.m. and on the road until 11 p.m. Fatigue no doubt accounted for her frankness: 'The empress is putting up with the journey very well; she speaks to me about you a great deal. M. de Metternich has told her that you are the most beautiful person at Court; I have told her that you are not that exactly but that you are very attractive and above all very good and lovable. The empress is blooming with health, of a beautiful figure, very amiable, very sweet, in fact charming, but not very pretty.'[5]

She found three letters from Joachim waiting for her, the first she had received since leaving Paris. They had been written some three weeks before, scolding her for not keeping him informed, telling her of Achille's delight in the electrical toy she had sent him, and Louise's progress at reading, and various appointments at court that he had made. She was still intent on overcoming his suspicions of the Austrian alliance and did not yet know whether or not he was on his way to Paris. She told him that Marie-Louise was very friendly. 'I am sure that what you say about her not liking you, and the other things, will prove to be wrong. This morning, when I said I was writing to you: *"I beg you sister to tell the king of Naples to give me his friendship: I desire it so much; I have heard him spoken of a great deal; I hope he will come to Paris and I shall look forward to meeting him."* She is excessively kind and sweet and never calls me anything but "Her sister the queen of Naples" . . . I promise you that she will not get involved in any sort of intrigue.'[6]

She told him that the king and queen of Bavaria were being kind to her, but 'I am very tired, although this is only the first day of the journey; but to remain in a carriage for sixteen hours without being able to get out even once, and having no convenience and being surrounded by equerries and guards, is terrible . . . The Empress, who is young, puts up with it marvellously, but for me, who have had children, it means great suffering. But I shall willingly forget all my burdens if the empress pleases the Emperor, makes us happy, and gives us a big boy.'[7] When they left Munich on March 19 Marie-Louise had lost her last link with home: her former governess, Countess Maria Lazansky, was sent back to Vienna that morning. 'I can truly make no greater sacrifice to my bridegroom than this,'[8] Marie-Louise wrote to her father. Madame Durand, later a member of her household, suggested that Caroline insisted on the countess's departure because she was jealous of her influence over the young empress, but Caroline did not usually behave in so clumsy a manner, and Marie-Louise's attitude towards her grew warmer rather than cooler.[9]

Tiredness, worry about Joachim's decision, and an increasing anxiety over Napoleon's possible reaction when he discovered that his bride was not very pretty, sharpened the tone of Caroline's letters as the journey continued. They reached the palace at Stuttgart in the afternoon of March 20, Caroline worn out and Marie-Louise developing a cold in the head. The bride's shyness and reserve did not make too happy an impression on the king of Würtemberg. 'The queen of Naples is very weary,' he wrote to his daughter Catherine, 'and truly that is the least to be expected; what a task they have given her; between ourselves, it is inconceivable; she is doing the best she can, but I think she is a bit tired of the job. The empress did not speak to anybody except me, the queen and the Princess Royal; your brother did not get a single word. The etiquette is a little extraordinary. Anyway it is over now.'[10] It was not entirely a matter of etiquette. 'I do not like any of the Royal Family, with the exception of the Queen and the Princess Royal,' Marie-Louise wrote to her father; and they did not endear themselves to her by taking her to hear an opera in a theatre 'so cold that the Queen of Naples and I have not yet been able to recover from it'.[11]

They jolted on to Carlsruhe next day and by March 23 were at Strasbourg, where Marie-Louise stayed in bed until 11 a.m. suffering from catarrh, headache and a sore throat. They were travelling through France now and Caroline was relieved to learn, when they got to Lunéville in the evening of March 24, that Joachim had arrived and was with the emperor at Compiègne. She assured him again that Marie-Louise had the most eager desire to visit Naples and was eating macaroni on every occasion that offered. 'From six in the morning to ten at night I have so much shouting of *Vive l'Impératrice* in my ears, that I wake up with a start during the night, and I begin to shout it too. I beg of you to warn Paulette and all the family that when they see me I shall reply to the first question they put to me with *Vive l'Impératrice* ... that's all I can say now, I'm just like Agnelet.'[12]

Next day they were at Nancy. It was Caroline's birthday. 'I was upset not to find a letter from you,' she told Joachim, 'and I am very annoyed that Madame Caramanica is one of the party – I thought I had told you that was something I did not want.[13] I had hoped that when it was a question of a *dame du palais* it was not too much of an assumption of power[14] to designate the one I liked best. But patience! I have put up with so much vexation in my life that I can put up with this little bit more.'[15] She reverted to the worry that was growing more insistent as they approached their journey's end. 'I hope the emperor is pleased with the letters I write him; I am afraid he may have the idea that the empress is beautiful, for all the young people who saw her from a distance have said that she was beautiful.'[16] Finally, because she could not be cross with him for long: 'Good-bye. I am sad because I am upset at your not having done what I wanted, but that does not prevent me from loving you very dearly. If you were kinder, and if you tried more often to please me, you would be too perfect and I should be too happy.'[17]

But next evening her resentment bubbled over when she received a letter from Pauline, telling her that Joachim had said she was not writing to him enough. 'So you will never cease being unfair! I arrive very tired, worn out with responsibility, and I often lose sleep to write to you, and still you complain! I write you more letters than I get from you. Good-bye! I shall be happy when you cease to be unfair, for your unfairness has always upset me. I kiss you and love you very tenderly. Let me know at once whether the Emperor is pleased with the letters I write him.'[18]

They were due to meet Napoleon at a field near Soissons where three large tents had been erected, one for the French party, one for the Austrian, and one in the middle for the ceremonial encounter. Here, according to the programme, 'the Empress will bow, preparatory to kneeling; the emperor will raise her and kiss her; and their Majesties will be seated'.[19] But long before they reached Soissons, outside the village church at Courcelles, the door of their carriage was flung open and in from the pouring rain sprang Napoleon and Joachim. Caroline moved to the front seat beside Joachim while the emperor embraced his startled bride. 'Your portrait does not flatter you,'[20] she said, referring to the picture that Berthier had brought to show her, and winning her bridegroom's heart at once. He asked her what advice she had been given, and she replied: 'To obey you in all things.'[21] He was so delighted with her that he ordered the coachman to drive straight to Compiègne, where they arrived at 9.30 p.m. in drenching rain. The family and royal guests saw little of her as Napoleon whisked her from the carriage up the windswept steps. She took her supper not at the great table in the Francis I Gallery but in her own apartments, with the emperor and Caroline, who soon excused herself on the grounds of sleepiness.

The civil marriage took place at St-Cloud on April 1; the religious ceremony was performed in Paris the next day, in a temporary chapel installed in the Salon Carré at the end of the long gallery of the Louvre.

Napoleon, who had an unhappy penchant for the gaudy on such occasions, and lacked the figure to carry it off, got himself up in a white satin gold-embroidered costume, a white satin cloak strewn with golden bees, and a black velvet cap with eight rows of diamonds and three white plumes held in place with the famous Regent diamond from the Bourbon crown jewels. He took Marie-Louise back to St-Cloud and then to Compiègne on April 5, remaining there with her until April 26, when they set out on a triumphal progress through Belgium, where many of the groom's subjects could remember having been those of the bride's father. He was an attentive husband. 'The emperor has become invisible to his family,' Catherine wrote to her father on April 13, 'and the empress receives nobody in her apartments except the Queen of Naples. None of the other sisters or sisters-in-law is admitted.'[22] Neither was Joachim, now eager to take his leave and get back to the problems of his kingdom. He sent a written request for permission to go on April 3, immediately after the wedding. While he waited in Compiègne he began to brood on past grievances.

On April 8 he addressed a long letter to the emperor protesting about his demands for money, the injustice of having to pay the French troops in Naples at active service rates when the war was over, the burden of paying for a French general staff and administration that he did not need, the uncooperative attitude of French agents and consular officials, the emperor's interference with his appointment of Neapolitan ambassadors, the emperor's failure to send the licences for export that he had been promised. His indignation swelled and next day he sent another letter: 'I have had myself announced to Your Majesty every day since my arrival at Compiègne. I do not complain at not having been received ... I must undoubtedly have merited it, for Your Majesty never acts unjustly to anybody and you were formerly well-disposed to me. However, Sire, I can no longer bear my suffering: ... It is time to put an end to this. I shall present myself this morning; I beg that you will do me the favour of receiving me.'[23] Napoleon did so and they had a violent quarrel, but it was not until midnight on April 18 that he finally got away, travelling as fast as he could go: despite a delay of twenty-four hours when his carriage broke down after leaving Florence, he arrived in Naples in a post-chaise accompanied by a single outrider at one o'clock in the afternoon of April 27. Still ringing in his ears was the sound of the emperor's voice, threatening to 'have your head cut off.'[24]

8

Caroline had not received the imperial permission to leave, and it is likely that she stayed with Joachim's approval. She herself suggested that 'if your expedition to Sicily takes place[1] it will not be a bad thing for me to remain, for if you need to ask the Emperor for something it would be better for me to be here to represent your interests'.[2] She accompanied Marie-Louise as far as Cambrai on the Belgian tour; dragooned by the emperor along jolting roads, called before dawn for the next day's journey, tramping round factories, standing interminably at civic receptions being dragged in boats through the tunnels of the Tronquay Canal with water up to their knees, and waiting in wet clothing while their carriages were dismantled and carried in sections over too-narrow bridges. 'This operation delayed us by a good hour and put the queen of Naples in such a bad humour that one could not speak to her for the rest of the day,'[3] Marie-Louise recorded in her diary on April 29. The testiness was infectious, for when Caroline, exhausted and suspecting that she was pregnant again, decided to return to Paris, the young empress noted, 'I am not sorry, I have a bone to pick with her, because ... but in this world one must forgive injuries; I resign myself to it, but I shall never have a high opinion of her again.'[4] Marie-Louise did not say what the injury was, but it was clearly pique that, after flirting with 'that wretched fop' Metternich and 'Uncle Ferdinand',[5] Caroline had encouraged both of them to return to Paris with her.

Napoleon had suggested that for the sake of economy[6] she should lodge in the Paris houses of the king of Westphalia or the king of Holland, both of whom had returned to their kingdoms. Louis had already given her a similar invitation, but when she arrived there she found that Hortense's equerry was unenthusiastic and belatedly realized that anything suggested by Louis would for that reason be resented by Hortense.[7] 'I perceived from M. Turgot's remarks that it might annoy you,' she wrote to Hortense, 'and I abandoned the idea immediately, for I should be too unhappy at the thought of having done anything that might be disagreeable to you.'[8] She returned to the Pavillon de Flore, and it was here during the next few weeks – if at all – that she began or renewed her affair with Metternich.[9]

She certainly met him in the course of her attendance on the empress, and equally certainly cultivated the friendship because of the influence that Austria could have on the continued tenure of the Neapolitan throne by Joachim and herself. During one of these meetings she said to him: 'Well, now France is united to Austria for ever. The two sovereigns and the two peoples can never be anything but friends.' 'I would not like to guarantee it,' Metternich replied. 'The emperor of the French is at the pinnacle of human grandeur; no other sovereign ever raised his glory and power to such heights. But does he know how to stop? Will he not try to submit all the states of Europe to his dictatorship? If that is so, then there is no purpose in his having become the emperor of Austria's son-in-law; in the end, all the powers will form an alliance against him, and we shall destroy him.'[10] She paid little attention to the words then, but she often repeated them to Agar four or five years later.

Laure Junot's claim that Caroline pursued Metternich and was unsuccessful because he found her physically disgusting is evident nonsense. The contrary suggestion that they were lovers, rests on a certain amount of gossip and two specific statements. One is by Stendhal, that about 1810 or 1811: 'I saw M. de Metternich, then at St-Cloud, wearing a bracelet of Caroline Murat's hair.'[11] The other is a letter written home by Lucien's daughter, Charlotte,[12] which was opened in the *cabinet noir* and forwarded to the Emperor. 'The queen of Naples is behaving in a very funny way,' wrote Lolotte. 'Her husband has gone back to Naples, and she has not gone with him, which Grandmama thinks very wrong; but what is worse is that she is always, every moment of the day, with a man named Meternick, an ambassador, who is quite young. There is a lot of talk about it. Princess Pauline is so unwell that she does not take much interest in pleasures. But on the whole the Grand Duchess E. and the queen of Naples cause Grandmama a great deal of sorrow by their conduct.'[13] After his return from Belgium, the emperor's quarrel with Lucien flared up again. When Caroline tried to defend him, Napoleon denounced the perfidy of his brood and produced Charlotte's letter. 'You think she has any affection for you? Well, see how she talks about you!'[14] Caroline dismissed it as childish prattle.

'Do not leave me as long without letters as you did on your first journey,' she wrote to Joachim on the day that he left Compiègne. 'You know how dear you are to me and that I cannot bear being apart for one moment from the father of my children.'[15] In her next letter: 'My dear, if I had known you were not leaving until midnight, I would have come to join you in Paris to see you for one more moment; I cannot tell you how sad I am without you here.'[16] And on April 22, urging him to take great care in the expedition against Sicily, and reassurring him of the emperor's good will: 'Will you be kind enough to have my apartments arranged as I wished? ... If you would give the Grand Marshal instructions, he has the plans and I shall find it ready for my return. I want to tell you too, how filled with grief I was at seeing you leave and above all how touched by your affectionate manner towards me; you have never been like that before, and I confess that it filled me with love; and it is that which has given me courage to ask what I want of you, without being afraid that you would get cross as you always used to, which made me not want to ask you for anything, or be indebted to you for anything.'[17]

By May 8 she had received his first letter from Naples, 'I cannot tell you how happy and how sad it has made me,' she replied. 'My poor children! I shed tears at the thought of them in your arms, asking again and again for their mother. Heavens! when we are united once more we must never be separated again ... kiss them for me and keep telling them that their mother can never know perfect happiness far from them, far from you. ...'[18] My dearest, this last separation seems to me even more insupportable than the others. You were so good, so perfect to me in those last moments, that your kindness brought me to tears and still fills me with affection. I confess that when you do justice to my true feelings for you, I am the happiest of women, believe me, my happiness, the happiness of my whole life, consists only in the joy of the father of my children, he whom I look upon as my dearest friend.[19] ... You will see one day: we shall be the happiest creatures in the world, and we shall owe it to our children. They will give us back all the love we have for them, and our old age will be adorned with their virtues. See as I do – far into the future. I think it is in the nature of mothers that they live in their children's future.'[20]

There was another sentence in this letter – one of great urgency though she did not dwell on it: 'You must make every effort to take Sicily, my dear. Above all lose no time about it; I advise this very strongly.'[21] For word had reached her – possibly through their friend Fouché – that the emperor was considering making peace with England: a peace in which Sicily might be used as a counter. The suggestion was plausible. It would be a graceful gesture to the new empress – refraining from throwing her grandmother out of the remnants of her kingdom. There were strong rumours that Napoleon was already in communication with Mary Caroline.[22] He was at that moment sending his troops into Holland and forcing Louis's abdication; there was no reason to believe that he would not suppress or give way their kingdom of Naples the moment it suited him.

'I am sure the emperor appreciates our feeling towards him, and that he is very fond of you,' she added. 'He is quick-tempered, but he is so well-disposed to us that we ought never to doubt his sentiments.'[23] But it was clear that *she* did, and two days later she repeated the warning. 'Everybody advises you to take Sicily. It is necessary and absolutely essential, for the emperor will readily sacrifice Sicily for peace. So borrow money on every side, do anything that needs be, but lose no time and take Sicily, because you may soon get a counter order, for there are negotiations in progress.'[24]

On May 6, he received a letter from Clarke saying that the emperor had approved his plans for the invasion. His Guard of Honour set off for Calabria on May 8, halting for the night at Torre Annunziata, which they renamed Gioacchinopoli in honour of their king and the approaching victory. Joachim made no secret of his impending descent on Sicily, nor of his confidence that he would succeed. On June 3 he set up his headquarters at Scilla.

One June 11 the bolt arrived from the blue; Clarke's aide-de-camp, Colonel Leclerc, brought instructions that no attempt should be made on Sicily unless there was certainty of success – 'the emperor regards the enterprise as impossible, unless there are the means of transporting 15,000 men at the same time'.[25] It was a stunning blow. He had the troops – and more. But the transport was strung out along three hundred miles of coastline and even when he had collected it all under the British guns across the straits he would not have enough to carry 15,000 men at one time.

There was worse to come. In case he should think of arguing or disobeying: 'the emperor desires me to remind you that the French troops are to be commanded by French generals.'[26] So, if it came to the point, they would refuse Murat's orders. And there was still worse. 'It is the emperor's will that [Colonel Leclerc] shall on his return give him a personal account of the condition of the fortresses of Naples, of Gaëta and many details whose multiplicity prevents their incorporation in an ordinary written report.'[27] The implication was clear and brutal. Napoleon was not satisfied with Murat's stewardship; he was prepared to take over with his own troops as he had in Holland, where Louis too, had tried to act like a king. And he sent a mere colonel to inspect and report.[28]

Murat replied with a torrent of indignation, a long repetitive letter that was sarcastic, pleading and defiant by turns. He regretted not being in Naples 'to assist the mission of the minister's aide-de-camp whom you have sent there to obtain secret information. Sire, nobody will provide you with any more truthful than I.' He bitterly resented the humiliation to which he would be exposed if he withdrew from the Sicily venture – 'at the moment when I was waiting only for my siege artillery before attempting the crossing – whose success nobody doubted, not even the English'.[30] He returned to the insult that he could not swallow: 'Why send junior officers into the heart of my capital to say that the emperor does not want the expedition? Private letters will soon send the news to the army and to Sicily.'[31] But he did not intend to abandon his project. 'I will see presently what is best to be done.'[32] He launched into a catalogue of advantages already gained – British troops withdrawn from islands they had occupied, brigandage reduced in Calabria; indications that the British were demoralized and the Sicilians ready to welcome an invasion. He stopped, apologized for writing at such length, and evidently sent the letter off without pausing to read it again. Even his correspondence he conducted at the charge.

On July 5 he moved to his advanced invasion headquarters at Piale. 'We are standing in battle array; army against army like the Israelites and Philistines in the Book of Samuel,' wrote General Campbell, Stuart's adjutant-general. 'Murat's large pavilion tent is pitched, his tricolour flag flying, and his eagles posted at the ridge above the Punta di Pezzo. . . . A large encampment surrounds him and the plains of Melia are white with tents; and the shore from Scilla to Pezzo and round that point is studded with gunboats and boats of debarkment.'[33]

He received a letter from Caroline saying that the emperor had given her permission to return. He told Lanusse, the Grand Marshal of the palace to suspend the refurnishing of the queen's apartments so that she could give her own instructions, and to go to meet her at Terracina. To the minister of Police he gave orders that 'she shall be received as I should be myself and with all the display possible within the short time that can be given to the preparations. My only regret is that I shall not be able to be at Naples at that time.'[34] His forces were almost built up to the point where Napoleon's stipulations could be met. 'You have forgotten me, my dear Letitia,' he wrote to his elder daughter, 'for it is a long time since I received a letter from you. Write to me quickly. Tell me how lucky you are to have your Mama returning. It is a long time since I was so happy.'[35] Caroline returning, the expedition about to be launched; he could ask for nothing more.

But before the crossing was made, he had to convince Grenier, the senior French general, that it was possible. And Grenier, though sympathetic, was bound by the emperor's orders. On July 25 there was a disheartening set-back: a large convoy bringing ammunition and provisions was intercepted in the Gulf of Santa Eufemia by a British frigate and two brigs. After a furious battle lasting two hours, the entire Neapolitan flotilla of twleve gun-boats and thirty-one transports was captured or sunk.

9

In Paris Caroline had spent the weeks since the emperor's return from Belgium in repeating her requests to be allowed to go to

Naples and in trying to get from him the concessions that he refused to Joachim. Her social life was restricted because of her pregnancy, but she attended the reception at the Hôtel de Ville on June 10, dancing the opening quadrille with Eugène as her partner, and went to Neuilly when Pauline[1] gave a fête for Marie-Louise on June 14. There had been many changes. Pauline, who believed her looks were best displayed against plain backgrounds, had reupholstered the rooms in monochromes, her bedroom all blue, her dressing room all orange, others all green or red or chocolate. There had been changes in the gardens too: new walks and summer houses, and, for tonight, a vast firework display as a background to the gymnastics of Madame Saqui, the rope-dancer, who lit the set pieces with torches she carried in each hand.

'I missed you very much,' she wrote to Joachim. 'I am a little tired. If a letter from you arrived for me today it would make me very happy.'[2] It did arrive. She assured him in reply that the emperor and the empress – despite her relationship with Mary Caroline – were enthusiastic about the attack on Sicily. She hoped that she would soon be able to leave, though each time she asked Napoleon answered testily: 'What, travel in this heat?'[3] She was growing more worried about the risks he would take when the chance came. 'Don't expose yourself more than your duty as a general demands, I implore you; remember that your life belongs to me and is not a property that you can dispose of. And take pity on my cruel anxiety.'[4] In the stiff boredom of St-Cloud she played hide-and-seek with Hortense's Napoléon-Louis – who was to be briefly king of Holland when Louis abdicated a fortnight later – and wrote to tell her: 'Our festivities will soon be finished and I shall be very glad, for in my present condition I find it quite fatiguing.'[5] Even more trying were the constant arguments with Napoleon over money.

On June 23 she slipped back to Paris for a few hours and sent her equerry, Arlincourt, with a secret letter to Joachim, telling him of the latest demand that had been presented to Campochiaro: five million francs by the end of the month, and another eight million over five years. 'The Emperor has made such large payments for his marriage, and the war in Spain is costing him so much, his treasuries are all empty, he is asking money from everybody ... He has just ordered the king of Westphalia to pay him immediately several millions of arrears . . . He is reclaiming debts from all the sovereigns and will not listen to any objection. So I advise you, my dear, to agree to what the emperor wants and appear willing.'[6] She had asked point blank for permission to return to Naples – a request that required courage, for when Pauline recently asked permission to go off to a spa, he had flown into a temper. He took it calmly, agreed, and she was able to tell Joachim that she planned to leave by July 1 or 2, and be home about July 15. Then, just as she was closing the letter, Campochiaro arrived to say that the emperor now agreed to deduct the money that he owed Joachim from the eight million that he claimed Joachim owed him. 'I think what I said to the Emperor must have made some impression on him,'[7] she added delightedly.

On June 24 she went to the ball given by the Imperial Guard in honour of the empress, excused herself from dancing, and left at 11 p.m. In Paris it was 'so hot you cannot breathe',[8] his letters had been delayed or stolen by the Calabrian bandits and she was afraid that he might have been out in the sun and been stricken with fever as in Spain two years before. There was more trouble over her leaving. Napoleon went back on his word and there was a scene when she insisted that she was going. And then there was the problem of all the presents she was expected to give before she left; she asked Joachim to tell Lechat to advance her next month's allowance and, fearful that Napoleon would scold her for pro-digality, or use it as an argument to demand more money for himself, added: 'Do not send me an answer on this matter by the estafette; there is no need for the emperor to be involved in details which only concern us.'[9]

Next day she received three letters from him, at the same time as Napoleon got his indignant protest of June 11. 'I cannot tell you, dear, how grieved I am,' she replied, 'to learn of your vexation. I would give anything in the world to comfort you. I foresaw that you would be annoyed by that officer's mission (they wrote from Naples to tell he had arrived) and two days ago I spoke to the Emperor, telling him how disagreeable it would be to you. The emperor seemed very surprised and answered that it was quite natural, knowing you to be in Sicily and too far away to help Naples if the English made an attempt on your coast . . . there was nothing to upset us in it, and that we were oversensitive people who took offence at everything. . . . I am very worried and sad, particularly when I know that you are unhappy and I am far from you, but allow me to say that you take things too much to heart . . . one must take words as they are and not for more than they are worth. . . . You see, my dearest, there is nothing really bad at the bottom of all this. The worst is the grief that you make for yourself. I beg you to calm down and to tell yourself that you do not have a single sorrow or a single care that I do not share a hundredfold.'[10]

She sent some of the ladies of her household off to Naples, then found herself commanded to Rambouillet, where the emperor was gay, charming, most pleasant to her, and jovially solicitous about the *King of Lazzaroni*. He believed – and so did Caroline – that Marie-Louise was pregnant. At last, on July 23, Caroline was able to get away. She travelled with such speed that she was at Caserta, holding the children in her arms, on August 3, and by August 5 she was in Naples, where the illuminations had been taken down and were hurriedly put up again.

But this time Caroline asked that no special celebrations should be held in her honour. That evening, when all the presents that she had brought from Paris had been unwrapped and the children taken off to bed, she sat in her bath and dictated to her confidential secretary a secret letter which she sent by an officer who had orders to destroy it if he were attacked by brigands. 'I found everybody eager to do everything they could to please me. I am very grateful for all the orders you gave for that, and they have been carried out as you instructed. But I am not inclined to accept anything, neither fêtes, nor police reports, nor anything that has been proposed to me . . . I do not want to give rise to stories that I have come here to govern in your absence and take part in administrative affairs. I want to prove to you that I have come back to show you how fond of you I am.'[11]

Her principal reason for writing was to pass on a conversation she had had with Napoleon just before she left. The events in Holland had worried her. Louis abdicated in favour of his son on July 1 as the French troops marched in; a little more than a week later Napoleon annexed Holland to France. He threatened to do the same in Naples if Joachim did not give preference to French trade and keep up the barriers against goods from abroad. He agreed that he was not as displeased with him as with Louis, but that Joachim 'always says he is doing what I want, yet he sometimes exceeds my orders, and in important matters he often does not consult me'.[12]

When she pointed out that Joachim's position was made untenable if he was forced to receive instructions from Clarke on whether or not he could invade Sicily, Napoleon replied, 'Why should he be upset at that? I have always regarded Murat, and I still regard him, as a general in my army, and I make no distinction when I give orders to my minister. . . . If the expedition had not succeeded it would have reflected on me.'[13] She was disturbed at the thought that the expedition might now fail and bring the emperor's wrath down on them. 'It would be better to retrace your steps, postpone it to another time, than expose yourself and your army. . . . Come back to us, and I will try to console you for the hardships you have undergone. . . . He is very irritable at the moment. So I will give you a piece of good advice: ignore a lot of the little things, so as to obtain the big ones and keep us in his good books. What is your object? It is to maintain our present position and preserve the kingdom. So you must do what he wants and not get annoyed when he demands something, for he is the stronger and you can do nothing against him. Perhaps one day he will calm down and then you can assume your rights.'[14]

She admitted with strange frankness, that 'the whole of Europe is crushed under the yoke of France. Even Joseph cannot hold out much longer . . . Louis has lost everything. Jérôme has been sent 15,000 men whom he is obliged to maintain, and he cannot possibly stand it more than six months. All the other States are similarly tormented. So you see you are still the least ill-treated. I enjoin you therefore to accept the situation in which you find yourself, bear with it, give no occasion for complaint; one day perhaps you will reap the reward of your patience.'[15] She thanked him again for the care he had taken in refurnishing her apartments. 'It would have increased my affection for you, if that had been possible. Here I am, surrounded by the children, and all that I lack for happiness now is to see you beside me. Come back as soon as you can. We could be very happy, but if that is to be so we must content ourselves with what we have; you must cool that head of yours which gets so easily overheated . . . My pregnancy is going very well; I cannot feel anything moving yet. I suffered a little, though, from the jolting on the roads ... I am a little on edge, but do not worry, my health is good and I hope by tomorrow I shall not feel any effects of the journey.'[16]

He was touched by her sincerity, moved by sympathy for her unenviable position, trying to keep the peace between a domineering brother and a headstrong husband. 'You are perfectly right in everything you say, my sweet Caroline ... With courage and careful behaviour and resignation we must wait and prepare ourselves for events that it is not in our power to avert ...' But his indignation bubbled over as he wrote. 'Holland has been ruined for France, by France, and the emperor has incorporated it in France, and the reason given is that it can no longer exist independently because it can no longer pay its debts. It is the height of impudence. Today he is imposing burdensome conditions on me; he makes me sign an unjust treaty and acknowledge an even more unjust debt, he reduces my revenues, crushes my trade, paralyses our industries, ... in fact puts me in a position where I cannot carry the enormous load with which he saddles me. He issues decrees over my head, lays down directives in Naples just as he does in Paris – and when the moment arrives and he decides, for the sake of policy or just for a whim, to turn me off the throne, the duc de Cadore will make another pompous report on the king of Naples as he did on the king of Holland. ... I realize that the emperor has the right to require us to conform to his policy and that we should consult him on political or important measures that we have to take: but he should be our Mentor, not our Master; it is not a king's duty to obey[17] ...

'My dear Caroline, I should never finish if I wanted to go on finding fault, but it would serve no purpose. ... I have decided to do everything the emperor desires or may desire, and when I can no longer support the burden I will ask him to assume it himself. So do not worry; I am not affected, I am calm, and I repeat that it is only for him and on his account that I have any fears if he does not change his policy.'[18] But as Caroline well knew, it was not within his nature to remain calm, and he was soon disputing Napoleon's demands: for the money which the treaty said he must raise by issuing five per cent government bonds; for the construction of two battleships and two frigates a year.

'I shall not write to you at length about Louis and the family,'
Caroline told him on August 11, 1810, 'because there are some
things that cannot be said aloud, and because you get too easily
excited; besides the couriers are not to be relied on ... I saw
Grosbois yesterday, and talked with him for a long time: I assure
you he will write in a favourable way, and is ours whenever we
wish.'[19] Her concern was not only for affairs of state. 'I have
handed your letter to the Prince Royal,' she wrote on August 13,
'but I am sorry to see, my dear, that you tell him in great detail
about your fleet and your army; he is still too young to share such
secrets and they give him too great a sense of importance. I think
you will agree with me and not talk about your affairs with him
any more.'[20]

Though she loved Naples, she found the summer heat burdensome, particularly now that she was expecting a fifth child. She
held her formal receptions of visitors before noon, dined at one
and then, as she told Joachim, 'after dinner I lie down until six;
I have supper at nine, go to bed at ten and get up at eight. I need
a lot of sleep; I have adopted Neapolitan habits: *mangiare, dormire
et la dolce farniente*' ('eating, sleeping and sweet idleness'). Joachim
had planted her terrace with trees and furnished it with tents and
awnings. 'I spend all my time there, when I am not sleeping – dine
there, paint there, receive my children there. Yesterday I had the
ministers and high officials to dinner there. It makes me happy to
think that I shall always dine there with you.'[21]

On August 15, 1810, Joachim celebrated Napoleon's forty-first
birthday by reviewing his troops at Piale, entertaining his officers
to dinner and a ball, and drinking the emperor's health by the light
of some thirty shells that landed in the camp from the guns of the
British fleet and set fire to the tents. In Naples, Caroline was less
happy. Firstly, very few of the Neapolitan notabilities attended the
reception at the palace and then, when Grosbois arrived, his
coachman tried to push in front of another vehicle and in the
ensuing scuffle a sentry gave the coachman a few slaps with the
flat of his sword. Caroline, recalling a similar set-to in Holland that
precipitated Louis's downfall, assured Grosbois that the offending
sentry would be suitably punished. At midnight she went for a
drive through the streets with Marshal Pérignon, Govenor of
Naples, – 'it is the only moment of the day when it is possible to

breathe,'[22] she wrote to Joachim. On August 19 she had the civic illuminations brought out in honour of Joachim's saint's day. On August 25 she drove to Castellammare to launch the *Capri*. Ten days later she lost the child whose birth she and Joachim had been eagerly awaiting.

Throughout the summer there had been a series of engagements between gun-boats in the Straits of Messina and the southern curve of the Gulf of Gioia, where Murat's transports lay under the protection of coastal batteries; but neither army had been able to land men on the opposite shore. On August 8, Napoleon sent orders that the troops were to be kept in position whether an invasion was practicable or not, so as to dissuade the British from sending reinforcements from Sicily to Spain, and to keep the British navy occupied while supplies were landed in Corfu, where the French garrison was threatened by attack from the Russians and Turks. Joachim suspected more strongly than ever that this had been the emperor's intention all along. He had been encouraged to make a fool of himself and would be kept on a leash until the other shore of the strait was impregnable.

While in this mood of exasperation, he received two letters from Caroline. In the first she told him how annoyed she was to learn that he had appointed General Cavaignac as his first aide-de-camp and had obtained the Grand Cordon of Westphalia for him from Jérôme. She was even more upset at the grant of property worth more than a million francs to Cavaignac's brother, Jean, the administrator of the National Estates. 'I cannot believe you can have done all that for the Cavaignacs without letting me know beforehand. I have a right to be astonished, considering how good-natured you are to me at the moment, so that I cannot believe it . . .' and so on with the repetition of haste and rage. 'You still have relations to marry off, to whom you could never give a sum like that . . . You know my aversion for the name of Cavaignac.'[23]

The criticism irritated him. The second letter, which he received four days later, produced a violent explosion. 'My dear,' she said, 'I am taking advantage of a trustworthy opportunity to write to you at some length and to speak freely about your interests.' After a brief mention of his quarrel with the emperor about the admission of duty-free French cloth, she came to the point of the letter – that on Joachim's feast day, as on the emperor's only ladies attached to the court had appeared at the Cercle: 'And that is because all the noble families are in the deepest poverty and have absolutely nothing to buy dresses with, since that cursed Commission [set up by Joachim to hasten the abolition of feudal rights] has been ruining somebody new every day ... In Paris nobody could understand why you should decide to throw away the love of your people in such a way. .... Foreigners were saying openly that there was no king – Revolution was established on the throne.'[24] It was a long letter, some fifteen hundred words of unrelieved nagging, more than half of them on this one subject. They shocked his republican principles; they set his suspicions aflame. He sent her a ferocious reply, accusing her of disloyalty and intriguing against him. She received it on September 6, two days after the miscarriage.

On September 8 Joachim sent thirty grenadiers of his Guard in two boats to make a landing on the outskirts of Messina, where they occupied a guardhouse and then returned. This expedition was probably intended to convince Grenier that a crossing was possible. In the morning of September 17 a gale blew up from the south, dispersing the British ships stationed off the Punta di Faro on the northeast tip of the island. In the afternoon it dropped as suddenly as it had arisen and the local boatmen declared that conditions were favourable. The big British vessels could not get back for lack of a strong wind; the sea was calm enough for the invaders to use oars as well as sail. Joachim gave orders for the troops to march to their points of embarkation, and at dusk they went aboard. Two thousand men under General Cavaignac were to cross from Reggio to create a diversion, while the rest of the invasion fleet – five hundred transports escorted by one hundred gun-boats – sailed from the bases between Scilla and Punta del Pezzo.

The boats of Cavaignac's division came ashore in Sicily a few miles above Scaletta, between San Stefano Mili in the north, where there was a garrison of the British Twenty-First Regiment, and San Placido, which was occupied by 400 light infantrymen. Two battalions of the Corsican Regiment led the assault, and moved up into the hills, making for the mountain paths that would bring them down on Messina from the west while the main army attacked from the east. Their progress was slow. The British troops were alerted, and at daylight the church bells called out the peasants who, contrary to Murat's expectations, joined the defenders with shouts of '*Viva il Re Giorgio!*'[25] The rising sun revealed, to Cavaignac's astonishment, that the straits were empty – the main force had not put to sea. He ordered his men to re-embark, but by this time the Corsicans had been cut off. The remainder set off for the Calabrian coast, pursued by marines who put out from Messina in rowing boats. Cavaignac lost his chief-of-staff and eight hundred men including forty officers. On the British side there were three casualties.

What happened during the night to prevent the main force from sailing is still unclear. Caroline expostulated to Grosbois about the lack of French cooperation, but at the same time alleged that Murat had never intended to do more than demonstrate that a crossing was a military possibility – and yet it was scarcely necessary for the whole army to be summoned for such a demonstration. The version recorded by Baron van Dedem, and widely whispered in Naples at the time, is that Joachim had already taken his place on the royal barge, ready to lead the assault, when Grenier told him he refused to commit the French contingents. Joachim ordered him to obey. Grenier produced his written authority from the emperor to exercise sole command of the French troops. Joachim, in an excess of rage, snatched the document and tore it to pieces. But there was nothing he could do.

Writing to Napoleon the same day, he stated that he was held up by a dead calm: 'It is painful for me to renounce the invasion of Sicily, but that is what I shall be forced to do if I do not get over on the first puff of wind that comes along, but I shall at least have gained the certainty of conquering Sicily when Your Majesty definitely orders it.'[27] The last phrase suggests that the French generals had refused him support. There is the same implication in the letter he sent Gallo five days later: 'It is to be feared that the emperor has made his generals too rich and important. Having nothing more to gain, they hesitate to risk losing what they have received from the imperial munificence.'[28]

In the same letter he claimed that Cavaignac's troops had triumphantly proved his point that the crossing could be made – their capture being due solely to an unfortunate failure in communication: the two star shells were not fired which would have warned them that the main force was becalmed. To Daure he was more outspoken about 'no longer confiding the conduct of the emperor's troops and mine . . . to men who have shown . . . that they do not believe the crossing to be possible'.[29]

On September 28 he hauled down his standard, struck camp and went back to his capital by sea.[30] 'He returned to Naples heartbroken at having spent his treasure to no purpose, at having sacrificed his navy, at having lost a great part of his artillery and his best soldiers, and at seeing himself so to speak tricked by his brother-in-law. Murat was a Gascon, not spiteful by nature, but capable of hatred and revenge . . . Napoleon had opened the way for the future defection of a prince who was absolutely determined to be an independent king.'[31]

There was the quarrel with Caroline to be resolved. On learning of the miscarriage, he wrote her an affectionate letter and asked for news of her health to be sent to him twice daily by telegraph. But Caroline was not to be easily placated. His latest message, she told him, 'would reduce me to tears, if I could forget the horribly unkind letter I received from you on the second day of my accident. After the way in which you expressed yourself in that letter, I can no longer attach any importance to your assurances of tenderness and sympathy; they do not come from your heart, and you have yourself given me proof of that . . . My own feelings are still the same, for I have never changed during the eleven years I have been with you.'[32] Two days later: 'I have just read it again and it is horrible. I do not want to upset you by sending it back to you, but when you are here I will make you read it again. I do not believe there is any reproach more cruel to a wife than to say she is siding with her husband's enemies, and so many other things that I must try never to remember.'[33]

10

Whatever may have been the true reasons for calling off the Sicilian invasion, Joachim was in no mood to accept the emperors' criticisms and demands and interference. At Piale on September

20 he learned that Napoleon had told Pérignon and Grenier to confiscate any ships carrying the forbidden colonial goods. 'As king and commander-in-chief of your army, I should be within my rights in punishing those generals if they gave such orders without reference to me. Nobody will carry out with greater alacrity than I whatever it may please you to command, Sire; but so long as I am sovereign I will never permit anybody other than Your Majesty to give orders in the States that you have confided to me.'[1]

He asked Napoleon to reduce the number of French troops on Neapolitan territory that he was obliged to pay and maintain. The emperor replied that the Neapolitans would not be able to defend their country against the British and he would merely have to send his troops back again. Joachim answered that the emperor was doing his Neapolitan soldiers an injustice but, in any case, there were only 12,000 British soldiers in Sicily 'and supposing they succeeded in persuading Your Majesty that they could beat all the Neapolitans, they would never succeed in persuading you that they could beat 12,000 Frenchmen. Well, you have 25,000 Frenchmen here; leave me 10,000 of them and you will certainly not have to make forced marches to come to my rescue.'[2]

Napoleon had no intention of removing his Trojan Horse. 'I have just made a careful study of your finance minister's report. I see that your deficit arises from the fact that you are foolish enough to maintain 40,000 Neapolitans who cannot be of any use to you. If instead of 40,000 you had not more than 15,000 or 20,000, you would be rich.'[3] He was as little inclined to allow Murat full diplomatic independence as he was to let him maintain a large national army. When Joachim appointed an ambassador to Russia and sent him to Paris for instructions on the imperial policy, the emperor refused to recognize him. For Murat to maintain embassies at Vienna and St Petersburg, would he said, be a 'useless expense'.[4]

In the course of these arguments Napoleon criticized Joachim for giving the title of 'colonel-general of the Guard' to La Vauguyon. 'In France, colonels-general of the Guard are marshals who have won several victories and made their names.'[5] Joachim used this as a pretext for altering the designations of all his senior officers, and in March he decreed new national colours of white, sky-blue and purple[6] and a new national flag.

When Baron Desvernois went to dine with the king about this time, he was intercepted by Daure, who said: 'If he asks you what they think of him in France, tell him frankly that they notice with regret that he is abandoning the Frenchmen who were devoted to his service and raising to the highest offices of state Neapolitans who will one day desert and betray him.'[7] Desvernois said he would do so if the king gave him the opportunity. He did not have to wait. He had scarcely been presented when Murat said: 'Well, I do not believe you are one of those Frenchmen that I have heaped riches and honour on and who calumniate me and write to their friends in Paris that since I have become king of Naples I have ceased to be a Frenchman; and let out yells as soon as I appoint one of my subjects to an employment of any importance. As king of a nation as susceptible as the Neapolitans I need to treat them with respect and consideration if I do not want to humiliate their pride and self-esteem; and proportionately speaking, for every ten appointments that I make, hardly one goes to a Neapolitan; the nine others go to Frenchmen and are more important.'[8]

Desvernois, who had been serving with the Neapolitan division in Spain, was posted to Calabria, under General Manhès, whom the king had appointed military governor of the province at the end of the Sicilian fiasco. Despite the large numbers of troops involved in that operation, banditry had continued to flourish throughout the region, outlaws had attacked and murdered people on the outskirts of the royal headquarters at Piale, and couriers and convoys had been held up on the main Naples–Reggio road. Pitched battles took place between the bandits – who were supported from Sicily with arms and money – and civic guards, a whole battalion of whom were put to flight near Cosenza by a bandit named Parafante who had for several years terrorized the surrounding district. Manhès waited for the winter to deprive them of easy food and shelter in the countryside, and then issued a proclamation promising rewards for the capture of the leaders, pardons for their followers, and death for any villagers who aided them. No food was to be carried outside towns or villages. Cattle were to be guarded day and night; if any were taken by the

bandits, the rest of the herd would be confiscated and the herds-
men shot as accomplices. Each villager was liable for guard duty
on two days a week.

The new regulations were received with a shrug. Terror, tor-
ture, extortion and acceptance of the invincibility of outlaws were
firmly implanted in the soil of southern Italy. But the Calabrians
discovered that Manhès was not content merely to issue pro-
clamations – he enforced them. Eleven women and children of
Stilo were arrested as they left the town to gather olives. They
were found to be carrying bread for their midday meal, and shot.
An old man was caught giving food to his son; both were publicly
executed in Cosenza. This sort of repression, though not notably
inhuman by Napoleonic standards, and certainly not by those of
the bandits themselves, increased the Neapolitans' distrust of the
French and their French king when the stories, inevitably exaggerated, spread across the country.

Murat, unwilling to leave Naples for another indefinite period
until the country was more peaceful, was nevertheless anxious to
reach an understanding with Napoleon. Early in January he sent
Pérignon to Paris: an emissary whose good faith could be accepted
by both parties. The approach was unsuccessful. Two months
later, when Manhès's campaign was evidently succeeding, Murat
wrote to ask permission to spend a fortnight in Paris. Before his
letter could arrive. Paris was ringing with the one hundred and one
gun salute that announced the birth of a son to Marie-Louise. The
news was signalled by telegraph to Milan and sent on from there
by Eugène. Joachim left at seven next morning, delighted with
this excuse to confront his brother-in-law.

He reached Paris in the evening of April 3. The day before,
Napoleon had flown into a rage about one of Murat's decrees
relating to the cotton trade, and had ordered Champagny to tell
Campochiaro that it must be rescinded immediately: 'The king
deceives himself if he thinks he is going to reign at Naples otherwise than in accordance with my will and the general interest of
the empire. Tell him firmly that unless he changes his ways, I shall
take possession of the kingdom and govern it by viceroy, as in
Italy ... Whenever the Continental System has been departed
from I have not spared even my own brothers, and I should be
still less inclined to spare him.'[9] Murat, though on a pacific errand,

was in no mood to refuse to fight if the alternative was surrender. Now that Marie-Louise had given Napoleon one son she might well give him two – and the whole of Italy, combined into one kingdom, would make a fine appanage for a younger son. In Rome, on his way to Paris, he had met the new French ambassador heading for Naples and, though receiving him in his usual friendly way, pointedly told him that the loyalty of his Neapolitan subjects 'had been even more strengthened by the rumours of annexation, which rallied more closely to the Throne a Nation jealous of its independence'.[10]

The scene was set for a violent quarrel, yet he failed to get to grips. Dinner with the emperor on the evening of his arrival; a day's hunting a fortnight later. He grumbled to Caroline about being cold-shouldered, and to an old friend whom he met one morning walking in the Champs-Elysées he was even more outspoken. 'He shouts loud enough that he made us kings,' he said of Napoleon, 'but was it not we who made him Emperor? My blood, my sword and my life are the Emperor's. If he summons me to a field of battle to confront his enemies and those of France, I am no longer a king but a marshal of the empire once more – but let him not ask more than that of me. At Naples I will be king, and I do not intend to sacrifice the existence, welfare and interests of my subjects to his policies.'[11]

Caroline was alarmed at what Joachim might say in the heat of the moment and what Napoleon might do in revenge. For six months she had lived in fear. 'I have received no letters from the emperor for a long time,' she wrote to Hortense at the end of October 1810 . . . 'I have just learned that [he] is vexed because he learned of my accident from another source. I beg you, dear sister, to find out if that is the cause of the emperor's silence.'[12] On April 28, 1811, she wrote in deep distress to Joachim that 'I can see from your letter that we shall end up by being obliged to quit the kingdom . . . When I think of the humiliations you are suffering . . . I weep for you and wish you would return; above all, I wish you would keep calm and act with a level head.'[13] 'For God's sake send me couriers,' she pleaded four days later. 'I am desperately worried.'[14]

In fact, Napoleon was anxious to avoid a direct break. When Julie Bonaparte urged him to relieve her husband of the burden of the throne of Spain and let him resume that of Naples, he replied sharply, as she reported to Joseph, 'that you had renounced that kingdom and that he was satisfied with Murat who was better liked than you'.[15] He knew that he might soon be in great need of Joachim's services, for he had good reason to believe that Tsar Alexander, foreseeing an attack from France, was planning to get his own blow in first. The tsar, irritated by the incorporation of his brother-in-law's duchy of Oldenburg in the French empire, resentful at Napoleon's failure to carry out promises to help Russia expand into Finland, Moldavia and Wallachia, suspicious of French intentions in Poland, and disturbed by the implications of the Austrian alliance, had already been forced to breach the Continental System because of its effects on his country's economy. Napoleon ordered Davout in Hamburg to be ready to occupy Danzig, and all senior officers of the army in Germany to return to their posts. And on the day following his dinner with Murat he told the minister of war to prepare to bring the cavalry reserve in Germany up to 34,000 men. He had learned the lessons of Aspern-Essling and Wagram: he must have Murat in command of the cavalry.

It is thus quite possible that Napoleon intended to end the quarrel when he invited Caroline to stand as godmother to his son. But to his sister it seemed equally likely that by snubbing Joachim and flattering her, he planned to widen the rift between them. That was the thought which sprang to Caroline's mind when she received the invitation at the beginning of May. She replied that she feared that she was not well enough to travel, and told the new French Ambassador, Durand, that she was pregnant. She sent copies of the correspondence to Joachim. 'You will see that in pleading my health, which in fact is not very good, I have still kept the door open . . . It is for you to let me know what you wish and what I should do . . . I could, with care, set out on the journey without any risk in eight or ten days.'[16] She begged him to send the courier back the same day, so that she could either give the emperor a definite refusal, or still have time to set off in the carriage which she would have waiting.

She wanted to know how many attendants she should take with her, and 'you could quietly get from the Grand Duke of Würz-burg[17] some information on the presents we ought to make to the

Governess and other people attached to the king of Rome. Find out what must be done and what is usual in such circumstances.'[18] She confessed that she would accept the invitation without hesitation if left to her own decision, 'but I cannot do anything – and do not wish to – without your consent'.[19] In case his decision was against her coming, she enclosed four invitations for various people to stand proxy for her. 'And mind you do not tell anybody I sent four,' she added, in a burst of impatience at her unpredictable husband, 'for you know that nobody will want to accept if it is known that I have made the same request to four people'.[20] Before she closed this nervously sprawling letter, she had a better thought: 'if you think I ought to come to Paris, you can let me know by telegraph – have them signal "the king wishes to know if the queen is on her way'.[21]

Joachim did not wish her to come. While the telegraph remained motionless, she sent him letters by the ordinary couriers – for the emperor's benefit – describing her ill-health and the failure of the remedies she was taking. On May 19 she had news from him by return of the same confidential courier. She was not happy about the tone of it and, while repeating that she would never do anything to displease him, accused him of still not understanding her. 'I know your heart is good and that you love me, but you are too ready to believe false reports in the newspapers and from our enemies.'[22] A new danger occurred to her. 'I am afraid that Joseph's arrival in Paris may decide the emperor to send you to Spain, and it seems to me that you greatly expose yourself to this by appearing to want to go to war. The emperor might well take you at your word. So I advise you to talk less about it and to arrange things so that nothing prevents your returning to Naples after the christening.'[23]

Joachim did not wait that long. He sent Caroline a prearranged signal to ask him to come back because of trouble in Calabria. She sent two messengers, but the emperor would not hear of his leaving. Joachim demanded an honest statement of Napoleon's intentions, telling him that 'he willingly consented to become his captain again, but he did not relish being kept any longer in suspense, only to be humiliated in the end like the king of Holland'.[24] The Russian envoy, Czernicheff, who reported this altercation to St Petersburg, added that 'it is said that he advised him not to get entangled in a quarrel with Russia, saying that things were at such a point that a single reverse could cost him his crown and his life. All these observations greatly displeased Napoleon, and they parted very discontented with each other.'[25]

Joachim doggedly set out his arguments again at great length in a letter which he sent to his Secretary of State, General Pignatelli Strongoli by public messenger. 'A man must be blind or totally ignorant of the political situation if he fails to perceive that England's only means of extracting herself from the impossible position into which the emperor's policy has forced her lies in the chance of rekindling hostilities on the Continent . . . The English are about to concentrate all their efforts on the Peninsula, and Masséna's retreat has just given fresh hope to the Spaniards. Is it likely that the emperor would transfer the seat of war to the Vistula with a formidable army within six days' march of his frontiers? . . . All the emperor's energies should be devoted to the maintenance of peace and the conservation of his possessions.'[26] Though it must have been opened and communicated to Napoleon, he did not react. Less than a week later Joachim received letters from three of his ministers urging his return. He wrote to Napoleon: 'My departure cannot interfere with your plans, while it may restore confidence among my people.'[27] He said good-bye to the emperor at Rambouillet on May 20 and left for Naples at dawn on May 22. On May 21 Napoleon had sent him a note suggesting a new expedition to Sicily, but he was not to be caught twice with the same trick.

II

He was in Naples by the morning of May 30, determined to do all he could to parry further threats of annexation. On June 7 he abolished the post of Governor-General of Naples, since Pérignon, though a friend of his, was a marshal under the orders of Napoleon. On June 14 he signed a decree that 'All foreigners holding civil employment in our realm must, in the terms of clauses 2 and 3 of Article II of the Constitution, make application for naturalization before August 1. Those who fail to satisfy this condition will be deemed to have voluntarily renounced such employment.'[1] His intention was quite clear: to force all Frenchmen in positions of authority to swear loyalty to him; and he made no secret of this in the letter he sent to the emperor. 'How could I repose any confidence in men under whose protection I lie down to sleep, if these same men hesitated to adopt the new country which I have been called upon to adopt myself? . . . I trust Your Majesty will approve of a measure dictated by the Constitution of which you are the guarantor, and which you have officially called upon me to administer.'[2]

He had underestimated the reaction of Napoleon and of his French ministers and staff. Agar and Daure said they would surrender their portfolios, Exelmans and Lanusse asked to be relieved of their appointments as Master of the Horse and Grand Marshal of the Palace. Joachim went off to Portici, where he continued the argument with Caroline.

Napoleon moved swiftly. He gave Clarke orders to disband the Army of Naples and form it into a *corps d'observation* (the usual title of an army poised for invasion) to be based between Naples, Capua and Gaëta, under the sole command of General Grenier, who would be responsible only to Clarke. 'It will not be employed in policing the country and will not be commanded by any officer in the service of Naples . . . You will notify the king of my decree, and tell him that . . . I shall leave this force in the kingdom of Naples until such time as I am certain that he can get on without it; that as long as it remains within his kingdom it will be fed, paid, maintained and clothed at the expense of the Neapolitan treasury.'[3] He followed this with instructions that Grenier was to ensure that Gaëta, the strongest fortress in the kingdom, was garrisoned with French troops. He then issued a proclamation that 'since the kingdom of Naples constitutes an integral part of the Grand Empire, and the prince who governs it is a Frenchman and a high dignitary of the empire, and he has been placed on the throne and maintained there only by the efforts of our people, we decree that: All French citizens are citizens of the kingdom of the Two Sicilies; the decree of the king of that country, dated June 14, is in no way applicable to them.'[4]

A copy reached Durand in the afternoon of July 16, and he communicated it to the Neapolitan foreign minister, Gallo, the same day. For Joachim it was almost literally maddening. He tore the Legion of Honour from his tunic and snatched up a pistol, threatening to take his own life. Caroline kept his ministers away from him for two days 'for fear somebody would see him in the state of frenzy into which he had fallen'.[5] He dictated a letter of reproach to Napoleon: 'If Your Majesty simply desires to be rid of me, do not seek pretexts to work your will . . . I do not know whether it will please Your Majesty but today the king of Naples is a laughing stock . . . so there is an end to my part in the play . . .'[6] He drove off in a closed carriage to Capodimonte and cancelled the court functions for August 15 – 'my health will not permit me to attend the *Te Deum* and the *Cercle* on the emperor's birthday',[7] he wrote to the Master of Ceremonies – and made only a brief appearance on the balcony for the traditional parade of the Royal Guard. It was not until August 22 that he returned to the palace for a meeting of the Council of Ministers.

Durand reported that 'the king will not give up the idea, *or at least wants to appear to be convinced,* that the initial objection and continued resistance to his decree by the French was prompted by the Minister of War, M. Daure, by the Master of the Horse and by M. de Longchamps'.[8] He also told Durand that Daure had been in correspondence with his enemy Savary, Napoleon's chief of police since Fouché's disgrace in 1810. 'The court interior is a hotbed of suspicions, distrust and poisonous gossip,'[9] continued Durand, who was certainly not slow in adding to them. On August 17, Joachim wrote to Napoleon that he had accepted Lanusse's resignation and deprived Daure of his appointments.

'I hasten to inform Your Majesty of the matter in order to forestall misrepresentations by these two men, who have been punished for the gravest personal faults . . . [Daure] aimed at forming a party against me. He did not hesitate to attack me in my tenderest affections, and although his efforts in that respect were far from obtaining the success that he dared hope for, Your Majesty may have in your own hands proof that they were not entirely without effect.'[10] To Campochiaro in Paris he had Gallo send a detailed account of Daure's offences: 'negligence in police administration . . . permitting widespread speculation in the Ministry of War and being personally involved in it. [Joachim had for some time been asking for a statement of Daure's accounts, but they had not been produced] . . . constantly intriguing and meddling to obtain an influence which the king did not think it proper for him to acquire, and to which he is forbidden as a minister to aspire.'[11]

Maghella, who succeeded Daure as minister of Police,[12] had served as Prefect of Police and was said to have precipitated the crisis by showing Joachim letters exchanged between the queen and Daure, 'which proved not only their intimacy, but also the attempts made to persuade Napoleon to withdraw the crown from his brother-in-law and give it to his sister'.[13] The statement has been repeated and enlarged on many times since then. That the second part of it is nonsense is proved by the fact that within a month Joachim sent Caroline to Paris to negotiate with the emperor, which he would certainly not have done had he suspected her of trying to edge him off the throne. As for the first accusation, 'influence which the king did not think it proper for him to acquire' might make a line in a farce but was not the way in which the hotblooded Joachim would refer to adultery with his wife.[14] A similar insinuation was made about Caroline and La Vauguyon, a few months earlier, yet Joachim was at that moment employing him as his confidential agent in Paris.

What is probable is that Caroline, anxious to know what was happening but fearing to stir up a storm like that of the previous autumn, had been obtaining reports from Daure, possibly passed on by Lanusse. 'It is only natural that I should want to be the first to know what is going on in my kingdom,'[15] she said to Hortense later that year, and only natural that she should be worried, for she learned from Louis of the ruthlessness with which Napoleon would drive them from their throne once he made up his mind to do so. 'My brother has not deigned to reply to me,' he wrote to her from his exile in Graz. 'He has had everything that belonged to me confiscated, I had to resort to subterfuge to get my clothes.'[16] Yet she was obliged to obtain information secretly from members of the Council and 'the king inspires so much fear that when the minister sees me next time he is pale and trembling and asks me nervously if I have burned the piece of paper that can ruin him'.[17] She could not forget that it was her kingdom as well as his; in any case, she could never long restrain herself from advising, organizing and, as Joachim would see it, interfering.

Napoleon kept up the pressure. On August 30, 1811, he wrote to Joachim: 'You are surrounded by men who hate France and who wish to destroy you. I have given you good warning before. . . . There is no point in your writing to me unless you have something important to tell me. Remember that I made you king only because it suited my plans. . . . Continue to correspond with the Minister of War.'[18] After dinner on September 9 at Compiègne Berthier wrote a letter evidently dictated by Napoleon in which he warned Joachim that the emperor had said: 'He torments the queen unceasingly, he is continually suspicious of her. Yet he is only king through her, as my sister.'

Berthier continued, 'Naples was conquered by the emperor; you, Sire, should govern that kingdom as if you were only the viceroy . . . The emperor said to me "He may have claims on my benevolence because of his military service, which I appreciate, but he has done nothing to be king: he owes that to his marriage with my sister and he should trust her and treat her well."'[19]

There was another turn of the screw: Savary arrested Aymé on August 23, 1811, on a charge of being involved in the theft of precious stones from the Spanish crown jewels – with the clear implication that Joachim was the real thief. (It was in fact Joseph who had filched the jewels, valued at between 15 and 18 million frances, and including the famous pearl *La Pelegrina*.) Savary imprisoned Aymé at Vincennes and went through the papers in his house in the rue de la Victoire. La Vauguyon was ordered to leave Paris.[20] Miollis, Governor of Rome, was told to take over the Farnese estates[21] which had been given to the Murats in part exchange for their French properties. Pérignon was sent back to Naples to resume the governorship from which Joachim had dismissed him with the message that, 'The emperor is content to have the king reign at Naples, but the emperor cannot overlook the fact that he is the emperor of Naples and its suzerain.'[22] Copies of these instructions were sent to Durand to be passed on to Joachim. If Murat demurred, Durand was to ask for his passports and tell him that 'the emperor intends to inform the Senate of the kings' conduct, to make known to France that he [Joachim] has closed to the French a city which they themselves conquered, that he has insulted the colours beneath which he had the honour of fighting

in the days before French blood won him his throne, and that he
has therefore ceased to reign'.[23]

On September 15, Joachim wrote to the emperor: 'The position
in which we find ourselves is so distressing and the means of
letting you know the truth so difficult, that I have decided to ask
the queen to attend upon Your Majesty. She will leave the day
after tomorrow.'[24] The going was slow – lack of horses, rivers
overflowing their banks, bad roads. At Turin she was dismayed to
learn that 'the emperor is no longer in Paris. I do not know what
I shall do during his absence, and I am very much afraid he may
disapprove of my journey.'[25] She was in Paris by October 2;
Napoleon and Marie-Louise were on tour in Holland, so she
lodged at her great-uncle Fesch's house in the rue du Mont-Blanc,
sending her attendants to furnished apartments. She at once set
about questioning her friends at court and reassuring Joachim:
'Calm yourself. . . . From everything that I hear, there will be no
annexation, it is just gossip.'[26]

Her health was not good. She suffered from frequent vomiting
and had grown so thin that she had to have her dresses made
smaller. The doctors ordered her to give up baths and prescribed
chicken broth and sedatives. Joachim anxiously implored her not
to drink too much lemonade. She in return begged 'do not keep
offering to give back your crown every day as you do; it is not
befitting . . . it is not befitting at all'.[27]

To Agar, who had attempted a kindly but too outspoken intervention as an old friend, she snapped back: 'I am unable to understand the phrase in your letter which says that *the King will be
unhappy until I let him know my real feelings and until I have dispelled his
regrettable distrust*. I cannot believe that the father of my children,
the one to whom I have given so many proofs of affection, and
continue to do so every day, could doubt my feelings and could
have a *regrettable distrust* and believe in *lying rumours*. That I cannot
imagine; I absolutely cannot believe that article. In any case, since
such a matter could only be adversely interpreted, you should not
have sent your letter by the estafette.'[28] To Joachim she wrote:
'You do not trust me enough, you do not see into my heart.
When it is a question of your happiness and peace of mind, I
forget the clouds and contrarieties. . . . It is true that I suffered in
Naples, that I was not happy, but I can bear my griefs. But the

thought that you are unhappy is for me unbearable. Everything will calm down, if only you desire it . . . I kiss you as I love you – kiss our children tenderly for me.'[29]

When the imperial couple returned on November 11, Napoleon gave her a friendly welcome. 'She has already received proof of her return to favour,' the Russian minister, Chernichev reported, "in obtaining a court carriage and permission to take up residence in the Tuileries at the Pavillon de Flore, which she formerly occupied.'[30] The season of grand festivals and balls was approaching. Napoleon was not on the best of terms with Pauline, who was said to have publicly insulted the emperor and empress with a rude gesture at a reception.[31] Hortense was out of town, taken up with other matters.[32] Caroline would be of the greatest value as a hostess. He was still thunderously sulking with Joachim and refused to communicate directly with him, but he was aware that his sister would be writing home diligently.

She sent a full account of her first interview with him on November 16, opening with the welcome news that 'the emperor began by telling me forcefully, and repeating several times in the conversation: "I have never planned to annex Naples; I do not want to annex it and I shall never do so, unless the king forces me to." '[33] Joachim was to remain in disgrace. He would receive no letters from the emperor until he had proved his loyalty by giving preference to the French over the Neapolitans, providing more ships for the fleet, and conforming in every respect to the Continental System. There was no precaution, however small, that must be neglected in order to avoid rousing Napoleon's envy and resentment. 'I advise you not to mention in the letters you send to Paris, your desire to accompany the emperor, because . . . the emperor might think that you consider yourself necessary, if he goes to war with Russia . . . If the talk of war is confirmed and you write to the emperor, you could say that you hope he will not forget his former pupil and most faithful friend. That would be enough, and could not displease the emperor, but anything you wrote to other persons on the subject would make him more annoyed with you.'[34]

The strain affected her weakened constitution – the trouble with her stomach and her chest grew worse, and for a time she seldom got out of bed until the evening, grew 'as thin as a cuckoo',[35] and had to drink ass's milk, as prescribed by Corvisart. 'I take very little dinner, for I can eat nothing and I am on a diet. After dinner I go down to be present at the emperor's. We then go to the private apartments and play a game of billiards, and it is at moments such as these that he always speaks of you in a very friendly fashion, saying to me: "Well, does our handsome king of Naples still love us, or is he sulky with us?" Sometimes he says to me: "Does he still believe that I do not like him?"'[36]

New Year's Day, 1812, brought the usual exchange of presents. Caroline gave the empress a cornelian *bonbonnière* with a bust of the emperor engraved on it, and the king of Rome a blue and gold barouche drawn by two sheep. For Pauline there was a necklace of the famous Neapolitan coral; for Uncle Fesch, who had been so kind a host before she moved to the Tuileries, she asked Joachim to send 'coffee, good Mocha, and a lot', and two of the finest pictures at Monte-Cassino 'the picture by Fra Bartolomeo and the Raphael or the Perugini that was at Monte Cassino and you gave me'.[37] For Joachim there was a writing-desk; and he in return delighted her with a fine diamond and an increase in her allowance from 41,000 francs a month to 50,000. When she went to offer seasonal greetings to the emperor she found him in the best of humours. He had a talent for denigratory nicknames and had thought up a new one for Joachim that morning. 'Have we any news of Bully-boy?'[38] he asked her. 'Is he still in a temper with us?'[39] She attended the formal reception of the diplomatic corps and dignitaries of state and then went off to dinner with her mother and early to bed.

12

Caroline's health improved a little and she was able to play the dominant part once more in the court revelries. By the emperor's command, the two principal events at the Tuileries were to be a costume ball on February 6 and a masked ball on February 11, at which the queen of Naples and the queen of Holland would present quadrilles. Workmen transformed the Tuileries theatre into a ballroom, with a dais for the imperial family at one end, the orchestra at the other. On the evening of February 6, fifteen hundred members of the court and their families, civil servants and persons who had been presented, were admitted to the dance floor, having made their way 'at the risk of their lives through an indescribable mob of people and horses',[1] outside the palace, while behind them, barred equally from the floor and the buffet in the grand foyer were eight or nine hundred very rich and resentful members of the upper bourgeoisie, ready to begin at 1789 all over again. The imperial couple took their seats at 10.30 and Caroline's quadrille began. The doors from the foyer were flung open and twelve divinities born of the stars entered: 'twelve men dressed in blue and white, more like Roman lictors and still more like Paris firemen; all so ugly that there was universal laughter.'[2]

Things improved with the appearance of the seventeen-year-old Madame le Grand as Iris, who executed a solo shawl dance and was followed by a bevy of beautiful nymphs pursued by zephyrs. And so to the entrance of Pauline, representing Rome, in a golden helmet and tunic embellished with the famous Borghese cameos. 'She was, that evening, the most perfect vision of beauty that can be imagined,'[3] said Laure Junot. The music changed to a martial beat and the Geniuses of Victory, Commerce, Agriculture and the Arts announced the entrance of Caroline as France. 'Her helmet was closed, and decorated with diamonds and coloured stones. The garnets and chrysoprases were as big as five-franc pieces. Her half-boots appeared to be made of steel set with diamonds; her golden shield with diamonds and turquoises.'[4] The purple cloak that she wore over her white satin robe was sprinkled with the golden imperial bees. She danced a mock combat with Pauline, then threw the cloak protectively around her and offered her a cradle, while Apollo led in twenty-four ladies who performed the Dance of the Hours. (These proved to have been chosen for their position at court rather than their youth or beauty; one was promptly nicknamed 'Well Past Midnight'.) Finally, in a brilliant confusion of costumes and jewellery, messengers of the Gods presented to France the portrait of a child which she handed to kneeling Rome, who surmounted it with the crown that she had discovered in the cradle.

The empress opened the ball, partnered by the prince de Neuchâtel. Supper was served at half-past one, the guests sitting ten or twelve to a table and the emperor circulating among them. An hour later the imperial couple withdrew and the guests went home. Next evening, if Hortense is to be believed, Napoleon upbraided Caroline for her choice of allegory: 'Rome has submitted to France, but she is not happy about it. Where on earth did you get the idea of showing her as happy and satisfied with her dependence? . . . I realize you only wanted to look pretty and wear a fine costume, but you could find other subjects and not bring politics into dancing.'[5] When Hortense presented her own quadrille on Shrove Tuesday, February 11, her entrance was greeted with a round of applause, and at supper Napoleon said to Caroline that the ballet was ' "Better, much better than yours . . ." The queen of Naples and Princess Pauline,' said Hortense in reporting this, 'never forgave me for such a complete success, even in so unimportant a matter.'[6]

On February 16 Napoleon had a conversation with his ardent admirer, the Countess Kielmannsegge. He told her that he was preparing for three years of war which would result in the formation of a new European kingdom of Russia, incorporating Poland and all White Russia from Odessa to the Baltic 'of which Caroline would be the ruler. She wanted an imperial title but would be called only queen of Russia.'[7] This deliberate indiscretion may have been another attempt to drive a wedge between Caroline and Joachim and she may have been momentarily seduced by it, for there was another change in the tone of her letters at this time. She was less patient with Joachim's complaints. When he took offence on hearing that on a visit to the empress she had been offered only a stool instead of an armchair,[8] she told him he was talking nonsense and reminded him of the humiliations he had subjected her to during their recent misunderstandings. 'You talk about *fauteuils* and yet you had mine removed everywhere as if I were dead.'[9] Joachim had done this as a reprisal when he suspected that she had deliberately had his own chair moved out of the royal box in the theatre. The petty quarrel still rankled.

'Do not talk to me about humiliations – I suffered them at Naples but here . . . it would be impossible to be treated with more consideration. And I have a great deal more credit here than in Naples, for I have only to ask the ministers for places and I get them. They do all they can to please me, and you should very well know what a nonentity I was in Naples, and that it was enough for somebody to be attached to me for them to be badly looked upon and turned out of office.'[10] She had not forgotten past slights, and she had not forgotten the men whom she held responsible for them. She used the same tactics as had been used against her, playing on Joachim's jealous independence. 'Is Zurlo king then?'[11] She did not mention Maghella, whom she blamed most of all, but this was perhaps because she knew that Napoleon was about to deal with him – possibly at her instigation. At the end of February Napoleon decided to order him back to France on the grounds that 'he has been acting in collusion with the English with a view to bringing about a rising on the part of the so-called patriots in Italy'.[12]

By the time that the emperor's recall of Maghella reached Naples – and for a day or two incapacitated Murat with another fit of fever born of rage and frustration – Caroline's letters were much occupied with the question of Joachim going to war. The year before she had feared that if he resumed his command in the Grande Armée his absence from Naples might lose them the crown. Now she saw it as a means of regaining favour with the emperor – perhaps, if she knew of Napoleon's conversation with Countess Kielmannsegge, an opportunity to lay indisputable claim to a greater kingdom.[13] As early as January she was asking him if he still wanted to serve and, if he did, to let her know at once. He wrote directly to the emperor, expressing his eagerness, but it was in his mind to try to drive a bargain – to get a reduction of his contribution to the imperial fleet or some other recompense for the services which he sensed Napoleon could not do without. He let the word filter through to Durand that, though willing, he might not be able to go.

Reporting on the king's continued ill-health – 'nervous attacks, sometimes feverish, complete lack of appetite, loss of weight' – Durand told Bassano that the few people who were allowed into his presence, 'say at one moment that if he were summoned to war all his trouble would cease, and at the next that it is not certain that his health would permit him to go on a campaign'.[14] But Joachim was dealing with too wily an opponent. Through Caroline – for he still refused to address him in person – Napoleon suggested that Joachim had lost his taste for battle, alternating veiled taunts with eulogies of his past triumphs and visions of future glories: 'The king does not want to go to war . . . He loves his kingdom more than me . . . He is brave, he has made so many campaigns with me, he is attached to me . . . A hundred thousand cavalrymen, do you know what that is? And Murat at the head of such a fine force . . . But he does not want to come; he does not wish it; they say he does not wish it.'[15]

It was too much for him. Forgetting the bargain he had hoped to drive, swallowing the insult of Maghella's recall, he wrote again: 'Sire! I shall die if you do not call upon me.'[16] Still no reply; until he wrote to Caroline telling her to ask permission for him to visit Paris – just for a few days, with the promise to leave again if there were no war. 'Certainly,' replied Napoleon, 'tell him to come.'[17]

He was on his way by April 26, having instructed his Council to meet every Thursday as usual, each minister taking the chair in turn: the minutes of the meeting to be sent to him each week. It was a system that the emperor followed. He was at St-Cloud on May 5. The palace was full of plans for war. He could not resist the excitement; he had been starved of battle for too long; yet he saw more clearly than Napoleon the folly of the coming adventure. 'The emperor does not see that Europe is ready to collapse under him,' he said to Cambacérès. 'Austria is wavering, Prussia is conspiring, the Confederation is waiting for the moment to throw off the yoke. If I follow him I shall perhaps get myself killed; but if I come back I must remember that I am a husband and father, and that I have duties as a king.'[18] With battle in prospect for him, and government for her, a partial reconciliation came quite naturally. On May 12 he left for Danzig, to take command of what was probably the greatest body of disciplined cavalry that Europe had ever seen. Caroline set out for Naples carrying with her a copy of his decree appointing her as Regent.

Napoleon, after meeting his reluctant German allies at Dresden, went off on May 29 to take command of the army of well over half a million men that was now ranged from Tilsit to Warsaw.[19] He was in Danzig on June 8. There was still restraint between him and Murat, a coolness that he needed to dispel before the campaign began. Joachim had asked permission to go to Danzig via Dresden and meet his fellow sovereigns. He was 'singularly shocked'[20] when Napoleon refused this, and did not accept the emperor's explanation that this was 'out of respect for his father-in-law, since the Austrian Kaiser still regretted the loss of his possessions in Italy'.[21]

Joachim said he was being treated as a lackey, Napoleon snapped that it was he who had made him a king. And as a king, Joachim replied, his first duty was to his people. Napoleon recalled his need to placate him and spoke of their early days together – the days when neither of them had any thought in mind except service to France and the quest for glory. Joachim, his heart and imagination always too easily touched, accepted the reconciliation with tears in his eyes.

'I used a bit of bad temper and a bit of sentiment turn and turn about,' Napoleon boasted to his staff at dinner that night. 'You need some of each with that Italian pantaloon. He's good at heart; he still likes me better than his *lazzaroni*; when he sees me he is with me, but when he is at a distance, like all these people with no character, he is an easy prey for anybody who flatters and makes up to him. He is under his wife's thumb. She's ambitious; she has put a thousand mad ideas into his head. He wants to have the whole of Italy. That is what he is dreaming about, and what prevents him wanting to be king of Poland.'[22]

13

On June 24, 1812, the Grande Armeé, with a total strength of approximately 356,000 Frenchmen and 322,000 foreigners, began the crossing of the Niemen. On June 29, Joachim entered Vilna with Napoleon close behind him; and here they had the first taste of what the weather might do to them. Stormclouds built up in the sultry summer sky. They burst with peals of thunder and blinding flashes of lightning, pouring down torrents of rain that continued for three days. Men soaked and shivered in the sudden cold. The commissariat, ill-organized for so large a venture, showed signs of breaking down before the campaign had ended its first week. The cavalry horses, fatigued by chasing the elusive Russians in the oppressive heat, had to be fed on green rye for lack of oats. The draft horses fared even worse, and as they died the transport problems became more acute. The mood of the troops was sombre from the beginning. And the leader himself, the legendary little corporal with lean cheeks, lank hair and eyes fixed on a distant tryst with destiny, was now fat-jowled, partially-bald, dozing the hours away in his carriage, not getting on horseback until the day's march was almost over, and even then 'he finds it more difficult to mount. The Master of the Horse [Caulain-court] has to lend a hand to get him into the saddle.'[1]

Joachim, on the other hand, more than two years his senior, regained his youth as he galloped across the vast Lithuanian Plain, dried out to dust again under the roasting sun, seeking but so seldom finding the retreating army under the Russian minister of war, Barclay de Tolly. 'I am well, despite the great marches these villainous Russians force upon us, running away in their seven-league boots,' he wrote to Letitia on July 18. 'Take good care of Mama, help her to forget my absence, make her happy, speak of me often to her, and tell her I can never be happy until I am home again with all my family.'[2] Vilia, Strasounouf, Vilna, Bojardly, Widzy, Braslaw, Disna, the strange names followed one upon another for three hundred undisputed miles. Then, at Ostrowno on the approaches to Vitebsk, the Russians turned. 'A light cavalry battle, very brilliant . . . eight pieces of artillery taken and 160 men. The king of Naples charged at the head of the Bruyère division.'[3] Barclay fell back on the hills about Vitebsk, placing 80,000 infantrymen on their slopes, with 10,000 cavalrymen in front of them, covered by trenches and earthworks. Next morning, leading the pursuit down the banks of the Dvina, Murat flung himself with a single regiment, the 16th Chasseurs, against the Russian cavalry. Behind him, Eugène de Beaharnais's infantry advanced under a devastating hail of grapeshot from Russian artillery in the lee of a wood. As Joachim and the remnants of his regiment fell back to reform, the Russian cavalry charged down on Eugène's wavering infantry; charged and charged again. The French were on the point of breaking when Joachim reappeared with a handful of officers and men, perhaps sixty in all, 'and flinging himself like a mere trooper into the midst of the Cossacks . . . broke the Russian lines, took their artillery and forced them to retire beyond the deep ravine of a little stream, a tributary of the Dvina'.[4]

Napoleon ordered the army to bivouac until the morning, when the set battle against the Russians would begin. But when dawn came on July 28 there were no Russians to be seen. With uncanny and disturbing discipline they had quit their positions silently during the short night, leaving the hillsides as empty as Vitebsk itself. Barclay had gone southeast towards Smolensk to link up with the Russian Second Army under Bagration. Napoleon entered Vitebsk, saying that he would go no further forward. 'We won't repeat Charles XII's folly. We must live here this year and finish the war next spring.'[5] To Joachim he said, as he had done to Countess Keilmannsegge, that they would take Moscow in 1813, and St Petersburg in 1814: 'The Russian war is a three-year war.'[6]

It was the sensible thing to do, but he was unable to do it. He must conquer the Russians to close the Baltic and complete the blockade against Britain, before all Europe – and France as well – perished from that same blockade. His economic advisers had told him he could not afford to begin the war; still less could he now afford to suspend it without victory. He waited in Vitebsk until August 13, hoping against all reason that the Russians would return to give battle, then ordered the advance on Smolensk of this limping, ill-provisioned and unwilling army, one third of its strength already drained by desertion, sweating under the hot sun by day, shivering through the damp, chilly nights, whittled away by illness and the hit-and-run attacks of Russians cavalry. On August 14 Joachim caught the Russian outposts near Krasnoé took five hundred prisoners and seven guns. By August 16 he was upon the main Russian army.[7]

The artillery commander, Griois, has left a typical picture of him as he led the two-day attack on Smolensk. 'Murat was beside me near my guns. Delighted with the liveliness and accuracy of our fire, he showed his appreciation to the gunners by shouting to them in his Gascon accent: "Well done, lads! Bowl that rabble over! You are firing like angels!" . . . His extremely theatrical dress would have drawn ridicule on anybody else, but it seemed made to his measure and the perfect accompaniment of a dazzling courage that was his alone. His rather long, handsome brown hair fell in ringlets on to his shoulders. He wore a turned-up hat trimmed with feathers and aigrettes ... crimson breeches and brown boots. A short green velvet cloak embroidered in gold ... was thrown across his shoulders. ... His bravery was so well known in the army, and one was so accustomed to seeing him in the thickest fire, that the aides-de-camp or orderly officers who had messages to take to him or information to give him, always headed for the sector where fighting was taking place, and the point where the attack seemed hottest; they were sure to find him there. He was the personification of courage.'[8]

During the night of September 17 to 18 the Russians set fire to Smolensk. In the morning the streets of the burning town were deserted except for the Russian wounded or dead; those of the inhabitants who had not been able to get away were huddled into churches and public buildings, feeding on potatoes, herbs, roots and the little flour that they had been able to bring with them and that the soldiers now threatened to steal from them. It was here, Metternich believed, that Napoleon intended to set up his winter headquarters.[9] It was quite impossible. He had to go forward.

'The King of Naples is in front, twenty-five miles on the road to Moscow. ... The Russians retire slowly, in good order,' Castellane noted. 'They burn the bridges, the villages; they spared Poland but they are devastating Russia; and that seems odd.'[10] The French were not advancing in such good order. Joachim continually warned the emperor 'that the troops were exhausted, that the horses, which had nothing to eat but thatch from the roofs, could not hold out against fatigue, and that continuing meant the risk of losing everything'.[11] But he was ordered to press on. After one engagement Joachim reproached Nansouty for lack of vigour in his cavalry. 'That,' Nansouty replied, 'is because horses have no patriotism; our soldiers will fight without bread; our horses will do nothing without oats.'[12] But even the soldiers could not be counted upon to support the emperor from patriotism, for half of them were unwilling foreigners. 'Our army is like the Tower of Babel; you cannot go near a bivouac without hearing, German, French, Italian, Spanish, Portuguese, Polish, Flemish, etc.'[13]

The sun still beat down, the dust rose in stifling clouds. The infantry marched in extended order because they constantly expected to make contact with the enemy. Some held pieces of broken window glass in front of their faces, others branches of leaves, and others 'marched with their shakos under their arms, their heads wrapped in scarves, leaving only just enough opening to breathe and see where they were going'.[14] The generals began quarrelling among themselves. Joachim alleged that Davout, whose 1st corps formed part of the advance guard, was slow in supporting him and that one of Davout's batteries had twice refused to fire without an order from Davout himself. Davout protested that Joachim was making too heavy a demand on the light cavalry seconded to him; and when the king ordered General Compans, commanding the infantry of the 1st Corps, to follow him into action, Davout rode up and forbade it. The argument grew so heated amid the burning ruins of Vyaza that Joachim wrote a challenge to Davout, which Belliard, his chief-of-staff, refused to deliver.[15]

Joachim had spent the previous night in a birch wood, protected by his Polish lancers, who stuck their weapons into the ground with their tricolour pennons fluttering among the tree trunks 'the colour of alabaster. . . . The ascending flames from our bivouac fires, the smoke from our kitchens, where huge braziers had encouraged false hopes; the activity and gaiety of these young men hungry for glory, taking a notch in their belts after an inadequate meal; it all produced a charming effect.'[16] It was the last of these pleasant nights: rain came again, with misty mornings, then more rain, then frosts at nightfall. When they reached Gzhatsk the storm raged so heavily that they halted in the smouldering ruins for three days.

Joachim was alarmed by the daily loss of horses that never even faced the enemy, the roads that had become rivers of mud, the limitless distances into which the Russians were forever disappearing. With Berthier and Ney he urged Napoleon to call a halt to the endless march towards disaster. But on September 4 the weather cleared. Galloping down the road at the head of his skirmishers in pursuit of the elusive Cossacks, Joachim suddenly discovered that he had outdistanced his men and that a group of the Russians had turned and were about to fire on him. In the nick of time, one of them, recognizing the white plume that was now almost as familiar to them as to the French, shouted: 'Present arms! Hurrah! Long live the King of the Brave!' Joachim rode over and gave him his gold watch.[17]

The Russians turned at Griednewo, stood again briefly at Kolotsko and Golowino. Hope returned that they were at last ready to give battle. There had, in fact, been a revulsion among the Russians themselves against the continued retreat. The tsar, against his better judgement, replaced Barclay by Kutusov: seventy-four years old, one-eyed, and so obese that he had to be driven about the battlefield in a drosky. And Kutusov determined to accept battle at Borodino on the Moskwa river. On September 5 the emperor ordered an attack on an enemy outpost at Schwardino by Murat's cavalry and an infantry division. The position was taken, retaken and taken again. It was two days before Napoleon was able to launch a full attack. The Russian left, under Bagration, was protected on the flank by woodland and in front by three redans.[18] The centre, under Bennigsen, was guarded by a large redoubt and the right, under Barclay, by a ravine with a shallow stream flowing through it. Davout, with two of his five divisions was to attack the Russian left, while Poniatowski and his Polish Corps tried to make their way through the woods to the old Moscow road and taken them in the rear. Ney, supported by Junot, whose madness was already prompting him to mistake hedgerows for lines of troops, covered the field between Davout and Eugène's 4th Corps, which stood beyond the new Moscow road, facing the village of Borodino. Behind the infantry, waiting for the ground to be clear enough for them to manœuvre, were Nansouty, Montbrun and Grouchy, with Latour-Maubourg in reserve and Joachim caracoling up and down in front of them. At the rear Napoleon retained both the Old Guard and the New.

At 6 a.m. the familiar three rounds from the artillery of the Guard gave the signal for the attack to begin. The fire was deadly on both sides. Davout, taking the place of the wounded Compans, was bowled off his horse by a cannon ball and, though still alive, unable to continue in command. Rapp, sent to replace him, was wounded four times within an hour. Bazout's 11th Infantry Division[1] pouring into the left of the three redans that guarded the heights of Semenowskoye was met by a withering Russian fire and driven back in disorder. Joachim, ordering his trumpeter to sound the charge, leaped from his horse, drew his sword, and led the infantry in a counter-attack. He brought up his artillery, ordered Nansouty to form his men on the right of the line, and set the whole right flank of the French army moving forward. In the centre, the main Russian redoubt had given way. Joachim called up Latour-Maubourg's corps and sent them smashing into the disordered Russian ranks. To the left and right he could see the Russian artillery pulling back. He sent Belliard to the emperor with an urgent request for the Imperial Guard. At one blow they could cut the enemy front in two.

Napoleon was seated, staring at the portrait of his son by Gérard that had just arrived from Paris, and guarded by his household troops – 'thirty-six thousand men, playing fanfares while the rest of army struggled for victory',[19] as one astounded officer noted. Refusing to commit the Guard, he sent Friant's division instead; but by the time they arrived Bagration had been reinforced by an army corps and the Russian Imperial Guard, both mounted and foot. Joachim tried to maintain his position with Friant's infantry while he threw in his cavalry from left and right. The Russian infantry was driven back, only to be replaced by their cavalry. Friant, twice wounded, was carried to the rear and Joachim took his place in the square against which the Russian cuirassiers[20] flung themselves in wave after wave. A young officer of the emperor's staff, Anatole de Montesquiou, son of the governess of the King of Rome, came upon him 'in the redoubt that his courage had won and his presence made impregnable. With his artillery thundering and the immense cloud of powder in which he disappeared entirely, or that his great stature enabled him to tower over from time to time, he seemed like one of the more terrible gods of Olympus.'[21]

Catching sight of Montesquiou through the drifting smoke, Joachim called, 'Tell the emperor to send me his reserve – if he's still got it.'[22] Montesquiou galloped back to where Napoleon still sat with the whole of the Imperial Guard drawn up behind him in the full-dress uniforms that they traditionally wore on days of battle. But the emperor gave no command for them to advance. At last the Russians drew back and did not come again. Joachim remounted, gathered the cavalry and charged against the sagging Russian lines. On the skyline to the right Poniatowski come into view. Once more Joachim, supported by Ney, implored Napoleon to throw in the Guards. He agreed, ordered the Young Guard to advance, then learned that the Russians had recaptured the central redoubt, recalled them and committed only Claparède's division. It was not enough to achieve the vital breakthrough. While Eugène attacked the redoubt from the front, Joachim sent the 2nd cavalry corps charging behind it, then wheeling left and driving in from the rear. The chance of total victory had passed. The armies faced each other, exchanging artillery fire, until nightfall.

It had been a day of appalling bloodshed, of pageantry, of bitterness, of disillusion.[23] It had been the king of Naples's day. Napoleon, who slept that night in his tent still protected by the square of the Old Guard, sent his second tent as a compliment to Joachim, bivouacked with his cavalry on the edge of the ravine. Deprived of the spare tent, the emperor's staff officers spent a cold uncomfortable night among the dead, 'putting two of their corpses, one on top of the other, to serve as chairs around the fire'.[24] The survivors collected broken musket stocks and the timber from shattered wagons to cook the plentiful supply of horse meat that lay about them. 'Around the flames that began to light up the gloom, we were soon outnumbered by the wounded and the dying. You could see them everywhere, like spectres, moving in the half-light, dragging themselves, crawling towards the glow of the fire. Some, horribly mutilated, used the last remnant of their strength in this supreme effort; they gave their last gasps and expired, their eyes fixed on the flames.'[25]

Napoleon had in fact put in an appearance once that day – in the late afternoon. 'Towards five o'clock,' recounted Rosetti, one of Joachim's aides-de-camp, 'the king sent me to tell the emperor that he could visit the battlefield. Napoleon mounted his horse and rode slowly to the king. Over an area of two to three miles square, the ground was covered with dead and wounded. . . . There were mounds of corpses across the plain, and the few spaces where there were none were covered with the debris of weapons . . . The most terrible to see were the ravines; almost all the wounded had dragged themselves there instinctively, to avoid further hits. And there these unfortunate creatures, piled one on top of the other, deprived of help and swimming in their own blood, uttered horrible moans and screamed loudly for death.

After examining this horrifying battlefield, the emperor turned to the king of Naples and said. "I had not imagined it so beautiful!"[26] 'I have had many killed and wounded,' he wrote to Marie-Louise next day. 'I was not exposed to any danger myself. My health is good, the weather a little chilly.'[27]

The Russians turned long enough at Mozhaysk to hold the town over night and the following afternoon they put up a bitter resistance at Forminskoyé,[28] where with 10,000 infantrymen and twelve regiments of cavalry they fought the French to a standstill. Davout again accused Murat of sacrificing the men attached to him from 1st Corps and they quarrelled publicly. After a day's rest, Murat continued on the road to Moscow.

In the morning of September 14, the advance guard came upon earthworks and barricades of newly felled trees and a line of cavalry on the heights.

A Russian officer, waving a white handkerchief above his head, brought a message that, in order to spare the city, the French would be allowed to enter unmolested if they undertook to protect the wounded who remained there. The battle would be resumed on the farther side. If the French refused these terms, the inhabitants had determined to set their houses on fire. Joachim replied that he accepted. The Russians turned about and, with the French advance guard marching at their heels, led the strange procession towards the gates of Moscow.

At 2 p.m. Murat entered at the head of the 1st Polish Hussars, followed by three cavalry divisions and 1st Corps. At the Kremlin he came under a hail of musketry fire from a group of franctireurs in the arsenal. 'I was never in my whole life in such wild danger,' he wrote to Caroline; 'but fortunately, having two pieces of artillery with me, which immediately opened fire with discharges of grape, I was rescued, and the assailants were dispersed: one of the demons, however, sprang upon a colonel of engineers on horseback, tore him to the ground, stabbed him in the back when falling, threw himself upon him to suffocate him, fixed his teeth in his neck, and perseveringly retained his hold until the surrounding French, recovering from their terror, dispatched him by beating out his brains with repeated blows.'[29]

He continued his ride through the city, surrounded by Cossack generals eager to speak with their famous adversary. 'I have known you a long time, Sire,' said one. 'You are the king of Naples; the difference between you and me is that since the Niemen I have always seen you ahead of your army, and for three months I have always been the last of ours.'[30] He asked for a keepsake and Joachim, blossoming in this congenial company, promptly gave him a watch, regretting that the circumstances prevented him from offering the Order of the Two Sicilies. Thus pleasantly gossiping and with Joachim handing out 'the watches of all his aides-de-camp and other officers of his general staff',[31] they arrived at the Vladimir gate, where the Russians begged him to halt. 'We have handed over the town to you, Sire,' they explained, 'but if you come any farther you will be our prisoner.'[32]

It was between six and seven in the evening. From the direction of the Kalouga Gate came the sound of a violent explosion, followed by the hiss of rockets: the signal for the fires which broke out half an hour later in several quarters of the city and spread rapidly before the stiff breeze. There was no serious attempt to deal with the fire, for those troops who had entered (they were camped outside the first day) in search of loot, were already too drunk to accept orders. The following day the streets were filled with pillagers, and the flames unchecked.

Joachim set up his headquarters some twenty-five miles down the new Kalouga road in the direction of Taroutina. In Moscow on September 19 the great fires were checked by rain; on September 27 a little snow came and melted and was followed by heavier rain. In the emperor's salon in the Kremlin, the flames crackled in the great marble and gold fireplace; in his study, by his orders, his gentleman usher set two candles close to the window each night 'so that the soldiers would exclaim: "Look, the emperor does not sleep by day or by night; he is always working."'[33] But there was nothing for the emperor to work at. He could not make up his mind what to do.

The weather outside worsened. By permitting indiscriminate looting in the city and by keeping his cavalry in the field instead of replacing a large part of them with infantry, Napoleon completed the moral and physical deterioration of his army. Joachim told an orderly officer who came out from Moscow: 'Report to the emperor that I have led the advance guard of the French army beyond Moscow with glory; but I am bored – bored, do you understand? I want to go to Naples and look after my subjects.'[34] He wrote to Caroline, saying the same thing. She replied anxiously: 'Calm yourself, my dear; reflect; do not lose the rewards of so perilous and brilliant a campaign.'[35]

There was talk of the emperor spending the winter in Moscow and sending to Italy for singers to entertain him. He wrote to the tsar, suggesting negotiations. The answer awaited the French troops who captured the village of Woronowo on October 2. The great manorial residence of Count Rostopchin, Governor of Moscow, had been burnt to the ground. On one blackened post was nailed a board on which was written, 'I have set fire to my castle, which cost me a million, so that no French dog shall find lodging there.'[36] He tried again on October 4. General Lauriston passed through Joachim's muddy headquarters at the Belfry with Five Spires in Winkovo. Kutusov refused to let him have a safe conduct for talks with the tsar, but promised to forward the general's message. That same day, the Russians attacked in strength and Joachim drove them off only after very hard fighting.

A tacit agreement – that each side would give the other three hours' warning of an attack – was resumed. 'Our scouts and theirs were stationed fifty paces apart and never spoke a word,' said Major Dupuy of the 7th Hussars. 'I have even seen the king of Naples, visiting our advance posts, find the Cossacks too close to us and go among them, making them draw back their vedettes and showing them the positions they should take up. The Russians obeyed; even the generals of their advance guard, whom we often had the opportunity of seeing, submitted without question to the slightest demands of the king, who had the air of commanding everything.'[37] But with the countryside ravaged on their side of the line, it was not easy for the French to stay within bounds without starving. And it was clear that the Russians were building up their forces. Joachim sent the news back, without results.[38]

'My situation is hideous,' he wrote on October 10 to Belliard, who was recovering in Moscow from a wound in the ankle he received at Moxhaysk. 'It is no longer possible to go foraging without running the almost certain risk of being captured. Not a day passes without my losing 200 men that way . . . Why cannot I see the emperor? . . . When will the emperor make up his mind?

What will happen to his army this winter?'[39] Belliard evidently transmitted the message to Berthier, and Berthier to the emperor, for late in the evening of October 12 Napoleon gave orders for two brigades of cavalry to escort him to Joachim's headquarters at 9 a.m. next day. But in the morning it was snowing and he changed his mind.

Joachim grew more and more worried about the future – and even the present – of Naples. The kingdom's defences had been weakened by the demand for troops for Russia; the British fleet was always ready to convoy an invasion from Sicily. He had received no reports from his ministers for two months; his doubts about Caroline's regency revived: 'I confess I am otherwise very satisfied with everything that is being done in Naples,' he told her in a mixture of pleasantry and bitterness. 'How could I not be? You tell me you understand affairs of state as well as I do, that you have been drilling my troops, in that case, come and take my place here; you would give a great deal of pleasure, the Russians would be beaten from the start, they would yield to valour and beauty, and the Bulletins would carry the news of your brilliant successes to Naples and Paris; they are silent about what little I do. . . . Farewell, most lovable of women; the emperor is in good health. Farewell!'[40]

From the Russian lines two miles away came the daily rattle and crash of firing practice with muskets and cannon. To the Frenchmen who visited them, the Hetman Platov and other senior officers said amicably: 'You are weary of war, and we are in the mood to begin it seriously. We intend to take your wagons, your booty, your baggage, your guns, everything.'[41] During the night of October 17–18, Bennigsen moved several Russian corps up to the right bank of the Nara, crossed it at midnight and began an advance in three columns astride the Taroutina–Moscow road that ran through the middle of the French position.

Bennigsen ordered his leading column to skirt round the wood at Teterinki which protected Sébastiani's division on the French left flank, and in the early morning of October 18, Sébastiani suddenly found himself attacked in the rear. He was no less surprised than his commander, for Joachim was still in bed when the first shots were fired. 'With difficulty he gained his horse before the Russians were in possession of his quarters: his baggage, silver canteens, and cooking utensils, in which were found cats and horse-flesh preparing for food, were taken. Desperate by a sense of the misfortunes menacing his comrades . . . he asserted to the highest degree all his energies and activity; his plume was seen waving in the thickest of every fray – now he was rallying the fugitives; now restoring order in the columns; now charging on the pursuers; now covering his line of retreat by the most energetic defensive measures and personal daring.'[42] He forced Bennigsen back across the Nara.[43] But it was impossible for him to hold against the weight of the Russian attack. Hit over the heart by a case-shot, Joachim miraculously escaped with nothing worse than a bruise eight inches wide. He sent an aide-de-camp to the emperor with a warning that he might be forced to retire.

14

Napoleon was reviewing the 3rd Corps when the message came. He at once decided on retreat. He ordered Eugène to lead the way, making first towards Mozhaysk and then turning left on the old Kalouga road. He intended to take a southerly route, thus avoiding the corridor of ravaged land along which he had advanced to Moscow. On the evening of October 19 he was at Troitskoë, the road behind him already jammed with thousands of private vehicles commandeered by officers and soldiers to transport their loot. Kutusov wheeled to confront him. The two armies met at Malojaroslavets on October 23. The French advance guard under Eugène held their ground but could do no more. The emperor passed the night in the village of Ghorodnia, two or three miles from the battlefield. When he went to observe the enemy positions the following morning there was a sudden burst of wild yelling and a group of Cossacks came charging towards him.[1] He was saved by Murat who drove off the attackers with a few cavalrymen and the officers of his household.

Napoleon's mind was made up. He would return by the old route,[2] and he would not stray from the protection of his mettlesome brother-in-law. From now on Joachim rode with him; when he got into his carriage he took Joachim to sit beside him; when he decided to walk it was with a long stick in one hand, his other arm supported by Murat, 'whose elegance contrasted with everything around him, and whom the cold and our sad circumstances had not robbed of the air of assurance and gaiety that was his by nature'.[3] The only change in his appearance was that the chilly air inflamed the scar on his face that usually passed unnoticed – the relic of his wound at Aboukir. They first retracted their steps northwards to Borowsk and then set off westward to Mozhaysk.

For some days the weather remained fine, but after Vyazma it turned very cold, with snow. Those who could not find sledges in the deserted villages knocked the wheels from their carts and dragged them on their axles – until a thaw bogged them down inextricably in the mud and they had to march on with what they could carry on their backs. There was optimism though, for the word had gone round that Marshal Victor was at Smolensk with 40,000 fresh troops and stores bulging with food: it was here that the emperor would set up their winter quarters. They reached Smolensk on November 9. As soon as the emperor and the Imperial Guard had entered the city the gates were closed. There was no Marshal Victor, no fresh troops, no distribution of food.

Griois, going to report to Belliard in Smolensk on November 13 found him in 'a quite vast building gutted by fire even before it was completed, but with a small staircase still remaining. I went up it; . . . I pushed open a half-broken door; I saw Murat and Belliard chatting happily. Belliard, still suffering from the wound he received at Mozhaysk, was stretched out on a shabby pallet with Murat seated at his feet. The spectacle was not without interest. A king – for such he was, and so recognized – keeping company with one of his wounded generals and seeming to be simply one friend looking after another – it was something rare, and I confess that I was touched.'[4]

When Napoleon left Smolensk on November 14 accompanied by Joachim, he was escorted for the first time by a battalion of infantry of the Old Guard, and rode at the head of the army, leading the retreat. The reserve of cavalry was reduced to 1,200 men, who were placed under the command of Latour-Maubourg; the cavalry units attached to the various army corps (originally about equal in total number to the reserve) amounted to 1,200 men, plus 2,000 with the Imperial Guard. The soldiers left the ranks to make their way *en amateurs*, rather than die of hunger with the colours. The eagles of the cavalry regiments were burned to prevent their falling into the hands of the enemy who harried this panic rout, picking off victims at their pleasure. For his personal protection the emperor ordered the formation of four companies of Guards of Honour[5] each composed of 150 cavalry officers, generals serving as captains, colonels as non-commissioned officers and so on.

On November 16, at Krasnoye, the Russians made their first attempt to bar the way westward. Napoleon, who had halted the flight long enough for the main body of the stragglers to catch up, pushed a way through with the Guard, leaving Ney and the rearguard to fend for themselves.[6] On that day, Junot counted his twenty infantry battalions of the 8th Corps and found they amounted to less than 600 men – a week later he had one gun, a hundred horses and not a single infantryman. Napoleon called in Oudinot with 2nd Corps and Victor with the 9th from his north flank. It was these two who held off the second Russian attack at the crossing of the Beresina river a few miles on above Borisov. Here dreadful scenes of panic and indiscipline confirmed the disintegration of the leaderless army. When the Russian guns, mounted on sledges opened fire in the afternoon of November 27 'thousands of men hurled themselves towards the bridges, . . . trampling on each other to get across'.[7] Napoleon ordered his own guns to fire on them to clear a way for the Imperial Guard. Castellane, thrusting his way over, came upon 'an unfortunate sutler woman, with water up to her waist, trying to get up on the bridge again, but pushed back by the soldiers. With despair written on her face, she held out her child to me; at the instant when I was going to take it, a wave of soldiers picked me up and carried me twenty paces backwards without my feet touching the ground.'[8] A few days later, at Molodeczno, Napoleon wrote his twenty-ninth bulletin, telling for the first time the truth about the 'terrible calamity'.[9]

It was at this time, passing through the great forest between Iliya and Molodezcno that Langeron, an émigré serving with the Russians, saw a French woman 'who had just given birth and expired beside her dead child. I saw a dead man with his teeth sunk into the thigh of a still palpitating horse. I saw a man dead inside a horse that he had disemboweled so that he could crawl into it and warm himself. I saw one tearing out the entrails of a dead horse with his teeth. I did not see the wretched French eating each other, but I saw dead men from whose thighs they had cut strips of flesh to feed themselves.'[10]

On November 29 Napoleon had written to Maret: 'The army is strong in numbers but shockingly dispersed . . . We shall soon be at Wilna: can we stand there? . . . Food, food, food! without it there are no horrors that this undisciplined mass will not commit against the town . . . I may think it possible that my presence in Paris is necessary for France, the empire, the army itself.'[11] Although Maret begged him to remain with the army – 'I cannot without terror imagine it abandoned to its own resources'[12] – Napoleon decided as he drove from Molodezcno to Biclitza on December 4, to quit.[13] At Smorgoni next afternoon he went through a brief charade in which Joachim, Eugène and others advised him to return to Paris as soon as possible and, when Bessières, commander of the cavalry of the Imperial Guard, pressed the point, Napoleon turned on him in simulated fury, his sword drawn, shouting, 'Only my most deadly enemy could suggest my leaving the army when it is in its present situation.'[14] Shortly afterwards he sent for Bessières and said: 'Since you all want it, I must go.'[15] He was away at ten o'clock, speeding through the night. Even before arriving at Smorgoni he had dictated the necessary instructions for the change of command to his chief-of-staff, Berthier. He confided the scattered remnants of the Grande Armée to the king of Naples, to the disgust of Eugène the dismay of Berthier and the mounting mistrust of Murat himself.

The emperor had assured Murat there were sufficient stores at Vilna for him to be able to set up winter quarters there and at Grodno, or at Grodno and Kovno, thus holding the Russians east of the Niemen. It was sheer fantasy. With the news of the emperor's desertion the last bonds of discipline snapped. Not only deserters and *amateurs*, but whole battalions raced to get ahead of the others. Generals ignored their orders of route and marched on as fast as they could, with or without their troops. The weather turned fiercely cold. They trudged towards Vilna in 27 degrees of frost. 'A frightening number of soldiers are lying dead on the road . . . They fall, a little blood comes to their mouths, and it is finished. Seeing this sign of approaching death, their comrades give them a nudge with the shoulder, throwing them to the ground, and strip them before they are quite dead.'[16]

They arrived on December 8. Hogendorp, the Governor-general of Lithuania, had signposted the town, directing the various corps to the buildings allotted to them; but when this great ragged mass began to pour in 'grenadiers with long moustaches wearing womens' bonnets and pelisses, others wrapped in Russian priests' garments, some in the embroidered robes of chamberlains that they had stolen . . .[17] they all, generals and soldiers alike, penetrated by force into the first houses that seemed suitable, sought out the best heated rooms, lay down and had food brought them. The strongest chased out the weakest; the generals and officers, if they could still exercise what was left of their authority, made the soldiers give way to them.'[18]

With the Russians hard on his heels, there was no time to organize a defence at Vilna. The following morning Joachim wrote to Caroline: 'H.M. has left me the command of the Grande Armée despite my entreaties. I am going to try to lead it to winter quarters, after which I am authorized to set off for Naples.'[19] He took the icebound road to Kovno, which he reached on December 11. He spent the following day trying to organize sufficient units to hold the line of the Niemen. But the river was frozen: the rabble swept across it, carrying with them the Kovno garrison and the large stocks of brandy they found in store.

On December 16 Joachim told Napoleon: 'It is no longer a question of fighting, but of reorganizing, administering, rallying the numerous debris of the army. . . . I shall therefore leave the command to the Viceroy, who . . . will carry out your wishes better. That prince has had more experience of administration than I. . . . If I have not received your decision within fifteen days, I shall be on my way.'[20] On the same day, Berthier said in a coded message to Napoleon: 'the king of Naples is the best man to carry out a commander-in-chief's orders on the field of battle. The king of Naples is the least capable man to act as commander-in-chief from any point of view. He should be replaced at once.'[21]

The letters crossed one from Napoleon, forbidding Murat to leave the army in any circumstances. Joachim replied, 'I wrote to you yesterday that nothing in the world will make me stay . . . I shall always be ready to hasten back to the colours when it is a question of fighting, but I cannot remain here when it is only a matter of organization and administration and when the care of my kingdom and the wishes of my subjects demand my presence.'[22]

At Königsberg he saw his first hope of making a stand. Marshal Macdonald, with his own 10th Corps and the Prussian Corps commanded by General Yorck, had been besieging Riga and was now withdrawing on Tilsit. Around these troops, undemoralized and untouched by hunger and the extreme cold, Murat could hope to rally the remnants of the Moscow army and hold a line along the Vistula from Elbing to Bromberg, or even from Königsberg along the Pregel. His southern flank was nominally covered by 40,000 uncommitted troops under the Austrian Schwarzenberg. So that when he received a pessimistic report from Belliard[23] he replied with an unselfconscious rebuke that 'Everybody wants to leave the army; I am truly indignant at the general state of demoralization.'[24] He put on his gaudiest clothes, spent part of each day reviewing troops in Königsberg as they were brought back into some semblance of order and directed to their posts along the Vistula, and 'talked ceaselessly of rallying the army, resisting, fighting'.[25]

On December 29 he again wrote to Napoleon saying that things were settling down, the Russians were unlikely to attack, and that he could therefore well be spared. But the Cossacks had cut communication with Macdonald's army and on New Year's Day 1813, the hope of making a stand was dispelled by the news that Yorck had taken the whole of his Prussian Corps over to the Russians. Murat withdrew to Elbing, where he arrived on January 3. From there on January 4 and again on January 7 he wrote to the emperor asking why he had received no reply and telling him that he had fever and jaundice. He fell back on Marienburg with Berthier, who was almost incapacitated with rheumatic gout. The two men, army commander and chief-of-staff, were constantly and openly at odds, Joachim wanting to turn and fight, Berthier insisting on further retreat. Joachim continued to Posen and there, on January 15, announced that he was handing over to Eugène. He left Posen at 4 a.m. on January 17. Caroline went to meet him at Caserta on January 31. He was still suffering from fever; but he wrote a cool and unconcerned note to Napoleon, announcing his safe return to his kingdom. He then arranged for his ceremonial entry into the capital on February 4 to be followed by three nights of illuminations and free theatre performances.

In the streets he received a welcome warm enough to bring tears to his eyes, but on arrival at the palace he retired at once to his private apartments and refused to see anybody. Letters came from the emperor which increased the jaundiced look that observers had noticed on his face. To Caroline, Napoleon wrote: 'Your husband is very brave on the battlefield, but he is weaker than a woman or a monk when he does not have the enemy in sight. He has no moral courage.'[26] His rage was tempered by his possible need of Joachim in the future, and he concluded, 'if he sincerely repents, if he seeks the right moment to prove to me that he is not as ungrateful as he is fainthearted, I may still forgive him the injury he has done me'.[27] In the *Moniteur* of January 27 came the public reproof 'Because of illhealth, the king of Naples has given up command of the army, which he has placed in the hands of the Viceroy. The latter is more accustomed to the administration of important affairs; he has the Emperor's confidence.'[28] Joachim closed his door on the French ambassador. He considered calling the Estates and having them proclaim him king of the Two Sicilies so that he could reign without benefit of Napoleon or France. Caroline dissuaded him, with great difficulty.

He knew that the Austrians were trying to act as mediators in a peace between France and Russia. At the end of February he sent one of his aides-de-camp, Prince Cariati, to ask Metternich for an assurance that Naples was not to be used as an expendable piece in the negotiations.[29] On March 25 there was an easy opportunity for Napoleon to show some sign of reconciliation, but no birthday wishes came.

Joachim sent for Durand at the end of the month. Caroline saw the ambassador first and told him how worried the king was that the emperor was considering making peace at his expense. Joachim then asked him to convey a message to the Emperor: 'I have thirty thousand men under arms; I shall soon have forty thousand. . . . My army ensures the safety of Italy. . . . I will defend it for the emperor, for his policies, with no thought for my personal interests. . . . If the emperor thinks my presence necessary with the Grand Armée, . . . [Prussia, after signing the Treaty

of Kalisch with Russia on February 28, 1813, had declared war on
France on March 17] let him say so and I will be there immediately;
but . . . let him accord me the confidence that I must have if I am
to serve him well, so that I at least know that he is doing justice to
me when I devote my life to him.'[30]

He followed this with a letter addressed directly to the Emperor
on April 13. Now that the enemy was advancing against the frontiers of France and Napoleon was about to take command again
he asked him, for their common good: 'to let nobody doubt your
confidence in me any more than my devotion to you and to
France. I acknowledge – and I have always openly affirmed – that
my political existence can only be supported by the might of the
empire. I acknowledge in particular, and I particularly declare,
that I would never wish for any existence which did not
have such support. Deign, Sire, for your part, to make it known
that I shall never lack the protection of the empire.'[31] As a proof
of good faith, he ordered two more squadrons of mounted
chasseurs to join the two already sent to the Grande Armée by
Caroline. The following day he left for a tour of inspection of the
provinces of Bari, Capitanata and the Terra d'Otranto. By the
time he returned on April 29, the situation had radically changed.

15

While Cariati was on his way to Vienna, Metternich sent instructions to Mier the Austrian ambassador in Naples, to obtain
Murat's views on a peace settlement: 'We are very willing as
mediators, to defend the interests of the king of Naples and we
wish to know his point of view.'[1] Joachim told him that he merely
required an assurance that he would not be deprived of his kingdom. He then received a messenger from Cariati, saying Metternich was ready to draw up a treaty if Cariati were given full
powers. These Joachim refused, since Cariati had already gone
beyond his instructions in suggesting that Joachim was ready to
enter into a military alliance with Austria and renounce his claim
to Sicily without receiving any other territory in compensation.
There was, in addition, a new factor in the negotiations – Lord

William Cavendish-Bentinck, second son of the third Duke of Portland, British minister to the court of Palermo and commander-in-chief of the British forces in Sicily.

Bentinck, a man of thirty-seven with a loose mouth and an obstinate nose, was a dedicated, unpredictable Whig. His liberal principles gave him as much dislike of Ferdinand's corrupt feudalism as of Napoleon's efficient dictatorship. His suspicions of the devious Mary Caroline, who was credited with secretly intriguing with Austria, Russia, Napoleon and Murat all at the same time, and his curt manner towards her, soon made them open enemies. He took up his appointment in July 1811, and in January of the following year forced Ferdinand to hand over the government to his son Francis.[2] Throughout 1812 he built up a spy system on the mainland and provided support for various minor insurrections. In February 1813 British troops captured the island of Ponza about 65 miles west of Naples. When its inhabitants were evacuated to the mainland, the senior British officer, Lieutenant-colonel Coffin, hinted to one of them that Bentinck was willing to discuss better relations with Naples.

On April 22 an employee of the Neapolitan ministry of Police, Giuseppe Ceruti, arrived at Ponza and asked to be informed of the British proposals. Coffin replied it was for Murat to make the first move. Ceruti went back to Naples again while Coffin reported to Bentinck, who told him that Murat must surrender the kingdom of Naples but, if he declared war on Napoleon, he would be given an equivalent kingdom elsewhere. Bentinck said he would visit Ponza towards the end of May on his way to Spain and was ready to come to terms with an accredited representative. He met two of Joachim's agents – Robert Jones, a British-born merchant, and Felice Nicolas, keeper of the Archives, on June 3. Nicolas, on June 5, broke off the negotiations on the grounds that Bentinck was not empowered to treat and that Austria had not yet declared herself. Bentinck, however, told Castlereagh that he believed Murat would resume them later. 'He broke off the negotiations, first, because the great inducement [his recognition as king of Naples] was not granted ... and, secondly, because being disappointed in that immediate object of his ambition, it was natural for him to hold back until he might be more accurately informed of the state of affairs in Germany.'[3]

In mid-April and at the beginning of May, Napoleon had asked for troops – still refusing to communicate with Joachim except through Clarke. Joachim turned a deaf ear. 'To go myself or to send my troops would, I am entirely convinced, be to lose not only my own kingdom but the rest of the Peninsula as well,' he wrote to Marie-Louise, adding an outspoken explanation for her to pass on to the emperor: 'Nothing can allay the anxiety aroused in me by the emperor's attitude since my return to Naples. . . . He has made requests which he knew I could not fulfil. . . . He has failed to give me the facilities to obtain in France the weapons and horses I need for his service. He has not let me have his views nor his instructions on the policy to follow in Italy. If I were less familiar with the genius of the Emperor and the close attention that he gives to details, I might believe the entire direction of affairs at the Tuileries has been in the hands of my enemies, with the intention of creating difficulties and working up grievances against me for use on some future occasion.'[4]

After his victories on May 2 and May 21 at Lützen and Bautzen, inconclusive because he lacked the cavalry to follow them up, Napoleon proposed an armistice and peace talks at Prague.

On June 27 at Reichenbach, Austria agreed to enter the war as an ally of Russia and Prussia if Napoleon refused the terms to be offered. It seemed he could not be madman enough to drag France into another bloody – and this time less than hopeful – adventure. So that when he wrote to Murat announcing he had agreed terms with Austria 'that would serve for the foundation of a general pacification' and 'he hoped that his brother-in-law would not be the last person to make up his differences',[5] Joachim saw the threat of a settlement without his participation. He appointed Caroline as regent and left for Dresden at ten o'clock on the night of August 2.

He had scarcely gone when Mier presented Caroline with a dispatch from Metternich, who wanted Joachim to sign a secret agreement to remain neutral in the event of Austria joining the Coalition against France (if he preferred, to join the Coalition as an active partner). Metternich required an answer by August 10, and added: 'The king's only means of assuring his continued existence as a sovereign is to join forces with Austria. He cannot honestly fail to see that he has gone too far not to have exposed himself to the full measure of the emperor's reprobation.'[6] It was too blunt a threat. Caroline promptly tore it up. Another copy enclosed in dispatches from Cariati which had to be decoded in Naples was sent on to Joachim, who reached Dresden at 5 p.m. on August 14.

The emperor greeted him in a friendly fashion and next morning took him in his carriage to his headquarters at Bautzen to review the troops, many of whom were arriving raw from France, scarcely knowing what companies they were in. Two days before, following his refusal of the Prague Peace terms, Austria had declared war. Murat, who had come to plead his cause at the peace talks, accepted the command of the cavalry instead. 'The army hears of his return with joy; for, on the field of battle, he is an incomparable cavalry general,'[7] said the artillery colonel, Noel.

Despite the accession of hundreds of thousands of untrained conscripts. Napoleon was outnumbered by the nations of the Coalition. He split his forces, hoping that a series of scattered lightning blows would demoralize his enemies; but Oudinot, on his way to attack Berlin, was met and defeated by Bülow (August 25); Macdonald, left without support, was overwhelmed by Blücher at the Katzbatch (August 26); Vandamme, with more than 30,000 men, on a hopeless mission to take the Austrians in the rear, lost half of them at Kulm (August 30); Ney, sent to repeat Oudinot's attempt on Berlin, was routed by Bernadotte at Dennewitz (September 6). Only at Dresden, to which he hastened with the bulk of his army when he realized he was in danger of being cut off by Schwarzenberg, did Napoleon score a victory, withstanding the Allied attack on the city and next day (August 27) driving them off. Joachim, commanding the right wing during the two days' engagement, captured 18,000 men and thirty guns, but the new French army had too few trained cavalrymen and horses to permit a pursuit. Napoleon exhausted his men still further in a series of fruitless marches, then returned to Dresden. He had failed to crush any of the Allied armies individually; they would now unite at their leisure.

During the pause that followed the inconclusive battles of late August and early September, Joachim and Metternich were in touch again. Bentinck had arrived in Prague, and Metternich pressed him to meet Murat's demand for an assurance that he would not lose his throne. On October 7, Schinina, the secretary of the Neapolitan embassy in Vienna, brought Joachim new proposals. In agreement with the British government, Austria would recognize him as the legal king of Naples if he would join the Allies.[8] It was clear proof of the renewed trust between them, that Joachim refused to give any reply until the proposals had been considered by Caroline.

When Schinina arrived on October 17, she realized that Joachim would not have consulted her had he not already halfway made up his mind to accept; and that her immediate task was to open exploratory talks. She sent for Mier next day, formally showed him her credentials – the Act of Regency – and asked him for a memorandum on Austria's requirements and proposals for guaranteeing the throne of Naples. On October 28, she learned that the king of Bavaria, Eugène's father-in-law, had joined the Coalition. She told Mier that she wished to open direct negotiations with Austria.

Napoleon retired on Leipzig to avoid encirclement. Joachim's cavalry covered the withdrawal, beating back the enemy advance at Walkirchen on the day before he received Metternich's offer, and routing Wittgenstein's corps four days later, at Borna on October 10. At Wachau, outside Leipzig, on October 16 he led his 10,000 cavalrymen with the old careless fury that carried them almost to the foot of the Wachberg where the tsar was standing. Had the infantry supported Murat's charge, the battle would have been over at that point. Next day Napoleon made an offer of an armistice, but it was refused. With appalling losses on both sides,[9] the battle was resumed. Driven back into the narrow streets of the town, the retreating Frenchmen choked the single bridge over the Elster. When the emperor had crossed, the bridge was blown, leaving 200 guns behind, and more than 30,000 men who fought, surrendered, or drowned.

The army fell back on Erfurt. Joachim's mind was finally made up: he would save himself from the mad destruction in which Napoleon would bring them all down. On November 24 he had a final stormy scene with his brother-in-law. He gave a clear warning of what he intended to do, then fell on his knees and begged the emperor to accept honourable terms for the sake of France. Napoleon raised the king of Naples to his feet and, after having embraced him said: 'I authorize Your Majesty to return to your states to do everything possible to preserve them; but let the king of Naples never forget that he is a French prince.'[10] Before leaving Erfurt that night, Joachim sent a coded message to Cariati telling him to inform Metternich he was on his way to Naples where he would bring his army up to eighty thousand in preparation for making common cause with the Allies. But, since he was king of the Two Sicilies, and the Allies were offering him a guarantee only of Naples, he would require the Papal Sates as recompense for renouncing Sicily. As soon as he had assurance on that point he would be ready to take the field.

He set off for Mainz and then up the Rhine to Bâle.[11] He left his carriage snowbound in the Simplon Pass and rode on to Milan, where he called on La Vauguyon (still living in exile since Napoleon ordered him out of Paris), and told him to be ready to take over as governor of the Papal States. In Florence he assured Elisa that she need have no worry: he would shortly set up his headquarters at Bologna with 40,000 men. In Rome he talked with the French Governor, Miollis, and 'without telling him that he was thinking of declaring against Napoleon, did not conceal from him that he considered Napoleon's cause to be lost'.[12] He was back in Naples late in the evening of November 4 and on November 8 summoned Mier for a secret conference in the house of the Grand Marshal of the Palace at 11 p.m. It continued until four o'clock in the morning.

He asked Mier to return to Vienna and inform Metternich that he was determined to join the Allies, but that he needed a guarantee of compensation. The Papal States, for instance, possibly territory north of them, and the island of Corfu. As he had come down through Italy, conscious of the dissolution of Napoleon's power behind him, the dream had grown of a united Italy with himself on the throne. On November 11 he issued a decree permitting the importation of all foreign goods in friendly or neutral vessels – thus virtually ending the Continental System in Italy. On November 12 he wrote to Napoleon, offering to march into Lombardy if the emperor would declare the independence of Italy. On November 21 he ordered his troops to advance northward, on division under Carascosa heading for Rome, and a second, under Ambrosio, for Ancona. On November 19 he had sent Schinina to

Sicily to tell Bentinck, now back from Prague, that he could move
no more men until he had a guarantee from Britain similar to that
of Austria, or at least an armistice for the period that he was out of
his kingdom.

It was a wise precaution. Aberdeen, writing to Castlereagh
from the Allied Headquarters at Frankfurt on November 10, had
said: 'In admitting the propriety of taking such measures as may
secure the most effectual co-operation of Murat, I have never
failed to impress on P.M. [Prince Metternich] the conviction that
as the assistance of Murat becomes less indispensable, the claims of
the Sicilian family rise in proportion.'[13]

16

There was a pause, a feeling that reason must prevail, the killing
would not begin again. The Allies halted on the Rhine; Napoleon
recovered his composure in Paris, where he arrived on November
9, and awaited the conscription of another 300,000 men. Joachim
waited for replies. Fouché, driven out of the Illyrian Provinces
where he had briefly ruled as governor, reached Naples on
November 30 with general powers from the emperor to do what
he could in the French interest, and almost certainly advised
Joachim to look after himself. Joachim wrote once more, 'Peace
is necessary to France . . . Peace is necessary to Italy . . . Why, Sire,
does Your Majesty refuse to treat on conditions which reconcile
both the honour and the interests of France?'[1] Another old friend,
Julie Récamier, appeared at the same time. She had been exiled by
Napoleon and was unsure how she would be received by his
sister, whom she had not seen for many years. But Murat provided
her with an escort on the road from Rome, and when she arrived
Caroline sent a page with a huge basket of fruit and flowers and
an invitation to visit her as soon as possible. Grateful for her company, Caroline showered attentions on her, boxes at the opera,
precedence over the ladies of the royal household, a specially
arranged excavation at Pompeii; and Julie fell under her spell
again.

On December 2 a note from Metternich, dated October 28,

repeated the offers already made but said Britain had withdrawn
her agreement because of the part that Murat had played in the
Dresden and Leipzig campaigns. On December 18, Schinina
returned from Sicily with a refusal from Bentinck to enter into
negotiations – on the same grounds.

On December 21 Joachim sent Napoleon his customary greetings for the New Year – though this year couched in more urgent
terms. 'May you rest for a long time in the shade of your laurels.
Your Majesty has done everything possible for your glory; may
you now do something for your happiness: give us peace!'[2] Four
days later, having received a letter from Napoleon asking him to
advance as far as Venice, he sent a detailed account of the position
of his forces and again called on Napoleon 'to proclaim the
independence of Italy ... The Italians are ready to entrust themselves to anybody who will make them independent. That is the
truth, the plain truth ... Time is passing, the enemy is gathering
reinforcements, I am compelled to remain silent, and the
day cannot be far distant when I shall in my turn be obliged to
make clear my position towards my nation and towards the
enemy.'

He concluded with a postscript that probably expressed the
hopes of millions of people: 'Sire, in the name of all you hold
dearest in this world, in the name of your glory, do not continue
in this obstinacy. Make peace, make it at any price ... If you
refuse the prayers of your subjects, of your friends, you will
destroy yourself, you will destroy us all!'[3]

On December 31, 1813, Lieutenant-general Neipperg arrived at
Naples, bearing a letter of introduction from the kaiser and
instructions from Metternich to present an ultimatum. Neipperg
was to confront Murat with an unvarnished picture of his contradictory behaviour during the past two years and his present
perilous position: 'An object of justifiable distrust to both France
and the Grand European Alliance, suspect to all parties, the king
has reached the point of having lost any claim to protection from
any of the powers.'[4] If Joachim refused to enter into an alliance,
Neipperg was to return, bringing the Austrian diplomatic mission
with him.

On January 3, 1814, Joachim wrote a letter of reproach and
apology to Napoleon, ending 'Sire, if harsh necessity compels me,

as I have cause to fear it may, to enter into relations that apparently conflict with your interests, but which may perhaps be of service to Your Majesty and to France by giving me influence in the negotiations for peace, I hope that you will judge my conduct with calmness, impartiality, with political judgement, taking into consideration all that I have tried to do to prevent such an unhappy situation.'[5] On January 8 he agreed with Neipperg a treaty of offensive and defensive alliance between their two countries in return for which Austria promised to guarantee the kingdom of Naples to him and 'a satisfactory military frontier in conformity with the political interests of the two powers'.[6]

Joachim still required assurance that he would not be attacked by the Anglo-Sicilians. Bentinck had received confirmation from the Austrian chargé d'affaires in Naples that both the Austrian government and Lord Aberdeen were prepared to recognize Murat, but he was unwilling to break his promise to the Sicilian Crown Prince that he would put the Bourbons back on the throne. He sent his secretary, James Graham, to Naples ostensibly to discuss an armistice but with secret instructions to 'arrive in the shortest possible time – first – at the headquarters of the [Austrian] Army of Italy and afterwards at the headquarters of the [Austrian] emperor where I suppose Lord Aberdeen to be'.[7] Graham was to inform Aberdeen and the Austrians that Bentinck did not believe Murat would venture north, for fear of attack from Sicily, and that Bentinck meanwhile was preparing to invade Corsica. Graham, refusing to listen to Neipperg's pleas to accept a truce, pressed on to Bellegarde's headquarters at Vicenza, where he found the British military observer, General Sir Robert Wilson. Wilson, who knew the strength of the Allied fears of an intervention by Murat in support of Eugène,[8] persuaded Graham to return to Naples, where he signed an armistice, which provided for the entire cessation of hostilities by land and sea, free commerce between the two countries, no resumption of hostilities without three months warning, and immediate consultation between general officers of the Austrian, British and Neapolitan armies to concert plans of action in Italy.

One task remained. 'Sire, I have just concluded a treaty with Austria,' Joachim wrote to Napoleon on January 15, 1814. 'He who for so long fought at our side, your brother-in-law, your

friend, has signed an act which appears to give him a hostile attitude towards you. That is enough for you to know. Your Majesty
can appreciate from that both the feeling of necessity to which I
have surrendered and the heartbreak that I suffer. . . . Your
Majesty was silent for two whole months, or the letters you sent
me gave neither reassurance nor guidance . . . I had either to fight
or to accept peace together with the conditions that were attached
to it. . . . Because the ties of politics are momentarily broken
between Your Majesty and myself, must those of friendship and
family be broken too? I need to learn you are still my friend, for I
shall always be yours.'[9]

Immediately before the Austrian treaty was made public,
Joachim went to Caroline's apartments. He found Julie Récamier
there. Knowing that Caroline had told her of his dilemma and the
country's desire for peace, he asked her what she thought he
should do. 'You are a Frenchman, Sire,' she replied ,'and you
must be faithful to France.'[10] Joachim threw open the window and
pointed to the British fleet entering the bay: 'Then I am a traitor!'[11]
he said, and sat down, covering his face with his hands. Caroline
gave him a glass of orange-flower water, and begged him to
compose himself.

Late on January 23, Joachim left Naples to take command of his
troops, once more confiding the regency to Caroline. Next day he
entered Rome, where La Vauguyon had already taken command
as military governor, and Maghella was charged with reorganizing
the government. On January 28 he left Rome for Ancona and
Bologna, planning to occupy all the territory south of the Po. But
neither Austria nor Britain intended him to lay permanent claim
to these rich central provinces. When Nugent reached Ravenna as
early as December 10 he had issued a proclamation promising
independence; early in February Bellegarde summoned the
Italians to throw off the foreign yoke; and in mid-February
Bentinck, with whom the armistice still rankled,[12] sent a message
that he proposed landing British troops at Leghorn. On February
3, Mier had arrived at Bologna with a note from Metternich saying
that the clause in the treaty of January 8 guaranteeing Murat 'a
satisfactory military frontier in conformity with the political
interests of the two powers'[13] must be strictly defined as territory
in the Papal States with a total population of 400,000, and Murat

must renounce all claims on the Kingdom of Sicily. Joachim protested at the changes, but Mier replied that the kaiser would not ratify the treaty without them. 'In the last resort,' commented Metternich's diplomatic adviser, Gentz, 'he must consider himself lucky to have preserved the kingdom of Naples, all the more so, since he cannot be unaware that in the Allied Councils the voices in his favour were very divided and, like all the other relations of Napoleon, he would have been sacrificed if Austria, and perhaps (secretly) England, had not given him protection before it was too late,'[14] Joachim, having declared against Napoleon, was at the mercy of Metternich.

Or was he? On January 21 he had assured Eugène that he would not attack him without warning, and he had not done so (although the mere presence of his troops on the Po forced Eugène to withdraw from the Adige to the Mincio). The revised treaty that he had been tricked into signing had now gone back to the kaiser for ratification. He was not fully committed until he received Francis's assent. Caroline was so alarmed by a letter from Bologna, in which he seemed to be convincing himself that he could rouse the Italians to support France and throw out the Austrians in the cause of their freedom, that she wrote to him on February 8, 1814, 'Your letter drives me to despair . . . Oh, my dear! . . . You are walking on the edge of a precipice . . . I feel it, I believe it, and I cannot convince you.'[15] Possibly in order to force his hand, she issued instructions as Regent on February 1 for 'the seizure of all French warships and merchant vessels in our ports' and 'the breaking off of all communication between the kingdom of Naples and the French Empire'.[16]

When the Austrian commander, Bellegarde, urged him to begin operations against Eugène, Joachim sent an official declaration of war (February 15) but did not move his troops. By the end of February, having received no word from the Austrians to state whether they had finally ratified the treaty or had increased their demands once more, he wrote again to Napoleon, via Eugène, asking for his recognition of a United Italy up to the Po.

On March 3 Francis's letter of ratification arrived. Joachim's throne was safe: now he had to worry only about expanding his territory, trying to hold the ground that he already occupied. He wrote to Metternich, thanking him for his good offices. 'I have shown that I am not motivated by ambition by accepting . . . an indemnity that was disproportionate to the sacrifices I agreed to make,'[17] he said, revealing his disappointment. The Austrians called for a joint attack on Eugène; Joachim sent him a warning. Unable to delay the assault on Reggio, because it was led by Nugent, he delayed it for an hour to allow the beaten French garrison to withdraw to Parma. 'The Kaiser has the right to expect active help from the king,' Metternich wrote to Mier, 'and if his co-operation is to be limited simply to his not attacking us, we might just as well recognize him as an outright enemy.'[18]

On March 9, at Laon, Napoleon launched the remains of his army at Blücher and was beaten back. As he retired on Rheims he issued a decree restoring the Papal States to the pope, and ordered Savary to release him from internment at Fontainebleau. 'Metternich, Murat and the pope can sort it out among themselves,' he said. 'At any rate Murat will not reign in Rome.'[19] But on March 12 he received the letter that Joachim had sent him by way of Eugène. He grasped at this very slender thread and wrote to Eugène: 'send an agent to this most extraordinary of traitors and make a treaty with him in my name . . . You may go as far as you like. . . . Later on we can do as we wish, for after such ingratitude and in such circumstances, no obligation is binding.'[20]

On March 15, Bentinck arrived at Joachim's headquarters at Reggio. He demanded the evacuation of the Neapolitan troops from Tuscany to make way for his own Anglo-Sicilian forces that had landed at Leghorn. Joachim proposed in reply that the British should sign a treaty with him similar to the Austrian one. Lord William answered that if the Neapolitan troops did not move out he would 'drive them out, reembark his troops, land them in the kingdom of Naples, and proclaim Ferdinand as king'.[21]

Mier, who tried unavailingly to persuade Bentinck not to be so aggressive, told Metternich that 'the king believes he has been sacrificed already . . . He must be relieved of his fears, which are not without foundation, and I am certain that he will then act honestly and vigorously.'[22] On March 18 Joachim sent Eugène some letters from Caroline for other members of the family. He asked for news of the emperor's health and that of the vicereine and assured the viceroy 'of my entire friendship'.[23] The letter reached Eugène on March 19, at the same time as the one that

Napoleon had written him exactly a week before. Eugène at once informed Joachim that he had the emperor's authority to negotiate a treaty and asked for a meeting of plenipotentiaries. The emissaries of both sides met at San Giacomo di Po, but Eugène, despite Napoleon's injunction to promise anything, refused to accept Joachim's demand for the independence of all Italy south of the Po and the Taro.[24]

Joachim set out his grievances in a letter to Campochiaro, who now represented him in Vienna: the delays by Austria, 'although her plenipotentiary gave us to understand that ratification was certain',[25] and the conduct of Lord Bentinck. 'It is quite beyond my power to describe to you my astonishment at the mad pretentions of this general. He claims nothing less than to turn me out of Tuscany which I occupy by agreement and by right of conquest . . . Lord Bentinck has issued a proclamation of independence for Italy; the words "Reunion of Italy" and "Italian Independence" are inscribed on his banners. The Prince-Vicar of Sicily has for his part issued a proclamation to the soldiers of the expedition in which he declares that Ferdinand has never renounced and will never renounce, the kingdom of Naples.'[26] He therefore proposed issuing his own proclamation of Italian independence and laying claim to all territory south of the Po. He sent word of his negotiations and intentions to Caroline, who foresaw that in his desire to seize more territory (and – to do him justice – in what does seem to have been a genuine concern for the independence and unification of Italy) he was in danger of losing what he already had: the kingdom of Naples. On March 25 she sent Agar to Joachim with pleas to change his mind, and threats that she would leave him if he did not.

By this time the negotiations at San Giacomo were already known in the Austrian camp at Verona,[27] where Bentinck had gone after his failure to reach agreement at Reggio. His reception there was cool. Bellegarde was interested only in persuading Murat to continue his long delayed advance up the Via Emilia to Piacenza, which would force Eugène to abandon his line on the Mincio. If Bentinck's stubborn, irrelevant and suspect insistence on British troops occupying Tuscany forced Murat to join forces with Eugène, the Austrians might well find themselves driven right out of Italy. It was agreed that Wilson should renew the talks with Murat, who had now withdrawn his headquarters to Bologna.

Wilson was impressed by his host's appearance: 'His hair curled in Roman coiffure – two ringlets or what *à la Parisienne*, are styled 'pensées', dependent on each shoulder. Blue uniform coat, red pantaloons, yellow shoes, with spurs; sword with three pictures in the handle; ... his countenance martial, his manner soft, his conversation easy and intelligent. ... The banquet was according to the rules of perfect gastronomy. The master's manners were very gracious. It was impossible for Lord Chesterfield to have done the honours better ... I fought with his Majesty all the battles over again which we had witnessed together [Wilson had served with the Russians in 1812 and with the Prussians and Austrians in 1813]. He was exceedingly interesting, very candid, and by no means a Gascon for himself or his brethren in arms ... My progress has been most favourable.'[28]

On April 7, Joachim received the necessary assurances from Wilson and Mier, and the promise that Tuscan administration would be left in Neapolitan hands, while the Anglo-Sicilian forces kept bases at Leghorn, Pisa and Viareggio. Joachim ordered his troops to advance.

At midday on April 15, Joachim was holding a conference with his chief engineer, General Colletta, in the garden of a villa just outside Piacenza, when an officer brought him two dispatches. 'Having read a few lines, he turned as pale as death, and it was with great apparent agony that he completed their perusal ... At length, in a low agitated tone, he briefly imparted to those around him the mournful intelligence':[29] the Allies had entered Paris and Napoleon had abdicated. Next day, without reference to Joachim, Bellegarde and Eugène signed a convention at Schiarino Rizzeno, bringing hostilities to an end. Bellegarde then told Joachim that the presence of Neapolitan troops in the former kingdom of Italy was no longer required, and called on him to withdraw them immediately. 'Opinions are divided on the attitude that the king of Naples will adopt,' wrote Gentz. 'I believe he will make the best of a bad job and not wait to be asked twice.'[30] Leaving Gallo to fix the new boundaries with Mier, Joachim returned to Naples on May 2. The following day, Louis XVIII entered Paris; Napoleon was on board the *Undaunted*, on his way to Elba.

17

It was a quiet home-coming, though the *lazzaroni*, with the customary bribes from the police, shouted loyal greetings as they ran beside the carriage which he shared with Caroline and Achille. Caroline was still in a state of depression brought on by the complete collapse of France and Napoleon. Julie Récamier noted the 'anguish and tears',[1] with which she received the news from France; and Nicola remarked on April 23 'she does nothing but weep; above all for her mother'.[2] There seems little doubt that, as Pasquier said, 'neither Murat nor his wife foresaw the complete downfall of their brother. They knew of the Frankfurt Proposals and they would have believed that the course they adopted would result only in forcing him to accept those proposals, contenting himself with being emperor of the French, with the Rhine, the Alps and the Pyrenees as the limits of his empire.'[3]

Joachim wore civilian clothes during the ceremonial entry, a tacit promise to her, as well as to the Allies, that he wished to leave his days of martial glory behind. On May 8 a *Te Deum* was sung in the Royal Chapel in thanks for the safe return of the king; in the afternoon Joachim and Caroline and the children drove in state to the cathedral to kiss the flask containing the blood of St Januarius, which that year was liquefying with propitious frequency and sparkle. As if in confirmation of this happy augury, Mier and the new Russian minister, General Balachoff, arrived that day. It was essential to peace that Joachim, doubly suspect as usurper of a Bourbon throne and member of the Bonaparte family, should be on good terms with at least one of the four Allies. Austria, the only power with whom he had a written treaty of Friendship, had forced him to withdraw from the territory he had hoped to keep; Britain, in the person of the forbidding Bentinck to whom he had hopefully presented a jewelled sword,[4] was merely on terms of a three-month armistice; with Prussia he had made no contact at all; it was a step forward to have a Russian at his court.

Caroline ran her household with model efficiency. She had the gift of organization and hated idleness; her delicate digestion frequently kept her in bed during the afternoon as well as the

morning, but her bedroom was furnished with a desk and tam-
bour-frame so that one of the two ladies-in-waiting, dressed in the
uniform of canary yellow silk with white slashed sleeves and white
caps surmounted by two white plumes, could get on with her
embroidery while the other took down letters at Caroline's dicta-
tion. She was called at seven each morning, and took her *petit
déjeuner* in bed. After her bath she often returned to the newly-
made bed until noon, to deal with her correspondence or to be
read to. The midday meal, if she ate alone, was more like afternoon
tea; she was the only member of the family who preferred tea to
coffee or chocolate, and accompanied it in the English manner
with toast, muffins and crumpets. This taste for English things
extended to English nurses for the children and, in Joachim's
case, to English grooms for his horses, English curricles, fowling
pieces from English gunsmiths, and 'English port wine'.[5] As soon
as the war ended in 1814, the English nobility resumed their
visits to Italy: the Oxfords and their daughter, followed by the
Bedfords, with their son Lord John Russell, the Hollands, the
Conynghams, Lord Gage, Lord Clare, the literary tourists, Rogers,
Baring and Mayne – and all came to Naples to observe this romantic couple, the most famous cavalryman of his age and the only
Bonaparte still occupying a throne, except for the deposed
emperor on his tiny little island.

Joachim, when he rose in the morning, dipped his head in a
silver-gilt basin of water, dried it and sat for a moment while his
valet rolled his naturally curly hair into corkscrews round his
fingers. Then, in a white dimity dressing gown and green slippers,
he strolled out on to the great terrace planted with lemon trees
which overlooked the bay and ran along the whole length of the
building, connecting his apartments with those of the queen.
Whenever he had a moment to spare, he unlocked the small door
in his dining-room and went up the concealed staircase to play
with Letitia and Louise whose rooms were immediately above.
This was for him the pleasantest part of the day. 'His greatest
delight was in the company of his children, spending many hours
playing with them and amusing them,'[6] and the girls rushed out
to embrace him and be bounced up and down on his knee. 'He
was our friend, I would almost say our playmate,' Louise recalled
fifty years later. 'We even went to far as to *tutoyer* him . . . but only

when we were alone. Custom did not in those days permit such a familiar way of speaking to one's parents as it does now, and we should never have dared to do it in front of our mother.'[7]

Caroline spoiled them less and paid more attention to their education. 'She loved us, but was not effusive,'[8] Louise remembered. After they had washed and dressed in the morning, and provided the timetable was not interrupted by games with their father, they prepared their lessons until breakfast at eight, and at nine were taken by Miss Davies or Mrs Pulford to the drawing-room where one of the governesses[9] supervised their studies under various masters until lunch at eleven, and again from twelve-thirty to six o'clock. Always dressed very simply in white, with black taffeta pinafores, they spent two or three hours each day at the piano and singing, to which were added dancing and languages – English and German as well as the French and Italian which were spoken around them all the time. On Sundays, Monseigneur Torre, the archbishop, instructed them in religion. Letitia, as pretty as her mother, had a very pleasant contralto voice; but Louise had nothing but a quick wit and sweet nature: 'I was never called anything but Plain Jane.'[10]

The boys' apartments were not in the royal palace but in the former Palazzo Acton, where all four children had at first been lodged. At all times, even during lessons, they wore uniform – Achille as colonel of the Lancers, Lucien as colonel of the Royal Bodyguard. Achille had outgrown the worst of the fits that clouded his early childhood but he remained headstrong and way-ward, already passionately pro-Italian and anti-French. Lucien plump and pink and pretty and the idol of the Neapolitan crowds, though more easily led, was too scatter-brained to concentrate on his work.

When both Joachim and Caroline were in the palace at midday, they took lunch together. At Portici they would often eat in the upper storey of the pavilion built by Joseph with a trick dining-table whose centre portion could be hauled down to the ground floor with the used dishes and pushed up again with the next course. On this Joachim had two dwarfs in a tureen served to some English visitors one day. (This distasteful sort of humour was popular at the time; even the gentle Josephine found it amusing to keep a pet dwarf.) But his robust sense of fun was better served in the palace's model dairy, where they often lunched in the hot weather and he could douse everybody by switching on the water sprinklers. The children took their meals in their own dining-room, with a tutor or governess present but not sitting at table with them. About once a week, usually after the Council of Ministers on Thursdays, they were invited to dine with their parents in semi-state, with uniformed pages standing behind their chairs. On other evenings, they ate alone and afterwards learned to play whist – the card game most preferred by Caroline.

On June 12, 1814, Achille received his first communion at the cathedral, with considerable pomp, for Joachim and Caroline, no longer hampered by Napoleon's quarrels with the pope, were eager to win the good will of their religious subjects. He returned in a grand procession through the streets, applauded by the populace who may or may not have been impressed by his devotion[11] but who never missed a chance of shouting. 'I cannot draw a comparison between any people I have yet seen and the Neapolitans, for making a noise,' said an English tourist who arrived in time for the festival of La Madonna dell' Arco on May 30. 'All those of the lowest class who could hire coaches had them, and crammed them as full as they could with their wives and families. Then, sticking oak-boughs all over their carriages and strings of nuts about their persons, they drove through the town as furiously as they could, singing and shouting in the most indecent manner, the women beating tambourins.'[12] They were not, of course, of the very poorest classes, for these did not have the money to hire a carriage, and it was fashionable to believe they did not want it. 'The Neapolitan does only as much work as is necessary to earn the two or three sous that will get him the handful of macaroni, the quarter of a watermelon, and the glass of ice-water that comprise his meal,' wrote Napoleon's literary admirer Arnault. 'After it, he stretches out on the quay to sleep and digest it, jumps into the water to refresh himself, then returns to the same slab to dry himself, thus passing from sun to sea and sea to sun, until the moment when the cool of the evening will allow him to finish off his day deliciously by prancing to the strains of the guitar . . . And his lodging, you ask? He finds it under the porticos of the great houses, in the cloisters of the churches; forty thousand individuals

live and multiply in Naples like the dogs in the streets of Constan-
tinople, without having any home.'[13]

Immeasurably poor yet extremely powerful, it was they who
held the balance in any popular uprising, and they whom the king
set out to win over, oddly but successfully, by his show of riches
and ostentation. Where the exiled Ferdinand, scion of the ancient
Bourbon line, had endeared himself to his subjects by exchanging
obscenities with them in the fish market, Joachim Murat, the
usurping inn-keeper's son, charmed them with his pomp and
bragadocio. Enchanted by this swaggering figure, 'the *lazzaroni*
had their peculiar way of describing with the fingers his gait on
horseback, and the waving of his plumes. . . . There was a jovial
kindness of temperament, which made his presence agreeable to
the public eye.'[14] On Corpus Domini day he went to the cathedral
in one resplendent uniform in a carriage drawn by eight cream-
coloured horses, then changed into another uniform and returned
to the palace on foot. Baring, who saw the royal couple on this
occasion and found Caroline 'elegant in her person and in her
manners; and, as far as these things are concerned, fitter to be a
queen than any woman in Europe',[15] was sturdily unimpressed by
Joachim: 'a stout middle-sized man, with strong black hair and
whiskers, dark complexion and black eyes; he is fond of parade,
and generally dresses in a showy manner.'[16]

On November 8 they greeted the arrival of Caroline of Brunswick, Princess of Wales, who was on a tour of Europe that had
already become the source of scandalous gossip. Six weeks before,
in Switzerland, she had visited Marie-Louise, who found her 'a
fairly good looking woman of forty-five, but too small and too
plump, and she says unimaginable things'.[17] Joachim eagerly
seized this opportunity of doing the honours to so prominent a
member of the British Royal family – and to William Austin, the
little London boy whom the princess had adopted. 'I have seen
the king and queen of Naples three or four times,' William wrote
to his mother on November 8, 'and the king has kissed me twice.
. . . The weather is beautiful, snow never falls here. The winter is
nothing but rain for two or three months. . . .'[18] The people are dirty
and full of flees.'[19]

The quaint unhappy Princess of Wales promptly fell in love
with her host. Her physician, Henry Holland, noted that 'the four

months we passed in Naples[24] were coloured in every way by the personal character of the man. . . . Tall and masculine in person; his features well formed, but expressing little beyond good nature and rude energy and consciousness of physical power . . . he was endowed with a large amount of pure animal vitality, which pleasureably expended itself in the active deeds of war, but found no sufficient vent in peace.'[20] He found the queen more interesting and complex. 'Under her fine and feminine features lay a depth of thought – at this time, as it seemed to me, verging on melancholy. I doubt not, indeed, from what I saw and heard, that she was keenly sensible of the crisis then hanging over the fortunes of her family. Her qualities were very different, and loftier than those of her husband, and both I believe to have been fully conscious of this disparity.'[21]

Another English visitor shared this opinion. The poet Samuel Rogers, who was present at the court ball on Sunday, February 26, 1815, noted of Murat: 'His countenance mild, his features handsome – the queen still beautiful, tho' *une peu maigre*, very graceful and wreathed with diamonds from head to foot. The queen danced like a gentlewoman – the king like a dancing master, perfect in his steps and affecting an ease not natural to him.'[22] John Mayne, an English traveller was at the masked ball at the San Carlo on New Year's Eve remarked that the king 'very good-humoured answered the salutations of the masks as they crowded under his box, but the queen did not attend much to what was passing. She seems passive and abstracted.'[23]

There was much for her to be pensive about, both in the state of the kingdom and the train of events abroad. On March 4, Agar the minister of Finance, gave a sumptuous ball that was attended by the king and queen, the Princess of Wales, the court and Neapolitan nobility, the Bedfords, Hollands, Conynghams, Oxfords and many other foreigners. 'Among the latter was the Countess Walewska, very recently arrived from Elba with her young son; and attracting much attention from her known relation to the great prisoner there, as well as from the graces of her own person and manner,'[24] noted Henry Holland, 'Her sudden presence at Naples, and certain other collateral incidents excited suspicions without defining them. It was that vague whisper which often precedes some event close at hand. The ball of which I am speaking afforded the solution in a sudden startling way. Everything went on according to the wonted fashion until about 11 o'clock – the king and queen, with the principal persons of their court, being at that moment engaged in the figures of an English country dance. Count Mosburg, our host, was suddenly summoned out of the room. He speedily returned, went up to the king, and whispered intelligence to him, which he instantly communicated in a smiling way to the queen. They both disappeared from the dance, and the assembly itself was at once dissolved; each guest carrying away some dim surmise of what had happened. The intelligence, in fact, was the escape of Napoleon from Elba.'[25]

A year of suspense was over. This was the moment of decision.

18

When Murat returned to Naples at the beginning of May 1814, depressed and resentful at having been forced by Austria to withdraw his troops and hand back the rich provinces that he had counted on making his own, he was already suspect to his new allies. 'The viceroy has given some strong evidence against him,' Castlereagh wrote from Paris to Lord Bathurst on April 27. 'He is a worthless dog.'[1] The following week Castlereagh reported that he had not yet received documentary evidence 'on which the Allies could justify a change of policy towards him', but 'the Austrian Government have no other reluctance on this point than what good faith imposes'.[2] Joachim was on bad terms with the pope. He was conscious of a growing chilliness on the part of the Russian envoy, General Balachoff. Within his own kingdom he was faced with the enmity of most of the clergy, a restiveness in the officer class which had already come near to mutiny in support of a demand for a new constitution, and open revolt from the Carbonari subsidized from Sicily. He had saved his crown – 'but what a crown! trembling like a dewdrop!'[3]

He hoped he could count on one friend – Austria – though as early as April 29 Gentz was noting that, 'It is even doubtful whether the brother-in-law of the dethroned Napoleon can keep possession of the throne of Naples,'[4] and within a few months the

Austrians were, as Castlereagh indicated, seeking a means of breaking their contract with Joachim without appearing to do so. Russia and Prussia were probably neutral. Britain was inclined to side against him, perhaps because she considered her interests in Malta and the Mediterranean would be less threatened by Ferdinand, but more from an antagonism to non-royal usurpers – 'Bonaparte was not a member of the College of Kings,' Barras warned Joachim when they met in Rome, 'nor do you belong to it.'[5]

All of the Allies were subjected to constant prodding from France, where the Big Four assembled for the discussions that produced the Peace of Paris but deferred the knottier problems of disentangling Europe to the Congress that was to meet in Vienna. Louis XVIII, urged them 'to remove the causes which still endangered the tranquillity of his realm: the presence of Bonaparte on the Isle of Elba and of Murat in Naples'.[6] In July he signed an agreement with the restored king of Spain to press the claims of Ferdinand to Naples and other Bourbons to their various Italian thrones. It was a duty to his family and a protection for his frontiers.

From midsummer onwards the plotting and chicanery increased rapidly. The euphoria of the meetings in Paris was dispersed by overlong contact between the victorious sovereigns in London where they went to celebrate with the Prince Regent. The cunning of Metternich was as feared as the avarice of Alexander. The unpredictable British were suspect to all. The delegates began gathering for the much-postponed conference, with a great mob of princelings clustered around them, clamouring for a place, or at least a hearing, at the conference table.[7]

Joachim's first concern was to establish representation in the foreign courts. He sent Campochiaro and Cariati to Paris, Vicenzo Ancilloti to London. None of them received recognition. He failed similarly to come to terms with the pope, to whom he offered to surrender the three provinces of the Papal States that he still occupied, in return for recognition, or Sicily; and on June 17 Balachoff packed his bags and went back to St Petersburg, explaining: 'My emperor declared at Paris that he will never negotiate with a member of the Bonaparte family.'[8] Refusing to be discouraged, Joachim announced on July 9, 1814, that he would henceforth be known simply as King of Naples (thus renouncing the other half of the kingdom of the Two Sicilies), and asked Lord Oxford to go to London with an offer of commercial privileges in return for recognition;[9] while Caroline commissioned Julie Récamier, on her return to Paris, to hire a political writer to produce a Memoir setting out their case, to be submitted to the Congress.

To Vienna, Joachim sent a succession of representatives, lobbyists and agents, his Master of the Horse, the Duke of Rocca Romana; Cariati, returned from London; Campochiari from Paris; and smaller fry such as Caroline's secretary, Guibourd. Baudus, who resigned as tutor when Naples declared war on France, volunteered to go but was unable to get there, in the hope of stemming the tide of feeling against him: 'Everybody here, with the exception of Metternich, is against Murat,'[10] wrote Mary-Caroline to her husband. Her death of apoplexy during the night of September 7, produced new complications. Since she was commonly believed to have been responsible for the horrible vengeance exacted at the previous restoration, it appeared that widowed Ferdinand would be more acceptable at Naples, and Murat had lost a weapon of fear. On the other hand, she had been such a tireless and persistent advocate of her own cause 'with a zeal and ardour that few accredited representatives could have equalled'[11] that some shrewd observers thought Murat lucky to have been 'delivered by death from a redoubtable opponent'.[12]

There was one other important consideration: Mary-Caroline was an Austrian princess, Ferdinand was a Bourbon. Metternich had as little desire to see France and Spain increase their influence in Italy as the French had to see it fall to the Austrians. With Mary-Caroline dead, Metternich would, for the moment at least, favour retaining Murat, provided he did not become a focus of discontent. For ill-feeling against the Austrians was growing daily in Northern Italy where, instead of their promised independence, the inhabitants found themselves paying the cost of an army of occupation while the Bourbon and Hapsburg princes struggled to resume their old autocratic sway. 'The entire bourgeoisie is against us,' noted Raab, head of the Austrian police in Venetia. 'The malcontents and men of ill-will are all looking towards the king of Naples; it is from him that they expect the longed-for succour; it is him that they rely on to drive the detested Austrians out of Italy.'[13]

The attitude of the Holy See was quite clear: 'They cannot understand [our] support for a prince of the proscribed family who is indelibly marked with the inherited taint, who is in the neighbourhood of the Isle of Elba, and whose conduct continues to be more than equivocal,'[14] the Austrian ambassador reported. The king of Bavaria, incensed on behalf of his son-in-law Eugène, now without a job of any kind and meeting with snubs from all the royal visitors to Vienna, roared: 'Of course we must turn the rogue out . . . He must be hanged. Who deserves the gallows more than he? There has never been a scoundrel like him.'[15]

Amid all the talk, it was only the British who prepared to take action. In August Castlereagh asked Wellington, who was in Paris, to discover whether France and Spain 'would be disposed to employ their arms to replace the king of Sicily on the throne of Naples'.[16] In the following month Wellington sent him his thoughts on how to turn Murat out. Since Austria would not like to see a French army in Italy again, 'the operation must be performed by the king of Sicily, the king of Spain and their Allies, and possibly a few French troops sent by sea into Sicily. I think we might get 10,000 men from Spain, 10,000 from Sicily, 12,000 from Portugal and 12 or 15,000, including cavalry, from England, or the English garrisons in the Mediterranean. England would be obliged to furnish transports for the whole, and a train of field ordnance of 60 pieces, equipped, and a battering train.'[17]

By this time Castlereagh was in Vienna, where Metternich persuaded him to agree to set aside the explosive question of Naples until the end of the conference for fear of setting off a revolution in Italy. He also received a visit from Campochiaro who, in the politest manner, informed him that Joachim had '80,000 men under arms, exclusive of the Militia, and, if driven to appeal to the Italian spirit, his means of resistance would be very formidable'.[18] Finally, on November 25, Liverpool wrote to Castlereagh warning him that 'if war should be renewed at present, I fear we should lose all we have gained, that the revolutionary spirit would break forth again in full force, and that the Continent would be plunged in all the evils under which it has groaned for the last twenty years . . . Though I should most deeply regret the continuance of Murat on the Throne of Naples as a sort of *taint* in our general arrangement . . . if the question should be whether any of the Powers of Europe should take up arms to drive him out of his dominions, my opinion would certainly be against such a measure.'[19]

The conference opened on November 1. Thanks to the conflicting cupidity of the victors and the brilliant manœuvring of Talleyrand, vanquished France was not only admitted to the deliberations but was soon taking a decisive part in the bargaining, and even threatening to resume the war if it did not have its way. The Neapolitan deputation failed to obtain recognition from the Congress. They let it be known once more that the king was 'determined to defend his throne to the death',[20] and when he received the news in Naples, Joachim at first 'could think of nothing but war – plans of campaign, plans of defence',[21] until Mier and Caroline managed to calm him down. Metternich, having urged on Talleyrand the wisdom of postponing a decision on Naples until the thorny problems of Poland and Saxony had been disposed of, wrote to Mier, telling him to assure Gallo that 'the kaiser has never violated the integrity of treaties and will never do so',[22] and to point out that, in view of this promise, Murat could afford to withdraw his troops from his land frontiers. Joachim, who earlier in the month had believed he was confronted with the certainty of war, received Metternich's assurances with joy. He sent a letter of gratitude to the kaiser, 'to whose powerful support I shall owe my crown',[23] and as a grand gesture of friendship offered to put his troops in the Ancona area at the disposal of Bellegarde, who was having trouble with the Italian patriots. But although Mier had urged him to take this step during the confrontation with Eugène in April, the Austrians now suspected that this was a move to get Neapolitan troops into Northern Italy, and there fan the flames of the insurrection that they were supposed to be quelling.

The problem facing Murat's many enemies was to clothe their suspicions with facts, so that the kaiser would be persuaded to repudiate the treaty. In France, Louis's closest adviser, Blacas, by agreement with Wellington, arrested Lord Oxford at Villejuif on November 26 on his way to Naples, on a charge of carrying private correspondence to various individuals in breach of the law which restricted all letter carrying to the official postal service. A day or two earlier, Joachim's physician, Andral, had been arrested on the same charge at Nemours. The two men had certainly broken the law: Andral had twenty-six letters addressed to Joachim and Caroline, and Oxford carried another large bundle. None was of any use in proving their case. Madame de Staël, it was true, told Murat, 'I adore you, not because you are a king, not because you are a hero but because you are a true friend of liberty.'[24] But that was merely her opinion. And there was nothing to indicate that Murat had solicited the offer contained in the letter from his former aide-de-camp and Grand Marshal, Exelmans, 'the admiration in which the French people hold Your Majesty will bring to his banners thousands of brave soldiers as soon as the signal is given',[25] or that 'in case of need, 20,000 brave Frenchmen were ready to draw the sword for him'.[26]

'I should have much desired that something had been found in his papers to compromise Murat with this court,'[27] Talleyrand wrote regretfully on December 7. Castlereagh, who told him he was delighted to hear of Oxford's arrest – 'a man who does not deserve any sort of respect',[28] – was still seeking proof of earlier duplicity on Joachim's part. On December 18 he asked Bentinck for 'every information that can throw light upon the conduct of Murat, under the engagements he had contracted . . . both as far as your own observation goes, and by recurring to any other sources you can avail yourself of, without attracting attention'.[29] To Liverpool he suggested on the same day that Murat should be offered compensation for his throne and threatened with war if he did not accept.

In Paris, Wellington had lent a sympathetic ear to the arguments of Blacas, the duc de Berri and Louis himself. He had, by agreement with Castlereagh, said nothing to the cautious Liverpool about his calculations of the forces needed to invade Naples,[30] but he now sent him the same list that he had made out for Castlereagh more than three months before. He warned Castlereagh that because of 'the temper prevailing in England, and the state of the finances, I think it most probable the Government will not enter into this scheme, and that Murat will escape'.[31] Before he left for Vienna, where he was to replace Castlereagh at the head of the British delegation, he received confirmation from Liverpool of 'the absolute impossibility in the present state of the circumstances and feeling in this country, of our engaging in military operations for the purpose of expelling Murat'.[32]

On January 13, Metternich sent a message to Blacas that the removal of Murat was 'an objective that his Imperial Majesty desires no less than the king'.[33] Nine days later he received the Neapolitan General Ambrosio, assured him that 'we are for you',[34] and passed him on to the kaiser, who said that if the Bourbons attacked Naples they would be dealt with by the Allies, who intended to preserve peace in Europe. Campochiaro and Cariati presented Metternich on January 25 with a demand that, since Louis XVIII had at Paris signed a treaty of peace and friendship with the Austrian kaiser and his allies, and since Joachim was one of those allies under the terms of the treaty of January 11, 1814, the kaiser should bring pressure to bear on Louis to give official recognition to Joachim. At the same time Joachim sent Castlereagh a reminder that Britain had not yet recognized him.

Wellington arrived at Vienna on February 1. To Prince Leopold of the Two Sicilies, he said: 'The Naples business is a stain that needs removing as completely and as quickly as possible.'[35] Castlereagh went to Paris, where, on February 27, he had a two-hour conference with Louis, at which he acquainted the king with a proposal that Metternich had not wished to put to Talleyrand: if Louis would withdraw the claims of the Bourbon ex-queen of Etruria to the duchy of Parma, which had been awarded to Marie-Louise under the treaty of Fontainebleau, Austria would cooperate in getting rid of Murat.[36] On February 28, Louis accepted. On March 1, Napoleon landed in France.

For months past the Allied secret services had suspected that Joachim and Napoleon were exchanging information. In August Bellegarde reported from Milan that Napoleon had flown into a rage because a Neapolitan vessel had been allowed to leave Elba without the dispatches he had intended to send by it. In September the Austrian minister in Rome, Lebzeltern, gave warning of 'the undoubted existence of a continuous exchange of clandestine letters between the Court of Naples and that of Porto-Ferraio'.[37] Napoleon's own merchant shipping, flying the white flag with the red bar and three golden bees, was busy in the Tyrrhenian Sea. In November the French consul at Leghorn mentioned that Joachim had decorated Captain Taillade, the commander of the brig *Napoleon*, when it arrived from Elba.

In December, Lord Burghersh, British minister in Tuscany, noted a sinister correspondence between the island and Naples. The spy known as 'the Oil Merchant', who landed at Porto-Ferraio on the last day of November, provided the French consul at Leghorn with a wealth of material in which gossip and firsthand information, fact and fiction were impartially mixed, but which aroused alarm when passed on to Vienna with the warning that Napoleon, with support from Naples, intended to lead a rising in Milan, where the Austrians had recently discovered a plot among Italian officers to declare independence.

In January the Oil Merchant affirmed that 'there is no longer any doubt about the king of Naples. He is entirely in league with Napoleon, for when an officer approaches Drouot [Governor of the kingdom of Elba] for employment . . . the general tells him . . . to go to Naples, and adds that those who serve that sovereign are serving the emperor.'[38] From Civita-Vecchia the British Consul notified Burghersh of an increase in correspondence between Elba and Naples. In the same port the apostolic delegate made a copy of a letter from one of Napoleon's officers to the governor of the fortress of Gaëta telling him that 'in a few days the *Inconstant* [Napoleon's brig] will leave with troops for Naples'.[39]

From the earliest days, Joachim and Caroline had been at pains – perhaps suspiciously so – to impress Mier with their determination not to intrigue with Napoleon. When Fesch forwarded from Rome a request from Napoleon for silverware, furniture and other articles to be sent to him on the British patrol ship *Curacao*, Caroline told her uncle that 'any sort of communication with Elba is forbidden to us in the present circumstances . . . I very much regret having to give you this answer, but the fate of the king and my children compel me to do so.'[40] She showed both letters to the Austrian minister, who was greatly impressed. It confirmed the reputation for hardness of heart which her enemies gave her. Mier would have been surprised to know of the letter she wrote to Lucien about this time, urging him not to publish his poem *Charlemagne*,[41] because of its implied criticisms of Napoleon.

'A month or two ago I should have read it with pleasure. Today, my dear brother, what was only a warning, a useful hint perhaps,

has become a wounding satire, an outrage committed against misfortune. . . . Fine though it may be to speak one's mind in defiance
of authority, yet, when circumstances change, it is just as fine and
grand to deny oneself that pleasure.'[42]

Robert Fagan, the British Consul-general in Rome who had
assumed the same post at Naples, reported that Gallo had talked
with him on September 25 and 'asserted that far from his master
having any correspondence with Buonaparte, he wished if possible
to cut off all communication and every connection with him'.[43]
Pons de l'Hérault, on the other hand, claimed to have possessed at
one time 'a letter from the king of Naples [to Napoleon], written
in his own hand', in which he set out the clauses of 'an offensive
and defensive treaty by which the Isle of Elba was ceded to the
Two Sicilies',[44] in return for his support. 'It is still considered
certain that Bonaparte and Murat are reconciled,'[45] a French
royalist agent reported in January. Napoleon certainly counted on
help from Joachim. He had said a few days before leaving Elba,
'Murat is ours. I had much to complain about him in the past.
Since I have been here he has regretted his mistakes and done as
much as he can to repair the wrong he did me. I have restored
him to my friendship and confidence. . . . He hasn't much of a
head, only arms and a heart, but his wife will guide him.'[46]

In the Murat family archives there are five documents which add
a final touch of mystery. The first, signed by Napoleon, is a letter
written from Porto-Ferraio on February 17, 1815, authorizing
Colonna 'to sign any agreement that Your Majesty may desire
concerning our affairs' and urging Joachim to 'believe everything
he tells you'.[47] The second, of the same date and place, bears a
note: 'The original of this letter, written entirely in Napoleon's
hand, is in the possession of M. Mercey who gave me this copy.'
The letter runs: 'My dear Murat, thank you for what you have
done for the comtesse de Valeska. I recommend her to you, and
especially her son who is very dear to me. Colonna will tell you
many great and important things. I count on you and above all on
the utmost speed. Time presses. My love to the queen and your
children.'[48] The third document is a copy[49] of a cipher said to have
been used by Napoleon on Elba. With it is a deciphered undated
note: 'Isle of Elba. The wind freshened three days ago and forced
the English patrol ship to move a little farther from our shores.

But she may return at any moment and my brig is not big enough to deal with her. If I had one of your ships I could leave by daylight and sink whatever stood in my path.'[50] The final document is marked, 'Ciphered despatch from King Joachim Murat to the Emperor Napoleon.' It is undated and runs: 'The 90-gun vessel *Capri* will leave during tomorrow night under the orders of Captain Bausan, bound for Portoferrajo, to be put at Your Majesty's disposal. God and your genius will do the rest. Your affectionate brother, Joachim-Napoléon.'[51]

There is no proof that these messages were ever received or sent. Certainly it is remarkable that even so unnautically-minded a Lord High Admiral as Joachim should describe the 74-gun *Capri* as a 90-gun vessel. But it is difficult to see what purpose could be served by fabricating the documents yet not publishing them. There is proof that the *Capri* left Naples about this time – 'several days ago', Mier wrote to Metternich on March 9[52] – and that same morning Captain Croker of the British sloop *Wizard* sighted her 'in Lat. 41 9 N and Long. 11 27 E, steering to the Northward'.[53] The Neapolitan minister of Marine later explained that the *Capri* had been sent to Elba to offer 'security and an asylum at Naples for the Mother and Sister of Napoleon'.[54] The evidence suggests that Murat knew Napoleon's plans in advance and decided to support him. Whether he had wished him to escape is another matter. Perhaps his attitude was expressed by Agar who, when asked what was the reaction in Naples, replied: 'A little hope, and a great deal of despair.'[55] But with so volatile a character as Murat, despair and exaltation were never far apart.

19

On March 5, the Royal Council met in the palace. Joachim invited Caroline to attend and after a short session he ordered his foreign minister to send word to London that his policy was not changed and to Vienna asking what the Austrian Government proposed to do. He than spoke with the Austrian minister – still with Caroline present – telling him he was certain Napoleon would have the army and the people on his side when he arrived in France, and asking for a statement of Austrian intentions. He talked for a couple of hours, 'extremely agitated', according to Mier, and 'not able to make up his mind what he wanted',[1] then, seeing from the window that several merchant ships had entered the harbour, he sent to find out where they had come from. On learning that one was from Elba he went to question the master, leaving Caroline to continue the conversation. Mier found her 'wise in her views and reasoning', though 'one could see from her face how much this event has upset her'.[2] She told him she was extremely anxious about her brother 'who is running into certain disaster',[3] and how much she wished he had remained peacefully on Elba. If he managed to mount the throne of France again he would evict them from Naples and turn Europe upside down once more. She assured Mier that she intended to do all she could to hold Joachim to the alliance with Austria.

It was a daunting task. The months of suspense had irritated his excitable spirit, inflamed his suspicious mind; he itched for action and for glory and an end to uncertainty. When Ambrosio arrived in Naples on March 7, he found the king indifferent to the news he brought from Vienna. Joachim said he was determined to march northward and unite Italy. Ambrosio pointed out that Austria had almost half a million men under arms, apart from her allies; that Napoleon would have difficulty in keeping them out of exhausted France and would certainly not be able to help Naples. 'I have need of nobody,' Joachim replied, 'once the Italians hail me as their sovereign, proclaim me as their liberator.'[4] He ordered his senior ministers to be ready to leave with him for Ancona.

He was confronted with warnings and pleas from many of his ministers and generals, from Mier, from Agar, and above all from Caroline, who became sick with worry and had to take to her bed. She received Mier on March 16 and told him: 'The king is calmer, more reasonable,'[5] and she hoped he would continue like that, but the recent exchanges between Metternich and the Neapolitan envoys in Vienna had convinced him that Austria was about to turn against him. She told Mier that Joachim had twice been on the point of setting out to take command of the army and she had been able to prevent him only by threatening to refuse to act as Regent and to leave Naples. The threat was not enough. Shortly after midday on March 17, alarmed by stories of Austrian troop movements, Joachim drove off towards Ancona in his eight-horse travelling carriage, leaving Caroline in tears. When the governor of Naples, Manhès, and the minister of Police, Maghella, called at the palace that evening to present their daily report, she would not receive them. To make her meaning clearer she went off to Portici with Letitia and Louise.

Joachim reached Ancona in the afternoon of March 19. On March 21, two of his divisions stationed north of Gaëta marched into Papal territory en route for Tuscany by way of Terni, Foligno and Perugia. On March 23, General Filangieri, whom he had sent to demand the release of Pauline,[6] arrived at Bellegarde's headquarters at Milan. Filangieri told him that, 'Joachim would rather die at the head of his army than descend shamefully from his throne at the command of the Great Powers.'[7] Bellegarde, not yet ready to receive an attack, sent General Starhemberg, who had been attached to the Neapolitan army in 1814, to present his compliments to the king and play for as much time as possible, giving him to understand that if he remained neutral Austria would renew her attempts to persuade the other powers to recognize him. But when Starhemberg reached Pesaro on March 25 he found Joachim in no mood to be played with. 'I see quite clearly that they will not have me, and in those circumstances you will agree that I have no other choice but war.'[8]

On March 4, Blacas sent Castlereagh copies of nine letters taken from the French Archives, which Castlereagh forwarded to Wellington as 'ample proofs . . . of Murat's treachery, at least of his double dealing'.[9] This 'coupled with Buonaparte's descent in France', Castlereagh told him, 'has removed all remaining scruples on the part of the British Government'.[10] Wellington was to 'concert measures with the other Powers . . . for the removal of Murat, either by negotiation or force'[11] – but to make it appear that the initiative came from Austria and France so as to avoid giving the Whigs more ammunition in Parliament. On March 13, Napoleon was declared an outlaw by the Congress. Exactly a week later he re-entered the Tuileries, from which Louis XVIII had fled.

Castlereagh promptly stood on his head. 'The Neapolitan question,' he wrote to Wellington in Vienna on March 24, 'has assumed a new shape under the late extraordinary events in

10. 'I have painted *real* princesses, and *they* never gave me any trouble!' protested Mme. Vigée le Brun, incensed by Caroline's habit of changing her hairstyle, gown and jewelry at each sitting

11. The Royal Children of Holland and Naples. Napoleon with Letitia, Hortense's sons Napoleon-Louis and Louis-Napoleon, Louise, Achille and Lucien

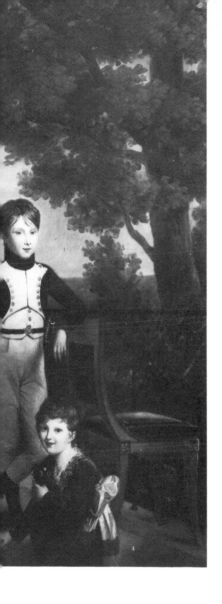

12. 'He behaved like a born King, and anybody who did not know his origins would have taken him for one.' (Colonel von Loewenstern on Joachim, 1814)

13. 'He looked for all the world like a fine athletic fellow who had been picked up in the streets, had a fine coat put on his back, and been turned loose to act the gentleman and king.' (Colonel Maxwell on Joachim, 1814)

14. 'Say a paternoster that it shall not be me.' Marie-Louise

15. The King of Rome takes the air in the carriage given him by Caroline

16. *Left:* The legendary little corporal . . . was now fat-jowled, partially-bald, dozing the hours away

17. *Below:* Retreat from Moscow

18a. September 23, 1815. He rode into Ajaccio with all his old swagger, on a handsome bay horse

18b. October 8, 1815. Three men were killed and others wounded before the peasants fell on them and dragged them up to the castle

19a. Joachim seated on the bench in the guardroom

19b. 6 P.M., Friday, October 13, 1815. 'Pointing one hand to his breast, he said, 'Fire!'

France. Whilst Louis XVIII was supposed to be firmly established on his throne, the difficulty was to consolidate the peace of Europe so long as a dynasty remained at Naples which neither France nor Spain would acknowledge. The case is different now; it is a question of public safety in Europe; and neither the King of France, nor even the king of Sicily, can expect that the policy to be observed towards Murat can be regulated upon considerations of minor importance.'[12] Castlereagh had just received Joachim's note affirming his desire to remain on friendly terms with Britain and repeating his request for recognition. So: 'if the Powers of Europe should consider this overture to be *bona fide* on the part of Murat', Castlereagh told Wellington, 'Your Lordship has full powers to conclude a treaty with him.'[13]

Wellington was not so easily dissuaded from his determination to get rid of Murat. On March 28 Clancarty took over from him at the Congress and he left for the Low Countries where he was to assume command of the British army. He sent instructions to Bentinck that if Murat attacked the Austrians they were to be supported by the British both on land and at sea. Near Würzburg he met the courier bringing Castlereagh's letter of the 24th. He read it and sent it on to Clancarty with a covering note: 'If I was at Vienna I should not act upon this dispatch . . . The Austrians are strong enough to beat Murat if they choose it, and present and future policy should induce them to do so.'[14] To Castlereagh he wrote: 'If we do not destroy Murat, and that immediately, he will save Buonaparte.'[15]

While awaiting instructions from Wellington, Bentinck sent Colonel Dalrymple from Genoa to ask Joachim for an explanation of the Neapolitan troop movements. Dalrymple arrived at Ancona on March 27, and during the afternoon had a long interview with Joachim, who harangued him about 'the falsity of the Austrians, the enmity of the French, his desire of peace, his determination to fight to the last if attacked. . . . He spoke very fast, and almost uninterruptedly going from one subject to the other, from Russian to Neapolitan politics. . . . "I trusted Austria, and she has deceived me," he said. "She has pledged herself to Talleyrand to destroy me because I am new. Everything has been new in its turn, and England surely would not find fault with a *new* and *liberal* government merely because it is not old and illiberal." '[16]

Joachim sent a message to Bentinck assuring him of the friendship of Naples for Britain. He explained that in the view of the menacing Austrian movements he was taking up his former position along the right bank of the Po. Bellegarde was that day writing to Bentinck that he would consider a state of hostility to exist at the moment when Neapolitan troops entered the territory of the Papal Legations.[17]

The opening shots were fired by the Austrians as Carascosa's divisions advanced on Cesena on March 30. From his headquarters in Rimini, Joachim issued a proclamation to all Italians: 'The hour has come for the accomplishment of the great destinies of Italy. Providence summons you to be an independent nation . . . 80,000 Italians from the State of Naples march forward commanded by their king, and swear they will not ask for rest until Italy is liberated . . . I call upon you, brave unhappy Italians of Milan, of Bologna, of Turin, of Venice, of Brescia, of Modena, of Reggio, of so many other illustrious oppressed regions. . . . I summon all brave men to join me in the fight.'[18]

He continued his march up the Via Emilia while the ringing proclamation died in the unechoing air. He reached Forli at midday on March 31. From there Dalrymple reported to Bentinck that Murat was prepared to negotiate with Austria on condition 'that she does not domineer over Italy', and that he did not have to subscribe to 'the declaration of the Allies respecting France . . . particularly so far as Bonaparte being a common Felon'.[19]

On April 2 he was in Bologna, the Austrians still withdrawing without offering serious opposition. That night he rode in triumph through the festively illuminated streets to the Teatro del Corso. The crowds cheered all the way, as they had in Imola, Faenza, Forli, Cesena, Rimini. 'It is impossible to describe the enthusiasm shown by the inhabitants of Bologna on my arrival,' he wrote to Maghella.[20] They were applauding the departure of the Austrians; he thought they were pledging support to him.

By April 4 he was in Modena, having defeated the Austrians in a stiff battle at the crossing of the Panaro; and Bianchi, commanding the Austrian troops south of the Po, was retreating again – this time northward towards Borgoforte. To Dalrymple, who had not yet left the Neapolitan headquarters, Joachim gave a letter for Bentinck, requesting a statement of British policy 'now that the

Austrians, contrary to my expectations, have opened hostilities against me'.[21] He asked Bentinck for a reply by return of the courier who accompanied Dalrymple. He got it; writing on April 5, Bentinck informed him that he regarded the armistice at an end and Great Britain at war with Naples. On the same day Metternich handed Cariati his passport and recalled Mier.

20

Joachim still held the initiative. His forces and the Austrians were almost exactly matched in numbers, a little over 34,000 men each, plus some Austrian garrison troops. He had not yet been rejoined by the household troops – 4,000 Infantry of the Guard, 1,500 Cavalry of the Guard – whom he had sent into Tuscany via Perugia and Arezzo, but the Austrians were themselves dispersed and unable to concentrate until they were certain of his next objective. They feared that he would advance as rapidly as possible to Milan and then into Piedmont, where nationalist agitation was strong, and raise the north against them. But the great crowds that thronged the streets of each city as he advanced, shouting *Long Live the King of Italy: Independence or Death!*, had gone straight home again, ignoring the patriotic appeals posted on the walls, and the open doors of the newly-established recruiting centres. The possibility of real popular support in Lombardy and Piedmont was not strong enough to outweigh the disadvantage of his lack of cavalry to operate on the great plain to the north-west, and the risk of exposing his right flank and rear to an Austrian thrust from the north. He decided to advance to the Po and secure his line there by seizing the two Austrian bridgeheads at Occhiobello and Borgoforte. In the late afternoon of April 6 he entered Ferrara where Austrian troops still occupied the citadel. The following day, his 2nd Division under Ambrosio was facing the Austrians at Vallunga, on the south bank of the Po, opposite Occhiobello. Their first assault was repulsed. Next day, Joachim ordered another attack which again failed. He returned that night to Bologna to study his position.

The infantry and cavalry of the Guard whom he had counted on joining him at least two days before were still in Florence, sixty mountainous miles away, and showing undue nervousness of a small Austrian force at Pistola. The 1st Neapolitan Division, based on Modena, protected his left flank and rear, while its commander, Carascosa, set up new administrations and committees throughout the Romagna in the hope of procuring the desperately needed men and supplies, a task that was more than ever difficult now that the Austrians were printing leaflets and posters announcing Britain's declaration of war on Joachim. The 3rd Division, under General Lechi, on the line of Cento, Finale, Bondeno, covered the gap between Carascosa's division and Ambrosio. North of the Po the Austrians awaited the arrival of regular reinforcements; south of the Po Joachim vainly looked for Italian volunteers, while the number of deserters from the Neapolitan army increased every day. On April 9 he issued a decree recalling to the colours all men who had been serving with Eugène's Army of Italy in March 1814. Next day he proclaimed the adoption of a new national cockade, purple and green – his own amaranth and the green of the former Cisalpine Republic and Kingdom of Italy – to be worn 'not only by the army but by Italians of every condition who are devoted to the cause of national independence.[1]

That day Bianchi, having come back over the Po at Borgoforte, attacked Carpi. The Neapolitans under General Pepe resisted bravely but, short of ammunition, without support and in danger of being cut off, abandoned the town just after nightfall and withdrew to Modena. This was in turn evacuated in the night of April 11 to 12. On April 12 the Austrians attacked and overran the Neapolitan position facing Vallunga; Ambrosio raised the siege of the citadel of Ferrara and withdrew beyond the Reno to Malabergo on the road to Bologna. Carascosa's division was behind the Panaro river at Castelfranco; Joachim was forced to straighten his line by withdrawing Lechi's 3rd Division from Finale and Creval-cuore to Cento. On the afternoon of April 13 he presided over a council of his generals and ministers at Bologna.

It was a forbidding outlook. He had failed to drive the Austrians across the Po. While their forces increased his dwindled. To avoid being surrounded, he must retreat back down the Via Emilia into the protective fork of the Appennines on one side and the Adriatic on the other. But first he must move out the stores, artillery, transport and wounded from his main base at Bologna. The great campaign for the liberation of Italy had ended almost before it began.

The Austrians, hampered in the north by spring-flooded rivers and marshes, sent a brigade across the Via Emilia below Modena and forced the Neapolitan 1st Division to withdraw to protect its left flank, while a second brigade pursued it along the high road. At Borgo Panigale, where the Reno obstructed their advance, they were held by another courageous stand from Pepe's troops. Bologna was successfully cleared of Neapolitan supplies and troops. Without difficulty, Joachim retired through Imola, Faenza, Forli and Forlimpopoli; there on April 20 he blew up the bridge over the Ronco and ordered the 3rd Division to turn and face the Austrians. At this moment, though he did not know it, he held numerical superiority. Bianchi had gone up into the Appennines with 12,000 men to take Joachim in the rear via Florence, Arezzo, Perugia and Foligno, while Neipperg followed him down the Via Emilia with 16,000. The infantry and cavalry of Joachim's Guard, badly led and frightened out of Florence by Nugent, were at Perugia in great confusion. Joachim's orders, four times repeated, for them to turn east and join his line of communications at Pesaro or Ancona, had not reached them. The enterprising Nugent was trying to outmarch and outflank them by taking the old Via Cassia through Poggibonsi, Siena and Viterbo to Rome.

Neipperg made no move on April 20, content to see Joachim halted while Bianchi progressed through the mountains. On April 21 Neipperg crossed the Ronco. Joachim, himself playing for time in which he believed the household troops would join him, sent a parlementaire to the Austrian outposts on April 22, suggesting that now that he had retired to the line at which the Austrians had opened fire on his troops because of what he assumed was a misunderstanding, they should agree to an armistice while he awaited a reply to proposals he had sent to Vienna. Neipperg replied that he was only the commander of the Austrian vanguard and had no authority to negotiate. Joachim decided to continue his retreat. Had he given way to his natural instinct to attack he would almost certainly have routed Neipperg and thrown the entire Austrian plan into confusion. But his eyes were now fixed on Naples, on the necessity to preserve his army intact

for the defence of his kingdom. And that army was rapidly dis-
integrating. The only recruitment was from those unfortunates
who had too hastily declared their support for freedom and now had
to flee from their homes to avoid retribution from the Austrians.

On April 26 he learned that Bianchi was making for Foligno:
he must race down the coast and up into the mountains to get to
grips with Bianchi. Leaving the 1st Division to hold off Neipperg,
he led the remainder of his army up towards Macerata. Between
Macerta and Foligno – which he had to reach in order to keep open
his communications with Naples – lay the valley of the river
Chienti, dominated by the small town of Tolentino. Here, on May
2, Bianchi set his forces in array. A little before midday Murat
launched his opening attack. By nightfall his cavalry had forced
back the Austrians in the valley and his infantry were established
on the crest of the hills overlooking them from the north. Even
more importantly, inspired by his own energy and courage, his
troops had recovered their confidence and dash.

On May 3, covered by the thick mist that filled the low ground,
Joachim thrust forward two columns, one on each side of the
river. These were to deliver the main attack, drawing off the
Austrians from the flanks so that the infantry of the 2nd Division
could swoop down on them from the wooded high ground on the
right, followed by the reserve under Lechi from the left. By 7 a.m.
the two armies were in contact. The Neapolitan centre drove in
the Austrian outposts, cleared the village of Cassone with a
bayonet charge and took possession of the ravine below it. This
was the moment for the infantry division to attack on the right,
but it was late because its temporary commander, General
Aquino (Ambrosio had been seriously wounded the previous day),
had forgotten to ensure that it had food and ammunition. When
it did move, the advance guard lost touch with the van and was
routed by the Austrian cavalry. Aquino, thinking to protect the
remainder of his men from a similar attack, marched them forward
in four squares, a formation impossible to hold on the broken,
sloping ground. Unexpectedly met by a hail of grapeshot from
three Austrian guns, followed up by a charge of both cavalry and
infantry, the first square broke and ran, communicating its panic
to the second.

Murat, galloping across the field with his staff, rallied the third and fourth squares, withdrew them out of range of the Austrian guns, and reformed the first two squares. In the nick of time he had prevented his right from collapsing and his centre being enveloped. But meanwhile the Austrians had recaptured the ravine at Cassone. It was mid-afternoon. Joachim had lost the impetus of his attack. He could not resume the battle next day, for fear Neipperg would advance along the road from Iesi to Macerata and take him in the rear. He dictated to his chief-of-staff, Millet de Villeneuve, orders for withdrawal towards Macerata, artillery and transport first, the two flanks forming behind the centre, which would remain in position as rearguard until after dark.

As he rode back to his base headquarters at Macerata he was met by two couriers, one from his minister of War, Macdonald, reporting that the Austrian column that Nugent had brought down was approaching the Via Casia Neapolitan frontier; and another that the Austrians had captured L'Aquila, far to the south. And behind him, though he did not yet know it, disaster had overtaken his army. Millet had in error ordered the commander of the centre division, Pignatelli Strongoli, to retire immediately instead of telling him to remain until the last. He discovered his mistake and sent an officer to convey the correction. But Pignatelli Strongoli, from stupidity, stubbornness or worse, insisted that his duty was to obey the written order, not the oral one. With the Neapolitan flanks preparing to retire and the centre in evident confusion, Bianchi saw his opportunity to attack. The Neapolitans were shattered, driven in disorder down the valley, and saved from utter destruction only by nightfall. Torrential rain completed their disarray. Failing to assemble at any of the points detailed in the king's orders, the fragments of the army made their way in small groups to Macerata.

The news of this catastrophe was brought to Joachim by a distraught aide-de-camp from the 2nd Division, followed by Aquino, in tears, who reported that in the darkness his men had walked straight into the pursuing Austrian columns. Aquino had not finished his account when Pignatelli Strongoli arrived, followed by Lechi. Pignatelli announced that his division no longer existed, there was not a single man remaining with him. Lechi had lost one of his two brigades, and the other was likely to run at the sound of the first shot. Joachim, unable to believe that the army he had left intact was now in shreds, jumped to his feet shouting, 'This is not true! It cannot be true!'[2]

Lechi answered: 'You are already a prisoner of the Austrians. Your Majesty: I can no longer answer for my division – it is entirely demoralized.'[3] All the generals agreed in shifting the blame for their shortcomings and mismanagement on to Pigna-telli ,who replied, 'I am not clairvoyant! My duty was simply to carry out the king's orders, not divine his intentions.'[12] Joachim let the impertinence pass. At last he succeeding in convincing them that their fears were exaggerated – the army could not have disintegrated entirely. He ordered them to reform their commands at dawn and march by different roads to Fermo and to Civitanova, where Carascosa could join them, coming down the coast from Ancona.[4] In the meantime Caraffa's uncommitted brigade was sent to occupy Monte Olmo, which dominated the valley from the other side.

Joachim was up at daybreak, receiving the local authorities, signing documents and bestowing decorations of the Order of the Two Sicilies. He reviewed his troops as they marched off. When he took his place in the rearguard, the Austrians were already entering the town. As the head of Joachim's column reached the cross roads at Santa Maria delle Vergini they came under fire from three Austrian guns and were attacked first by cavalry and then by a battalion of infantry; Caraffa's brigade, whose mission was to prevent the Austrians penetrating down the valley, had fled towards Fermo at the first sight of them. Here, at least, after a night of putting a brave face on misery, was a situation in which Joachim could act. He galloped the length of the column, dis-mounted, took personal command of the 6th Infantry Regiment and, with a squadron of cavalry on each flank, drove off the Austrians. Without reinforcements from Neipperg, who was still bringing his tired troops from Iesi, Bianchi decided not to press the pursuit. Joachim was again committed to the road along the Adriatic; the Austrian commander sent Mohr's division to dog him as far as Fermo and then keep on his western flank through Ascoli, Piceno, Teramo and Penne, skirting the Gran Sasso to Popoli. Bianchi himself set off on a circuitous march through Foligno, Spoleto, Terni and Rieti to L'Aquila, and sent a brigade by the shorter route through Sarnano to keep contact between the two columns which were thus moving roughly parallel, with the Austrians always between Joachim and his capital. 'We are making terrible marches to cut off the king of Naples,' Neipperg wrote to Marie-Louise on May 8. 'We shall pass very close to the Sibyl, the highest mountain in the Appennines; it is covered with snow and resembles the Jungfrauhorn, if Your Majesty still remembers that.'[5]

At Civitanova food and lodging had been prepared by Carascosa's troops, and supplies had been sent to Monte San Giusto for Caraffa's brigade, but by the time the Neapolitans reached these two points they had again been overtaken by panic and by a rainstorm – this time a howling hurricane in comparison with which the previous night's downpour had been only a shower. Despite their officers, perhaps even encouraged by them, they refused to halt; a blind, incoherent mob, they stampeded down the coast road. Nobody dared give them further orders, lest this silent disobedience turned to active mutiny; it was not until they reached San Benedetto del Tronto, and were physically exhausted, that they began to accept discipline again. Fortunately the great tempest had caused so much damage inland, flooding the roads, carrying away bridges and bringing down landslides, that Mohr's division could make only very slow progress.

Joachim sent to each divisional commander an appeal to respect 'the honour of the army and of the nation' and an order 'to march, you and the general commanding your vanguard, at the rear of your division'.[6] (Thus ensuring that this time they would not actually take the lead in any flight from the enemy.) But, as he had conclusively demonstrated in 1812, he was not the man to lead a successful retreat. Seeing that Mohr's division, separated from the main Austrian force by a series of impassable mountain ranges, might still be trapped and defeated, he decided to turn and face his pursuers on the river Tronto. On receiving these orders, the whole of Caraffa's brigade disappeared into the hills, the cavalrymen selling their horses as they went. Mohr, unable to catch up with him, nevertheless swept up a thousand prisoners in a single day.

At Pescara Joachim turned south-west, up the Pescara river towards Popoli and Sulmona, where he held a sad review of the 10,000 demoralized men who still followed him, harangued them, saw that his words had no effect, and continued over the mountains and down to the Sangro. He knew that, even if he could lead them intact to Naples, they had no will to defend it.

21

On the evening of April 13, when Joachim in Bologna was taking his decision to retreat, Caroline appeared in the Royal Box at the San Carlo with Madame Mère[1] and Jérôme, who had escaped from Trieste disguised as a sailor on a Neapolitan gunboat. Caroline, realizing that the tide of war was about to run against them, had returned to Naples to restore confidence. But to Jérôme 'she predicted in detail what would happen and how her husband would behave . . . she was morally as well as physically depressed.'[2] Mier had left for Vienna that day; and the withdrawal of troops had given boldness to the brigands, who were now operating on the trunk roads and close to the capital.

She no longer hesitated to accept appointment as Regent. As the Neapolitan troops fell back on their own frontiers and deserters spread stories of the deepest gloom, she struggled by word and action to fend off the approaching catastrophe. 'After his brilliant successes, the king has decided to concentrate the army and take up new positions,' she wrote to Desvernois on April 22, urging him to keep a strict watch against invasion attempts in Calabria. 'From another quarter the news of affairs in France is daily more satisfactory. Just today I received some which could not be better; thus there can be no doubt about the result of this struggle.'[3]

But there were some things that could not be disguised by a bold front and optimistic interpretation. On April 26 two British men-of-war, *Tremendous* and *Rivoli*, with the brig *Alcmene*, entered the bay of Naples, took up moorings and cleared for action. Their commander, Captain Campbell, demanded the surrender of the Neapolitan arsenals and naval vessels. Early in the morning of April 30 Captain Dickson in *Rivoli* sighted a French frigate, *Melpomène*, between Ischia and Procida, forced her to surrender and sent her in to Palermo. The battle lasted scarcely half an hour and sent a shudder through Naples with its threat of renewed attacks by the British fleet – and the even more terrifying threat of an invasion from Sicily. Caroline continued outwardly calm, 'I had a long audience of the queen yesterday (who by the way, I like very much),' the duke of Bedford wrote to Lady Holland on May 1, 'and was very pleased with the firmness, moderation and propriety which govern her conduct in the very critical situation in which she is placed.'[4]

On May 6 she received news from Joachim of the disaster at Tolentino, which she published in the *Monitore* next day as a victory. At noon she had the fortress guns fire a salute to another fictitious victory in which 'the king has taken twelve pieces of artillery and many thousands of prisoners, completely routing the enemy'.[5] But on May 8 the Grenadiers of the Royal Guard, the only regular soldiers still in Naples, marched off to face the oncoming Austrians. Crowds gathered in the streets next day, anxious and menacing, Caroline took Jérôme, who had recently lent her more than half a million francs to pay some of the troops, on a drive through the streets, smiling serenely. But when Belliard arrived that afternoon from Toulon, sent by Napoleon as ambassador to Naples, she did not try to hide her anxiety from him.

She gave him a rapid account of what had happened and told him she had sent Macdonald, the Minister of War, to try to block the advance of the Austrian troops under Nugent, coming down the western flank of the Appennines. Belliard, in avoiding the British patrol, had landed without baggage. Caroline gave him some of Murat's clothes, a carriage and horses and sent him off that night. He found Joachim next day at Castel di Sangro. 'Ah, my good Belliard!' he said. 'So you have come to die with me?'[6]

Caroline made plans to save the others. Her mother, her brother and uncle could make for France; her children must not quit their kingdom, but they needed a place of greater safety than the open palace in this seething city. She arranged for the adults to escort the children to the fortress of Gaëta by road and then be picked up by the *Dryade*, the French vessel that had brought Belliard; that way the town would not so quickly be filled with rumours that the royal family was fleeing. As Miss Davies was packing her trunk Lucien came to her room. It was a week short of his twelfth birthday. He was wearing his uniform. Taking her hand, he asked her: 'Davies, are you afraid of the enemy?' 'No, Your Highness,' she replied. 'And you need not be,' he assured her, 'whilst I have this sword by my side.'[7] But there were tears in his eyes when the family gathered in the drawing-room at two o'clock for Caroline to say good-bye.

There was talk of a hundred brigands on the road. Their departure was put off to seven o'clock. In the end it was midnight before they left the palace. An hour before dawn they were warned of an ambush. Mademoiselle Lavernette, hearing a musket shot, shrieked and threw herself on her knees in the carriage that she shared with Letitia and Louise. The girls, horrified that their escort should think they had any part in this display of cowardice, promptly stifled the poor woman's cries under a shower of cloak and scarves. At Gaëta Madame Mère was so distrustful of the villagers that she took the children by boat to the fortress. On May 13 she left with Fesch and Jérôme in the *Dryade*.

On May 11, Caroline put on the uniform of the Guardia di Sicurezza and reviewed the handful of troops that remained to her in the villa Reale, the gardens from which she had so often admired the view out over her beautiful bay of Naples. At the palace her council debated Campbell's ultimatum to bombard the town if the arsenals at Naples and Castellammare and ships of war in harbour and on the stocks were not surrendered. Caroline told them she was not frightened of the bombardment but she would not expose the city to the violent excesses that might follow it. She appointed Cariati as her negotiator with Campbell, at the same time protesting at the breach of the armistice and at the threat of hostilities without three months' warning. Campbell replied that it was Murat who had broken the armistice. On May 13 he signed an agreement with Cariati under which the Neapolitan warships and arsenals were surrendered to him 'to be disposed of as the respective governments may hereafter decide,'[8] in return for Campbell's promise to spare the city, and to 'offer every protection to the Queen Regent, her family and private property and such other individuals as may claim the protection of the British flag'.[9] He also agreed, though not in writing, to provide her with transport to France.

The *lazzaroni* gathered menacingly, working themselves into a fury, clamouring for a march on the palace. In the evening she drove through the ominous streets 'in a carriage drawn by six white horses. Her face composed, she waved graciously to right and left . . . Naples owes to her the calm that has reigned here until the present time.'[10] It was true; she imposed calm by her own cool courage, so that when she returned to the palace the howling mob was cheering and clapping its hands. The struggle was lost, but she would not admit defeat: she ordered Gallo to send new ministers to Vienna and London. During the night of May 16–17, the Army of the Interior, commanded by Macdonald since May 13, was utterly defeated at Mignano, leaving the road to Naples open to Nugent's division. Caroline told Gallo to make a direct approach to Bianchi for peace. On May 18 Joachim rode into Naples, having handed over command of the army to Carascosa. The evening strollers in the streets gave him a polite, almost warm, welcome. To Caroline he said, 'All is lost, except honour; there is nothing left for me but death.'[11]

In this extremity of misfortune he managed to remain as calm as she. He had already sent word to Gallo not to approach Bianchi on his behalf.[12] The following day he appointed Carascosa and Colletta to make the best terms possible but to insist upon a guarantee of the reforms that had been made during his reign. Since the king had made no stipulations on his own account, Colletta asked exactly what he was to offer. 'Everything, except the honour of the army and the interests of the people.' Joachim replied. 'I wish that all the burden of adverse fortune should fall on me alone.'[13]

At Gaëta, where the commander of the fortress, General Begani had enough food for six months, the Austrians were taking up siege positions. The children's apartments were on the seaward side, divided only by a narrow alley from the ramparts where roses grew picturesquely among the batteries. Their meals were frequently interrupted by broadsides from the British fleet, whereupon their nurses bustled them down to the safety of a casemate, Achille escaping whenever he could to help and encourage the gunners. Soon the visitations became so regular that they spent every night in the damp cellar beneath the batteries, wrapped in blankets and stretched out on the seats of their travelling carriages, which had had their wheels removed.

Before leaving Naples, Joachim spoke with all his ministers and household, thanking them and offering them parting gifts. 'He was as generous with his presents as a man who was just ascending the throne,'[14] noted Colletta. At 9 p.m., having said good-bye to Caroline, Joachim set out for Gaëta. Since the fortress was now inaccessible by land, he made for Pozzuoli. It is possible that he intended to hold out in Gaëta, but more probably his plan was to say farewell to the children, and then make for France and continue the war in the service of Napoleon.

On May 20, while Colletta and Carascosa were signing what was virtally a capitulation[15] at Bianchi's headquarters at Casalanza, Lord Exmouth[16] arrived with his squadron at Naples. On May 12, the day before the signing of the convention with Campbell, Caroline sent off to Toulon the most treasured exhibits from the private museum she had constructed in two rooms at the top of the palace. And according to the duke of Bedford she had sent 'a hundred small chests of gold to Gaëta with her children'.[17] Having appointed a Regency Council and received confirmation of the terms agreed upon at Casalanza, she left the palace late in the evening. To get to the passage leading to the seafront and the Castel dell' Ovo on the mole below the Villa Reale, she had to walk the length of the building. She did it 'with a firm step and unaltered countenance . . . She only made one observation . . . that Ferdinand would find the palace in a better state than when he left it.'[18]

At midnight she sent an officer to Lord Exmouth asking for a ship to be placed at her disposal in accordance with her agreement with Campbell. She was rowed out to the *Tremendous* which she boarded at 2 a.m. Shortly afterwards she asked Exmouth to land British patrols, because she did not believe the Guardia di Sicurezza was strong enough to preserve order. He sent 500 Marines ashore at 9 a.m. They held the city quiet until the arrival of the Austrians.

Since Exmouth's arrival there had been an ominous change in the British attitude. During the course of May 20, he told Agar that he would not wish the *Tremendous* to call at Toulon, because it was a military port, nor at Marseilles, because of the strict quarantine regulations, and would prefer Antibes. On May 21 arrangements were made for the duchess of Bedford to travel with Caroline to France[19] but the following day, when Caroline expected the vessel to sail, she was told first that the duchess could not be allowed to accompany her, and then that her own departure would be delayed. She guessed that this was connected with the triumphant arrival in the city of the Austrians, bringing with them Leopold of the Two Sicilies to claim the throne on behalf of his father. Gun salutes and the cheering of the crowds greeted the return of the Bourbons; from the balconies of the via Toledo the ladies showered rose petals on Leopold; boatmen brought parties of jeering sightseers wearing the Sicilian cockade to circle round the *Tremendous* and shout insults at yesterday's queen; at night she could see not only Naples but all the towns along the coast lit up in celebration. It was while she was discussing the transport to France of the members of her suite who did not wish to stay in Naples that she became aware of the reluctance to discuss taking her to France at all. Suddenly discovering that she was a prisoner, she wrote to Exmouth protesting that this was a breach of the convention signed with Campbell and contrary to the spirit of all the discussions of the past week.

Exmouth had received Campbell's dispatch enclosing a copy of the agreement on May 19, while he was still at sea. And, though he later said that he disapproved of what Campbell had done, he admitted that 'from my conviction that he had been actuated by the purest motives and placed in a peculiar situation, I thought it right in acknowledging his Letter, to express my approbation of his general proceedings'.[20] On arriving at Naples he received letters from Lord Burghersh, who was with the Austrian army. One, dated from Rome on May 16, said, 'It is most desirable that the property of Marshal Murat and his family should not escape from Naples under the cover of any Flag whatsoever';[21] the other told him that the Neapolitan army would capitulate at any moment. Exmouth had his fair share of the naval officer's fear of the Admiralty. Horrified at the prospect of an unfavourable report, he declared that he did not recognize Campbell's agreement and that Campbell had no powers to enter into it. Murat's property, which Burghersh was so anxious about, had already left for France; but he could at least prevent Caroline from following it.

It was undoubtedly a staggering breach of Campbell's promise. Lady Langdale, one of the English visitors, confirmed that Campbell gave his word, 'that Her Majesty should be received on board the *Tremendous* with her property and immediate attendants, and a free passage granted her to any port in France',[22] and that he was so well aware of this concession that 'addressing himself to some English who were present, he said: "If I have erred it has been on the side of mercy, and you great people must stand my friends for it in England."'[23] The duke of Bedford's account was similar. 'Campbell put the copy of the Convention into my hands the day after it was signed and said: "if I am attacked at home for this (which I dare say I shall be), you will, I hope, defend me."'[24] Bedford also asserted that 'Lord Exmouth, upon receipt of the Convention, wrote an official Letter warmly approving of Campbell's conduct, which Letter I saw,' but 'Lord Burghersh wrote [Exmouth] a private Letter . . . slily urging him to find a pretext for breaking the treaty'.[25]

Hearing that the charming Count Neipperg had led the Austrian advance guard into Naples, Caroline asked him to come and see her. He found her despondent and suffering from the motion of the ship. He told her bluntly that neither she nor Joachim had any bargaining rights; they were no longer recognized by Austria, and were not mentioned in the treaty signed by Colletta and Carascosa. She replied that they had not abdicated and would never do so. But she was in a hopeless position. She had lost faith in British promises and was anxious to leave Naples before the Bourbons took control. After two hours of argument she agreed to accept the protection of Austria, though not as a prisoner of war, and to be conveyed on the *Tremendous* to Trieste to await the Kaiser's decision as to her future residence. She promised that neither she nor her retinue would return to France or Italy without permission from the Austrian government. 'A fine conclusion to a 28-day campaign,' Neipperg wrote gleefully to Metternich, 'placing in our power as a hostage the queen, who is much more the king of this country than her fool of a husband.'[26]

She sailed northward on the *Tremendous* on May 25, to Gaëta, where the valiant Begani still kept the blue, white and amaranthine flag flying. A boat from the *Tremendous* carrying General Livron[27] went ashore under a flag of truce, but at first Begani refused to hand over the children, fearing that the queen was acting under duress; it was only when Macdonald went ashore and, in his capacity as minister of War, ordered the general to release his royal wards, that the children were rowed out to the *Tremendous*, where Campbell was pacing up and down in a tearing rage brought on by the delay, the unfavourable report he rightly feared Exmouth had sent to the Admiralty, and the consciousness of the breach of faith with Caroline in which he had unwillingly been involved. Of the numerous party of governesses, tutors and servants who had accompanied the children, only two valets de chambre, the two English nurses and the timorous Mademoiselle Lavernette volunteered to go into exile with them. The others sent out to the ship a petition asking to be paid off and given the means of returning to France or Naples. The document, read out to Caroline, began, 'On leaving the service of the ex-queen. . . .'[28] The children glanced covertly at their mother. There was not a flicker of emotion on her face.

The *Tremendous* put about and sailed down the length of Caroline's former kingdom. The girls astonished Campbell by their efficiency as interpreters, the boys romped with him, running around the quarter-deck and leaping on him from the rigging until Caroline had to curb them for fear they would overstep the bounds of politeness. Louise, whom Campbell always addressed as 'My old grandmother', jumped about so comically with her Chinese bonnet flapping over her serious face that his great fat cheeks grew as red as his hair; and in return for all this entertainment he had the sailors sing shanties to them in the long summer evenings. At the entrance to the straits of Messina they encountered Rear-Admiral Penrose's flagship, the *Queen*, bringing Ferdinand IV to resume his reign. As the ships were about to pass, Campbell warned Caroline not to be frightened if she heard the sound of gunfire – it was only a salvo in honour of the king of Naples. 'She who was alike royal in her nature and her bearing,' General Colletta admiringly recorded, 'replied that such sounds were neither new nor displeasing to the ears of a Bonaparte'.[29] The *Tremendous* arrived at Trieste during the night of June 7. The next morning Caroline went ashore after presenting Campbell with a gold and diamond snuff box and a watch with her portrait set in diamonds for his wife. She made separate gifts to the officers and £100 to the crew. Campbell, impressed by the courage she had shown during the six weeks that he had known her, ordered his gunners to fire a twenty-one-gun salute, which was answered by the shore batteries. He went with her in his launch. When they had landed she turned to thank him again but, overcome by embarrassment, he was already on his way back to the *Tremendous*.

22

When Joachim sailed from Miniscola in the night of May 19, he failed to penetrate the British blockade and was forced to take refuge the following day on the island of Ischia. There, on May 21, he was picked up by the chebec *Sainte Catherine*, flying the British flag but chartered by Manhès and carrying the general and several of his relations. With Joachim, his secretary, Coussy, and his valet de chambre, Armand, they set sail for France and reached Cagnes on May 25. He was uncertain of his welcome from Napoleon but had a strong suspicion that it would be frigid. 'It is certainly a great misfortune,' he wrote to him in an attempt to excuse the loss of his kingdom, 'that a letter I received from Joseph . . . speaking on your behalf, decided me to begin operations which it was so important to coincide with Your Majesty's. But I was told to move swiftly up to the Alps . . .'[1] He asked to be allowed to serve in the forthcoming campaigns.

It was true that Joseph had written to him, asking for his help 'militarily and politically . . . March up to the Alps but do not pass beyond them';[2] and towards the end of the month Napoleon had sent him a note entirely in his own hand saying: 'I have an army in Flanders, one in Alsace, one in the interior, one being formed in the Dauphiné. Up to this moment I am at peace with everybody. I will support you with all my might. I rely on you.'[3] He told Joachim to send ships to Marseilles as soon as the port had submitted, so that they could correspond. 'Send me a minister. I will send you one shortly on a frigate.'[4] Neither of these letters, of course, reached Joachim before he had committed himself; but the fact that Napoleon initially approved of his advance northward is shown by the emperor's instructions to Caulaincourt on April 7 to prepare a report to be read to the Council of Ministers and published in the *Moniteur*, 'making known our relations with the king of Naples, the advantages which should result from it, and what we know of his operations',[5] and by his appointment of Belliard on April 13 as Envoy Extraordinary and Minister Plenipotentiary to the Court of Naples. But now that the picture had been changed by misfortune, 'he put in the plague-house this man infected with the disease of the vanquished'.[6]

He sent Baudus, the young princes' former tutor, to tell Joachim that he would not be received in Paris but should 'choose some agreeable country place between Grenoble and Sisteron to live until the queen arrives and the news from Naples can be clarified'. Baudus was to inform him of 'the emperor's regret that the king attacked without any consultation, without agreement',[7] and 'make it clear to him that he ruined France in 1814; in 1815, he has compromised her and ruined himself'.[8]

Baudus found the king at Plaisance, a country house a mile outside Toulon that he had rented from Admiral Lallemand, after spending a fortnight in 'a wretched little inn near the town',[9] The message he brought drove Joachim into a fury. On June 7, he learned that Caroline had left Naples with the children, and realized that 'she must be either in Germany or England',[10] as he wrote to Napoleon from Cannes the next day. To Madame de Civrieux, his close friend and probably his mistress, then in Paris, he wrote: 'The country is in danger, I offer my services; they put off accepting them. I do not know whether I am free or a prisoner. I shall be involved in the Emperor's ruin if he falls, and they deprive me of the means of serving him and of serving my own cause.'[11] On June 14, Desvernois, who had brought a party of 134 French officers and men with him from Calabria, was allowed out of quarantine at Toulon and went to pay his respects to the king who greeted him in almost the jovial and expansive manner of old, insisting that he should join 'his military family', assuring him that 'a place will be set for you at my table as long as we remain at Toulon. We breakfast at ten and dine at six'.[12] It was an honour not without its dangers. The soldiers of the Toulon garrison openly insulted Joachim by name and his men to their faces. Five duels took place the first day and eight the next.

Fouché, who amid graver preoccupations had been trying to advocate Joachim's cause in Paris, advised him to move up to Lyons and await events there. He made preparations to go at once – the message reached him in the evening of June 18 – but he had a bitter premonition that it was too late: 'The emperor leaves me kicking my heels here,' he said to Desvernois, 'whereas if I were with him my sword might perhaps be of powerful help against his enemies.'[13] He got no farther than Aubagne before meeting the Marseilles garrison fleeing from a royalist rising. Their commander, General Verdier, gave him the news of Waterloo. It was exactly as he had feared.[14] He returned to Plaisance.

He told Coussy to go on to Paris and ask Fouché's help in obtaining Metternich's permission for him to join his family in Austria. Fouché not only set this negotiation on foot but also obtained from the Provisional Government, which he now presided, an order restoring to Joachim the property in France that he had surrendered at Bayonne. Three days later, on July 8, 1815, Louis XVIII returned to Paris once more. The Royalist White Terror which accompanied this second restoration was particularly violent in the South of France. Joachim was now in danger of losing his life as well as his liberty. Exmouth's squadron arrived at Marseilles on July 12 and Joachim sent Rossetti to ask for a passage to Britain. The admiral replied that 'he will be received on presenting himself to any of His Majesty's Ships, and protected in his person; but he must consider himself at the disposition of the British government and he will not be permitted to go to England without an order from thence to that purpose.'[15]

In Paris, the duke of Wellington told Maceroni, an Anglo-Italian adventurer who had attached himself to the king that Mura could not be given asylum in Britain unless he abdicated. Maceroni then approached Castlereagh. Joachim in Toulon wrote to Coussy to say he would not abdicate without the agreement of his wife and children; in the meantime he wished permission to reside in France as an ordinary citizen with the title of Prince Joachim Murat. The next day, July 14, Armand, the valet de chambre, brought a letter from Fouché asking for Joachim's authorization to sign an agreement with Metternich, who offered a refuge in Austria if Joachim would abdicate.

These long-distance, cross-purpose negotiations were interrupted by the arrest in Paris of Maceroni and Coussy on the orders of Decazes, Hortense's former admirer, now Prefect of Police. The police at Cuges had intercepted a message which Maceroni sent to Joachim in a metal tube inserted in a Bologna sausage.[16] It contained the depressing news that the Prince Regent would not allow Joachim into England. While Fouché was having Coussy and Maceroni released from their Paris prisons, Joachim's niece Clotilde, Duchess of Corigliaro, and his nephew Colonel Eugène Bonafous were arrested on their way to Cahors.

On August 2, a royalist mob recognized Marshal Brune in Avignon and murdered him. The time for bargaining was over; Joachim needed to quit France as quickly as possible. He left the house at Plaisance and went into hiding. He sent his other Bonafous nephew, Joseph, a naval captain, to Marseilles to charter a merchant vessel, and the marquis de San Giuliano to Paris where he was to offer Wellington the surrender of Gaëta in return for passports to Britain. San Giuliano would take these to Le Havre and there await the arrival of Joachim in the merchant ship. Joachim's money and baggage was loaded on to the ship and those members of his suite who had decided to accompany him went on board. Joseph Bonafous was to hire a small fishing smack to take Joachim out on August 10 to meet the merchant vessel off a quiet part of the coast. But on that morning Joseph was arrested. Joachim found himself another boat, set out for a rendezvous whose location he did not know, spent the night fruitlessly searching a stormy sea, and returned at dawn soaked to the skin. The merchant vessel cruised around the meeting place for some hours and then headed for Le Havre.

Joachim, stranded on the beach, was being pursued by three different groups: the soldiers of the garrisons of Marseilles and Toulon, who had orders to arrest him; royalist vigilantes who intended to kill him; and the police who had been instructed by Fouché to provide him with a safe-conduct to the British fleet or the Austrian army. But it was the Bonapartists who denounced him to the Prefect of Marseilles.

Making his way back to the house at Plaisance, he learned from the gardener's wife that a reward had been offered in Toulon that morning for his capture. He took refuge in a cave in the mountains, with no food except sea-biscuits and a bottle of rum; and later found lodging with a sympathetic farmer who 'installed him in his finest room and, just in case, prepared him a compartment in the big chicken house, concealed by a plank'.[17] To make contact with Joseph Bonafous, who had been released but was being kept under observation. Joachim ventured back to Plaisance, spending each night in the gardener's cottage but hiding in the countryside during the day. Bonafous now arranged a different and successful plan: to get Joachim to Corsica on the regular packet from Toulon, which the king – heavily bearded and dishevelled after a stormy trip in a leaky boat – boarded at sea, south of the Iles d'Hyères. At Bastia he was allowed to land and went to a coffee house where a former battalion commander in the Neapolitan army found him a horse on which he rode to Vescovato, a large village sixteen miles south, whose mayor, André Colonna-Cecaldi, was father-in-law to one of Joachim's former aides-de-camp, General Franceschetti.

On August 28, he wrote to the Governor of Elba, urging him not to surrender the island to the Tuscans. 'All the departments of the North are in arms. . . . Austria's policy has decidedly changed, and in agreement with Russia seems to have decided for Napoleon II. . . . I am ready to join you with as many troops as you wish . . . I have in any event a claim on the Island of Elba in virtue of a Treaty made with Napoleon at the time of his departure for France, Monsieur Lapi should know about it.'[18] The governor replied that it was too late. The Allies feared that he might attempt to seize control of Corsica; but Joachim's eyes were on a larger prize. He was sending messengers eastwards, to Florence in the hope of getting letters through to Caroline and Naples, to sound out the amount of support he might count on for a return to his throne. Despite his recent unhappy experiences he was still fascinated by the image of himself as the popular leader of a movement for Italian liberation. With a handful of brave men, he could land somewhere on the long Neapolitan coast, raise his banner and win back his throne and liberty for Italy.

On September 17, he left Vescovato and set off into the mountains on his way to Ajaccio, sending Franceschetti ahead to hire boats for an expedition, and recruiting in the villages as he went. Followed by several hundred veteran soldiers and many eager novices he rode into Ajaccio with all his old swagger, on a handsome bay horse that had been presented to him by a country curé. He put up at the Hôtel de la Croix de Malte which he immediately transformed into a headquarters by posting a guard on the door and flying his amaranthine standard over the gateway. The garrison prudently retired to the citadel: the Prefect quit the town and only the Mayor remained to represent civil authority.

His immediate problem was money. The local bankers in both Ajaccio and Bastia could not, or would not, cover the whole of the drafts he gave them on his banker in Paris. He had arrived in Corsica with about 10,500 francs in cash and a collection of diamonds which he valued at 100,000 francs. Commandant Poli, who had married the grand-daughter of Napoleon's wetnurse, but was on bad terms with the Ramolinos who refused to help Murat, lent Joachim 90,000 francs for these; he possibly raised another 200,000 francs from the Gregori brothers in Bastia. His expenditure merely to get his small force of 300 men (chosen from three times as many volunteers) to sea, came to 60,000 francs, of which in round figures 32,000 went on the charter of five *gondoles*[19] and a felucca; 10,000 for advance pay to a score of seamen; a similar amount for food for the voyage; 2,000 for the costs of printing pamphlets, including a proclamation to the people of Naples; 6,000 for 50 uniforms, arms and ammunition and a new coat for himself.

On September 28, Maceroni arrived bringing with him an offer from the kaiser signed by Metternich, for Joachim to reside anywhere he chose in Bohemia, Moravia or Upper Austria, provided he gave his word not to leave without permission. He was not asked for a formal abdication, but Metternich stipulated that 'the king shall take the name of a private individual. The queen having taken that of countess of Lipona [an anagram of Napoleon] the same is suggested to the king.'[20]

Joachim welcomed Maceroni warmly, but made it clear at once that his mind was already made up. 'You are come too late . . . the die is cast.'[21] He clearly understood that this time he was playing for the highest possible stakes. The thought invigorated him; and in any case 'I have now gone too far: I have compromised three hundred brave officers and soldiers by accepting their services, and if I now abandon them and leave them here behind me, they must infallibly fall victims to the vengeance of the Bourbon government.'[22]

Maceroni asked for a formal reply to the letter he carried and the king dictated one, accepting the passport which 'I count on using to make my way to the place stated therein. As for the conditions that His Imperial and Royal Majesty imposes on the offer of a refuge in Austria, I reserve the right to discuss that important subject when I have rejoined my family.'[23] But after dinner he led Maceroni to his private apartment and dictated a second letter: 'I will in no way accept the conditions that you are charged with offering me, Monsieur Maceroni. I regard them as an abdication, pure and simple, under the sole condition *that I am allowed to live*, but in eternal captivity. . . .' I have not abdicated. I have the right to resume my crown if God gives me the strength and the opportunity . . . I shall succeed or I shall end my misfortunes with my life. . . . It is only the fate of my family that makes me tremble.'[24] He gave Maceroni a draft for 40,000 francs to cover his expenses and the cost of clothes and other items that he had brought for the king. While they were talking, Franceschetti came in to announce that everything was ready for departure. The fleet of six small ships sailed a little before midnight, carrying Joachim and 298 seamen, officers and men.

By daylight on September 29 they were off the island of Asinara, at the northwest corner of Sardinia, but a strong east wind prevented them from getting through the Straits of Bonifacio that day. After sheltering overnight farther along the coast, they passed the island of Maddalena in the morning of September 30 and sailed down the east coast of Sardia to Tavolara, where Joachim landed his troops, reviewed them, and distributed new uniforms to those in the most need. On October 1 they began their slow crossing of the Tyrrhenian Sea. The troops did not know which part of the Neapolitan coast they were heading for; possibly Joachim himself was not yet decided. Towards dusk on October 6 they sighted Paola, in Upper Calabria; but just as they were preparing to anchor for the night a sudden storm dispersed them. In the morning, only the felucca and the royal *gondole* carrying Joachim, four servants and twenty-four officers and men remained in position. Joachim sent the felucca to look for the other craft while Colonel Ottaviani and a sailor rowed ashore to reconnoitre.

The colonel and the sailor failed to come back, for the local authorities were more watchful and less friendly than Joachim had believed.[25] The felucca returned with one of the missing *gondoles*, commanded by Colonel Courrand; but within a short time two of the colonel's officers rowed across to tell Joachim that Courrand was trying to get his men to desert the expedition. Joachim ordered the colonel to come aboard and told him of the accusation; the colonel swore it was false, but Joachim took the precaution of securing the other vessel to his own with a tow rope. With darkness and the danger of the two boats colliding, the rope had to be cast off, and in the morning – Sunday, October 8 – Courrand had gone.[26]

Joachim recognized defeat. 'Gentlemen,' he said to his officers, 'I am deeply conscious of your devotion to me, but I do not believe it would be prudent to land when I have no information and so few men. Return to your country, gentlemen, in the little felucca.'[27] He offered them a purse containing a thousand francs There were tears in his eyes and it seems that he had made up his mind to sail to Trieste and join Caroline and the children.

What happened next is in dispute. His servant Charles claimed that General Franceschetti argued against giving up when so close to success and began shouting, 'Let us land! Land! Long live Joachim!'[28] Franceschetti's own account makes no mention of this but says that Baron Barbara, who commanded the royal *gondole*, warned Joachim that they needed more supplies and, if possible, a sounder ship if they were to get to Trieste. Before going ashore in search of these, he asked Joachim for the passport signed by Metternich. This request annoyed the king, possibly because he suspected that Barbara planned to desert, or alternatively because he thought Barbara was hinting that Joachim might sail away and desert *him*. It may be that both accounts are true, and one incident followed the other. In any event, Joachim exclaimed; 'I will go on shore!'[29] Putting on a blue coat with gold epaulets, and a sabre and two pistols, he told Barbara to cruise up and down just out of musket-shot for an hour and then anchor beside some fishing nets.

They had drifted farther south during the night and were now in the bay of Santa Eufemia with the small town of Pizzo just above them. It was about midday when Joachim jumped from the ship's boat on to the beach followed by a score of officers and men. Having forgotten to bring a drum, they marched up the steep path towards the town shouting *Vive le Roi! Vive le Roi! Vive*

Joachim! 'Seeing the Sicilian colours he called out "Haul down that White Rag" and one of his officers took from under his Cloaths one of Murat's flags.'[30] There was a Sunday market in Pizzo and the small square was crowded, but it emptied as they approached. Armand says the king was saluted by an artillery serjeant, whom he ordered to accompany him with his men, but there is no indication that they did so: the great crowds that should have rallied to the liberator failed to appear. Two young men told him to hurry on to Monteleone. 'You are here surrounded with enemies who will not give you time to explain yourself,'[31] they warned. Too late, he realized that for them he was not a king but an alien: a Frenchman, like the detested Manhès who had so ruthlessly repressed brigands in these parts; worse the Frenchman who had *sent* Manhès.

He led the way out of the town, stepping briskly. His blue military coat was heavy, the road up through the olive groves was steep, he was in his forty-ninth year. He got the stitch and had to halt for a while. Between the olive trees he could see a party of armed peasants coming up the road, led by the local captain of gendarmes.[32] Another group were circling inland, evidently aiming to cut him off. His pride, his dignity were bruised by the thought of running from his own subjects. Despite protests from Franceschetti and the others he insisted on turning and facing the peasants. The gendarme came on alone. Joachim told him why he had come, and ordered him to obey his king. The gendarme replied that his king's name was Ferdinand. As soon as he was back on the road the peasants opened fire.

There was nothing for it now but to make a dash for the beach. Barbara, cruising beyond range in the *gondole*, made no attempt to help them. They were not able to reach their own boat and made instead for a fishing vessel. As they tripped and struggled, heaving at the boat stuck on the sandy beach, the bullets and buckshot whistled among them. Three men were killed and others wounded before the peasants fell on them and dragged them up to the guardroom at the castle. Along the way they beat Joachim and ripped his clothes: 'Punched in the face, cuffed, spat upon in the face, stripped of his epaulets and the cross of his order, his uniform torn, struck in the face with his own hat after they had taken from it 15 diamonds of great value, and one wretch had the wit to hit him in the face with his own shoe,'[33] according to the disjointed account of the British vice-consul, Antonio Perri, to whom the king sent for help. Perri found him wearing a borrowed shirt and breeches. Joachim told him he had a passport from the Allie Powers to go to Trieste and asked for Perri's assistance, but his captors refused to allow Perri to intervene.

At 5 p.m. the Calabrian divisional commander, General Nunziante, arrived from Tropea and had Joachim and four others transferred to an upper room. Joachim claimed that he had landed only to take on provisions, again produced the passport signed by Metternich, and demanded his release. Nunziante refused, but next day moved him to a private room, where he was attended by Armand.

An English officer, Colonel William Robinson, R.N., who commanded the Army Flotilla in the Straits of Messina, called on him and they talked for several hours. 'He affected to believe that he had done nothing which gave a right even to detain him, but at most as a prisoner of war for the decision of the Allies. But he never had nor never could resign his right to the Crown of Naples. He endeavoured to keep from thinking on his situation, I conclude, by a constant talking. He enquired how Ferdinand served his horses, if he took care of his carriage. Boasted how well he had used him by leaving his palaces furnished and that he had expended *3 millions* (I think) of his *own money* . . .[34] He said he had passed six months of misery – that he had overheard people in the next room to him at Marseilles planning how to cut his throat. In short, he ran on all subjects but failed not to regret beyond all things that he was not at Waterloo!'[35]

The news of his arrest sped to Naples. A jubilant order sped back: General Nunziante was to appoint a court-martial to try his prisoner as a public enemy. The sentence (there was no question what it must be) would be read at once to the prisoner, who would be given a quarter of an hour for spiritual preparation before his execution. The court assembled at 10 a.m. on October 13, but the accused was absent, having refused to plead, defend himself, or in any way recognize its jurisdiction. 'I know it is useless. The Government wants me dead, and there is no doubt that I shall die,'[36] he said; but he protested that 'these are my subjects, and it is not permissible for them to judge their sovereign . . . Sovereigns have only God as their judge. If I am a marshal of France, only a council of marshals may judge me; if I am considered to be a mere general, a council of generals is necessary. To reduce me to the level of the judges whom you have appointed you would have to tear up too many pages of the history of Europe!'[37] While the court was sitting he asked for a meal. They brought him soup, a pigeon with the bones removed, bread cut into small squares and a spoon. There was no knife with which to cheat the firing squad. 'Even if I were not already certain of dying, this would be proof enough,'[38] he said. The officer who came to announce the sentence was accompanied by a seventy-year-old priest from the local church, who found him finishing a letter:

'My dear Caroline, My last hour has come; in a few moments I shall have ceased to exist; you will no longer have a husband, and my children will have no father. . . . Good-bye, my Achille! Good-bye, my Letitia! Good-bye, my Lucien! Good-bye, my Louise! Show yourself worthy of me in the world. I leave you without realm and without property, among my many enemies. Remain united always. Show yourselves always superior to misfortune, and think more of what you are than what you have been. May God bless you.'[39] It was a bleak, miserable end to the brave life that he and Caroline had in their separate ways fought to make and preserve for them. A doleful ruin that he had brought crashing down on them through his hastiness and his pride. 'Do not curse my memory,' wrote this prodigal father to his sons and daughters. 'Understand that my greatest sorrow in the last moment of my life is to die far away from my children! Receive my paternal blessing! Receive my tears and my kisses! Never forget your unhappy father.'[40]

He sealed the letter, enclosing a lock of his hair, added to it his watch, which had a portrait of Caroline inside the case, and handed it to the officer. Then he rose to greet the priest, Canon Antonio Masdea. 'What do you want of me?' he asked. 'To know if you die a good Christian,' the priest replied. 'I recognize God, the Trinity,' Joachim answered. 'I have never done evil and I die a Christian.'[41] Masdea reminded him that he had two years earlier made a gift of 1,000 ducats to the church of San Giorgio at Pizzo. 'I ask you to do me another favour,' said the old man. 'I?' said Joachim. 'Am I in any position to do favours?'[42] The priest asked him to sign a written affirmation of his faith, so that there should be no questioning of it later. He did so, and the priest asked him to make confession. The officer who had brought the death sentence shook his head, pointing out that they had wasted five minutes already. Masdea told him sternly that no power on earth would prevent his hearing the confession and giving absolution. Joachim sat with the priest, confessed and was absolved. 'Now let us go and accomplish the will of God,'[43] he said, getting to his feet.

It was six o'clock in the evening. The firing squad was drawn up on the castle esplanade. Joachim refused the chair that had been set for him, and the blindfold to cover his eyes. He asked the soldiers to aim at his heart, not his face. 'Then, pointing one hand to his breast, he said, "Fire!" and they fired twelve bullets into his chest from which he died immediately; then another three bullets in his head when he was on the ground.'[44] His body was put into a rough wooden coffin and carried by the soldiers to the churchyard, where they tipped it into the common grave.

'Thus perished the greatest fool in Europe,' Admiral Penrose wrote to Exmouth, 'a vain empty coxcomb, but of kind and pleasant manners, possessing however not one of the great qualities but personal courage . . . You will have more particulars via Naples, but I have put down these things for your amusement.'[45]

Byron, less amused, wrote to Tom Moore: 'Poor dear Murat, what an end! You know, I suppose, that his white plume used to be a rallying point in battle, like Henry IV's.'[46]

On St Helena, where the news did not arrive until February 7, 1816, Napoleon remarked bitterly. 'The Calabrians have been more human and generous than those who sent me here!'[47] Lucien's comment was even briefer: 'The duc d'Enghien!'[48] And in Paris, Louis XVIII's courtiers 'went into transports of joy'.[49]

PART IV

The Countess Alone
1815 – 1838

I

Caroline landed at Trieste a comparative pauper. Unlike her mother, who had never really believed that her little Napoleone's luck would last, unlike the cautious Joseph and the eager Fesch who had pursued wealth wherever they perceived it, unlike even Pauline and Lucien, who had grasped whatever came their way and not expended all of it, she had almost no riches outside her kingdom of Naples, and the greater part of those – perhaps obeying a royal instinct that no true crowned head would have given way to – she had left in her Neapolitan palaces out of pride. The crates that she brought with her on the *Tremendous* contained some furniture and works of art; she also had most of her personal jewels, and her determination and charm. 'I cannot sufficiently praise the wit, the grace, the vivacity, the simplicity[1] and the gentleness that she possesses,' the enraptured Baron Lilien wrote to Hager, head of the Austrian ministry of Police and Censorship soon after her arrival. 'It is impossible not to be entranced by the amiability that she brings to everything she says.'[2]

The Austrian police kept a very close eye on the house where Caroline was staying[3] for this was the one from which Jérôme had at Easter slipped past their guard. As soon as she had settled in, she wrote to ask the kaiser for his help in getting her to France in accordance with the convention she had signed with Campbell. She sent a similar appeal to Metternich the same day; and on June 19 she wrote to Napoleon. But he was no longer in a position to welcome her back to France. June 18 was the day of Waterloo.

She had no idea what had happened to Joachim. 'I am so miserable,' she told him in mid-June, in a letter written entirely in her own hand, 'that the merest trifle upsets me; I am putting on a good appearance and showing a cheerful face, but with no peace at the bottom of my heart. News from you would set me up again. I need it so much.'[4] A few days later, she sent off a whole batch of letters, carried for safe keeping by eight servants whom she was having to send back to France for reasons of economy. 'I am very sad, very worried,' she wrote to Joachim. 'The children are very anxious, and so am I, that we should not stay any longer here. We need to see you, to look after you. We talk about it all the time, and all our thoughts are with you. . . . They get up at 6, study till ten, lunch, and a walk till midday. When they get back they work until 6, walk or talk till 7. Then dinner, play for a while, and bed.' Achille, who had been feverish for some days, was a little better, and making good progress, with Agar as his tutor. 'Write to me and do not forget the slightest detail. If you think it proper, send me my valet de chambre. If you do not send him to me, keep him for yourself, or try to do something for him. It is distressing to abandon these people. Farewell again. Always love your loving Caroline.'[5]

The rest of the family were silent. Elisa, whom Metternich had interned at Brünn immediately upon Napoleon's escape from Elba, was doubly vexed with Joachim who had turned her out of her Tuscan states in 1814 and thwarted her hope of getting them back by his impetuous attack in the spring. Pauline was at Bagni di Lucca. Hortense was in Switzerland, where she had been temporarily joined by her lover, Flahault. Madame Mère, Fesch and Louis were in Rome. Jérôme and Catherine were at Ellwangen, in Würtemberg. Lucien was being held in Turin by the Sardinians. Only the cautious, downy Joseph had got clear away, with a fortune in banker's orders,[6] and by August 28 was safely in New York. Caroline began to look for a home in Austria in which she and Joachim could resume and repair their shattered life.

In August she decided to take a lease on the castle of Hainburg, conveniently near Vienna, where she intended to press claims for restitution of her property in France and Naples. There, on September 27 she received a message from Metternich that Joachim was in Corsica, but would soon be in Trieste now that the kaiser had sent him a passport. Caroline's secretary forwarded this news to Agar who had remained in Trieste to look after affairs; and the next day, to amuse the aide-de-camp Livron, sent him the latest gossip: that Murat was forming a small army in Corsica. 'Really! Even if one *assumed him to be mad*, one could not imagine anything less likely.'[7]

Caroline, hoping to repair the rift, wrote to Elisa, who replied politely. The days passed and the news of Joachim's strange conduct in Corsica filtered through. Writing to Joachim's niece, Antoinette, Caroline, said: 'You may imagine my uneasiness. As soon as I know anything I will tell you.'[8] Meanwhile there was sad news of the girls' governess, Madame de Roquemont: 'she was so affected by our departure from Naples that she died of fright.'[9]

On October 29 Caroline acknowledged a letter Catherine had sent her from Ellwagen four weeks before. 'Yes, they wrote to me what you said [about the issue of a passport for Joachim] but that was five weeks ago, and if things had gone as they should, he would be back here by now.'[10] Elisa wrote that she believed Joachim had been taken prisoner, and Caroline replied on November 2 that she had heard the same thing. She had written to the kaiser to beg his release. Next day she knew that he was dead. The news was broken to her by Macdonald, who had learned it the previous day but had concealed it from her, trying to prepare her for the shock by talk of a serious illness that had overtaken Joachim.

Elisa summed up the general opinion of the family when she wrote to Jérôme on November 4 that she was very sorry to hear of Joachim's death but 'how can one imagine such madness?'[11] To Catherine she admitted frankly that 'I am very far from being able to commend his behaviour to me; he is the cause of my ruin and the loss of my entire fortune, yet I could not bring myself to hate him and, now that he is dead, I have only tears for his sad end.'[12] Her compassion was genuine. She told Caroline that she had asked the Austrian authorities for permission to spend a few days with her. Caroline replied: 'I have received your letter. Permit me to say no more about it. You can imagine my grief. I try not to give way to it so that it shall not rob me of the little strength that I have left and I do not wish to add another word on this subject, for I should not be able to hold back the tears that oppress my heart.[13]

In a house of woebegone servants and weeping children, she had to face a future that, even financially, was bleaker than ever. With Joachim dead, loans became more difficult to obtain, creditors quicker with demands for repayment. Even the home that she had just rented was not to be hers much longer. Metternich, fearing that the other Allies would be suspicious of her living so close to the Austrian court – and to her nephew the king of Rome, who after Waterloo was given the title of prince of Parma and then duke of Reichstadt – urged her to leave Hainburg as soon as possible. It was a melancholy Christmas and New Year. In France the decree of January 12, 1816, banished all members of the Bonaparte family, their wives, husbands and children; deprived them of their possessions, incomes and all civil rights in France and of the protection of the French embassies in whatever land they inhabited. Fearful that they might engineer Napoleon's escape from St Helena, the Allies agreed that they should not be allowed to move from one place to another without permission from an Allied Commission to be summoned to Paris by the French foreign minister.

Metternich suggested she should find her new home in Prague or Brünn (he had specifically mentioned Bohemia or Moravia in his invitations to her and to Joachim), but Caroline did not intend to be hurried or dictated to. She protested to the kaiser at the inhumanity of ordering her and her children, accustomed to much warmer climes, to move to an even colder one in the middle of winter; and in any case she did not have the necessary capital to make another move so soon. Metternich accepted defeat and allowed her grace until the spring of 1816. She spent a fortnight with Elisa at Brünn in April, but could not find a suitable property, and she was still at Hainburg in August, when Jérôme and Catherine, now Prince and Princess of Montfort, received permission to leave Würtemburg. She invited them to use Hainburg as a temporary home while they looked for an estate of their own. Like many such arrangements, it was agreeable at first but went on too long. It was clouded by her debt to Jérôme, which he was constantly pressing her to pay; and it was a relief to all of them when the Montforts bought a house at Erlau. In this intensely competitive and mutually envious family, Catherine had the disadvantage of being touchy, suspicious and an outsider, royal by birth. But relations between the two sisters-in-law remained superficially amicable. When Caroline found herself an estate at Frohsdorf, a few miles north of Wiener Neustadt on the Vienna road, and the Austrians objected that the Montforts, at Erlau, were too close to Schoenbrunn and the duke of Reichstadt, they moved to Schönau, only ten miles from Frohsdorf.

Caroline was forced to sell many of her clothes and her valuable collection of *vermeil de Rome* to make a deposit on Frohsdorf, which she bought, together with the Katzeldorf estate, for 100,000 florins, hoping to pay off the outstanding debt with profits from the estate. She approached her mother, who had throughout the days of imperial opulence been putting away money in preparation for a time like this, but Madame Mère replied tartly through her chamberlain that 'what she has belongs entirely to the Emperor and she has already placed it at his disposal'.[14] Caroline then suggested that her mother and Pauline should come to live with her at Frohsdorf. It would bring most of the family together in Austria. Whether or not this was her true reason for the proposal, Catherine and Elisa (who had previously asked Letitia to live with her) assumed that Caroline was trying to get her hands on the considerable fortunes of Madame Mère and Pauline. Both of them urged Pauline not to exchange the sun and comparative freedom of Italy for the cold climate and strict surveillance of Austria.

The affair swelled up into a misery of suspicion and oblique recrimination. Pauline was upset that Catherine wrote to Madame Mère behind her back. Caroline wrote on July 10, 1817 to Louis in the neutrality of Rome: 'Jérôme and Catherine are still annoyed with me, they think self-interest was the reason for that proposal',[15] but she protested that her only aim was to unite the family so that they could forget past glories, renounce future ambitions, and live quietly together. 'If one does not get involved in anything, one can live at peace, free from any unpleasantness. But if one has descended from the throne and still demands the same marks of respect, the same deference, it is clear that one will be disappointed. . . . The only seemly thing to do . . . is to live in the most profound retirement.'[16]

To Hortense, with whom she had determinedly kept in touch,[17] she wrote: 'Music, drawing and languages take up all our time. Letitia has recently developed a taste for etching and is getting on quite well with it. You will be able to judge for yourself, for she intends to send you a view of Frohsdorf . . . I have passed on all your messages to Jérôme and his wife; they were touched by your remembering them. We live two post-stages apart, which is not enough to prevent our seeing each other frequently; though they do most of the journeying because it is not easy for me to get about with all my children. But I am on the point of going to them with my whole household – the 15th is Jérôme's birthday and he is expecting us. His estate is charming, the park very agreeable and everything well appointed; but I prefer my own, which, without being as elegant, has everything that one needs in the country, from which I do not budge.'[18]

Neither Catherine nor Jérôme was happy with the country life. Their discontent worked itself off on Caroline, since she was the relation nearest to hand, and was exaggerated in their letters to the rest of the family. The unhappy Pauline, lonely and broken in body, begged them 'Let us love each other! What happiness can there be for me, without husband, without children, if I am at odds with my brothers and sisters as well?'[19] She reconciled Lucien with the others and he wrote a friendly letter to Caroline[26] announcing that Alexandrine 'has just given me my fifth boy; mother and child are doing marvellously. I take this opportunity to give you the names of my children, since you may not know them, the bizarre events of fortune having kept us apart for so many years: Charlotte, Christine, from my first marriage; Anna, from my wife's first marriage; Charles, Letizia, Paul, Jeanne, Louis, Pierre and Antoine.'[20]

But in February, 1819, Catherine wrote to Elisa that she and Jérôme no longer visited Frohsdorf, where they encountered nothing but vexatiousness. 'We have to assume that Caroline is well pleased that we should be on this footing, because when Jérôme was ill she did not come to see him, and when I was myself ill twice recently, she did not even send to inquire how I was. . . . Would you believe that after I had had the courtesy to inform her of the death of my sister-in-law [Caterina-Pavlovna of Russia, her brother William's second wife] she did not come to see me. Achille, now completely recovered, has not even come to thank us for our attentions during his long and terrible illness. It is not the poor child's fault, and I will say more – Caroline is not her own mistress to do as she wishes, she herself is subjugated and dominated'[21] – a reference to General Macdonald whom Caroline was believed to have secretly married.

Later in the year the Montforts bought themselves a second house: in Trieste, to be near Elisa, who had obtained permission to move there in 1816, and to spare their son and Catherine the rigours of winter at Schönau. They did not long enjoy Elisa's company. Plagued with depression and gout, the eldest of the Bonaparte sisters died on August 7, 1820.

Achille had a serious illness in the autumn of 1818 which seemed at first to be a recurrence of his childhood fits, but then developed into a form of paralysis. This was eventually cured, though he was for months unable to make full use of his hands. The trouble was almost certainly as much psychological as physical, for he had suffered more acutely than the other children from the shock and circumstances of his father's death. Raised in the shadow of the towering, heroic Joachim, he was orphaned to the harsh clamour – from relations as well as strangers – that his hero was a traitor and a villain. He had spent his impressionable boyhood in Italy, from seven to fourteen. France for him was the gross Bourbon whose cousin had shot his father, or the tubby little dictator with cold eyes and a fondness for pinching small boys' cheeks and pulling their hair. France was the nation that accused his father of treason. Italy was streets full of cheering people, lines of rattling, glittering cavalrymen saluting him as their colonel, rich palaces in which he was crown prince.

He stated his position with an emotionalism inherited from his father, and clung to it with his mother's stubbornness: 'I am not French; I never want to be. I am Italian; I shall always be Italian,'[22] he would exclaim. 'Even at table,' Maret's wife wrote in November 1817, 'he flies into ridiculous rages about France. . . . Scarcely sixteen, he is already as big and strong as a man of twenty-five . . . Yet they say his health is undermined by debauchery . . . But all agree on his courage, too.'[23] He was restless, energetic, unruly. Disillusioned with France, irked by the strait-jacket of the Austrian police, resigned to the impossibility of a return to Naples, he looked across the Atlantic to the United States where his uncle Joseph pursued a life of princely splendour at Point Breeze and the simpler citizens lived in the freedom and equality of which he regarded his father as the shining champion.

Count Sedlnitzky, the new chief of Police, refused to believe that Caroline had no ambition to return to the throne of Naples, and saw in Achille's sympathy for liberal ideas the first steps towards an understanding with the Carbonari. In June 1819, he reported that Joachim's niece, Clotilde, was on a visit to Frohsdorf and that he suspected that 'Madame Murat is still maintaining a faction in Naples and Madame Corigliano has been appointed to work for her there'.[24] Metternich thought this an unjustified scare and the kaiser agreed with him, but they changed their minds in the summer of 1820, when a revolution against the Bourbon monarch of Spain was followed by a similar uprising in Naples. The Austrian police entered and searched Frohsdorf. 'If that sort of thing is to continue,' Caroline protested to Metternich, '. . . I shall beg His Majesty to put me and my family into a fortress which would be a great deal more suitable.'[25]

It might even have solved some of her troubles, for she was chronically short of money, and being pressed for the repayment of debts which Joachim had contracted in the last months of his life. Some she resisted firmly, notably in a protracted legal suit brought by General Franceschetti. But where she believed the claim to be genuine, she did her utmost to meet Joachim's commitments – as in the case of Maceroni, who claimed payment of the draft for 40,000 francs. In June 1819 she gave Armand, Joachim's valet, a pension of 300 francs and to Mercey, her former secretary who was helping to look after her affairs in Paris, she wrote: 'I am upset at not having been able to do more for him but you will be able to judge my unhappy position when I tell you that the little pension I have promised him embarrasses me a great deal.'[26] She asked for his advice about Clotilde. On her marriage to the duke of Corigliano, Joachim had given her a pension which Caroline was still having to pay. It was this – not a revolutionary plot – that Clotilde went to Frohsdorf to discuss in the summer of 1819. 'I want to do what the king would have done in my position,' Caroline told Mercey, but did not conceal 'the difficulty in which I find myself at the moment, having nothing more that I can sell and being obliged to borrow small sums at considerable interest to meet my current expenses. My estate costs me more than it brings in; this is only temporary, but none the less embarrassing for that.'[27]

Mercey sold some investments for her in March 1820, and she gradually came to rely on him more and more, as a business agent, as an adviser, and as a sympathetic listener. Thanking him for the greetings that he sent her for New Year 1821, she said. 'You have good reason . . . to wish me a happier future, for Frohsdorf is a very sad place – everything is bearing down on me at the same time. . . . You know how much the General [Macdonald] would like to help me, but he does not understand this sort of thing.'[28] A few days later weariness reduced her to uncharacteristic self-pity. She asked Mercey to find her a companion, healthy and able to take walks – but middle-aged. 'If she is young there will be love affairs and intrigues, and I need peace. I feel myself getting old, and my task is becoming too much for me.'[29]

It was a passing mood. She had lost none of her skill as a hostess. Her guests fell under her charm as she sat with them in the garden room, where the curtains embroidered by the girls and herself with red hortensias on a white background[30] were drawn back and the doors opened on to the terrace, the aloes in tubs, the balustrade, the fountains beyond, and the wood in the distance. 'It grew dark. . . . The evening air was so aromatic, the nightingales sang so sweetly, the full moon stood so bright and still in the sky . . . An optimistic smile flitted across her features, softly lit by the light of the moon. "You will see, things will go well for us again," she exclaimed, "we were never a brake on spiritual progress; we loved glory, greatness, truth and beauty – that sort of thing is not forgotten." '[31]

Napoleon's death on May 5, 1821, brought some relaxation in the supervision of members of his family who were suspected of plotting his return, but the watch on Caroline, the only Bonaparte with the remotest chance of regaining a kingdom, continued. She had unsuccessfully asked for permission to go to Rome in December 1819 and February 1820; now she repeated the request, on the grounds that her mother needed comforting. It was again refused.

Unable to go herself, Caroline sent General Macdonald at the beginning of November, 1821. There was talk of his arranging a marriage between Achille and one of Lucien's daughters; but his visit had a more important purpose. In April 1816, when Jérôme first asked Caroline to repay his half-million francs, she wrote to her uncle Fesch saying that the only way Jérôme could be prevented from pressing the matter in the courts was for her mother to oppose the repayment on the grounds that Jérôme owed her 300,000 francs which Caroline ought to pay to her instead of to him. The shrewd old lady did exactly that – and promptly insisted on Caroline settling the debt. Macdonald's mission – to persuade

her to grant a period of grace – was unsuccessful. Letizia's demands became more frequent and more sharply worded. Caroline
was compelled to reverse her argument. 'My very dear Mama,'
she wrote, 'I will remind you, that at the beginning of 1815 my
capital, where I had the happiness of having you, was threatened
with imminent revolt because of lack of funds to pay the garrison . . . I asked you for money and you refused. It was in the
extremity that I turned to my brother Jérôme and asked him for
the loan of 500,000 francs. . . . Not having the entire sum that I
requested, he asked – and obtained – from you 300,000 francs. . . .
I gave him a receipt, and acknowledged that *I had received it from
him, and owed it to him*. In my agreement with Jérôme your name
was not mentioned.'[32]

Caroline sold some of her pictures[33] – ironically to the marquess
of Londonderry, whose half-brother Castlereagh had been
Joachim's implacable opponent – and used part of the proceeds to
finance Achille's journey to America, for the Allies had at last
granted him permission to leave, after receiving his written
promise not to return to Europe without their consent. Caroline
was heartbroken to see him go, but he was thoughtful enough to
write frequently to her, and to tell her how much he appreciated
her past affection for him though he may have been too boorish to
show it. 'I want to share with you all the happiness he has brought
me, my good Mercey,'[34] she wrote three weeks after his departure.
'His behaviour has been perfect and his heart excellent. If my
affairs can be set in order I do not think I shall be able to resist the
pleasure of joining him and living close to him. All his little outbursts and contrarieties which often grieved me, have completely
disappeared; for six months past I have had nothing but praise for
his change of manner and his tender affection.'[35] Her other son was
delighting her too. (The girls were never any worry.) 'Tell
Mosbourg,' she said in the same letter, 'that Lucien is absolutely
the living portrait of his father. . . . He has the same impulsiveness,
the same good looks, the same contempt for danger. . . . It is a pity
that he will have to spend his life hunting stags and hares.'[36]

Achille left Frohsdorf on December 17, 1822, and arrived at
Hamburg ten days later, but the icebound harbour delayed his
departure for America until the spring of 1823. He had scarcely
arrived at his uncle Joseph's palatial estate at Point Breeze than he

learned that the French had invaded Spain to restore Bourbon absolutism. He sailed across the Atlantic again, determined to offer his sword to the revolutionaries, but by the time he arrived at Gibraltar the French army was in control of the whole of Spain. He was back in America by October. He had broken his word to the Allies not to return to Europe without permission, and had attempted to aid a rebellion against the king of Spain, ally of the king of France. Caroline wept, wrote reproaching him for embarking on such a stupid adventure, and told him that when Macdonald heard the news he was so aghast that he turned pale and lost his breath.

Early that year, Metternich, without consulting the Allies, had given her permission to take the waters at Battaglia and then to move to Venice, partly for the sake of her health and partly so that she might raise some capital by selling Frohsdorf, which continued to be more of a liability than an asset. 'The countryside here is charming,' she wrote to Mercey. 'I am delighted to have found my Italian tongue again, and I talk to everybody I meet. I have been almost deaf and dumb for eight years, for you know that I do not understand German.'[37] Now, following Achille's mad escapade, she learned that the French refused to consider her claim for compensation and that Metternich was acceding to the Neapolitan request to have her sent back to Frohsdorf.

She had found a suitable though undistinguished husband for Letitia – the thirty-four-year-old Guido Taddeo, Marchese Pepoli, conte di Castiglione – but the worry of meeting the cost of the marriage made her ill. She was in bed for six days with a fever and the ceremony, on October 27, 1823, had to be conducted in her room. In February 1824, she warned Metternich that if she did not soon receive a settlement of her claims she would have to apply to the kaiser for help in supporting her family. As for the continued pressure for her to be ejected from Venice, she would consider going to Trieste, or right out of Austria to live with Antoinette in Switzerland, or with Joseph's wife, Julie Bonaparte[38] in Holland. When her claims against France and Naples were settled, she would go to the United States, where her younger boy Lucien, intended to emigrate as soon as permission was granted. Meanwhile she moved into an apartment that she rented in Trieste.

The Conference of Ministers assembled in Paris on the last day of June 1824. They refused to let Caroline live in Switzerland or Holland, since these were too close to France; nor in Venice or Trieste because they were too close to Naples. They preferred her to be kept in Austria, but raised no objections to her going to America with Lucien. Caroline exploded with rage. 'I am exhausted; my patience is at an end . . . I cannot understand all these contradictions,' she wrote to Metternich. 'They are compelling me to quit every country in which I can find peace, and closing every town to me with the exception of those which are unsuited either to my taste or my health – or my means.'[39] She made no attempt to move from Trieste.

To Julie Récamier, who had spent three months in Naples and from whom she was delighted to receive a letter on her saint's day, she replied: 'Only if I saw you could I tell you of the persecutions that are inflicted on me in the name of the French Government . . . my second son left me a fortnight ago . . . my second daughter will soon be settled . . . Why do they refuse me what my family has so easily obtained? They are peaceful in Rome, they travel and meet with no difficulties . . . I am the only one who is persecuted.'[40] In May 1825, after spending the winter in Rome, Julie made a detour through Trieste on her way back to Paris. She called on Caroline and found her in bed – it was eleven at night – but they talked for an hour or more and in the morning a bouquet of flowers was brought to Julie's bedside with a note from Caroline: 'What a day I am going to have, dear Juliette! . . . Tell my valet de chambre at what hour you wish to have the carriage, and what you wish to do today.'[41] When Julie arrived at the house, Caroline introduced Louise and General Macdonald and then they all went to call on Elisa's daughter, Napoléone. Julie's own niece noticed that Caroline had with Louise 'a relationship of the most confiding tenderness; with General Macdonald, a feeling of affection mixed with a shade of domination.'[42]

On August 21, 1824, Caroline's first grandchild was born, and named after her. Letitia came to stay in October, bringing the baby with her in an attempt to lessen Caroline's grief at Lucien's departure for America. Sorrow soon turned to exasperation. When the ship on which Lucien was travelling called at Malaga for repairs, he foolishly accepted an invitation to go shooting and was clapped into prison as soon as he set foot ashore – brother of the man who had tried to join the revolution of 1823, son of the man who had crushed the nationalist rising of the *dos de Mayo* – a useful captive for almost any propaganda purpose. Achille appealed for help to President Adams and the United States Ambassador prevailed on the Spanish Government to release Lucien, who finally arrived in America on June 19, 1825. Macdonald wrote to a friend, 'I am distressed to see new incidents occurring every day to fill the queen's life with bitterness. All the sacrifices she has imposed on herself are of no avail to mitigate the hardships of her fate.'[43] But they did not break her spirit – nor her resolve to remain in Trieste.

Metternich ordered her to move to Görtz. She answered that she would not go unless force was used, and then it would be as a political prisoner to be supported at Austria's expense. From month to month, and then from year to year the most powerful minister of the most powerful state in Europe, representing the entire anti-Bonapartist force of the Continent, failed to put down this woman. And in the summer of 1826 Metternich admitted defeat. So she was allowed to stay where she was.

2

The prolonged battle had left her outwardly unscarred, unlike Jérôme, whom the countess von Kielmannsegg had seen in Rome a year before and found 'so grey and aged that I scarcely recognized him.'[1] Caroline, approaching her mid-forties, had put on a little weight but, in the words of Julie Récamier's niece, 'was still remarkably pretty; she had preserved almost the full radiance of her youth'.[2] A legacy from Pauline, who died on June 9, 1825, at the age of forty-five, enabled her to buy the Villa Campo di Marzo from Elisa's widower Felix Baciocchi. But she had no success with her claims against the French and Neapolitan governments. The Conseil d'Etat had in July 1823 refused to recognize the validity of the decree, signed by the five members of the provisional government on July 5, 1815, which restored his French properties to Murat. Franceschetti took his claims against her to court.

Caroline put in a reply. He lost, appealed; lost and appealed again; lost the third time and did not return.

In June 1828, while Jérôme and Catherine were in Italy, she went to stay in Schönau to negotiate the sale of Frohsdorf to the Russian general, Aleksandr Yermoloff. Elisa's daughter, the twenty-two-year-old Napoléone Camerata, joined the party and went for a day's outing with Caroline's *dame de compagnie*, Mademoiselle de Braig, to nearby Baden. There, on the promenade, they caught sight of the duke of Reichstadt; Napoléone, a fervent admirer of her dead uncle, leaned out of the carriage window and shouted indignantly, 'Aren't you ashamed to wear Austrian uniform?'[3] Fortunately there were no repercussions, and Metternich even paid a friendly private call on Caroline before she left Schönau.

She was back in Trieste by early October, when she gave help to another of Joachim's lame ducks – Louis Ferrari, who had accompanied the king on the expedition to Pizzo but had fallen on evil days. She engaged him as a cook (but had to discharge him two years later because all his recipes were too expensive). To Mercey she wrote: 'I expect Letitia here at any moment, I have at last persuaded Louise to have her baby here. I hope to have her with me by the end of November; so you see the winter will be very happy for me.'[4] But as usual there were clouds in the sky. 'I am very distressed by the letters I receive from Achille. My sons think I am not giving enough attention to our claims, and as they are very embarrassed for money they want to act without me. My daughters are a little of the same opinion as their brothers.'[5]

To add to her worries, there was argument about the terms of sale of Frohsdorf which involved her in a new lawsuit, dragging on into 1829 and 1830. 'I am grateful for the letter you wrote to Achille,' she told Mercey in the summer of 1829. 'I receive letters from both my sons which are extremely distressing; they are completely mistaken about my financial position, constantly asking me for money and believing that I refuse them because I want to. I beg you, good Mercey, to repeat the sad truth to Achille that I have not a penny in income, that I am making sacrifices to give them the pensions they receive, that Frohsdorf is all I have left and it is entirely impossible for me to make fresh sacrifices.'[6] Her favourite niece, Lucien's second daughter, Christine, brought her second husband, Lord Dudley Coutts Stuart[7] to stay for several weeks in July, and at the end of the month Caroline went to Vienna to deal with new developments in the Frohsdorf case.

The peculiar fear with which the Bourbons regarded her was demonstrated in their opposition to her visiting her mother in Rome, where they suspected she might hatch some unspecified plot against Naples. The Montforts had been allowed to make long stays with Madame Mère, and Hortense was a frequent visitor, but Caroline's applications were stolidly rejected. On April 22, 1830, the Letizia, now in her eightieth year, fell and broke her hip while walking in the garden of the Villa Borghese. Hortense wrote to Caroline, who replied on May 2, thanking her and adding indignantly, 'I was totally unaware of it, and I am very grieved that my brothers sent me no news. I am very sorry that I am not permitted to leave for Rome, and I cannot tell you how anxious and upset I am. I enclose a letter for Mama; give it to her yourself and tell her of my distress at not being able to come and nurse her.'[8] She asked Louise to go to Rome on her behalf and wrote to Metternich for permission 'to embrace my dying mother',[9] adding that if the answer were a refusal, she demanded that it be given to her in writing. Metternich approved. She left on May 24, Macdonald staying behind in Trieste to deal with the money from the Frohsdorf estate, which had finally been paid and now needed to be invested. But for her it truly seemed that as one door opened another shut – she had just learned from America that 'Lucien continues to get into debt; he already has new ones amounting to 10,000 francs and the 30,000 francs that I lent him are all spent.'[10]

On hearing of Metternich's compassionate gesture, Ferdinand of the Two Sicilies complained to the Allied Commission, asking that Caroline should be ordered back to Trieste. On June 13, Caroline arrived in Rome and saw her mother for the first time for fifteen years. In Paris, the commission agreed to ask the Pope to expel her immediately. Caroline learned of this on June 20. She applied to the Austrian ambassador for a few days longer with her mother. The ambassador went to consult the papal Secretary of State. The pope, with a gesture hallowed by tradition, washed his hands of the affair, asking the ambassador to submit the problem to the Allied Envoys.

Caroline was visited by Henry Edward Fox,[11] who found her

amid a confusion of 'half-packed trunks, boxes, waste-paper',[12] in Hortense's apartment in the Palazzo Ruspoli. Fox, a prominent liberal who had many friends in common with Caroline, including the Dudley Stuarts, was 'much struck by the great remains of beauty she still possesses. She is stout, and her figure is not good, but rather thick and stumpy; however, notwithstanding that, she is very graceful and dignified in her motions. Her complexion, which I had heard was blotched and bad, was very clear and her features are regular and small. Her mouth has a very peculiar expression of firmness and decision, which when it relaxes into a smile is uncommonly pretty and playful. . . . Her voice is very sweet. She speaks French with a very strong Italian accent but with great fluency.'[13]

She was noticeably agitated, having just been told she must leave the next day. Although her servants had begun to pack, she assured Fox that 'having come to Rome to fulfil a sacred duty to her mother, probably on her death bed, she would yield to force alone and not go into her carriage till the military came to order her to do so'.[14] She had asked her Rome attorney, Giuseppi Vannutelli, and Louise's husband, Giulio Rasponi, to plead with the papal Secretary of State on her behalf and was to meet them in the Colosseum. She invited Fox to accompany her if he 'did not fear to be seen in her carriage'.[15] She spoke bitterly of the way the Allies were treating her, though Fox detected a touch of vanity when she spoke of 'the importance all the foreign courts seem to attach to her movements and the persecuting distinction they shew her, in contrast to the other members of the Bonaparte family'.[16]

Another little vanity still remained to her, too: the conviction of her ability to attract other women's husbands and lovers. Walking in the Colosseum, she confessed to Fox that 'had it not been for her affection for Christine *"elle aura volontiers fait tourner la tête à ce cher Dudley."*'[17] After half an hour pacing up and down the arena 'while her black skeleton dame-de-compagnie struggled to the summit',[18] they were joined by Rasponi and Vannutelli. The papal decision was that Caroline could stay for one more day, but must leave in the morning of Wednesday, June 23. She turned pale and, her voice shaking with emotion, said: 'Well, I will leave when they come to chase me out. One insult more or less will mean nothing to them.'[19] When she set off two days later for Trieste by way of Viterbo, her revenge was very close at hand: the July Revolution that removed Charles X from the throne of France. She spent twelve hours with Letitia on the Pepoli estate near Bologna, then 'fled as quickly as possible from the papal States where I had been so ill treated'.[20] She was home in Trieste by June 28.

The upheaval in France brought a new tremor to the Bonaparte family. Caroline, Lucien and Jérôme saw in it the promise of the repeal of the law that prevented them from returning to France and prosecuting their claims there. Joseph, hearing the news of a revolt but not its outcome, wrote to Jourdan and Belliard, calling on them to proclaim the duke of Reichstadt as Napoleon II. Lucien Bonaparte was frankly furious at the fuss his elder brother was making. He had been hoping for permission to return to France – but now: 'Joseph's protest, declaring war on the king of the French from his camp in New York, where he is safe and sound, has ruined everything.'[21]

Hortense, though letting it be known that Madame Mère strongly condemned Caroline and her two brothers for making approaches to the new French government that were 'unworthy of the name they bore',[22] was herself in no hurry to oppose it, for she had a claim for a million francs that she wanted to press in the French courts. Nor was she in any hurry to see the duke of Reichstadt come to the throne. He was sickly: only Joseph and Louis stood as elderly, improbable candidates between her two sons and the title of heirs to the Empire. Ever since her step-father's death on St Helena her ambitions had grown. Her friend, the countess of Kielmannsegge, had noticed as early as the spring of 1822 that she 'was beginning to throw off the mask',[23] and that the 'gentle, very sentimental'[24] side of her nature was spoiled by her 'inclination towards intrigue which makes her a creature who can neither attract nor hold people'.[25] She took to wearing a crown when receiving visitors, and for her Sunday receptions she revived the ceremonial of the former imperial *cercle*.

The revolutionary explosion in Paris was only one of many. The Poles turned against their Russian masters, the people of the Southern Netherlands declared themselves an independent nation under the ancient title of Belgians, the Greeks won freedom from the Turks – and in Italy, counting on support from France, the nationalists rose in rebellion in the Papal States. Both of Hortense's sons enlisted with the rebels. The Austrian troops marched in, Louis-Philippe failed to support the patriots, and the revolt collapsed. Hortense's elder son, Napoléon-Louis, struck down not by bullets but by measles, died at Forli on March 17, 1831.

His death brought genuine sorrow to Caroline, who had been an indulgent aunt in his childhood and had met him frequently since he had been living with his father in Florence. It had been another bitter-sweet winter. Macdonald was in Paris, still pursuing the claim for restitution of the Murat properties in France. When Mercey wrote to Caroline, evidently with some flattering reference to Macdonald's good fortune in spending his life with her, she replied: 'You have too high an opinion of my character. Believe me, the general is not to be envied. For fifteen years, far from his family and his native land, faced with problems of every sort, his devotion has only grown the more, but I suffer to see him deprived of everything that is dear to him and I am only too sensible that my character, embittered by sorrows, can do nothing to recompense him. I confess that I like you too much to wish you such a fate.'[26] In January 1831, she told him: 'The weather is magnificent. We have had no winter this year and yet I catch cold walking from one room to another; you can see, good Mercey, that we are growing old – and despite all the ills of old age, I would not wish to go back.'[27] Three days later she learned that Louise had given birth to her fourth boy:[28] 'so I am a grandmother for the eighth time!'[29] Unfortunately her sons brought her less joy than her grandsons.

Achille, burning to lead the liberation of Italy, arrived in London on February 14, 1831, with his wife,[30] a great-grand-niece of George Washington. He was fat and prematurely bald. The past eight years in America had not greatly increased his fortune; neither had his marriage. 'My wife did not bring me a penny in her dowry,' he told Mercey. 'She had some property of her own which according to the law of the country, is mine now. This property consisted of ten negroes, seven of them children, eating and bringing nothing in, and an old house in Virginia that they have not been able to let for the past three years and whose sole value is a fire insurance for 3,000 dollars.'[31] He had tried his luck as a planter on two estates in Florida which he nostalgically named Parthenope and Lipona; he had dabbled in various wild-cat development schemes; he had set up as a lawyer; he had taken part in skirmishes against the Seminole Indians and retired with the rank of colonel of militia; he had cured his youthful physical disabilities with a diet of mint-juleps; he had lost half the little finger of his right hand in a duel; and he had enthusiastically adopted the new-world habit of chewing tobacco. (During his courting days he considerately took with him a shaggy snuff-coloured dog in case his future mother-in-law forgot to provide him with a spittoon.) The new world was not quite as favourably impressed by some of his old world tastes and habits. 'He boasted of never removing his boots from the first use until worn out,'[32] and disliked water so much that, when he fell into a vat of warm sugar his first fear was, he later said, not that he would be scalded but that "Kate will make me wash". His taste in food was catholic; he claimed to have tried all the birds and reptiles in Florida, found buzzards not good but alligators acceptable. During one of the Indian skirmishes, wild hogs which had been feeding on the enemy dead were shot and roasted. Achille, eating a large chop, saw his commanding officer, General R. K. Call, look at him askance. "I know why you no eat de pork – because he eat Indian,' he remarked. 'But I just soon eat Indian if he well fried.'[33]

He found to his dismay that Louis-Philippe had no intention of intervening in Italy, nor of allowing him to enter France. The other Allied Powers tried, but failed, to have him expelled from England. By April he was in touch with conspirators in France who proposed that he should lead a revolution by the combined Bonapartist and Republican factions. The Duke of Reichstadt would be proclaimed as Napoleon II, but with a constitution modelled on that of 1791, and with Achille as Regent until the young emperor could get out of Austria.

Hortense and Louis, fleeing from the Italian fiasco, arrived in London in May 1831 and rented a house at 30 George Street. Achille called to pay his respects to his aunt and to present his wife, who unfortunately did not speak French. He returned in the evening and with his customary confidence gave the company an exciting account of his future plans and past exploits, painting a rosy picture of the state of his finances and claiming an income of

£15,000 a year from his plantation, 'the most beautiful in the region, which people come to see from miles around',[34] and where 'he gives balls for which his Negroes form the orchestra'.[35] All this, he told them, he had mortgaged, then borrowed another 50,000 francs from the bank, and hastened to Europe as the representative of his uncle Joseph,[36] who in turn represented the claims of Napoleon II. 'When it is a question of the fate of Europe,' he declared, 'one has no right to consider one's personal interests!'[37]

This talk of senior members of the family and the duke of Reichstadt did not fall too kindly on Hortense's ears. She wished her nephew would 'remember the urgent letters in which his mother preaches moderation and prudence to him'.[38] Her companion, Valérie Masuyer, noted that 'Queen Hortense adheres to the same point of view as Queen Caroline. She wants to have her million francs returned first'.[39] When her son Louis was approached by one of Achille's associates asking for support for the coup in favour of the duke of Reichstadt, he dutifully replied that 'in the unfortunate circumstances in which he found himself, the things of this world no longer interested him, and having no personal ambition, he would never introduce trouble or civil war into his native land'.[40] Achille's own interest waned when the great anti-monarchical uprising which he had expected to take place in Paris on July 14, 1831, turned out to be only a few scattered scuffles. He was by then doubtful whether he wanted either Hortense or Louis as associates. 'She is too sly for my taste and I too frank for her,' he wrote to Caroline. 'She keeps her son in swaddling clothes, which makes him a laughing stock';[41] though this did not prevent his getting involved in a plot later in the year in which Hortense opened an account in Paris of 12,000 francs to be used in bribing garrisons in Eastern France.

Caroline, deeply disturbed by the behaviour of her nephews in Italy and the incautious talk of her son in London, was seeking some means of seeing Achille again. If she could not go to England, perhaps he could get permission to visit her in Austria or Italy. She had not met his wife – and never did. Neither had she met the other American girl[42] whom Lucien was to marry that year. But she by now had plenty of accounts of Lucien's escapades. Faced with a violent rainstorm after a night of playing billiards in a Bordentown tavern, he saved his clothes from getting wet by tying them in a bundle and running home naked. He appeared in court on a charge of kicking a stable boy, for which he was found guilty and fined six cents – one for each kick. And he had given more than one smart rap on the knuckles to his uncle Joseph. 'You were born a miserable Corsican peasant,' he told him on one occasion. 'You happened to have a brother who had more brains than is frequently allotted to mankind. He grasped the sceptre of the world and elevated you to the rank of a sovereign ... I, on the contrary, was born on the steps of a throne.'[43]

Caroline wrote to Christine and Dudley to thank them for the kindness they had shown to Achille. 'I beg you to help him in a society of which he knows nothing,' she said anxiously to Christine. 'Your advice and that of the excellent Dudley will certainly be welcome to him. Although I am happy that my son is in England and enjoys being there, I have some anxiety about the expenses which he will be obliged to incur.'[44] To Dudley she was more explicit: 'I shall be most distressed if he undertakes engagements in the hope that our claims [on the French Government] will be met and that he would later find it embarrassing to fulfil, and that he should return to America without the slightest means ... you to watch over my son. Money worries are cruel things – he does not yet understand this.'[45] And to Christine: 'I should have liked to send some good presents to my daughter-in-law, but the ruinous lawsuit over Frohsdorf and all the expenses of our claim [in Paris] have made it impossible ... I cannot do more than ask you to give her the muff, the tippet and the fur trimming that I sent you to sell for me, to tell her the price I was asking, and help her to sell them if that is agreeable to her.'[46]

In August she learned that Achille was in Belgium, where King Leopold gave him permission to set up headquarters in Ath and recruit a Foreign Legion. This was too much for the horrified Allies. Leopold received a sharp rebuke and Achille found himself confronted with a series of unexplained and insurmountable obstacles. He had now created so much disturbance and alarm that Caroline could have no further hope that he would be able to visit her. 'I could not be more grieved by my son's visit to Brussels, his petition to the Chambers, his plans to stay a good deal longer on the Continent,' she wrote to Mercey. 'He thinks he is expediting our claims, and I am sure he is doing the opposite.'[47]

Her courage sapped by more than fifteen years of battle and almost unrelieved reverses, she succumbed in September 1831 to the epidemic of cholera that began to sweep through Europe that year. 'For a week past,' Macdonald wrote to Mercey on September 9, 1831, 'the queen has kept to her bed. The illness that attacked her, characterized at first by gastric trouble, has become much more serious: continual spasmodic agitation, constant fever, pains in the nervous system – these are the symptoms.'[48] She was fortunate in one thing: that she had two daughters to comfort her. When they had nursed her back to health, she applied to Metternich for permission to move to Tuscany.

Metternich, touched by the plight of the woman who had once been his friend and perhaps his mistress, warmly recommended Caroline's request when he submitted it to the Paris Conference. The Neapolitan envoy raised the inevitable objections, but this time there was no support from France. Louis-Philippe, though he still did not want Bonapartes in his own country,[49] was aware of the outcry which harsh treatment of the ailing countess might arouse in the liberal press. His representative announced that if the proposal was acceptable to Austria, who had the greatest interest in preserving peace in Italy, then France would raise no objection. Caroline was granted a six-month permit. She stayed for a time in Louis's appartments in Florance, close to the Palazzo Corsini the brilliant setting of her early married life, thirty years before, but now her situation was 'very restricted and precarious'.[50] Jérôme and his family also moved to Florence in 1831. Caroline rented the Casa Capponi in the Via del Mandorlo, which was 'convenient, but very small and quite new',[51] and where the smell of paint gave her a cold. In June 1832 she rented the Palazzo Griffoni[52] in the via Borgo Ognissanti and in November she bought it outright. The six months came to an end. There was no mention on either side of a renewal or withdrawal. Achille, after a final mad fling in April 1832, when he planned to rally the patriots of Italy but got no farther than Portugal, practised his literary skill in London for a while and then went back to Florida in the summer of 1833.

Settled at last in the congenial atmosphere of Florence, spending the summer months in the house Pauline had left her at Viareggio, Caroline renewed her onslaught on the French government. The 500,000 francs a year that the Murats were paid while they were in

Naples represented five per cent interest on the 10,000,000 francs' worth of property that they surrendered in France. Caroline demanded either the return of the property in accordance with the decree signed by Fouché and the other members of the Provisional Government in 1815, or the payment of the capital, plus accumulated interest – a total of well over 20,000,000 francs.

In 1834, Hortense published an account of her travels in Austria, France and Italy three years earlier. It appeared in a magazine, and separately as a slim book. Two sentences were devoted to the Murats. 'In London, I found Murat's son, who had just arrived from America with his young wife,' she wrote. 'His views are entirely republican, but I could have wished that he had been brought up with more recognition of the fact that he was French, and that he only became prince of Naples by the grace of France and the emperor.'[53]

It was a malicious reopening of old wounds and, after Caroline's affectionate correspondence over so many years, entirely unexpected. Hortense feigned surprise that Caroline should have taken the remark amiss, and promised to remove it if the book were reprinted. 'It is of little consequence to me that the duchesse de St Leu has cut in the second edition what she stupidly wrote in the first,' Caroline told Mercey. 'What wounded me, and hurt me, and still hurts me, is to have to give up an illusion that was dear to me, and to experience a bitter disappointment that I would never have anticipated.'[54] It brought on a physical distress and – though there were other graver reasons for her increasing ill-health – she wrote to Mercey several days later that 'I am suffering a great deal from my stomach attacks, which have started up again, very violently'.[55] The pain from now on became almost continual, though she seldom let it show. She still entertained her friends with music and cards, and above all with conversation. 'About midnight, the habituées of the Palazzo Griffoni gathered round to talk, exchanging stories until morning. There was an inexpressible charm in those vigils; the room was still in all the disarray of the concert or the ball, but the dancers and the artistes had disappeared, the parts were still scattered on the music stands, the lamps extinguished on the whist tables and the four chairs vacant around each of them; after all the joyful noise, the family conversation – with tea and beautiful waffles stamped with the arms of the queen of Naples.'[36]

The death of Jérôme's Catherine in November 1835 was followed by that of Madame Mère on February 2, 1836. The painter Gigoux arrived in Rome that day with letters from Caroline whom he had visited in Florence. The one addressed to her mother he was unable to deliver. The one for Fesch the cardinal refused to accept. The publication of the will produced a fresh family squabble. Lucien and Caroline considered that Joseph and Louis had been unfairly favoured. The men, Joseph, Lucien, Louis and Jérôme, demanded that the will should be executed under Roman law, which gave them larger shares of the residue than the women; Caroline and Elisa's daughter, Napoléone Camerata, insisted on the Code Napoléon, which treated them as equals. Furious letters were exchanged. Louis sent Caroline a lengthy opinion provided by his lawyers, proving the justice of his case. 'I am much too ill to reply at length,' she answered. 'We have different points of departure, my dear brother, you believe that I do not have any rights, and I am certain that I do. I should have to have none at all to accept the proposition that you offer me.'[57]

Hortense wrote to her when her mother died, but she was in no mood to forgive her. 'I am too ill to be able to reply in detail to everything you tell me in justification of what you wrote about Achille; perhaps you have forgotten the lines that distressed me so much; read them again and you will see that they are a peculiar way of expressing affection for him . . . Give my best wishes to Louis, my dear Hortense, and be sure that I can never forget our friendship and the happy days when we had mutual trust in each other.'[58]

In July, Thiers, Louis Philippe's *président du conseil*, gave permission for the countess of Lipona to visit Paris if she undertook 'not to stay more than a month, act with the greatest reserve while in France, and prevent any demonstration on the part of her friends that might disturb the peace'.[59] She had waited so long for the news that its coming upset her. The stomach pains became more severe 'so that I have no strength to do anything or concentrate on anything'.[60] She asked Mercey to try to find her former cook, Potain. 'Not to do any grand cooking for me, but because he knows what I can eat – for I am quite ill.'[61] It was a rough three-day crossing from Leghorn on the steamer *Sully*. She landed at Marseilles on September 3, very unwell, with the noise of the paddlewheels still banging in her head. It was raining and she could not get used to not seeing the sun, but, as she wrote to Louis, 'I am in my seventh heaven – travelling in France.'[62]

While looking for more permanent accommodation she stayed several weeks at No. 6 rue Royale with Meneval whose daughter Pauline had married Joachim's nephew Pierre-Gaetan. She found the legend of her past riches still endured; the price rose as soon as her name was mentioned. Finally, in the rue de la Ville-l'Evêque she came upon one of her rare admirers. 'The person who is letting it is Madame la comtesse de C . . . V . . . [Chateau-Villars] (the one who blew her husband's horse's brains out),' Stendahl wrote to a friend. 'When the critical moment arrived to say, "It is for Madame Murat", the person who was negotiating was very surprised: "Why did you not name Madame Murat earlier: for her it will be only five thousand francs a month and I will leave her the little ornaments that are on the tables." '[63] Caroline declined the loan of the ornaments for fear they should get broken, but was grateful for the kindness in a city where royalists hated her because she was a Bonaparte, and Bonapartists hated her because she was a Murat.

The faithful Agar was there, eager in support of her claims, unflagging in defence of his dead master. Laure Junot was back in Paris too, famous for the Memoirs that Balzac had helped her to get published; riddled with debt, buoyed up by increasing doses of opium, neglected by the last of her many lovers, the two beautiful rivals of thirty years before did not meet.[64] Lechat and Coussy called on her on the evening of her arrival in Paris and the former spent an afternoon with her a week later. He found her unwell but 'not as much changed as I had feared, after 22 years of absence – she still has her delightful smile'.[65] But she wept a little when she poke of her embarrassment at coming to beg favours from Louis-Philippe. 'I told Exelmans yesterday that I was braver than he . . . when I decided to return to France; but I have two sons in America who have gone through all the substance they had, and now have nothing.'[66] She faced difficult situations with courage and a cool dignity. While she was visiting Juliette Récamier at the Abbaye-aux-Bois, another caller was announced – Sosthène de la Rochefoucauld, who had distinguished himself at the Restoration by climbing up the column in the place Vendôme and putting a rope around the neck of the statue of Napoleon. Juliette asked Caroline if she should say she was out. 'No,' said Caroline, 'the statue has been restored to its place: I have forgotten the people who made it fall.'[67]

But some memories remained. She went to the Théatre-Française, discreetly out of the public view in a *loge-grillée*. As she listened to the voice of Mademoiselle Mars, as clear and youthful as it had been a quarter of a century before, the years suddenly fell away. 'I saw myself in that same theatre, not hidden ... but as a queen, beside the emperor, among his family and his court. All the past came back to me; it was only a momentary illusion, but it was delightful and very strong.'[68]

When Gigoux called on her she told him: 'I am going to Gérard's tomorrow; I shall walk up the little staircase where all the celebrities used to throng – yes, all the notabilities and all the interesting people and all the beauties of the time climbed that little staircase – and I shall be so happy to be back in those elegant, sympathetic little rooms.'[69]

At the end of October there was a new moment of anxiety. Since the death of the duke of Reichstadt, Hortense's surviving son had modified his decision 'never to introduce trouble or evil into his native land'. He attempted a *coup d'état* in the city of Strasbourg which failed miserably, but for a time looked like ending Caroline's stay in Paris. 'I hear ... that the Council of Ministers ... wishes her to leave,' Meneval wrote to Joseph on November 18. 'This poor princess will perhaps be forced to leave in ill-health, in a harsh season, and go to face the cholera that is raging in Italy.'[70] Fortunately Louis's escapade had been so clumsily planned and executed that it strengthened the government's position, though it upset the rest of the family. Joseph exclaimed indignantly: 'That ambitious young wretch might at least have given his father and me time to die first!'[71]

The claim for compensation dragged on. Her stay in Paris was extended from the winter of 1836 through the summer of 1837. In June she heard that the government refused to present her petition to the Chamber of Deputies, at any rate during that year. Meneval told Joseph that this was on the instructions of Louis-Philippe, perhaps out of pique because Caroline had in the end not brought herself to plead with him in person. 'One must in justice admit that the countess of Lipona has in no way fallen short of the reserve and dignity demanded by her brothers' position and her own name. I am not in her business confidence, but I fear that she may be in a precarious financial state ... These vexatious complications have cast her into a dejection which will arouse your concern. If you are kind enough to reassure her with a few friendly words, I think you will do her a great deal of good.'[72] But Joseph remained silent. On August 19, General Macdonald, whom she had left in charge of her affairs, died in Florence. And in October Hortense died at Arenenberg. Louis, in banishment, was unable to accompany his mother's body to its burial beside Josephine in the parish church at Rueil.

On the bitterly cold morning of January 8, 1838, Caroline took her place at the head of the mourners who advanced along the black-draped nave to the choir where the candle-lit coffin rested beneath a rich catafalque. By a trick of fate, she alone among the emperor's family brought her bitter-sweet memories to the burial of his adopted daughter. 'You would have found her very changed from when you saw her before,' Valérie Masuyer wrote to her aunt, 'because of the stomach complaint which she suffers from, and which killed her brother'. Yet she was 'still well preserved, above all in the nobility of her bearing'.[73]

On May 5, 1838, the seventeenth anniversary of Napoleon's death, she invited Marchand, with his wife and daughter, and Meneval to dinner. The talk was all of the empire and Caroline spoke kindly of Josephine, perhaps remembering the days of forty years past when she first fell in love with handsome Colonel Murat, and General Bonaparte's elegant wife did all she could to encourage the match. 'She was infinitely generous,'[74] she said. Her task was almost over. The lawyers were drawing up an agreement with the government, which proposed to pay her, not the 20 million francs capital, nor the yearly interest 500,000 francs, but a pension of 100,000 francs during her lifetime and of 50,000 francs to her children after her death. She returned to Florence in July.

The following month the Paris journal *La France*, revived the accusations of Joachim's deep involvement in the Enghien murder. Agar sprang to his defence, and was reminded of his former project of writing an account of Murat's actions in 1814 and 1815. He asked Caroline if she would lend him the necessary documents. 'Tell the whole truth,' she urged him when she sent them on September 4; 'that alone will command lasting belief. ... It is often the apparent contradictions that give portraits the stamp of truth. ... The king's character is rich enough for there to be no need to disguise the truth. Like all warmhearted men, the king had his weaknesses, but they were generous ones.'[75] She went to Viareggio, hoping that the sea air would do her good, but by now she was declining rapidly. She went back to Florence. Julie Bonaparte's daughter, Charlotte, died suddenly at Sarzana on March 2, 1839. Caroline visited her sister-in-law every day in an attempt to comfort her, but 'the spectacle of grief on one hand and the coldness of the house on the other', as her secretary Clavel wrote to Mercey on May 12, 1839, 'increased her sickness. ... She has been in bed for two months. ... The jaundice has become worse during the past week ... her stomach cannot tolerate anything ... she grows weaker and weaker.'[76] On May 18 she died.

Notes
Sources
Index

Notes

1

1 Giuseppe (1768), Napoleone (1769), Luciano (1775), Anna (1777), Luigi (1778), Paola (1780), Nunziata (1782), Girolama (1784); one son (1765) and three daughters (1767, 1771, 1773) died at birth or soon after; all the girls, like their parents, Maria-Letizia and Carlo-Maria, were called Maria

2 He spent a year at Ajaccio; returned Jan.-Jun., 1788, and again Sep. 1789–Jan. 1791

3 Nasica, 208

4 Son of Franz Fesch, Swiss officer in the Genoese army, 2nd husband of Angela-Maria Ramolino

5 Lautard, II, 76

6 *Ibid.*

7 Said to have been given her by Napoleon in memory of Caroline du Colombier, to whom he made tentative advances when newly commissioned

8 Larrey, I, 249

2

1 Originally La Bastide de Fortanier; since 1852 La Bastide-Murat

2 Not 12th, as usually stated, see Vanel, *Origines*

3 Lumbroso, *Corr.*, 6; Oct. 1972

4 Thiébault, I, 525

5 Bertrand, III, 86

6 May 10, 1796. Effective disproof of the legend – doubtful on other grounds – that Murat had an affair with Josephine during his visit to Paris; though Napoleon affected to believe it when it suited his purpose. See Agar's notes in Murat, *Murat en 1808*, 7

7 Arnault, II, 341–2. 'Pékins': Army slang for civilians

8 Ricard, 340–1

3

1 Napoleon had removed him from Juilly and sent him to Patrick MacDermott's Irish College, next door to Mme Campan's school

2 Now 61 rue du Rocher. Joseph bought it in 1798, sold it to Letizia 1801. Lucien lived at the present No. 30

3 Arjuzon, 89

4 *Ibid.*, 83–4

5 Hortense, *Mémoires*, I, 55–6

6 *Ibid.*, 56

4

1 Lumbroso, *Corr.,* 18–19
2 Montbel, 364
3 Nap. I, *Corr.,* V, 542 (4323), Alexandria, Jul. 28, 1799
4 Murat, *Lettres,* I, 26–7, Alexandria, Jul. 28, 1799
5 Nap. I, *Corr.,* V, 537 (4316), to Dugua, Alexandria, Jul. 27, 1799
6 Miot, 249

5

1 Arnault, IV, 393
2 *Ibid.*
3 Bonaparte, Lucien, *Mém. Sec.,* I, 74
4 Vandal, *Avènement,* I, 388
5 Hortense, *Mémoires,* I, 63
6 Abrantès, *Salons,* IV, 298
7 Campan, *Journal Anecdotique,* 29
8 Bertrand, I, 234
9 *Ibid.,* 193
10 *Ibid.,* II, 100
11 Caroline, whose name was given as Marie-Anonciate, had a dowry of 40,000 francs from her brothers. It was a civil ceremony, in the village hall at Plailly
12 Murat, *Lettres,* I, 35–6
13 Roustam, 93
14 Récamier, I, 111
15 Chastenay, I, 419. The occasion was a ball at Mme de Montesson's
16 Arjuzon, 163
17 In the angle of the present rue de Villiers and boulevard du Château. It had a salon, music-room, billiards-room and dining-room on the ground floor, three bedrooms, a boudoir and library upstairs. Murat's staff officers and Caroline's attendants were lodged in five other buildings. It was at first separated from the river by the rua de la Procession, but this was ceded to the Murats by the parish in exchange for land to be used as a cemetery near the church
18 Thiébault, III, 141
19 *Ibid.,* 142
20 Murat, *Lettres,* I, 39, Paris, Aug. 6, 1800. He enclosed money for his mother, brother and sisters: 'If you need any more, write to me at once and I will send you whatever you want.' *Ibid.* He was unfailingly generous to his family
21 Hortense, *Mémoires,* I, 92–3
22 *Ibid.,* 23–4
23 Abrantès, II, 83
24 Murat, *Lettres,* I, 95, Paris, Dec. 16, 1800
25 Rapp, 21

6

1 Murat, *Lettres,* I, 101, Milan, Jan. 1, 1801
2 Nap. I, *Corr.,* VI, 569 (5283), Paris, Jan. 13, 1801
3 Murat, *Lettres,* I, 107, Paris, Jan. 7, 1801. *Bouillotte:* a card game for four players; the first to get three cards of the same value wins
4 In the Palazzo Riccardi, moving in March to the splendid Corsini Palace overlooking the Arno. Others shared his view. 'Brune lost respect and became the object of mockery.' Marmont, II, 172. 'General Brune has fallen

into such discredit, that it really arouses one's pity.' Conegliano, 180, Moncey to Macdonald, Jan. 23, 1801

5 A small pun, because *bonne maman* could now be used in its meaning of 'granny'

6 Murat, *Lettres*, I, 121, Paris, Jan. 21, 1801

7 AM, 24/438 *ter* (1)

8 Murat, *Lettres*, I, 129–30

9 *Ibid.*, 170–1, Ancona, Feb. 14, 1801

10 *Ibid.*

11 *Ibid.*, 183, Foligno

12 Boulay, *Docs. . . . Concordat*, II, 28, to Spina, Roma, Feb. 25, 1801. In a ciphered postscript, Consalvi added: 'This General Murat is the best, absolutely the best.' *Ibid.*

13 Murat, *Lettres*, I, 203, Paris, Mar. 3, 1801

14 *Ibid.*, 219, Florence, Mar. 7, 1801

15 April 5 or 10, 1801

16 Murat, *Lettres*, I, 232–3, Paris, Mar. 14, 1801

17 Nap. I, *Corr.*, VII, 136 (5546), Paris, Apr. 24, 1801

18 Murat, *Lettres*, I, 389, Florence, May 17, 1801. To Joachim, His Holiness gave a Raphael painting no wood of the Holy Family

19 Murat, *Lettres*, II, 166, Morfontaine, Oct. 10, 1801

20 *Ibid.*, 169, Paris, Oct. 18, 1801

21 Murat, *Lettres*, II, 185, Milan, Oct. 25, 1801

22 *Ibid.*, 210, Paris, Nov. 19, 1801

23 Mary Caroline, II, 216

24 Damas, I, 332. According to Allonville, VII, 458, Murat asked

for a Neapolitan decoration. The king, Ferdinand, replied that he could have 'as much money as he wants, but none of my ribbons'. Whereupon, 'the first consul's brother-in-law contented himself with 800,000 francs, and Salicetti, who accompanied him, received a similar sum'. He was also said to have asked for 100,000 scudi from the Pope

25 Remacle, 84

26 Murat, *Lettres*, II, 303, Milan, Nov. 20, 1802

27 Nap. I, *Corr.*, VIII, 266–7 (6666), Apr. 2, 1803

7

1 Cavaignac, 269

2 Hortense, *Mémoires*, I, 163. He was at this time having an affair with the actress, Mlle Georges

3 Iung, III, 119

4 Rémusat, I, 353–4

5 Boulay, *Docs. . . . Enghien*, II, 206

6 Murat, *Lettres*, III, 93, Paris, Mar. 20, 1804

7 *Ibid.* (Agar's notes in AM, 44/2)

8 Chateaubriand, II, 287

9 Murat, *Lettres*, III, 92

10 *Ibid.*, 94

11 *Ibid.*

12 *Ibid.*

13 *Ibid.*, 95

14 *Ibid.*

15 *Ibid.*, 102

8

1 Meneval, III, 219

2 *Moniteur*, May 21, 1804, p. 1094, col. a

3 Masson, *Revue d'Ombres*, 60

4 Marie - Félix - Constance - Euphrosiné Aubert du Bayet, wife of General Henri-François-Marin Charpentier, Murat's chief of staff 1801–3

5 Joseph's sister-in-law, née Désirée Clary

6 Masson, *Revue d'Ombres*, 55

7 *Ibid.*, 60. Two aides-de-camp were on duty each day (four when Murat paid calls on the Emperor). One accompanied Murat; the other took messages. They were paid on the same scale as officers of the Imperial Guard and Murat gave them an additional 1,000 francs a month and four uniforms

8 *Ibid.*, 61

9 *Ibid.*, 64

10 Hortense, *Mémoires*, I, 187

11 Roederer, III, 514–15

12 Hortense, I, 200, says: 'The Princess Joseph and I were the only ones who were willing'; but it is clear from Roederer (who has no axe to grind here) that this is untrue

13 Indeed mythical. Bonaparte crossed on May 20, 1800 – four days after Lannes

14 Murat, Lettres, 312–13, Paris, Feb. 6, 1805. As a prince, Joachim was entitled to a seat in the Senate, and to accompany Caroline into the Throne Room

15 Nap. I, *Corr.*, X, 134 (8303), Paris, Feb. 1, 1805

16 Hortense, *Mémoires*, I, 90

17 The date is usually given as Friday, Mar. 22, and thus recorded in the Murat Archives, but Mme Saint-Cyr says plainly 'Elle accoucha à quatre heures du matin du jeudi' (Masson, *Revue d'Ombres*, 98) while Caroline herself, writing to her mother-in-law on March 27, says 'Je suis au septième jour de ma couche'. (Murat, *Lettres*, III, 359)

18 Murat, Lettres, III, 358, Malmaison, Mar. 22, 1805

19 Hortense, *Mémoires*, I, 237

20 Murat, Lettres, III, 359, Paris, Mar. 27, 1805

21 Murat, Lettres, III, 359, Paris, Mar. 26, 1805

PART II The Emperor's Lieutenant 1805–1808

I

1 The Grande Armée was composed of seven army corps; the Cavalry Reserve; and the Guard, both mounted and foot, which always remained with the Emperor. Most army corps had a division of light cavalry which could be reinforced from, or detached to, the Cavalry Reserve

2 Murat, Lettres, IV, 30, Sept. 20, 1805. This nervousness over Murat's reactions has been represented as mere bossiness, but she was as ready to accept advice as to offer it. On Sep. 22, when Josephine invited her to go to

Strasbourg, Caroline asked
Joachim: 'Do you advise me to
make the journey? I will act
according to whatever you say'
Murat, *Lettres*, IV, 37

3 Murat, *Lettres*, IV, 41

4 *Ibid.*, 54, Pforzheim

5 *Ibid.*, 70, Wertingen, Oct. 8, 1805

6 Lejeune, I, 30

7 *Ibid.*, 31

8 Nap. I, *Mil. Corr.*, III, 422,
Moelk, Nov. 11, 1805

9 Murat, *Lettres*, IV, 143,
Hütteldorf, Nov. 12, 1805

10 Deceptions like this were used by
generals on both sides – though
not always approved by their
subordinates. 'Bayard was doubtless no braver than Prince Murat,'
a captain of Oudinot's grenadiers
recorded in his diary, 'but
certainly in similar circumstances
he would not have trifled with
his honour in this fashion'.
Fantin des Odoards, 63

11 Nap. I, *Corr.*, XI, 415–16 (9497),
Schoenbrunn, Nov. 16, 1805

12 To which he made only one
public reference – five months
later when opening a session of
the Corps Legislatif: 'Storms
have caused us to lose a few
vessels, after a battle imprudently
engaged.' *Moniteur*, Mar. 3, 1806,
p. 243, col. b

13 Bailleu, II, 611

2

1 Achille had undergone a minor
operation which 'has succeeded
perfectly. He has never been
more gay and never looked

better.' Murat, *Lettres*, IV, 95,
Oct. 19, 1805

2 Le Brethon, 603, Munich, Dec.
21, 1805. The original letters are
in AM 11/54

3 *Ibid.*, 606–7, Dec. 25 (in error for
24), 1805

4 *Ibid.*, 607

5 *Ibid.*

6 *Ibid.*, 609, Dec. 26

7 *Ibid.*, 611, Jan. 11, 1806

8 Hortense, *Mémoires*, I, 234

9 Murat, *Lettres*, IV, 168 (1).
(Agar's notes)

10 *Ibid.*

11 *Ibid.*

12 'If you knew what I have just
seen,' Josephine exclaimed to
Volney. 'I caught the Emperor –
the Emperor, do you understand?
– in Pauline's arms!' Favre, 216.
This was in the Tuileries, where
he was in residence from Jan.
27 to Mar. 31, 1806. On Mar. 30
he created Pauline Princess and
Sovereign Duchess of Guastalla.
Josephine once said to Mme de
Rémusat: 'Has he not seduced
all his sisters, one after the
other?' Rémusat, I, 368. But this
was no doubt exaggeration in a
moment of anguish

13 Deutz, Königswinter and Willich,
plus lordship over a group of
mediatized princes and control
of the North German postal
services. Berg and Cleves extended along the right bank of
the Rhine from a few miles above
Bonn to just below Wesel

14 During his March visit he learned
of the death of his mother, aged
85. He had two lines from

Petrarch inscribed on her tomb-
stone:

Non la connobe il mondo mentre
l'obbe;
Connobil' io ch' a piangere qui
rimasi
(While she lived, the world did
not know her;
I did, who remained to mourn
her)

15 AM 11/54 (7), July 1806
16 Nap. I, *Corr.*, XIII, 33 (10,587),
St-Cloud
17 *Ibid.*
18 Murat, *Lettres*, IV, 299, Aug. 7,
1806
19 *Ibid.*
20 *Ibid.*, 311, Benrath, Aug. 14,
1806
21 Murat, *Lettres*, IV, 291–2
22 Pelleport, I, 234
23 Murat, *Lettres*, IV, 418–19
24 Nap. I, *Corr.*, XIII, (11, 121)
25 Murat, *Murat en 1808*, 84
26 Thoumas, 451
27 Colbert, IV, 149

3

1 Nap. I, *Corr.*, XIII, 419, (11,093),
Potsdam, Oct. 26, 1806
2 Abrantès, *Mémoires*, VI, 199
3 Potocka, 102. The countess, who
accused Joachim of making
improper advances to her, disliked him because he interrupted
her liaison with the universal
lover, Charles de Flahaut, by
returning him to regimental
duties
4 Barante, I, 207
5 Potocka, 104
6 Abrantès, *Mémoires*, VI, 252

7 Nap. I, *Corr.*, XIV, 10 (11,349),
Posen, Dec. 1, 1806
8 Murat, *Lettres*, V, 64, Paris, Dec.
16, 1806
9 *Ibid.*, IV, 503, Paris, Dec. 2,
1806
10 *Ibid.*, V, 65, Paris, Dec. 16, 1806
11 Nap. I, *Corr.*, XIV, 11 (11,350),
Posen, Dec. 2, 1806
12 Murat, *Lettres*, V, 80, Sousk, nr.
Golaczyna
13 Charles, comte Léon, b. Dec. 13,
1806
14 Gonneville, 60
15 Murat, *Lettres*, V, 106, Feb. 6,
1807. The operational journal of
4 Corps claimed 11 pieces of
cannon, 3,000 Russian dead,
2,500 wounded, 1,500 prisoners.
The Russian official figures were
'2,500 killed or wounded, 5
cannon and 2 standards'.
Bennigsen, I, 202. Joachim's
figures seem to be accurate and
restrained
16 Formerly 5th Corps; 7th and 10th
Corps were disbanded and their
remnants used to bring other
corps up to strength. Mortier's
8th Corps had rejoined the
army. Bernadotte, wounded,
had handed over 1st Corps to
Victor
17 Gonneville, 68
18 Norvins, III, 196
19 Commanding the 3rd Division of
the Cavalry Reserve (4th, 6th and
7th Cuirassiers)
20 Gonneville, 68
21 Pouget, 105
22 François, 171
23 Gonneville, 77
24 Durand, 40

25 Murat, *Murat en 1808*, 11–12 (Agar's notes in AM 45/2)

26 *Ibid.*, 37

27 *Ibid.*, 73

28 The emperor and the tsar dined together almost daily. The seating at the top table was: Murat on the right, then the tsar, Napoleon in the middle with the king and Grand Duke on his left

29 Thiébault, IV, 90–1

30 From the tsar he received the Grand Cordon of the Order of St Andrew

31 Prusse, 258

32 *Ibid.*

4

1 They were neighbours in the rue du Faubourg St-Honoré since Caroline had moved to the Hôtel de l'Elysée (Nos. 55–57, now the Presidential Palace). It was used as a dance hall after the Revolution and, when Murat bought it in April 1805, was divided into shops and apartments. Napoleon bought the Hôtel Thélusson from Murat and presented it to the Russians as an embassy

2 Murat, *Lettres*, V, 128, Paris, Feb. 28, 1807

3 Abrantès, *Mémoires*, VI, 231

4 Junot did not receive his title until several months later

5 A reference to Caroline and Joachim, not Junot

6 Abrantès, *Salons*, V, 241–3

7 No. 6, now part of the rue Boissy d'Anglas

8 Laure's pet name for her husband

9 It was first published by Turquand, *la générale Junot*, from Laure's *Journal Intime* in the possession of the Institut de France, Bibliothèque Spoelberch de Lovenjoul, Chantilly. The manuscript, written by Laure in her wretched later years, was left by her to Balzac. Dumas might have been a more suitable recipient, pp. 182–3

10 Included among those she sent (Am 26/532) was a poem from Junot, which scarcely suggests a guilty conscience

11 Murat, *Lettres*, V, 148–51, Paris, Mar. 25, 1807. In fact it was she who was unfair to him. In the Murat Archives there is a rough, in his his own hand, of verses 'To Caroline, on her birthday', written at the foot of the draft of a letter to Napoleon on March 16. Evidently it did not arrive in time

12 *Ibid.*, 148

13 Meneval, III, 219 and Durand, 31

14 Hortense, *Mémoires*, I, 363, Finkenstein, May 20, 1807

15 Murat, *Lettres*, V, 152, Finkenstein, Apr. 3, 1807

16 That Murat and Junot challenged each other to a duel but were forbidden to fight by Napoleon is another oft-repeated legend that owes its origin to Laure. Neither man, once committed in such an affair, was of the kind to turn back

17 The counties of Mark, Lingen and Tecklenberg; the principalities of Munster and Siegen

18 Murat, *Lettres*, V, 215, Paris, Aug. 21, 1807

19 *Ibid.*, 215–6, St-Cloud, Aug. 21, 1807

20 Schlossberger, I, 65–6. Catherine's mother died when she was 5 years old. She seldom wrote to her stepmother, Charlotte Matilda, daughter of George III, whom she disliked at this time, though after Napoleon's fall she was grateful for her sympathy and support

21 Murat, *Lettres*, V, 222. (Agar's notes)

22 *Ibid.*, 222–3

23 Beugnot, 256. He took over Agar's post in the Grand Duchy the following year

24 AM 44/3. (Agar's notes)

25 The maid of all work whom Joseph brought back from Pisa in 1788; usually referred to in more affluent days as 'the children's governess'

26 On Nov. 8, 1807, the King of Portugal sent the marquis de Marialva to Paris to offer Napoleon money and 'to propose a marriage between the Prince of Beira, future heir to the throne, and one of the daughters of the Duke of Berg'. Foy, II, 376. The Prince of Beira was 9; Letitia 5

5

1 Abrantès, *Mémoires*, VII, 43

2 *Ibid.*, 44. The younger of the two was known as *Princess* Louis, because of his gentle manners and the fine light hair that he inherited from Hortense

3 *Ibid.*, 158

4 Abrantès, *Salons*, VI, 258

5 Less than six months after Caroline's attempt to steal her husband – according to Laure's own story

6 Abrantès, *Mémoires*

7 Isabey, on this and several other occasions. Fouché, who could be prudish in these matters, administered a rebuke in the daily Police Bulletin that he sent to the Emperor. 'It is said that the Emperor appeared very gay at Princess Caroline's ball; that H.M. appeared in different disguises and that he was recognized because he allowed himself more liberties than the other masks.' *Bulletins*, IV, 83 (176)

8 Abrantès, *Salons*, VI, 262

9 Abrantès, *Salons*, VI, 268

10 Murat, *Lettres*, V, 304, Bayonne. 'Few generals have ever received such an enigmatic mission ... nor in a more off-hand and vague manner.' Grasset, I, 311. Napoleon was still studying the possibility of an expedition against Turkey and had no clear idea of why he had sent his troops into Spain

11 *Ibid.*, 338

6

1 Murat, *Lettres*, V, 358–9, Castillejo, Mar. 19, 1808

2 *Ibid.*, 364, Buitrago, Mar. 20, 1808

3 *Ibid.*

4 Thoumas, 464

5 Murat, *Murat en 1808*, 136

6 O'Meara, II, 96

7 Nap. I, *Corr.*, XVI, 450 (13,695), St-Cloud, Mar. 27, 1808

8 Grasset, I, 372

9 A son of the Revolution, he had no strong religious beliefs, though in moments of indecision or surprise he would very rapidly cross himself. As Governor of Paris he had been honorary churchwarden of Notre-Dame de Lorette, where he acted as server on his patronal festival

10 Murat, *Lettres*, V, 394–5, Madrid, Mar. 27, 1808

11 *Ibid.*, 405, Mar. 29

12 *Ibid.*, 417, Mar. 31

13 *Ibid.*, 418, Mar. 31

14 *Bulletins*, IV, 118 (251)

15 Castellane, I, 15

16 Nap. I, *Corr.*, XVI, 426 (13,664), Paris, Mar. 19, 1808

17 *Ibid.*, 435 (13,675), St-Cloud, Mar. 23

18 *Ibid.*, 438 (13,682), Mar. 25

19 Murat, *Murat en 1808*, 193–4, Bordeaux, Apr. 4, 1808

20 Nap. I, *Corr.*, XVI, 476–7 (13,721)

21 *Ibid.*, 487 (13,733), Bordeaux, Apr. 10, 1808. On Apr. 26 he wrote: 'It is time to show the necessary force. I assume you will not spare the Madrid rabble if they get restive.' Lecestre, I, 184 (270), Bayonne, Apr. 26

22 Murat, *Lettres*, VI, 5–6, Madrid, Apr. 23, 1808

23 *Ibid.*, 6. Others, less enthusiastic, referred to the Grand Duke of Berg as *el gran trocho de berzas*, a poor pun meaning the Big Cabbage Stalk

24 *Bulletins*, IV, 159 (335)

25 Dedem, 127

26 Murat, *Lettres*, VI, 29, Madrid, May 1, 1808

27 Murat reported that at least 1,200 Spaniards had been killed. Napoleon increased this to 'more than 2,000'. *Corr.*, XVII, 72 (13,821), to Jérôme, Bayonne, May 6. Grandmaison, 203–5, arrived at a figure of 300 Spaniards and 145 French

28 Murat, *Lettres*, VI, 48, Madrid

29 *Ibid.*, 54

30 Nap. I, *Corr.*, XVII, 55 (13,801), Bayonne

31 Murat, *Lettres*, VI, 65, May 6, 1808

32 *Ibid.*, 79, May 10

33 *Ibid.*

34 *Ibid.*, 75, May 9

35 *Ibid.*, 89, May 11

36 *Ibid.*, 81, May 10

37 *Ibid.*

38 Nap. I, *Corr.*, XVII 97 (13,859), Bayonne, May 11, 1808

39 Nap. I, *Corr.*, XVII, 147 (13,913), Bayonne, May 17, 1808

40 Murat, *Lettres*, VI, 166, Madrid, May 23, 1808

41 *Ibid.*, 179, May 28

42 La Forest, *Corr.*, I, 47, to Champagny, Madrid, May 26, 1808

43 He had moved to the Duke of Alba's villa, La Floride, outside Madrid

44 Murat, *Lettres*, VI, 182–4, La Floride, May 31, 1808

45 *Ibid.*, 187–8, Jun. 2

46 *Ibid.*, 201, June. 4

47 Murat, *Lettres*, VI, 211, Chamartin, Jun. 14, 1808

48 Marquiset, 143

7

1 Turquand, 222, quoting from Laure's *Journal Intime*, see chap. 4, note 13, above

2 *Ibid.*, 225

3 *Ibid.*, 231

4 *Ibid.*, 223

5 Abrantès, *Mémoires*, VII, 275

6 'She considered herself out of place anywhere except on a throne, and it must be admitted that she seemed fitted for it by her strength of character and highmindedness.' Beugnot, 257

7 Murat, *Lettres*, VI, 212–13, Paris, Jun. 17, 1808. Julie-Andrieu, daughter of Joachim's eldest sister, Jacquette, had married Agar in 1807 at the age of 17. She was, according to Beugnot, 258, 'a little simpleton, lacking nothing but wit, looks and health'

8 Typical of the misrepresentation suffered by Caroline and Joachim from contemporary and subsequent detractors is this passage from General Dedem de Gelder's *Mémoires* (p. 123): 'Joseph arrived too late at Bayonne [to get Lucien appointed as his successor]. The Grand Duchess of Berg had travelled by post on the pretext of her husband's illness but in fact to canvass for the throne of Naples, and she succeeded.' The truth is that Joseph arrived on Jun. 7, Caroline in the afternoon of Jun. 26, and the throne had been offered to Murat on May 2. A similarly inaccurate account is given in *Mémoires secrets sur la vie ... de Lucien Bonaparte*, I, 218–19; and Hortense, *Mémoires*, II, 7, makes the same point by implication

9 Barère, III, 143

10 Murat, *Lettres*, VI, 219, to Napoleon, Barèges, Jul. 14, 1808

11 Murat, *Lettres*, VI, 219

12 Near Lectoure (Gers), the ancient capital of Armagnac, where Lannes was born. The ill-feeling between the two men – and between Murat and Ney – has been exaggerated. It sprang from rivalry for glory on the battlefield and died each time that tempers cooled

13 Lecestre, I, 226 (332), Agen, Jul. 30, 1808. Mlle Avrillon has a similar story that Caroline stripped the Elysée of furniture and valuable objects. Leroux-Cestron questions this, pointing out that she certainly took nothing, apart from a few family portraits, from Neuilly and Villiers. From the Elysée she took the small collection of Old Masters which she and Joachim began forming with Cacault's help in 1801

14 *Ibid.*, 253

PART III Their Majesties 1805–1815

1

1 Sister of Marie-Antoinette. Ferdinand credited her with having the evil-eye, and told his court after their wedding night that she slept as if pole-axed and sweated like a pig. She had 17 legitimate children and many lovers

2 Dedem, 130. The population of the city of Naples was about 350,000

3 AE, Naples, CXXXII, 240, to Champagny, Sep. 15, 1808

4 Murat, *Lettres*, VI, 323, Naples. She arrived on September 20

5 *Ibid.*, 347, Oct. 13

6 *Ibid.*, 351–3, Oct. 16

7 *Ibid.*

8 Murat, *Lettres*, VI, 355, Naples, Oct. 18, 1808

9 Nap. I, *Corr.*, XVIII, 35 (14,436), Bayonne, Nov. 4, 1808

10 Murat, *Lettres*, VI, 426, Portici, Nov. 25, 1808. They stayed at Portici below Vesuvius and adjoining Herculaneum from Oct. 21 to Nov. 30 and Caroline acquired a lasting interest in archaeology. She made frequent visits to Pompeii and subsidized the excavation with an annual grant of 2,400 ducats from her own purse. The value of the ducat varied between 4 and 5 francs

11 Murat, *Lettres*, VI, 437–8, Naples, Dec. 1, 1808

12 *Ibid.*, 442, Dec. 9

2

1 Nap. I, *Corr.*, XVIII, 85 (14,519), Aranda, Nov. 27, 1808

2 Murat, *Lettres*, VI, 448, Dec. 12, 1808

3 AM 45/2

4 'He is an idiot, but he has dash and boldness. He's done nothing but make war all his life. Murat is an idiot and he is a hero,' Napoleon said to Roederer (III, 536) on Feb. 11, 1809. It was his policy never to credit his generals with any quality other than bravery

5 Murat, *Murat en 1808*, 8 (1)

6 AE, Naples, CXXXII, 357b, to Champagny, Dec. 25, 1808

7 *Ibid.*, CXXXIII, 20, Jan. 11, 1809

8 Murat, *Lettres*, VII, 11, Naples, Feb. 7, 1809. The tone of these letters refutes Espitalier's criticism: 'He crawled to the Emperor so long as Napoleon was the stronger and controlled money, places, honours and kingdoms.' Espitalier, 26

9 Murat, *Lettres*, VII, 19–20, Naples, Feb. 14, 1809

10 *Ibid.*, 20, Feb. 15

11 *Ibid.*, 59–61, Paris, Mar. 5, 1809. Berthier had said the same thing in a letter to Joachim six weeks before. Murat, *Lettres*, VII, 53 (2)

12 *Ibid.*, 60 (1)

13 Jacques-Marie-René; his brother, Charles-Jean-Louis, was a general

in Joachim's service. Joachim had ordered him to come to Naples in November 1808

14 *Ibid.*, 57–8, Paris, Mar. 5, 1809

15 *Ibid.*, 87–8, Mar. 17

16 Larrey, I, 484

17 Murat, *Lettres*, VII, 57 (1)

18 *Ibid.*, 82, Naples, Mar. 13

19 Dedem, 165

20 Nicola, II, 458

21 Murat, *Lettres*, VII, 107, Naples, Mar. 26, 1809

22 *Ibid.*

23 Nicola, II, 458

24 Murat, *Lettres*, VII, 45–6, Belvedere, Mar. 1, 1809

25 Nor was he accustomed to such resistance. 'I have only one passion, only one mistress, and that is France,' he said to Roederer on Feb. 11. 'I go to bed with her. She has never failed me, she lavishes her blood and her wealth on me. If I have need of 500,000 men, she gives them to me.' Roederer, III, 539

26 Murat, *Lettres*, VII, 78, Naples, Mar. 13, 1809

27 *Ibid.*, 108, Mar. 29

3

1 Murat, *Lettres*, VII, 142, Naples, Apr. 6, 1809

2 *Ibid.*, 158, Apr. 13. Napoleon was pressing for payment of his half of the annual million francs that he claimed from the kingdom. Joachim refused to pay on the grounds that (a) Joseph had never done so; (b) the million francs were to be levied on Naples and Sicily and the latter should pay at least one third, therefore only 660,000 francs were in question; (c) of these, 500,000 were due to Joachim under the terms of the Treaty of Bayonne, leaving 160,000 for Napoleon; (d) this sum was more than cancelled out by the revenue from Berg for the fiscal year up to August, 1808, which the Emperor had retained

3 Nicola, II, 462

4 Murat, *Lettres*, VII, 195–6, Naples, Apr. 28, 1809

5 Bunbury, 240

6 Ironically, this was the eve of the battle of Aspern-Essling, which was to shatter Napoleon's personal reputation for invincibility as Baylen had that of the French army ten months before

7 Murat, *Lettres*, VII, 235, Naples, May 20, 1809

8 He was right. 'If I had had [him] at the head of my cavalry at Wagram,' Napoleon said to Berthier, 'not a single Austrian would have escaped.' Vandal, *Le roi et la reine*, 489

9 AE, Naples, CXXXIII, 245b, to Champagny, Jun. 10, 1809

10 Nicola, II, 473. The semaphore system invented by Claude Chappe in 1792 was first used by the French army in 1794

11 Nicola, II, 474

12 Bunbury

13 Murat, *Lettres*, VII, 333–4, Jun. 24, 1809

14 Bunbury, 249

15 Murat, *Lettres*, VII, 345, Jun. 27, 1809

16 *Ibid.*, 358, Naples, Jul. 1, 1809

17 *Ibid.*, 375 (1)
18 'No more kid gloves. He is a raving lunatic; he must be locked up.' Napoleon to Murat (Lecestre, I, 317 (459) Jun. 20). 'I am annoyed that the Pope has been arrested. It is sheer madness.' Napoleon to Fouché (Nap. I, *Corr.*, XIX, 265 (15,555) Jul. 18)
19 AE, Naples, CXXXIII, 307, to Champagny, Jul. 18, 1809
20 Bunbury, 248
21 Murat, *Lettres*, VII, 446 (2). Agar to Joachim, Aug. 12, 1809
22 Manhès, who joined Murat as major aide-de camp in April, 1807, acted with considerable brutality. In this he could plead the example of Napoleon but not of Joachim, who later that year wrote to General Cavaignac: 'Make it known to your division that I shall severely punish any officer who in future has anybody shot without a preliminary trial. It is a disgrace to the French name that detachments escorting brigands shoot them en route, and the French officer who recently had a woman, a child and a priest shot deserves to be sent before a court-martial himself. This sort of behaviour is the real cause of the brigandage.' Murat, *Lettres*, VIII, 92, Nov. 7, 1809

4

1 Whose date varied from year to year: the first Sunday after Aug. 15, the feast of the Assumption of the Virgin, St Joachim's daughter
2 Murat, *Lettres*, VIII, 17, Naples, Sep. 16, 1809
3 *Ibid.*
4 Nap. I, *Corr.*, XIX 575 (15,941), Schoenbrunn, Oct. 14, 1809
5 Murat, *Lettres*, VIII, 75, Portici, Oct. 27, 1809
6 *Ibid.*, 74 (1)
7 *Ibid.*, 59, Oct. 12
8 *Ibid.* Despite Mme Campan's efforts, Caroline was largely self-educated. She was very fond of reading and being read to, and her quick mind benefited from the talk of the scholars whom she welcomed at her table. She usually dictated her correspondence, because her spelling was erratic and her handwriting difficult to decipher
9 Abrantès, Salons, V, 139
10 *Ibid.*, 138. Laure was no slave to consistency. She says of this same occasion in her memoirs: 'The Queen of Naples, whose gracious and charming smile was intended to make the Parisians say "Welcome back among us!", spoke to everyone with extreme affability.' Abrantès, *Mémoirs*, VII, 502–3
11 Murat, *Lettres*, VIII, 122, Paris, Dec. 13, 1809
12 Schlossberger, I, 275. Catherine to Friedrich, Dec. 22, 1809
13 Murat, *Lettres*, VIII, 129, Paris, Dec. 16, 1809
14 *Ibid.*, 140 (2), Dec. 14
15 Nicola, II, 509
16 Nap. I, *Corr.*, XX, 104 (16,118), Paris, Jan. 9, 1810

5

1 Marie-Louise's mother, Maria Theresa, 2nd wife of Francis of Austria, was the daughter of Mary Caroline and Ferdinand
2 Murat, *Lettres*, VIII, 168 (1). Agar's notes
3 *Ibid.*
4 Lavalette, *Mémoires*, II, 5: which confirms in broad outline Agar's detailed account
5 Cambacérès, speaking first, had cautiously opposed it
6 Murat, *Lettres*, VIII, 168 (1)
7 *Ibid.*
8 *Ibid.*
9 *Ibid.*, 165–6, Paris, Feb. 3, 1810
10 *Ibid.*, 167, Feb. 5
11 *Ibid.*, 167–8, Feb. 6
12 *Ibid.*, 168–9, n.d.
13 *Ibid.*, 171–2
14 *Ibid.*, 175, Feb. 11, 1810
15 *Ibid.*, 176, Feb. 12
16 *Ibid.*, 202, Feb. 27

6

1 Nicola, II, 515
2 Murat, *Lettres*, VIII, 187, Naples, Feb. 20, 1810
3 *Ibid.*, 191, Feb. 23
4 *Ibid.*, 210, Mar. 3
5 *Ibid.*, 199, Paris, Feb. 27
6 *Ibid.*
7 *Ibid.*
8 *Ibid.*, 200
9 *Ibid.*
10 *Ibid.*
11 *Ibid.*, 205, Feb. 28
12 And the conjectures of subsequent commentators. Janvier wrote to Caroline on the 9th that the king was 'preparing to get on his way to Paris' (*Ibid.*, 227) and Nicola (II, 518) reported on the same day that the 'messenger arrived this morning' and the king 'will leave in three or four days'
13 Murat, *Lettres*, VIII, 220, to Napoleon, Mar. 12, 1810

7

1 Murat, *Lettres*, VIII, 215, Munich, Mar. 8, 1810
2 A sincere appreciation, since it was nearly thirty years later, in 1838, that she gave it to Marchand, *Mémoires*, I, 152
3 Helfert, *Maria-Louise*, 119, to the Kaiser, Braunau, Mar. 16. She came as a brave but very unwilling bride of the 'Anti-Christ' Bonaparte. 'I pity the unhappy woman that his choice falls on. . . . Say a paternoster that it shall not be me.' Brouwet, 221
4 Murat, *Lettres*, VIII, 225, Munich, Mar. 18, 1810
5 *Ibid.*
6 *Ibid.*, 226
7 *Ibid.*, 227
8 Helfert, *Maria-Louise*, 124, Strasbourg, Mar. 23, 1810
9 Bourgoing, *Coeur de Marie-Louise*, I, 13, states definitely that Berthier received the order from Napoleon and asked Caroline to convey it to the Empress, but she refused
10 Schlossberger, III, 146
11 Helfert, *Maria-Louise*, 124, Strasbourg, Mar. 23

12 Murat, *Lettres*, VIII, 228–9, Lunéville, Mar. 24, 10 p.m. Thomas l'Agnelet, the rascally shepherd in the 15th Century farce *Maître Pathelin*, answered questions by bleating

13 In her secret letter of Feb. 27 – because 'she has a very, very bad reputation here for gambling'

14 Caroline's sarcastic phrase is '*trop grande acte de pouvoir*'

15 Murat, *Lettres*, VIII, 232, Nancy, Mar. 25

16 *Ibid.*

17 *Ibid.*

18 *Ibid.*, 233, Vitry-sur-Marne, Mar. 26

19 Norvins, *Mémorial*, III, 279

20 Durand, 15

21 Marchand, I, 153. See Gourgaud, II, 276

22 Schlossberger, I, 295. 'The Queen of Naples is full of charm,' Marie-Louise wrote to her father. 'She is smaller and plumper than I am, but very pretty, and you can read in her face the kindness that inspires her. She is very intelligent and the dearest to me of the three princesses.' Helfert, *Marie-Louise*, 164

23 Murat, *Lettres*, VIII, 242–3, Compiègne, Apr. 9, 1810

24 Vandal, *Le roi et la reine*, 503

8

1 Napoleon had agreed to it in general terms on Mar. 22. *Corr.*, XX, 278 (16,356)

2 Murat, *Lettres*, VIII, 274, Paris, May 6

3 Bourgoing, I, 39

4 *Ibid.*, 40

5 The impressionable Grand Duke of Würzburg, formerly of Tuscany, brother of Kaiser Francis

6 Attendance upon the emperor was an expensive honour. Agar had to send Joachim 700,000 francs during his short stay, and Caroline needed another 100,000 francs before she left

7 Who had been ordered by Napoleon to rejoin Louis in Holland. They had moved in June 1804 from 16 rue de la Victoire to the former Hôtel St-Julien in the rue Cerutti, close to the Hôtel Thélusson

8 Murat, *Lettres*, VIII, 268, Paris, May 2, 1810

9 Who used the marriage as a pretext for coming to Paris to talk with Napoleon. 'Metternich is still in Paris, fettered by the charms of the Queen of Naples.' Stroganov to Czartoryski, St Petersburg, June 20. Mikhailovitch III, 266–7. He had succeeded Stadion as Austrian Chief Minister in 1809

10 Murat, *Lettres*, VIII, 168 (1). Agar's notes

11 Stendhal, *Corr.*, III, 396, to Balzac, Oct. 16, 1840

12 Napoleon had brought her to Paris, promising to find her a husband – possibly the Prince of the Austrias – and hoping thus to bind Lucien to him

13 Fleuriot de Langle, *Alexandrine*, 108

14 *Mém. Sec. de Lucien Bonaparte*, II. 15

15 Murat, *Lettres*, VIII, 248, Compiègne, Apr. 18, 1810

16 *Ibid.*, 249, Apr. 21

17 *Ibid.*, 250, Apr. 22

18 *Ibid.*, 277–8, Paris, May 8

19 *Ibid.*, 286, May 11

20 *Ibid.*, 291, May 13

21 *Ibid.*

22 A letter that he allegedly wrote to her was published in Spain. It offered Sardinia, Corsica, Malta and the Ionian Isles if she formally relinquished Naples. Mary Caroline gave the British Minister 'her most solemn assurance that no such letter had reached her by any channel whatsoever'. FO 70/39 No. 46, Amherst to Wellesley, Palermo, Jul. 15, 1810. She had sworn earlier in the year that 'no consideration should ever induce her to humble herself so far as to accept a boon from the favour of Bonaparte'. *Ibid.*, No. 32, Mar. 27. The British suspected her of planning with Napoleon another Sicilian Vespers, to massacre them as soon as a French force landed. See Bunbury, 257–8

23 Murat, *Lettres*, VIII, 291, Paris, May 13

24 *Ibid.*, 295, May 15

25 *Ibid.*, 367 (1), Clarke to Murat, Paris, May 25

26 *Ibid.*, In fact, all the senior commanders were French: Lamarque and Partouneaux of the French divisions, Cavaignac of the Neapolitan division, Dery and La Vauguyon of the Royal Guard, Compère of the Gendarmerie

27 *Ibid.*

28 Espitalier's statement, p. 72, 'Fortunately for Joachim's peace of mind, Leclerc, though he made no secret of his visit, carefully refrained from disclosing the object of it' is quite untrue. Leclerc showed Clarke's letter to Daure, who communicated it to at least one other person (Murat, *Lettres*, VIII, 366). Similar instructions were sent by Clarke to Pérignon who, to his credit, replied: 'Everything that concerns me in the contents of your letter will be carried out punctually, but almost the whole of it is the business of the king, as king and commander-in-chief of the army, and it will therefore be for His Majesty to carry out the Emperor's orders.' *Ibid.*, 381

30 *Ibid.*, 356

31 *Ibid.*, 358

32 *Ibid.*

33 Bunbury, 317. Messina, Jul. 12, 1810. Bunbury returned to England and became Undersecretary to Lord Bathurst at the War Office

34 Murat, *Lettres*, VIII, 434, Jul. 6, 1810

35 *Ibid.*, 446, Piale, Jul. 11

9

1 Napoleon retained Villiers but gave Neuilly to Pauline, Jan. 1809

2 Murat, *Lettres*, VIII, 372, St-Cloud, Jun. 15, 1810

3 *Ibid.*, 373, Jun. 16. Oddly, Joachim wrote to Napoleon two days later, 'We have not yet had a single hot day, which much surprises the locals.' *Ibid.*, 379, Scilla, Jun. 18

4 *Ibid.*, 374, St-Cloud, Jun. 16

5 *Ibid.*, 380, Jun. 19

6 *Ibid.*, 388, Paris, Jun. 23

7 *Ibid.*, 390

8 *Ibid.*, 397, St-Cloud, Jun. 25

9 *Ibid.*, 409, Jun. 29

10 *Ibid.*, 413–14

11 *Ibid.*, 493, Naples, Aug. 5. Although she 'had not slept well and was still feeling the effects of the journey' (*Ibid.*, 488), she wrote him four letters in all that day

12 *Ibid.*, 491–2

13 *Ibid.*, 492

14 *Ibid.*, 490–1

15 *Ibid.*, 491

16 *Ibid.*, 493–4. In fact she found the heat excessive and, when writing to him two days later, said, 'I am drooping over the table as I write to you'. AM 27/566 (77). The published *Lettres* end with these four from Caroline on Aug. 5, 1810

17 *On n'est pas Roi pour obéir*

18 AM 27/566 (66 *bis*). Cadore's report was published in the *Moniteur* on Jul. 10, p. 747, cols. a–c

19 AM 27/566 (70)

20 *Ibid.*, (72)

21 Vandal, *Le roi et la reine*, 767

22 *Ibid.*, 771

23 AM 27/566 (75), Naples, Aug. 20

24 *Ibid.*, (79), Aug. 24

25 WO 1/309, Stuart to Amherst, Messina, Sep. 23, 1810

26 Amherst reported that as soon as the British troops (the 21st Regiment, riflemen of the 3rd and 4th King's German Legion, a troop of the 20th Light Dragoons and a detachment of Royal Artillery, approximately 1,900 men) launched their counter-attack, 'the enemy, with precipitation as dastardly as it is unaccountable, hurried to his boats'. FO 70/39 (58,) to Wellesley, Palermo, Sep. 23. Some of the boats had already returned to the Calabrian coast without waiting for orders

27 AM 46/1, Piale, Sep. 18

28 Valente, 221 (1), Reggio, Sep. 23

29 *Rambaud*, G., 702

30 Espitalier, 84, and other detractors suggest this was because his pride would not allow him to face the crowds who had cheered him on his way down. It is much more likely, and in keeping with his character, that he chose this as a way of heartening his people by showing his disregard for the enemy navy. He landed at Massa, in the bay of Salerno, on Oct. 3, a gale preventing his continuing to Naples. He joined Caroline at Portici, where she had been since Oct. 1

31 Dedem, 182

32 Vandal, *Le roi et la reine*, 776

33 AM 27/566 (90), Sep. 17

10

1 AM 46/1

2 Espitalier, 96

3 Nap. I, *Corr.*, XXI, 271 (17,128),

Fontainebleau, Nov. 12. There were approximately 3,000 in the Household Regiments, 37,000 in the others, of whom 6,000 were serving in Spain. The army was less than 18,000 strong when Murat came to the throne

4 *Ibid.*, 9 (16,754), to Champagny, Trianon, Aug. 4

5 *Ibid.*, 222 (17,052), Fontainebleau, Oct. 17

6 White for Imperial (formerly Royal) France; sky-blue, the traditional Neapolitan colour; purple, his own amaranth livery. *Général de division, général de brigade, adjudant-commandant* became *lieutenant-général, maréchal de camp, adjudant-général*

7 Desvernois, 420

8 *Ibid.*

9 Nap. I, *Corr.*, XXII, 8 (17,546), Paris, Apr. 2, 1811

10 AE, Naples, CXXXVI, 145b, Durand to Champagny, Rome, Mar. 27

11 Saint-Hilaire, II, 359–61

12 AM 54/37, Naples, Oct. 31, 1810. On Jan. 10, 1811, Catherine of Westphalia noted that 'the Kingdom of Naples is said to be going to be united with the Kingdom of Italy; the Queen of Naples has been invited by the Emperor to the Empress's lying-in; she has written to Madame Mère begging her to tell the Emperor that, since they wanted to take her crown away, she would rather receive that insult in Naples than in Paris.' Jérôme, V, 18. And on Apr. 15: 'The King of Naples, who came without being invited,

wants to leave but the Emperor does not seem to agree; it is even said that he will never return to Naples.' *Ibid.*, 34

13 AM 27/567 (4)

14 *Ibid.*, (5)

15 ADD 51,528/54, Julie to Joseph, Paris, Jan. 15, 1811

16 Vandal, *Le roi et la reine*, 783, Naples, May 12, 1811

17 Proxy for the kaiser; Joseph and Madame Mère were the other godparents

18 *Ibid.*

19 *Ibid.*, 784

20 *Ibid.*, 785. Hortense accepted. The other three were Pauline, Julie and Berthier's wife, niece of the King of Bavaria

21 *Ibid.*

22 *Ibid.*, 787

23 *Ibid.*, 788

24 Czernicheff, 199

25 *Ibid.*, 200

26 Espitalier, 122–4, May 12, 1811

27 *Ibid.*, 129, May 11, 1811

11

1 *Monitore delle Due Sicilie*, Jun. 18, 1811

2 Espitalier, 135, Castellamare, Jun. 18, 1811

3 Nap. I, *Corr.*, XXII, 284 (17,849), St-Cloud, Jun. 24, 1811

4 Espitalier, 1400

5 Meneval, II, 469

6 AM 46/3, Naples, Jul. 20, 1811

7 *Ibid.*, Capodimonte, Aug. 13

8 AE, Naples, CXXXVII, 70, to Bassano, Aug. 4, 1811

9 *Ibid.*, 83, Aug. 18

10 AM 46/3, Capodimonte, Aug. 17
11 Espitalier, 155
12 Daure's other two ministries (War and Marine) went to Tugny; Exelmans succeeded Lanusse as Grand Marshal of the Palace but returned to France in 1812, to command the mounted grenadiers of the Imperial Guard.
13 Cavaignac, 301
14 Several of Murat's biographers have argued that he introduced the naturalization law in order to force the resignation of Daure. If Murat wanted to get rid of him he had only to dismiss him. Daure, a hard worker but fat, ugly, coarse-mannered and in his late forties, was almost as unlikely a lover for Caroline as Cacault, the French Ambassador to Rome, with whom one of her biographers claimed she had an affair in 1801. (In fact, Cacault, wise, witty and nearly 60 years old, was 'loved and esteemed' by Murat, while Caroline 'called him her father'. Artaud de Montor, *Pie VII*, I, 133). Shielded by an iron censorship, Napoleon presided over as immoral a court as any of his predecessors and it would be unlikely that Caroline did not indulge in extramarital affairs; but some of those attributed to her are not so much a slur on her memory as an insult to the reader's intelligence
15 Hortense, *Mémoires*, II, 135
16 Wertheimer, *Verbrannten*, Nov. 15, 1810
17 Hortense, *Mémoires*, II, 135
18 Norvins, *Portefeuille*, I, 89

19 AM 25/482 (12)
20 Joachim sent Agar to Capua to meet him. To avoid further imperial wrath he did not offer him his former place at court, but told him he could have command of the Neapolitan forces in Spain. When this was refused, he told him to remain in northern Italy for the time being, and continued to pay him his full salary and allowances. Scarcely the treatment he would have given his wife's lover
21 Consisting of the Farnese palace, the Farnesina palace, the Palatine gardens, the villa Madame and the castle of Caprarola
22 AE Naples, CXXXVII, 161b, Clarke to Pérignon, Paris, Sep. 16, 1811
23 *Ibid.*, 646, Bassano to Durand, Compiègne, Sep. 17
24 AM 46/3. On arrival in Rome at 10 a.m. Sep. 19 she had to wait for her carriage to be repaired. 'I sent for General Vauguyon,' she told Joachim, 'but they did not find him at home.' AM 27/567 (16). From Florence she wrote that she had seen La Vauguyon before she left
25 AM 27/567 (18), 25, 1811
26 *Ibid.*, (19), Paris, Oct. 3
27 *Ibid.*, (23), Oct. 10
28 *Ibid.*, 43/1, Oct.
29 *Ibid.*, 46/3, Oct. 10
30 Czernicheff, 262 (wrongly dated 7/19 Sep.)
31 'She made a sign with two fingers that the common people derisively use to credulous and deceived husbands.' Fouché, 316

32 On Oct. 21 she gave birth to an illegitimate child by Flahault: the future duc de Morny

33 AM 27/567 (42), Nov. 17, 1811. 'The Emperor dictated practically all' of this part of her letter, she told Joachim on Dec. 9. *Ibid.*, (51)

34 AM 46/3, Dec. 14

35 AM 27/567 (57), Dec. 20

36 *Ibid.*

37 *Ibid.*, (51), Dec. 5

38 *Fier-à-bras*; he also called him Orlando, after Ariosto's *Orlando Furioso* and, of course, Franconi (the circus master) and King of the Lazzaroni. He was envious of all his marshals, but probably more of Murat than the others because of their closer relationship

39 AM 27/567 (57), Dec. 21

12

1 Kielmannsegge, 95

2 Kielmannsegge, 96

3 Abrantès, *Mémoires*

4 Kielmannsegge, 97. At a ball given by Hortense on Jan. 17, and at another given by Bassano on Feb. 8, Caroline wore jewels estimated to be worth 40,000,000 francs. The cost of the costumes and presentation of the quadrille on Feb. 6 was put at 100,000 francs

5 Hortense, *Mémoires*, II, 139

6 *Ibid.*, 142. Marie-Louise, dressed as a Normandy peasant, was attended by Caroline as a Provençale; other members of her suite represented departments of France; Pauline, as a Neapolitan, danced a solo tarantella

7 Kielmannsegge, 104

8 A nicety of etiquette on which Napoleon insisted when he found Hortense, Julie of Spain and Madame Mère in *fauteuils*. Since Madame Mère was not a queen she was not entitled to more than a *tabouret*. He therefore ordained that they should all sit on stools. (Durand, 54). Caroline soon put an end to this when she arrived at court: 'I only had to speak to the Emperor once ... and we had chairs immediately.' AM 27/568 (12 *bis*)

9 *Ibid.*

10 *Ibid.*

11 *Ibid.*

12 Lecestre, II, 196–7 (926), Paris, Feb. 29. As a Genoese, Maghella was a French citizen

13 Although 'it is only in Naples that one can reign *well*', as she once said to Josephine. Avrillon, I, 341. She told Agar that although the doctors had ordered her 'all sorts of remedies, blisters, douches, pills, milk, quinine' none of them had had any effect and it was five months since she had taken solid food. 'I know they are saying in Naples that I do not want to come back again; I cannot understand how they can think that I could live far away from my husband and my children . . . If he has any fears on that subject, assure him of the great pleasure I shall have in seeing him again; but I should like to think that he has no

doubts on that score.' AM 43/1, Paris, Apr. 1, 1812

14 AE Naples, CXXXVIII, 248, Mar. 28, 1812

15 AM 27/568 (27), Mar. 12, 1812

16 Masson, *Famille*, VII, 231-2

17 AM 27/568 (38), Apr. 13, 1812

18 Lamarque, II, 175. When Joachim urged him to settle the war in Spain first, Napoleon replied: 'I am bored with Europe, everything is so familiar, so monotonous.' AM 45/1. It must have reminded Joachim of a conversation almost ten years before, when Napoleon said to him: 'I shall be unhappy to die in Europe. I want to found an empire in Asia . . . One day I will let you reap that harvest of glory.' *Ibid.*

19 A few days later, Marie-Louise left Dresden to spend a month with her family at Prague, where she was given as *chevalier d'honneur* a tall, witty Swabian officer with a romantic patch over his right eye: Count Albrecht Adam von Neipperg

20 Rapp, 169

21 Vandal, *Nap. et Alex.*, III, 406. Naples had never formed part of the Hapsburg domains.

22 *Ibid.*, 464

13

1 Castellane, I, 112

2 *Revue Napoléonienne*, Jun. 6, 1908, p. 171

3 Castellane, I, 120, Jul. 25, 1812

4 Lejeune, II, 189

5 Willemain, I, 199. Charles XII, King of Sweden who penetrated too far into Russia and was disastrously defeated at Pultawa in June 1709

6 *Ibid.* Joachim, who made his headquarters at the castle of Belmonte, near Matuzero (the property of Count Mamerchi, Russian Ambassador to Bavaria), amused himself by composing a set of verses which his First Equerry, Caraffa, set to music. 'Un moment à Belmonte abandonnons Belone. / Adieu, soucis guerriers; fuyez, soucis du trône!/ Que j'aime à m'égarer dans ces lieux enchanteurs / Où les yeux et les ris, les grâces et l'amour / Auprès de ma Constance ont fixé leur séjour. / Ici l'on n'entend plus ces foudres, ces foudres destructeurs. / Ici la douce paix règne malgré la guerre. / Le silence des bois, leur ombre hospitalière, / Invitent au repos le guerrier désarmé / Et tout respire ici Bonheur et Volupté, / Et tout respire ici Bonheur et Volupté, / Bonheur et Volupté, / Bonheur et Volupté.' AM 19/249 *bis*

(Now we, at Belmonte, abandon Bellona –

Begone, royal burdens! Begone cares of war! –

What solace to sport in these glades so beguiling,

Where Graces and Cupid my Constance adore!

Where the warrior, wearied, his weapons discarding,

Reposes remote from the grim battle's roar;

Where bright eyes are dancing;
where sweet lips are smiling;
Where all is enhancing our Joy
and Delight!
Joy and Delight!
Joy and Delight!
Where all is enhancing our Joy
and Delight!)

7 Barclay made junction with Bagration on Aug. 4

8 Griois, II, 21

9 With some reason. Otherwise why had Napoleon wasted time and men on assaulting the city when an encircling movement would have been more likely to force the Russians to battle?

10 Castellane, I, 140, Aug. 22

11 Fezensac, 35

12 Chuquet, *Etudes*, VI, 260

13 Castellane, I, 146, Sep. 4

14 Brandt, 269

15 'The evening of August 29, when I was at Murat's headquarters, I learned that things had gone so far that the prince's officers had had great difficulty in preventing him from going sword in hand to the marshal to demand an explanation.' Baudus, II, 58. Davout was distrusted by his fellow-marshals; he had long had the reputation of being the Emperor's spy

16 Lejeune, II, 201, Aug. 28

17 The trooper, Tchernozouboff, was promoted by the Hetman Platov for his chivalrous conduct. He later refused 20,000 roubles for the watch, which was inscribed: 'Joachim Murat, capitaine de chasseurs à cheval: Eléonore to Joachim – do not

forget her.' *L'Estafette*, Feb. 2, 1841

18 Redan: two-sided defensive position, shaped like an arrowhead. Redoubt: multi-sided and stronger

19 Dedem, 237

20 His old friend Prince Constantine's regiment, who were at first mistaken for friendly Saxons because of their similar uniforms of white tunics with black facings.

21 Montesquiou, 36

22 *Ibid.*

23 The Russians lost probably 50,000 killed and wounded, the French 30,000. Among the Russian cavalry were Kalmuk and Baskiri archers who carried their arrows in quivers and were nicknamed 'Cupids' by the French. Ney was so incensed at Napoleon's behaviour that he roared: 'What's he doing at the rear? . . . If he no longer wants to fight . . . let him go back to the Tuileries and leave us to be generals for him.' Chateaubriand, III, 209. Dedem, 237, remarked that 'He was never less great than on that day'

24 Castellane, I, 151

25 Brandt, 279–80

26 AM 10/42 (3). Rossetti's *Journal*. This passage, with the last sentence omitted, appears in Labaume, 153–4

27 Nap. I, *Lettres inédites ... à Marie-Louise*, 70. Sep. 8, 1812. Early that morning the admiring Sergeant Bourgogne and a friend saw Joachim 'superintend the amputation by his own surgeon

of the legs of two gunners of the Imperial Russian Guard. When the operation was over, he gave them each a glass of wine.' Bourgogne, 8–9

28 Chuquet says Murat launched the attack because he was 'drunk with the smell of powder'. *Etudes*, VI, 260. Dedem, 243, who commanded a brigade in the 2nd Division of 1st Corps, attributes it to his desire to spend the night in a château instead of a tent. Joachim prided himself on not allowing war to interfere with his comfort. 'It was a sort of defiance, one more way of outfacing danger,' says Colbert, I, 93. '"But if you go to bed, and are surprised by the enemy, what will you do?" somebody asked him. – "Why, I'll get on my horse in my shirt; they'll see me all the better!"'

29 Wilson, *Narrative*, 167
30 Dedem, 250
31 Combe, 102
32 Dedem, 250
33 Castellane, I, 161
34 *Ibid.*, 159, Sep. 22
35 Reboul, I, 379–80, Portici, Oct. 16
36 Brandt, 300
37 Dupuy, 185–6
38 Elie Baudus, son of Achille's tutor, and one of Bessières's aides-de-camp, was sent with a joint warning from Joachim and Bessières (commanding the Cavalry of the Guard) that the cavalry would disintegrate if kept on active duty much longer. 'Are those buggers frightened?'

was Napoleon's reply. 'Tell them that if they are frightened I will replace them.' Baudus, II, 154–5. Berthier gave him a more tactful reply to carry back

39 Derrécagaix, *Belliard*, 511
40 Reboul, I, 382–3, Vinkowo, Oct. 13
41 Roos, 144
42 Wilson, *Narrative*, 210, Wilson, British Military Observer with the Russian army, had an opportunity to discuss the campaign with Joachim eighteen months later

43 Bennigsen was wounded and Dery, Joachim's Grand Marshal of the Palace, was killed in this engagement 'remarkable for the ferocity on both sides'. Seruzier, 230. 'There never was a cavalry combat in modern warfare where the antagonists continued so close and commingled for such a length of time.' Wilson, *Narrative*, 211. Murat, with a total force of less than 30,000 men, was faced with 90,000 Russians and 100 cannon

14

1 He feared being captured, having heard that 'the Hetman Platow had promised his daughter's hand to anybody, even a simple Cossack, who brought him Napoleon alive'. Dedem, 270. Admiral Chichagoff, commanding the Moldavian Army brought up from the southern frontiers, had issued his description: 'small, stout, pale-complexioned, short

thick neck, big head, dark hair'
and ordered that all prisoners of
low stature be brought to his
headquarters for identification.
Langeron, 134

2 A fatal mistake. Kutusov had
'resolved on falling back behind
the Oka' if Napoleon pressed on.
Wilson, *Narrative*, 236

3 Griois, II, 140

4 *Ibid.*, 126

5 The 'Escadron Sacré', commanded by Grouchy under the
direct orders of Joachim

6 Ney marched his 6,000 men
through the Russians, rejoining
the main body on the 21st. He
had only 900 men left. It was on
this occasion that Napoleon
named him 'The Bravest of the
Brave'.
A week later he had one gun, a
hundred horses and not a single
infantryman
Nov. 26, 27 and 28
Which they conveyed on sledges

7 Suckow, 242

8 Castellane, I, 196

9 *Moniteur*, Dec. 17, 1812, p. 1,391,
col. a. The Bulletin ends: 'His
Majesty's health has never been
better,' *Ibid.*, col. c

10 Langeron, 92. General Wilson,
horrified at the 'complication of
misery, of cruelty, of desolation,
and of disorder, that can never
have been exceeded in the history
of mankind' *Narrative*, 261,
recorded that the French prisoners 'were immediately and invariably stripped stark naked and
marched in columns in that
state, or turned adrift to be the

sport and the victims of the
peasantry'. *Ibid.*, 256

11 Nap. I, *Corr.*, XXIV, 322
(19,362), Zanivki

12 Eronouf, *Bassano*, 462

13 There is no substance in the
suggestion that he hurried back
because he heard of the Malet
conspiracy at Molodeczno; he
had learned of this four weeks
before, on Nov. 6

14 Chateaubriand, III, 241

15 *Ibid.*

16 Castellane, I, 203, Dec. 7. He
made no further entries in his
journal because his hands were
frostbitten. Langeron, 88, says:
'The cold began to make itself
felt at Zembin (on December 1).
It was 7 or 8 degrees [of frost];
three days later it was 15 to 18;
on December 11 it was 28.'
Larrey, Chief Surgeon of the
Grande Armée, who wore a
thermometer in his buttonhole,
confirms the temperature of
28 degrees (Réaumur, which in
this instance is approximately the
same as Fahrenheit). *Mémoires*,
IV, 107. The cold which had so
demoralized the French forces
had not until now been more
severe than normal; but
Napoleon 'had not, it seems, even
investigated what the weather
was likely to be in the enemy's
country'. Angervo

17 Langeron, 90

18 Hogendorp, 337

19 AM 19/248 (4), Vilna, Dec. 9.
Lechat, who met Joachim at
Vilna, denies Maret's accusations
that he had lost his nerve. 'He

was a tired man, certainly, but not demoralized.' *Journal*, 136. Coussy was working with Joachim on plans for the defence of Vilna when Ney entered the room on the morning of the 13th and said: 'Sire! there is fighting in the suburbs, and I do not know if our men can hold out for long ... Do you want to be taken like a conscript, like a mouse in a trap?' *Ibid.*

20 Reboul, I, 386 (1), Wirballen, Dec. 16

21 *Ibid.*, 386–7

22 *Ibid.*, 386 (2), Stallupönen

23 'Some corps have not as many as 25 to 30 men all told, and they will vanish if you try to keep them on the Vistula; there may not be even one left, for the officers have not the power, nor even the will, to stop them, and are even the first to set an example of disorder.' Derrécagaix, *Belliard*, 519

24 *Ibid.*, 519–20

25 Hogendorp, 351

26 Brotonne, *Lettres inédites*, 422 (1032), Fontainebleau, Jan. 24, 1813. This is one of the batch of letters falsified by Blacas to mislead Castlereagh, see n. 50, p. 080. It may have been sent the following year

27 *Ibid.*

28 *Moniteur*, Jan. 27, 1813, p. 103, col. a

29 Mier told Metternich that Joachim was greatly concerned by a remark Berthier made to him – that 'he considered him too good a Frenchman not to be certain that he would willingly sacrifice his crown if the interests of France demanded it' Helfert, *Joachim Murat*, 133, a suggestion which Joachim believed came from Napoleon

30 Weil, Eugène, I, 52. Durand again warned Bassano a few days later that Joachim 'feared he would find himself abandoned' and 'intended to provide his own means of self-preservation'. *Ibid.*, 53

31 AM 25/500 (1)

15

1 Weil, *Eugène*, I, 53 (3)

2 Ferdinand tried to resume power early in 1813; Bentinck overbore him and obtained the exile of Mary Caroline

3 FO 70/58, at sea, Jun. 10, 1813

4 AM 25/500 (1), Portici, May 11

5 ADD. 43,073/318, Bentinck to Castlereagh, Prague, Sep. 14, 14, 1813

6 Weil, *Eugène*, I, 158 (2)

7 Noel, 204

8 The British resistance to Murat's retaining the throne of Naples had now been modified. On Aug. 6 Castlereagh wrote to Aberdeen that 'It will probably be found necessary ... to enter into an Understanding with Murat. ... The Prince Regent persuades himself that a liberal Establishment may be found for Murat in the Centre of Italy, without prejudice to the rights of the Sicilian Family to the Crown of Naples.' But in a Secret and

Separate dispatch which was presumably not laid before the Prince Regent, he told Aberdeen that the Bourbons should be found a new home since 'Murat might find a stronger inducement for exertion if his claim to the Throne of Naples depended on an equivalent for the Sicilian Family being conquered elsewhere'. FO 7/101, No. 3

9 Nearly 100,000 men killed and wounded. The French lost 40,000, plus 30,000 prisoners and 260 guns. With this battle Napoleon forged the nationalist spirit of modern Germany; four months later, by failing to accept the Chaumont proposals, he let her learn that she could successfully invade inviolable France. Of all his crimes against his country and Europe, these two are perhaps the worst

10 Desvernois, 438

11 Pasquier, II, 97

12 Bellaire, 5–6

13 ADD. 43,075/153

16

1 AM 25/500 (1), Dec. 16

2 AE Naples, CXXXIX, 565

3 AM 25/500 (1)

4 ADD. 43,076/22–3, enc. in Aberdeen to Castlereagh, Frankfurt, Dec. 11, 1813

5 AE Naples, CXL, 8, Jan. 3, 1814

6 Weil, *Eugène*, III, 647. Elisa learned of it the following day and at once sent the news to Napoleon. It was signed on Jan. 23

7 FO 63/52 enc. in Bentinck to Castlereagh, Palermo, Jan. 4

8 'If he comes in support of the Vice-Roy, the Austrian army of Italy will for a time be considerably embarrassed.' Aberdeen to Castlereagh, Dec. 11, 1813. ADD. 43,076/19

9 AM 20/300

10 Récamier, I, 249

11 *Ibid.*

12 'This Treaty is a sad violation of all publick and private principle,' he wrote to Castlereagh on Jan. 14. FO 70/63. And to Bunbury on Feb. 17: 'This monstrous connection with Murat can end in no good.' ADD. 37,050/236

13 Weil, *Eugène*, III, 617

14 Gentz, *Theilnahme*, 172, to Caradja, Vienna, Feb. 11. Metternich changed the terms on the insistence of Castlereagh, who arrived at Allied HQ at Bâle on Jan. 18

15 AM 27/580 (1)

16 Helfert, *Joachim Murat*, 142

17 Weil, *Eugène*, IV, 316

18 Helfert, *Joachim Murat*, 148, Chaumont, Mar. 8

19 Despatys, 196. A few days before he had written to Marie-Louise: 'You asked me if you should write to the Queen of Naples. I answer no; she has behaved in an inconceivable way to me, who transformed her from a little nobody into a queen.' Nap. I, *Lettres inédites à Marie-Louise*, 214, Besut-St-Germain, Mar. 4

20 Beauharnais, X, 215, Soissons, Mar. 12, 1814. He told Eugène he had sent the Pope to Murat's

21 Helfert, *Joachim Murat*, 151, Mier to Metternich, Reggio, Mar. 29

22 *Ibid.*, 153

23 AE Naples, CXXXX, 121, Reggio, Mar. 18

24 On the 18th Joachim wrote to Fouché asking him to persuade Napoleon to issue a proclamation saying: 'My army will cooperate with whichever power desires the independence of Italy and will save her from the return of the former dynasties.' 'That,' Joachim said, 'would give me a pretext to break with the Austrians.' Weil, *Eugène*, IV, 403–4

25 AM 20/309, Reggio, Mar. 21

26 *Ibid.*

27 Eugène revealed Joachim's proposal 'from hatred of the man as well as of the line of conduct that he has pursued', as Wilson shrewdly noted at the time. Wilson, *Diary*, II, 354

28 *Ibid.*, 343–5

29 Maceroni, *Life*, II, 115

30 Gentz, *Theilnahme*, 325, To Caradja, Vienna, April, 22

17

1 Herriot, I, 319

2 Nicola, II, 712

3 Pasquier, II, 137. 'Nobody ever dared mention his removal to me beforehand,' Joachim told Wilson. 'If I had ever thought that was their intention I would have sacrificed my crown and my life to prevent it.' Note in outposts 'wishing to embarrass him'. *Ibid.*

Wilson's handwriting on a document in AM 25/513 (1)

4 'It is a severe violence to my feelings to incur any degree of obligation to an Individual whom I so entirely despise,' Bentinck wrote to Castlereagh from Genoa on May 1 – and asked him to pass the sword on to the Prince Regent. FO 70/64, No. 26

5 Macirone, *Interesting facts*, 358. The author was using this spelling when he wrote to Caroline and General Macdonald in 1817, 1818 and 1819 (AM 21/358) but later changed it to Maceroni, under which style he published his *Life*

6 Davies, 17. Catherine Davies was the nursemaid, assistant to Mrs. Pulsford

7 Murat-Rasponi, 483

8 *Ibid.*

9 Mlle de Paraviccini or Mlle de Mirvaux who assisted the official Governess, the short, plump, much-loved Mme de Roquemont. Each *sous-gouverante* was on duty in alternate weeks, spending every hour of the day with them and sleeping in an adjoining room at night

10 Murat-Rasponi, 486

11 'Another scene in the comedy,' noted Nicola, II, 736. 'It's all a farce.' They remembered at the last moment that Achille, born at a time when such things were not so popular, had never been baptized, a ceremony which was hurriedly and discreetly performed in Caroline's library

12 Baring, 220–1

13 Arnault, III, 196–7
14 Henry Holland, 131–2
15 Baring, 233
16 *Ibid*. Baring was not one for enthusing. Of the Bay of Naples he remarked: 'The view would be greatly improved if, in casting your eye upon the city, you could descry some turrets and steeples. The whole place appears at a distance to be a huge mass of stones thrown together.' *Ibid.*, 251–2
17 Bourgoing, *Coeur de Marie-Louise*, II, 139
18 GOUL. 4A/2/2 (5)
19 *Ibid.*, (10)
20 Henry Holland, 131
21 *Ibid.*, 132
22 Rogers, *It. Journ.*, 258. Caroline opened the ball with Achille and Joachim with Letitia; later Caroline waltzed and Joachim joined in the country dances. Joachim treated the poet with his usual affability. 'He would invariably call out to me, rising in his stirrups, "Well there, Sir, are you inspired today?"' Rogers, *Table Talk*, 226
23 Mayne, 275–6
24 Henry Holland, 133
25 *Ibid.*

18

1 Bathurst, 274
2 Castlereagh, *Corr.*, X, 3
3 Iung, III, 184
4 Gentz, *Theilnahme*, 337, to Caradja, Vienna
5 Barras, IV, 280
6 Polovtzov, 51

7 One representative, Franz von Gaertner, appeared on behalf of no less than fifty minor German feudatories
8 Weil, *Murat, D.A.*, I, 161
9 Oxford asked Castlereagh to appoint him British Minister to Naples. Castlereagh sent a curt refusal and a warning 'to abstain in your language and conduct, whilst you may remain at Naples, from taking any step whatever which might be construed into an Act of the British Government', FO 70/66, London, Jul. 26, 1814
10 Weil, *Congrés*, I, 53
11 Weil, *Congrés*, I, 73, Gentz to Caradja
12 *Ibid.*
13 Weil, *Murat, D.A.*, I, 309–10
14 *Ibid.*, 338, Lebzeltern to Metternich, Rome, Sep. 3, 1814
15 Weil, *Congrès*, I, 240
16 Castlereagh, *Corr.*, X, 76, London, Aug. 7
17 *Ibid.*, 114–5, Paris, Sep. 12
18 *Ibid.*, 145, to A'Court, Vienna, Oct. 2
19 Wellington, *Supp. Desp.*, IX, 285
20 Weil, *Congrès*, I, 442, spy's report to Hager, Nov. 1
21 Helfert, *Joachim Murat*, 165, Mier to Metternich, Nov. 12
22 *Ibid.*, 164, Nov. 6
23 Weil, *Murat, D.A.*, II, 125
24 *Ibid.*, II, 533
25 Polovtzov, 131
26 Weil, *Murat, D.A.*, II, 149 (2)
27 Talleyrand, II, 514
28 *Ibid.*, 513–14
29 Castlereagh, *Corr.*, X, 221
30 And seems to have deliberately misled him over his reaction to

Oxford's arrest. Lieven, the Russian ambassador in London, was informed, evidently semi-officially, that Wellington 'has not been satisfied to ask for excuses; he has demanded an explanation of the outrage'. Weil, *Congrès*, I, 724

31 Castlereagh, *Corr.*, X, 228, Paris, Dec. 26

32 *Ibid.*, 244

33 Weil, *Murat, D.A.*, II, 335

34 Croce, 390

35 Weil, *Congrès*, II, 275

36 Castlereagh's fee as middleman was a promise that France would abolish the slave trade

37 Weil, *Murat, D.A.*, I, 291

38 Pellet, 147, Jan. 6, 1814

39 Weil, *Murat, D.A.*, II, 353

40 *Ibid.*, I, 181

41 Written while he was interned at Thorngrove. He arrived in Rome from London on May 27, 1814

42 Fleuriot de Langle, *Alexandrine*, 149

43 FO 70/66, enc. in Fagan to Castlereagh, Palermo, Oct. 20

44 Pons de l'H'erault, 376–7. See Joachim's letter to Alesme, p. (387 of MS), below

45 Firmin-Didot, 234

46 Fleury de Chaboulon, I, 102. In the copy of Fleury's book which he read and annotated on St Helena, Napoleon let this passage stand unchallenged

47 AM 20/334 (1)

48 *Ibid.*, (2)

49 AM 25/510 (3)

50 *Ibid.*, (1)

51 *Ibid.*, (2)

52 Helfert, *Joachim Murat*, 180

53 ADM 1/430, No. 88, Penrose to Croker, *Queen*, Messina, Mar. 12

54 *Ibid.*, No. 94, Palermo, Mar. 29. Madame Mère was hooted in the streets of Leghorn when she left for Elba in August 1814. 'That woman may have a kind heart, as some people say,' the chevalier de Sobiratz wrote to the comtesse d'Albany, 'but hers is certainly the most culpable belly that ever existed.' Pelissier, *Portefeuille*, 211

19

1 Helfert, *Joachim Murat*, 177, Mier to Metternich, Mar. 9

2 *Ibid.*, 177–8

3 *Ibid.*, 178

4 Croce, 403

5 Weil, *Murat, D.A.*, III, 84

6 Returning from Elba, she was arrested by Austrian troops at Elisa's Villa di Compignano, near Massarosa on the Lucca-Viareggio road

7 Weil, *Murat, D.A.*, III, 170

8 *Ibid.*, 189

9 Wellington, *Supp. Desp.*, IX, 592, London, Mar. 12. These are the letters that Blacas falsified. For a discussion of their real dates see Johnston, II, App. E. The argument is not of importance here

10 Wellington, *Supp. Desp.*, IX., 593

11 *Ibid.*

12 *Ibid.*, 609

13 *Ibid.*

14 Webster, 321

15 Wellington, *Dispatches*, VIII, 15

16 WO 1/284 (133), Ancona, Mar. 28

17 Under a secret article of the treaty
of Jan. 11, 1814, Joachim had
'the incontestable right' to occupy the Marches 'until the definite
settlement of his affairs', including his recognition by the
Pope. But he was now literally
across the Rubicon and it was
because of the Pope's 'incessant
complaints and jeremiads' and
the 'personal animosity of the
Austrian representative in Rome
towards Murat' that the Austrian
government was forced to call on
him to withdraw. Gentz, *Theilnahme*, 617

18 Nicola, II, 793–4

19 WO 1/284 (168)

20 AM 20/337 (15)

21 WO 1/284 (235), Bologna, Apr. 4

20

1 Schoell, V, 77–8

2 Weil, *Murat, D.A.*, IV, 407

3 *Ibid.*, 408

4 *Ibid.*

5 Fournier, 289, Muccia, on the
Foligno road, May 8. A reference
to their visit to the Oberland the
previous September when Marie-
Louise made Pauline's rude ges-
ture come true by cuckolding
Napoleon with Neipperg at the
Inn of the Golden Sun

6 Ayala, 289 (1)

21

1 Who arrived at Naples on Apr. 4.
Caroline's younger daughter
Louise remembered her playing
interminable irritable games of

whist with the ruddyfaced, youth-
ful-looking Fesch, who came
down from Rome some days
earlier

2 Jérôme, VIII, 17

3 Desvernois, 487–8

4 ADD. 51,665/201

5 Nicola, II, 812

6 Derrécagaix, *Belliard*, 604

7 Davies, 37

8 ADM 1/430, No. 107, enc.

9 *Ibid.* That day a dispatch from
Metternich caught up with Neipperg at L'Aquila. It told him to
offer Joachim a pension of two
million florins a year if he agreed
to abdicate. With Murat so evidently beaten, Neipperg took
it upon himself not to forward
the proposal

10 *Bibl. Univ.*, II, 70–1

11 Desvernois, 493. Meneval,
Mémoires, III, 474, has: 'All is
lost except my life; I have not
been lucky enough to find Death';
while according to Colletta,
History, II, 240, Joachim said,
'We are betrayed by Fortune, all
is lost', and Caroline answered,
'Not all – if we preserve our
honour and constancy'

12 The message arrived too late;
Bianchi replied that Joachim
must throw himself on the mercy
of the Austrians – they would not
treat with him

13 Colletta, *History*, II, 240

14 Colletta, *Opere Inedite*, I, 198

15 The surrender of all forts, ports
and arsenals with the exception
of Gaëta, Pescare and Ancona
(which were besieged and not
under Carascosa's command);

the surrender of Capua on May 21, withdrawal of all Neapolitan troops to Salerno and entry of the Austrians into Naples on May 23. In accordance with Joachim's instructions, his negotiators got promises of protection for investors in state funds, purchasers of state properties, and a universal amnesty.

16 Better known as Admiral Pellew, he had come out from England in the *Boyne* to take command of the Mediterranean fleet

17 ADD. 51,665/235, Woburn Abbey [? Sep. 6, 1815]

18 *Ibid.*, 36,457/150b, Broughton Correspondence

19 The Duke and Duchess acted as interpreters. On May 20 the Duke wrote to Caroline: 'My wife has one more favour to ask of Your Majesty and that is to permit her to accompany you in the ship as far as the coast of France – as the captain speaks only English, she dares suggest that she could be of some service to Your Majesty during the voyage.' AM 27/587

20 ADM 1/430, No. 107, Exmouth to Croker, *Boyne*, Naples Bay, May 24

21 FO 79/23

22 ADD. 36,457/150

23 *Ibid.*

24 ADD. 51,662, to Lord Holland, Westminster, Sep. 13 [?1816]

25 *Ibid.*

26 Weil, *Murat D.A.,* V, 249. 'It was my intention to have landed the Queen on the frontiers of France,' wrote Exmouth, 'but as

objections have been stated to that arrangement, I have determined (in compliance with her own request) that she should be landed at Trieste.' ADM. 1/430, No. 197

27 Louise Murat-Rasponi's memory is at fault when she says Caroline sent her physician, Andral. He was already with the children; Caroline sent him a letter by Livron, asking him to take all her property from Gaëta to Naples and from there to France, where he would find Joachim. Brouwet, 241, on board *Tremendous*, May 25

28 Murat-Rasponi, 846

29 Colletta, *History*, II, 250

22

1 AM 20/348 (1), in the Bay of Cagnes in quarantine, May 25

2 AM 20/335. This has slightly more detail, but does not vary in essentials, from the version published by Iung and Espitalier

3 Nap. I, *Corr.*, XXVIII, 52 (21,745)

4 *Ibid.*

5 Nap. 1, *Corr.*, XXVIII, 80 (21,777), Paris

6 Chateaubriand, IV, 317

7 Nap. I, *Corr.*, XXVIII, 112–13, Paris (wrongly dated Apr. 19)

8 *Ibid.*, 113

9 AM 21/361 (1) Armand's account

10 AM 20/348 (3)

11 Chateaubriand, IV, 318

12 Desvernois, 515. Finding that Desvernois had no money, Joachim lent him 10,000 francs

13 Desvernois, 517. Napoleon is

said to have replied to Fouché's advances, 'What peace treaty has been signed between France and Naples since 1814?' Saint-Hilaire, I, 270

14 'Ah!' he said to Maceroni, 'how must the Emperor on that day have regretted having refused *me* the command of that cavalry. Two or three only – perhaps one – of the British squares of infantry broken – and the battle was surely ours! I would have broken their square!' Maceroni, *Life*, II, 302

15 ADM. 1/431, Marseilles, Jul. 13

16 Maceroni prided himself on his ingenuity in these matters; on another occasion he carried a written message stuffed down the barrel of his loaded pistol, so that he could destroy it with a squeeze of the trigger

17 Desvernois, 534. Realizing that the Bourbons would wage a vendetta as fiercly as the Bonapartes, Joachim wrote to the newspapers denying any guilt in the Enghien murder

18 ADM. 1/431, No. 197, enc.

19 Single-masted lateen-rigged craft capable of carrying about 50 men each

20 Macirone, *Interesting Facts*, 160

21 Maceroni, *Life*, II, 298

22 *Ibid.*, 299

23 Macirone, *Facts*, 160–1

24 *Ibid.*, 162

25 For the arguments for and against the theory that a deliberate trap was laid for him, see Sassenay and Dufourcq. There is no indication that Joachim's decision

was influenced by any of the alleged lures

26 On his way back to Corsica he encountered another of the *gondoles*, commanded by Captain Ettore, and told him the king had decided not to land, whereupon Ettore also turned back

27 Masson, *Revue d'Ombres*, 203, quoting from an account by Charles. These passages do not occur in the incomplete manuscript *Relation de Charles* in AM 21/362

28 *Ibid.*, 204

29 Maceroni, Life, II, 323

30 ADD. 35,651/294. Penrose to Exmouth, *Queen* at sea, Oct. 25

31 Maceroni, *Life*, II, 325

32 Trentacapelli, two of whose brothers had been hanged by Manhès

33 ADD. 41,537/83b, Perri to A' Court, Pizzo, Oct. 15

34 The claim was true: many of Joachim's and Caroline's treasures remained in Naples

35 ADD. 35/651/294–5

36 Fortunato, 13

37 Saint-Hilaire, II, 282

38 AM 21/361 (1). Armand's account

39 AM 21/362. Charles's account

40 *Ibid.*

41 Fortunato, 15

42 *Ibid.*

43 *Ibid.*

44 ADD. 41,537/81b. Perri's account

45 ADD. 35,651/295

46 Byron, *Letters and Journals*, III, 245, Nov. 4, 1815. In his *Ode from the French* he apostrophized 'Thou, too, of the snow-white

plume, Whose realm refused thee ev'n a tomb!' *Works: Poetry*, III, 433

47 Las Cases, I, 368

48 Bonaparte, P-N., I, 155. Murat, guessing that the Bourbons would wage a vendetta as fiercely as the Bonapartes, had written to the newspapers while in the South of France, denying any guilt in the Enghien murder

49 Noailles, II, 63

PART IV The Countess Alone 1815–1838

I

1 '*Naiveté*' in the original; probably the only time this noun was used to describe Caroline's character

2 Wertheimer, *Verbannten*, 136 (2), Trieste, Jun. 14, 1815

3 The Palazzo Romano, which Jérôme bought in Feb., 1815, for 100,000 florins. On the plinth of a statue in the garden was the inscription: 'Greater virtues are needed to sustain good fortune than bad.' Duhamel, 20

4 *Ibid.*, 142 (1)

5 Weil, *Murat, D.A.,* V, 447–8. This, together with 32 other letters carried by the servants, was discovered by the Austrian customs officers at Opicina

6 'I think he has about twenty millions,' Napoleon told Bertrand on Jul. 28, 1816. Bertrand, I, 93. By July 1815 Caroline had already sold some of the gold lace and embroidery from Joachim's uniforms and her own court dresses for 14,000 francs. She arrived in Trieste with 100,000 francs in cash, and jewels which she sold for 400,000

7 Weil, *Congrès,* II, 712, Sep. 28

8 *Ibid.*, 721, Oct. 20

9 *Ibid.*

10 *Ibid.*, 723

11 *Ibid.*, 729

12 Wertheimer, *Verbannten,* 119 (1)

13 Weil, *Congrès,* II, 731

14 Wertheimer, *Verbannten,* 153 (2). From Colonna di Lecca, Rome, May 3, 1817

15 *Ibid.*, 154 (2)

16 *Ibid.*

17 'Three letters without a reply,' she wrote to her in Dec. 1816. 'I hope this one will be luckier and will reach you, for I am using the address that Catherine has given me.' AM 11/54 (39)

18 *Ibid.*, (41), Nov. 13, 1817

19 Wertheimer, *Verbannten,* 154, to Elisa, Rome, Apr. 16, 1817

20 Fleuriot de Langle, *Alexandrine,* 164, Nov. 2, 1816. Two more daughters were born later

21 Catherine, *Corr.,* 250, Schönau, Feb. 4

22 Iung, III, 394, letter from Mme Maret, Nov. 9, 1817

23 *Ibid.*

24 Schlitter, 44

25 Wertheimer, *Verbannten,* 156 (1), Jun. 12, 1821

26 FM 58/11, Jun. 14, 1819

27 *Ibid.*, 58/9

28 *Ibid.*, 58/22, Jan. 28, 1821

29 *Ibid.*, 58/25, Feb. 3

30 'We are sketching a lot, making music, and at the moment we have a mania for tapestry.' *Ibid.*, 58/42, Caroline to Mercey, Frohsdorf, Jun. 8, 1822

31 L., Ernestine von, 259

32 AM 22/397 (3), Frohsdorf, Mar. 30, 1822

33 November 1822. The fifteen pictures included two Carrachis, two Corregios, two Veronese, an Andrea del Sarto, a Guido Reni, a Perugino, a Raphael and a Titian. Caroline sold them all for £9,200 payable in three instalments. They are now in the National Gallery

34 Caroline always addressed him as 'bon Mercey', a pretty little untranslatable pun

35 FM 58/79, Frohsdorf, Apr. 23, 1823

36 *Ibid.*

37 *Ibid.*, 58/83-4, Battaglia, Aug. 26, 1823

38 Who had remained in Europe ostensibly because her health did not permit her travelling to America. She was also sickened of Joseph's innumerable affairs with other women

39 Wertheimer, *Verbannten*, 165, Aug. 8, 1824

40 Récamier, II, 144-5, Nov. 11, 1824

41 *Ibid.*, 174, May 9, 1825

42 *Ibid.*, 176

43 FM 57/258b, to Joseph de Girard, Mar. 8, 1825

2

1 Kielmannsegge, 331

2 Récamier, II, 175-6

3 L., Ernestine von, 271

4 FM 58/136b, Nov. 2, 1828

5 *Ibid.*, 136b-7

6 FM 58/151b, Jun. 29, 1829. She made each of them an allowance varying from £200 to £300 a year, according to the state of her own finances, but it was never sufficient. 'Lucien's affairs are in a deplorable state,' Achille wrote to Mercey on Jun. 27, 1827. 'I do not think he has enough to pay for his house, and that is all he possesses in the world.' *Ibid.*, 63/93b

7 Christine was first married, in 1818, to Arved de Possé, a Swede who disappeared in South America, and then, in 1824, to Lord Dudley – whereupon Possé reappeared and the next four years were spent in anxious but finally successful attempts to get the Vatican to annul the first marriage

8 AM 11/54 (48)

9 Wertheimer, *Verbannten*, 168, May 10, 1830

10 FM 58/167b, to Mercey, May 23, 1830

11 Later the 4th Lord Holland

12 Fox, 375

13 *Ibid.*

14 *Ibid.*

15 *Ibid.*

16 *Ibid.*

17 *Ibid.*, 376. 'She would gladly have turned dear Dudley's head.'

18 *Ibid.* An ungallant reference to

either Hautmesnil's wife, Sylvie Boucot, who previously held a similar post with Pauline, or more likely to Mlle Elisa Braig, 'very musical, very witty, very erudite' (Masuyer, 31), but unfortunately a mischief-maker whom Caroline was forced to get rid of in the following August

19 Fox, 376. Caroline's words are in French in the original

20 AM 11/54 (51), to Napoléon-Louis, Jul. 16, 1830

21 Bonaparte, J., *Lettres d'exil*, 157

22 Masuyer, 35. The fierce old woman was never really reconciled to her youngest daughter, though when Caroline left Rome she told Hortense that 'she was extremely kind to me; she even made me a present of a superb gold snuff box with the portrait of my children on it'. AM 11/54 (50), Florence, Jul. 10, 1830

23 Kielmannsegge, 325

24 *Ibid.*, 324

25 *Ibid.*

26 FM 58/189. Trieste, Nov. 9, 1830

27 *Ibid.*, 58/202, Jan. 15, 1831

28 Pierre. Of the previous three, all named Joachim, two had died within a month of birth

29 *Ibid.*, 58/204, Jan. 18

30 Catherine Daingerfield Gray, née Willis, a 23-year-old widow when she married Achille on Jul. 12, 1826. 'Pretty, sweet-tempered, kind, an accomplished woman; they are much in love and very happy,' wrote Joseph's elder daughter, Zénaïde, in May 1827. Bertin, 295

31 FM 63/92, Jun. 27, 1827

32 Long, 5

33 *Ibid.*, 7

34 Masuyer, 221

35 *Ibid.*

36 Joseph followed him to London much later, leaving America at the end of July 1832 and arriving in England at the beginning of September, only to learn that the Duke of Reichstadt had died on July 22

37 Masuyer, 223

38 *Ibid.*

39 *Ibid.*

40 *Ibid.*, 244

41 Weill, 83, Jul. 23, 1831

42 Caroline Georgina Frazer, daughter of a British army officer who settled in South Carolina. She later opened a girl's boarding school to help support the family

43 Bertin, 302

44 HARR, XXIV, 257, Mar. 11, 1831

45 *Ibid.*, 169–70

46 *Ibid.*, 257

47 FM 58/225, Aug. 29, 1831

48 *Ibid.*, 58/484

49 In April 1832 a new law continued the banishment of all descendants and relations of Napoleon, adding to them those of Charles X

50 Lumbroso, *Misc. Nap.*, V, to Achille, Florence, Jan. 10, 1832

51 FM 58/239, to Mercey, Mar. 6, 1832

52 From Carlo and Ugolini Griffoni; the site is now occupied by the Hotel Excelsior Italia

53 Hortense, *Italie*, 256–8; and *Mémoires de tous*, I, 236–7

54 FM 58/298b, Sep. 20, 1834

55 *Ibid.*, 58/299, Sep. 29

56 Méry, 92 (originally published in 1835 in *Le Correspondant* and elsewhere). One of Caroline's favourite stories at this time was of Joachim's lenient treatment of a mutinous garrison at Leghorn in 1801. Having announced that he would shoot one man in ten, he reduced the total to three, then faked their execution with blank shot and had them smuggled on to a boat bound for America – where Achille met one of them in the autumn of 1830. During this visit to Italy, Méry called on Madame Mère in Rome. 'Motionless in her chair, she seemed to me to be in pain, from physical suffering, from age, from her memories, but heroically resigned. Her tightly fitted dress revealed an extraordinary state of emaciation; her hands were skeletal; her face retained only the thinnest pale skin; her eyes though open, wandered at random.' *Ibid.*, 187–8

57 AM 11/54 (56)

58 *Ibid.*, (55) Florence, Mar. 26, 1836

59 FM, 58/339, to Agar, Paris, Jul. 2, 1836

60 FM, 58/343, to Mercey, Florence, Aug. 16, 1836

61 *Ibid.*, 58/345

62 AM 11/54 (54), Nevers, Sep. 17, 1836. It was exactly twenty-five years since she left Naples on her last visit to Paris. 'There is the flag of a French frigate just below my window,' she wrote to a friend from Trieste in July, 1831. 'The

sight of it made me forget for a moment that I was exiled.' AM 28/592 *bis*

63 Stendhal, *Corr.*, III, 222, to Mme Jules Gauthier, Paris, Nov. 1, 1836

64 Laure died on Jun. 7, 1838. Caroline would on occasions amuse her company by reading Laure's *Mémoires* to them. 'The Duchess of Abrantès,' she confided to them, 'could never bear me; Junot asked for my hand first and, although I refused, he always showed a weakness for me – his wife could not forgive me for it.' L., Ernestine von

65 Lechat, 151

66 *Ibid.*

67 Stendhal, *Corr.*, III, 222. The one pulled down in 1814 represented Napoleon as Caesar; the substitute put up by Louis-Philippe in 1833 showed him in modern uniform. When Caroline returned to Florence she commissioned from the sculptor Bartolini the statue of her brother as a Roman Emperor that now stands in the place St-Nicolas at Bastia

68 Collet, II, 305 (1)

69 Gigoux, 95. The painter, François-Pascal-Simon Gérard, died in 1837

70 Bonaparte, J., *Lettres d'exil*, 225

71 *Ibid.*, 227

72 *Ibid.*, 233, Jun. 21, 1837

73 Masuyer, 459–60

74 Marchand, 152

75 Murat, *Murat en 1808*, ix

76 FM 58/406. In January 1852 Clavel, in common with many

former adherents of the Bonaparte cause, was given a minor
government post by Louis, President of the French Republic and
about to become Emperor as
Napoleon III. In his private
diary, Horace de Viel-Castel
wrote the cynical and unsup-
ported comment that Clavel had
received the appointment 'because he was kept by the late

Queen of Naples, Mme. Murat'.
Mémoires, II, 31. Caroline's biographers have repeated this allegation that Clavel was her lover
without citing the source, revealing the flimsiness of the
evidence, or examining its distasteful improbability. Her fellow
countrymen cannot be accused of
an excess of gallantry towards
her

Sources

This list comprises the sources from which I have drawn material for this book.

There have been several biographies in French of Joachim and Caroline, individually and jointly. This is the first joint biography to appear in English; it is also the first in any language to be based on the complete Murat family archives now preserved in the private sector of the Archives Nationales. For permission to consult this very large collection of documents I am deeply indebted to Prince Charles Murat and the Director of the Archives of France.

For making other hitherto unpublished material available to me, I am equally indebted to: the Institute of France and Mlle Hélène Michaud, Librarian of the Bibliothèque Thiers; the Director of Diplomatic Archives, Ministère des Affaires Etrangéres; the Trustees of the Harrowby MSS Trust and the Archivist, Miss Rosemary Dunhill; the County Librarian and County Archivist, Lincolnshire; the Trustees of the British Museum; the Keeper of Public Records. I am especially grateful to Jean Vanel, Président des Amis du Musée Murat, for his help in identifying collateral members of the Murat family.

The following abbreviations have been used:
- ADD Additional MS, British Museum
- ADM Admiralty records, Public Record Office
- AE Archives diplomatiques, Ministère des Affaires Etrangéres
- AM Archives Murat, Archives Nationales (where they carry the prefix 31 AP)
- FO Foreign Office records, Public Record Office
- FM Fonds Masson, Bibliothèque Thiers
- GOUL Goulding Collection, Lincolnshire County Archives
- HARR Harrowby MSS, Sandon Hall
- WO War Office records, Public Record Office

BOOKS AND PERIODICALS

ABRANTÈS, LAURE JUNOT, duchess d', *Histoire des salons de Paris* (Paris, (1837–8)

——, *Mémoires* (Paris, 1905–13)

[ALLONVILLE], *Mémoires tirés des papiers d'un homme d'état* (Paris, 1831–8)

ALOMBERT, PAUL-CLAUDE, and J. COLIN, *La campagne de 1805 en Allemagne* (Paris, 1902–8)

AMBROSIO, ANGELO D', *La campagne de Murat en 1815* (Paris, 1899)

ANGEBERG [ps. for Jakob Leonard Chodzko], *Le Congrès de Vienne et les traités de 1815* (Paris, 1863)

ANGERVO, JUHO MAURI, *How Cold was 1812?*, in *The Times*, Feb. 8, 1961, p. 14, col. 6–7

Annales historiques de la Révolution française, see Dayet

Archeografo Triestino, see Plitek

Archivio storico italiano, see Palmarocchi, Ricciardi

Archivio storico per le province napolitane, see Cortese, Cutolo, Lemmi, Rambaud G.

ARJUZON, CAROLINE D', *Hortense de Beauharnais* (Paris, 1897)

ARNAULT, ANTOINE-VINCENT, *Souvenirs d'un sexagénaire* (Paris, 1833)

ARTAUD DE MONTOR, ALEXIS-FRANÇOIS, *Histoire du pape Pie VII* (Paris, 1837)

AULARD, FRANÇOIS-VICTOR-ALPHONSE, *Paris sous le Consulat* (Paris, 1903–9)

AVRILLON [ps. for Charles-Maxime-Catherinet de Villemarest], *Mémoires* (Paris, 1896)

AYALA, MARIANO D', *Le Vite de Piu Celebri Capitani e Soldati Napoletani* (Naples, 1843)

B., V. C. DE, *La Campagne des Autrichiens contre Murat en 1815* (Brussels, 1821)

BADEN, WILHELM, MARKGRAF VON, *La Guerre de Russie* (Paris, 1912)

BAILLEU, PAUL [ed.], *Preussen und Frankreich von 1795 bis 1807. Diplomatische Correspondenzen* (Leipzig, 1881)

BARANTE, AMABLE-GUILLAUME-PROSPER BRUGIÈRE, BARON DE, *Souvenirs* (Paris, 1890–1901)

BARÈRE, BERTRAND, *Mémoires* (Paris, 1842–4)

BARING, THOMAS, *A Tour through Italy, Sicily, Istria, Carniola, the Tyrol and Austria in 1814* (London, 1817)

BARRAS, PAUL-FRANÇOIS-JEAN-NICOLAS DE, *Memoirs* (London, 1895)

Bathurst, Report on the Manuscripts of Earl (London, 1923)

BAUDUS, MARIE-ELIE-GUILLAUME, *Etudes sur Napoléon* (Paris, 1841)

BAUSSET, LOUIS-FRANÇOIS-JOSEPH DE, *Mémoires anecdotiques sur l'intérieur du palais . . . pour servir à l'histoire de Napoléon* (Paris, 1827–9)

BEAUHARNAIS, EUGÈNE, *Mémoires et correspondance politique et militaire* (Paris, 1860)

BELLAIRE, J. P., *Précis de l'invasion des Etats Romains par l'armée napolitaine, en 1813 et 1814, et de la défense de la citadelle d'Ancône, etc.* (Paris, 1838)

BELLIARD, AUGUSTE, *Mémoires* (Paris, 1842)

BENNIGSEN, LEVIN-AUGUST-GOTTLIEB VON, *Mémoires* (Paris, 1907–8)

BERTHOLDI, GIUSEPPE, *Memoirs of the Secret Societies of the South of Italy* (London, 1821)

BERTIN, GEORGES, *Joseph Bonaparte en Amérique* (Paris, 1893)

BERTRAND, HENRI-GRATIEN, *Cahiers de Sainte-Hélène* (Paris, 1959)

BEUGNOT, JACQUES-CLAUDE, *Mémoires* (Paris, 1889)

BIANCO, GIUSEPPE, *La Sicilia durante l'occupazione Inglese (1806–1815)* (Palermo, 1902)

Bibliothèque Universelle des Sciences, Belles Lettres et Arts, faisant suite à la Bibliothèque Britannique, see Malet

BOIGNE, CHARLOTTE-LOUISE-ELÉONORE-ADÉLAIDE DE, *Memoirs* (London, 1912)

BONAPARTE, JÉRÔME, *Mémoires et correspondance du roi Jérôme et de la reine Catherine* (Paris, 1861–6)

BONAPARTE, JOSEPH, *Lettres d'exil inédites* (Paris, 1912)

———, *Mémoires et correspondance politique et militaire* (Paris, 1854)

Mémoires secrets sur la vie privée, politique et littéraire de Lucien Buonaparte (Paris, 1818)

BONAPARTE, PIERRE-NAPOLÉON, *Souvenirs, traditions et révelations* (Brussels, 1876)

BOULART, JEAN-FRANÇOIS, *Mémoires militaires* (Paris, n.d.)

BOULAY DE LA MEURTHE, ALFRED, *Documents sur la négociation du Concordat* (Paris, 1881–2)

———, *Documents relatifs au duc d'Enghien* (Paris, 1904–13)

BOURGOGNE, ADRIEN-JEAN-BAPTISTE-FRANÇOIS, *Memoirs* (London, 1926)

BOURGOING, JEAN DE, *Le Coeur de Marie-Louise* (Paris, 1938–9)

———, *Le fils de Napoléon* (Paris, 1932)

BOURRIENNE, LOUIS-ANTOINE-FAUVELET DE, *Mémoires* (Paris, 1831)

BRANDT, HEINRICH VON, *Souvenirs d'un officer polonais* (Paris, 1877)

BROTONNE, LÉONCE DE, *Les Bonapartes et leurs alliances* (Paris, 1901)

———, *Dernières lettres inédites de Napoléon 1 er* (Paris, 1903)

———, *Lettres inédites de Napoléon 1 er* (Paris, 1898)

BROUWET, EMILE, *Napoléon et son temps. Catalogue de lettres autographes, de documents et de souvenirs napoléoniennes... Troisième partie* (Sold by Sotheby's, Dec. 8, 1936)

Bulletins quotidiens adressés par Fouché à l'Empereur. La police secrète du Premier Empire [ed. E. d'Hauterive] (Paris, 1908–63)

BUNBURY, HENRY EDWARD, *Narratives of some passages in the great war with France from 1799 to 1810* (London, 1927)

BYRON, GEORGE GORDON NOEL, 6th Baron, *Letters and Journals* (London, 1899)

———, *Works: Poetry* (London, 1900)

CAMPAN, JEANNE-LOUISE-HENRIETTE GENET, *Correspondance inédite . . . avec la Reine Hortense* (Paris, 1835)

——, *Journal anecdotique* (Paris, 1825)

CANTU, CESARE, *Della independenza italiana* (Turin, 1875)

CASTELLANE, ESPRIT-VICTOR-ELISABETH-BONIFACE, COMTE DE, *Journal* (Paris, 1895–7)

CASTLEREAGH, ROBERT STEWART, VISCOUNT [2nd Marquess of Londonderry], *Correspondence, despatches and other papers* (London, 1848–53)

CATHERINE, QUEEN OF WESTPHALIA, *Correspondance inédite* (Paris, 1893)

[CAVAIGNAC, MARIE-JULIE], *Les mémoires d'une inconnue* (Paris, 1894)

CHANTEMESSE, ROBERT, *Le roman inconnu de la duchesse d'Abrantès* (Paris, 1927)

CHARLES-ROUX, FRANÇOIS, *Rome, asile des Bonapartes* (Paris, 1952)

CHASTENAY, LOUISE-MARIE-VICTORINE, COMTESSE DE, *Mémoires* (Paris, 1896)

CHATEAUBRIAND, FRANÇOIS-AUGUSTE-RENÉ, VICOMTE DE, *Mémoires d'outre-tombe* [ed. Biré and Moreau] (Paris, 1947)

CHAVANON, JULES, and SAINT-YVES, G., *Joachim Murat* (Paris, 1905)

CHÉNIER, LOUIS-JOSEPH-GABRIEL DE, *Histoire de la vie politique, militaire et administrative du Maréchal Davout* (Paris, 1866)

CHLAPOWSKI, DEZYDERY, *Als Ordonnanzoffizier Napoleons in den Kriegen 1806–1813* (Berlin, 1910)

CHUQUET, ARTHUR, *Etudes d'histoire* (Paris, n.d.)

——, *La jeunesse de Napoléon* (Paris, 1879–99)

CLARETIE, JULES, *L'Empire, les Bonaparte et la Cour* (Paris, 1871)

COCKBURN, SIR GEORGE, *A voyage to Cadiz and Gibraltar, up the Mediterranean to Sicily and Malta in 1810 and 11* (London, 1815)

COIGNET, JEAN-ROCH, *Narrative* (London, 1897)

COLBERT, NAPOLÉON-JOSEPH, MARQUIS DE CHABANAIS, *Traditions et souvenirs, ou mémoires touchant le temps et la vie due Général Auguste Colbert* (Paris, 1863–74)

COLET, LOUISE, *L'Italie des Italiens* (Paris, 1862)

COLLETTA, PIETRO, *Opere inedite o rare* (Napoli, 1861–2)

——, *History of the Kingdom of Naples, 1734–1825* (London, 1858)

COMBE, MICHEL, *Mémoires sur les campagnes de Russie, etc.* (Paris, 1896)

CONEGLIANO, CLAUDE-ADRIEN-GUSTAVE DUCHESNE DE GILLE-VOISIN, DUC DE, *Le Maréchal Moncey* (Paris, 1902)

CONSTANT, BENJAMIN, *Journal intime* [ed. J. Mistler] (Monacco, 1946)

——, *Lettres à Mme Récamier* [ed. A. Lenormand] (Paris, 1882)

Copies des lettres originales et dépêches des généraux, ministres, grands officers d'Etat, écrites de Paris à Buonaparte pendant son séjour à Dresde, ainsi qu'une correspondance de divers personnages de cette famille entre eux; interceptées par les avant-postes des alliés dans le Nord de l'Allemagne (Paris, 1814)

Le Correspondant, see Melegari

CORSINI, ANDREA, *I Bonaparte a Firenze* (Florence, 1961)

CORTESE, NINO, *L'esercito napoletano nelle guerre napoleoniche* in *Archivio storico per le province napolitane,* 1926, anno LI (o.s.), XII (n.s.), 164–339

COSTA DE BEAUREGARD, CHARLES-ALBERT, MARQUIS, *Un homme d'autrefois* (Paris, 1877)

COVONI, PIERFILIPPO, *Il Regno d'Etruria* (Florence, 1894)

[CRESCERE, GIANGIACOMO, FREIHERR VON] *Memorie segrete del Gabinetto di Napoli e di Sicilia per servire all vera Storia di quel Paese dal 1790 fino al 1816 trovate nel Portafoglio d'un Viaggiatore Americano,* in *Sitzungsberichte der philosophisch-historishen Classe der Kaiserlichen Akademia der Wissenschaft,* Band 122 (Vienne, 1892)

CROUZET, FRANÇOIS, *L'économie britannique et le blocus continentale* (Paris, 1958)

GUGNAC, GASPAR-JEAN-MARIE-RENÉ, *Campagne de l'armée de réserve en 1800* (Paris, 1900–1)

CUSSY, BARON FERDINAND DE, *Souvenirs du chevalier de Cussy* (Paris, 1909).

CUTOLO, ALESSANDRO, *Il regno di Napoli ai tempi di Gioacchino Murat* in *Archivio storico per le province napolitane,* 1936, anno LXI (o.s.), XXII (n.s.), 380–423

CZERNICHEFF, ALEKSANDR IVANOVICH, PRINCE, *Correspondance* (St Petersburg, 1877). (Vol. XXI of *Imperatorskoe Russkoe Istoreschkoe Obschestvo Sbornik*)

DAMAS, COMTE ROGER DE, *Mémoires* (Paris, 1914)

DAVIES, CATHERINE, *Eleven Years' Residence in the Family of Murat, King of Naples* (London, 1841)

DAYET, MAURICE, *Caroline Murat et les Carbonari* in *Annales historiques de la Révolution française,* 1957, XXIX, 289–95

DEDEM, BARON ANTOINE-BAUDOIN-GISBERT DE, *Un général hollandais sous le Premier Empire. Mémoires du général baron de Dedem de Gelder, 1774–1825* (Paris, 1900)

DERRÉCAGAIX, VICTOR-BERNARD, *Le lieutenant-général comte Belliard, chef d'Etat-Major de Murat* (Paris, 1908)

——, *Le maréchal Berthier, prince de Wagram et de Neufchâtel* (Paris, 1904–5)

DESMAREST, PIERRE-MARIE, *Quinze ans de haute police sous le consulat et l'empire* (Paris, 1900)

DESPATYS, PIERRE-CAMILLE-AUGUSTIN-OMER, BARON, *Un ami de Fouché, d'après les mémoires de Gaillard* (Paris, 1911)

DESVERNOIS, BARON NICOLAS-PHILIBERT, *Mémoires* (Paris, 1898)

DIDIER, EUGÈNE, *The Life and Letters of Madame Bonaparte* (London, 1879)

DITO, ORESTE, *La campagna murattiana della independenza d'Italia; con un' appendice sulla morte del Murat a Pizzo* (Rome, 1911)

DU CASSE, BARON PIERRE-EMMANUEL-ALBERT, *Les rois, frères de Napoléon* (Paris, 1883)

DUCREST, GEORGETTE, *Mémoires sur l'impératrice Joséphine* (Paris, 1828–9)

DUFOURCQ, ALBERT, *Murat et la question de l'unité italienne en 1815* in *Mélanges d'archéologie et d'histoire*, 1898, année XVIII, 207–70; 315–61

DUHAMEL, JEAN, *A Trieste sur les pas des Français* (Trieste, 1950)

DUMAS, MATTHIEU, COMTE, *Souvenirs* (Paris, 1839)

DUNAN, MARCEL, *Napoléon et l'Allemagne* (Paris, 1942)

DUPUY, VICTOR, *Souvenirs militaires* (Paris, 1892)

[DURET DE TAVEL, LT.-COL.], *Calabria during a military residence of three years, etc.* (London, 1832)

DURAND, SOPHIE COHONSET, *Napoleon and Marie-Louise* (London, 1886)

DUVEYRIER, HONORÉ, BARON, *Anecdotes historiques* (Paris, 1907)
English Historical Review, see Johnston

ERNOUF, BARON ALFRED-AUGUSTE, *Maret, duc de Bassano* (Paris, 1878)

ESPITALIER, ALBERT, *Napoléon et le roi Murat, 1808–1815* (Paris, 1910)

FABRY, GABRIEL, *Campagne de Russie* (Paris, 1900–3)

FANTIN DES ODOARDS, LOUIS-FLORIMOND, *Journal* (Paris, 1895)

FAVRE, LOUIS, *Le Luxembourg, 1300–1882* (Paris, 1882)

FEZENSAC, RAYMOND-EMERY-PHILIPPE-JOSEPH, DUC DE, *Journal de la Campagne de Russie en 1812* (Paris, 1850)

FIRMIN-DIDOT, GEORGES, *Royauté ou Empire. La France en 1814 d'après sel rapports inédits du comte Anglès* (Paris, 1898)

FLEURIOT DE LANGLE, PAUL, *Alexandrine-Lucien Bonaparte* (Paris, 1939)

——, *La Paolina, Soeur de Napoléon* (Paris, 1946)

FLEURY DE CHABOULON, PIERRE-ALEXANDRE-EDOUARD, BARON, *Mémoires ... avec annotations manuscrites de Napoléon I er* (Paris, 1901)

Fortescue, Report on the manuscripts of John Bevill (London, 1892–1927)

FORTUNATO, GIUSTINO, *Le ultime ore di Gioacchino Murat* in *Nuova Antologia di Lettere, Scienze ed Arti*, 1925, CCXLI, 8–16

FOUCHÉ, JOSEPH, *Mémoires* [ed. L. Madelin] (Paris, 1945)

FOURNIER, AUGUST, *Studien und Skizzen*. Zweite Reihe (Vienna, 1908)

FOX, HENRY EDWARD, BARON [Lord Holland], *Journal* (London, 1923)

FOY, MAXIMILIEN-SEBASTIEN, *Histoire de la guerre de la Péninsule* (Paris, 1827)

FRANCESCHETTI, DOMINIQUE-CÉSAR, *Mémoires sur les évènements qui ont précédés la mort de Joachim Ier ... suivi de la correspondance privée de ce général avec la reine, Comtesse de Lipano* (sic) (Paris, 1826)

FRANÇOIS, CHARLES, *Journal. From Valmy to Waterloo* (London, 1906)

GAFFAREL, PAUL, *Les Bonaparte à Marseille* in *La Révolution française*, 1912, LXII, 255–76, 289–314

GARNIER, JEAN-PAUL, *Murat, roi de Naples* (Paris, 1959)

GARROS, LOUIS, *Quel Roman que ma Vie! Itinéraire de Napoléon Bonaparte (1769–1821)* (Paris, 1947)

GAUTHEROT, GUSTAVE, *Un gentilhomme de grand chemin: le maréchal de Bourmont, 1773–1846* (Paris, 1926)

GAUTIER, PAUL, *Mme de Staël et Napoléon* (Paris, 1903)

GAYOT, ANDRÉ, *Une ancienne Muscadin, Fortunée Hamelin* (Paris, 1911)

GENTZ, FRIEDRICH, *Oesterreichs Theilnahme an den Befreiungskriegen* (Vienna, 1887)

GIGOUX, JEAN, *Causeries sur les artistes de mon temps* (Paris, 1885)

GIRARDIN, LOUIS-STANISLAS-CECILE-XAVIER, comte de, *Journal et Souvenirs, Discours et Opinions* (Paris, 1828)

GISQUET, HENRI-JOSEPH, *Mémoirs* (Paris, 1840)

GONNEVILLE, AYMER-OLIVIER LE HARIVEL DE, *Souvenirs militaires* (Paris, 1876)

GOURGAUD, BARON GASPARD, *Journal* (Paris, 1899)

——, *Napoléon et la Grand Armée en Russie* (Paris, 1825)

GRANDMAISON, GEOFFROY, *L'Espagne et Napoléon, 1804–1809* (Paris, 1908)

GRANVILLE, GRANVILLE LEVESON-GOWER, EARL, *Private Correspondence, 1781–1821* (London, 1916)

GRASSET, ALPHONSE-LOUIS, *Guerre d'Espagne* (Paris, 1914–32)

GREATHEAD, BERTIE, *An Englishman in Paris, 1803* (London, 1953)

GRIOIS, LUBIN, *Mémoires* (Paris, 1909)

GUILLON, ????, *Les complots militaires sous le Consulat et l'Empire* (Paris, 1894)

——, *Les complots militaires sous la Restauration* (Paris, 1895)

HANDELSMAN, MARCELI, *Napoléon et la Pologne* (Paris, 1909)

HANNA, ALFRED JACKSON, *A Prince in their Midst* (Norman, Oklahoma, 1946)

HAUTPOUL, ALPHONSE, *Mémoires* (Paris, 1906)

HELFERT, JOSEPH ALEXANDER, FREIHERR VON, *Königin Karolina von Neapel und Sicilien im Kampfe gegen die französiche Weltherrschaft, 1790–1814* (Vienna, 1878)

——, *Joachim Murat, seine letzten Kämpfe und sein Ende* (Vienna, 1878)

——, *Maria Louise, Erzherzogin von Oesterreich, Kaiserin der Franzosen* (Vienna, 1873)

HENNET, LÉON, and E. MARTIN, *Lettres interceptées par les Russes durant la campagne de 1812* (Paris, 1913)

HERRIOT, EDOUARD, *Mme Récamier et ses amis* (Paris, 1904)

HOBHOUSE, JOHN CAM [Lord Broughton], *Recollections of a Long Life* (London, 1909–11)

HOGENDORP, DIRK THIERRY VAN, *Mémoires* (The Hague, 1887)

HOLLAND, SIR HENRY, *Recollections of Past Life* (London, 1872)

HORTENSE [DE BEAUHARNAIS], QUEEN OF HOLLAND, *Mémoires* (Paris, 1927)

——, *La reine Hortense en Italie, en France et en Angleterre pendant l'année 1831* (Paris, 1834)

Imperatorskoe Russkoe Istoreschkoe Obschestvo Sbornik, see Czernicheff, Polovtzov

Instructions et Dépêches des Résidents de France à Varsovie [ed. M. Handelsman] (Cracow, 1914)

IUNG, THÉODORE, *Lucien Bonaparte et ses Mémoires* (Paris, 1882)

JACKSON, SIR GEORGE, *Bath archives* (London, 1873)

JAUCOURT, ARNAIL-FRANÇOIS, COMTE DE, *Correspondance avec le Prince de Talleyrand pendant le Congrès de Vienne* (Paris, 1905)

JOHNSTON, ROBERT MATTESON, *Lord William Bentinck and Murat* (a review of Weil's *Prince Eugène*) in *English Historical Review*, 1904, XIX, 263–80

——, *The Napoleonic Empire in Southern Italy and the Rise of the Secret Societies* (London, 1904)

KIELMANNSEGGE, AUGUSTE CHARLOTTE, GRÄFIN VON, *Memoiren . . . Über Napoleon I* (Dresden, 1927)

L. D.***, *Journal historique sur la campagne du Prince Eugène en Italie, pendant les années 1813 et 1814* (Paris, 1817)

L., ERNESTINE VON, *König Jérôme und seine Familie* (Leipzig, 1870)

LABAUME, EUGÈNE, *Relation circonstancié de la Campagne de Russie en 1812* (Paris, 1815)

LA FOREST, ANTOINE-RENÉ-CHARLES-MATHURIN, COMTE DE, *Correspondance* (Paris, 1905–13)

LAMARQUE, MAXIMILIEN, *Mémoires et souvenirs* (Paris, 1835)

LAMARTINE, ALPHONSE-MARIE-LOUIS PRAT DE, *Mémoires inédites* (Paris, 1870)

LANGERON, LOUIS-ALEXANDRE-ANDRAULT, COMTE DE, *Mémoires* (Paris, 1902)

LANSDOWNE, HENRY WILLIAM EDMUND PETTY-FITZMAURICE, 6th Marquis of, *The First Napoleon* (London, 1925)

LAPLACE, MARIE-ANNE-CHARLOTTE DE, *Lettres . . . à Elisa Napoléon* (Paris, 1897)

LARREY, DOMINIQUE-JEAN, *Mémoires de chirurgie militaire et campagnes* (Paris, 1812–17)

LARREY, FÉLIX-HIPPOLYTE, BARON, *Madame Mère* (Paris, 1892)

LAS CASES, MARIE-JOSEPH-EMMANUEL-AUGUSTE-DIEUDONNÉ DE, *Le Mémorial de Sainte-Hélène* [ed. M. Dunan] (Paris, 1951)

[LAUTARD, LAURENT], *Esquisses historiques: Marseille depuis 1789 1789 jusqu'en 1815, par un vieux Marseillais* (Marseille, 1844)

LAVALETTE, ANTOINE-MARIE CHAMANS, COMTE DE, *Mémoires* (Paris, 1831)

LECHAT, JEAN-CLAUDE, *Journal* in *Nouvelle Revue Retrospective*, 1901, XIV

LE BRETHON, PAUL, *Le voyage de Caroline Murat à Munich en 1805* in *Revue de France*, 1921, III, 601–15

LECESTRE, ALEXANDRE-LÉON, *Lettres inédites de Napoléon Ier* (Paris, 1897)

LEJEUNE, LOUIS-FRANÇOIS, BARON, *Mémoires* (Paris, 1895)

LEMMI, FRANCESCO, *La fine da Gioacchino Murat* in *Archiviox storico Italiano*, 1900, Quinte Serie, XXVI, 250–294

——, *Gioacchino e le aspirazione unitarie nel 1815* in *Archivio storico per le province napoletane*, 1901, XXXVI, 169–222

LEROUX-CESBRON, CHARLES, *Le château de Neuilly* (Paris, 1923)

LEVAILLANT, MAURICE, *Deux livres des Mémoires d'Outre-Tombe* (Paris, 1936)

LOEWENSTERN, WOLDEMAR VON, *Denkuürdigkeiten eines Livländers* (Leipzig, 1858)

LORD, WALTER FREWEN, *The Story of Murat and Bentinck* in *The Nineteenth Century*, 1898, XLIV, 626–40

LUMBROSO, ALBERTO, *Correspondance de Joachim Murat* (Turin, 1899)

——, *Miscellanea napoleonica* (Rome, 1895–9)

——, *Il re Gioacchino Murat e la sua Corte* in *Nuova Antologia*, 1898, CLX, 446–75

MACDONALD, ETIENNE-JACQUES-JOSEPH-ALEXANDRE [duc de Tarante], *Souvenirs* (Paris, 1892).

MACERONI, FRANCIS, *Memories of the life and adventures of Colonel Maceroni* (London, 1838)

MACIRONE, FRANCIS, *Interesting facts relating to the fall and death of Joachim Murat, etc.* (London, 1817)

MACKESY, PIERS GERALD, *The war in the Mediterranean, 1803–1810* (London, 1957)

MALET, G., *Lettres sur Naples* in *La Bibliothèque Universelle*, 1816, II, 62–85

MARBOT, JEAN-BAPTISTE-ANTOINE-MARCELIN, BARON DE, *Mémoires* (Paris, 1891)

MARCHAND, LOUIS-JOSEPH-NARCINE, *Mémoires* (Paris, 1952–5)

MARIE-LOUISE, EMPRESS, *Correspondance, 1799–1847. Lettres intimes . . . à la comtesse de Colloredo et à Mlle de Poutet* (Vienna, 1887)

MARMONT, AUGUSTE-FRÉDERIC-LOUIS VIESSE DE [duc de Ragusé]

MARMONT, AUGUSTE-FRÉDERIC-LOUIS VIESSE DE [duc de Raguse], *Mémoires* (Paris, 1857)

MARMOTTAN, PAUL, *Murat à l'Elysée* (Paris, 1919)

MARQUISET, ALFRED, *Napoléon sténographié au Conseil d'Etat, 1804–1805* (Paris, 1913)

MARTEL, RENÉ, *Napoléon en Lithuanie* in *Revue de Paris*, 1932, XXXIX (4), 897–912

MARY CAROLINE, QUEEN OF NAPLES, *Correspondance inédite . . . avec le marquis de Gallo* (Paris, 1911)

MASSON, FRÉDERIC, *Jadis* (Paris, 1905)

——, *Napoléon dans sa jeunesse, 1769–93* (Paris, 1907)

——, *Napoléon et sa famille* (Paris, 1897–1918)

——, *Revue d'Ombres* (Paris, 1921)

MASUYER, VALÉRIE, *Mémoires, lettres et papiers* (Paris, 1937)

MAXWELL, ARCHIBALD MONTGOMERY, *My Adventures* (London, 1845)

MAYNE, JOHN, *Journal during a tour on the Continent . . . 1814* (London, 1909)

MAZOIS, FRANÇOIS, *Les ruines de Pompeii* (Paris, 1812–38)

Mélanges d'archéologie et d'histoire, see Dufourcq

MELEGARI, D. ????, *Une reine en exil* in *Le Correspondant,* 1898

Mémoires de tous: collection de souvenirs contemporains (Paris, 1834–7)

MENEVAL, CLAUDE-FRANÇOIS, BARON DE, *Mémoires pour servir à l'histoire de Napoléon Ier* (Paris, 1894)

——, *Napoléon et Marie-Louise* (Brussels, 1843)

MENIÈRE, PROSPER, *Journal* (Paris, 1903)

MÉRY, FRANÇOIS-JOSEPH-PIERRE-ANDRÉ, *Les nuits italiennes* (Paris, 1853)

MIOT, JACQUES-FRANÇOIS, *Mémoires pour servir à l'histoire des expéditions d'Egypt et de Syrie* (Paris, 1814)

MONTBEL, GUILLAUME-ISIDORE, COMTE DE, *Souvenirs* (Paris, 1913)

MONTESQUIOU-FEZENSAC, ANATOLE DE, *Souvenirs de la campagne de Russie* in *Revue de Paris,* 1948, LV, 34–63

MONTHOLON, ALBINE-HÉLÈNE DE VASSAL, COMTESSE DE, *Souvenir de Sainte-Hélène* (Paris, 1901)

MORVAN, JEAN, *Le soldat impérial* (Paris, 1904)

MURAT, JOACHIM, KING OF NAPLES, *Lettere alla figlia Laetitzia* (Florence, 1893)

——, *Lettres et documents* [ed. Le Brethon] (Paris, 1908–14)

MURAT, COMTE JOACHIM, *Murat Lieutenant de l'Empereur en Espagne, 1808* (Paris, 1897)

MURAT-RASPONI, LOUISE, *A la cour du roi Murat* and *La fin du royaume de Murat* in *Revue de Paris,* 1928, XXXV, 481–511, 826–35

NABONNE, BERNARD, *Pauline Bonaparte* (Paris, 1948)

NADAILLAC-PÉRUSSE, ROSALIE MARQUISE DE [duchesse d'Escars], *Mémoires* (Paris, 1912)

NAPOLEON I, *Correspondance* (Paris, 1858–69)

——, *Lettres inédites à Marie-Louise* [ed, L. Madelin] (Paris, 1935)

NASICA, T., *Mémoires sur l'enfance et la jeunesse de Napoléon* (Paris, 1852)

NICOLA, CARLO, *Diario napoletano, 1798–1825* (Naples, 1906)

NICOLAS MIKHAÏLOVITCH, GRAND DUKE, *Le comte Paul Stroganov* (Paris, 1905)

Nineteenth Century, The, see Lord

NOAILLES, EMMANUEL-HENRI, MARQUIS DE, *Le comte Molé* (Paris, 1922–30)

NODIER, CHARLES, *Histoire des sociétés secrètes de l'armée et des conspirations militaires, etc.* (London, 1815)

NOEL, JEAN-NICOLAS-AUGUSTE, *Souvenirs militaires* (Paris, 1895)

NORVINS, JACQUES MARQUET, BARON DE MONTBRETON DE, *Souvenirs* (Paris, 1896–7)

——, Portefeuille de 1813 (Paris, 1825)

Nouvelle revue retrospective, see Lechat

Nuova Antologia di Lettere, Scienze ed Arti, see Fortunato, Lumbroso

ODELEBEN, ERNST OTTO INNOCENZ, BARON VON, *A Circumstantial Narrative of the Campaign in Saxony in the Year 1813* (London, 1820)

O'MEARA, BARRY EDWARD, *Napoleon in Exile* (London, 1822)

PALMAROCCHI, ROBERTO, *Le riforme de Gioacchino Murat nel primo anno di regno* in *Archivio storico italiano*, 1914, LXXII, 18–60

PARQUIN, DENIS-CHARLES, *Napoleon's Army* (London, 1969)

PASQUIER, ETIENNE-DENIS, DUC, *Histoire de mon temps* (Paris, 1894)

PELISSIER, LEON-GABRIEL-JEAN-BAPTISTE, *Le Portefeuille de la comtesse d'Albany* (Paris, 1902)

PELLEPORT, PIERRE, VICOMTE DE, *Souvenirs militaires et intimes . . . de 1793 à 1853* (Paris, 1857)

PELLET, MARCELLIN, *Napoléon à l'Ile d'Elbe* (Paris, 1888)

PERCY, PIERRE-FRANÇOIS, BARON, *Journal* (Paris, 1904)

PICHOT, JOSEPH-JEAN-MARIE-CHARLES-AMÉDÉE, *Napoléon à l'Ile d'Elbe* (Paris, 1873)

PIÉTRI, FRANÇOIS, *Lucien Bonaparte* (Paris, 1939)

PIGNATELLI-STRONGOLI, FRANCESCO, *Memorie intorno alla storica del del regno di Napoli dall'anno 1805 al 1815* (Naples, 1820)

PINGAUD, LÉONCE, *Un agent secret sous la Révolution et l'Empire: le comte d'Antraigues* (Paris, 1893)

PLANAT DE LA FAYE, NICOLAS-LOUIS, *Souvenirs* (Paris, 1895)

PLITEK, V., *I Napoleonidi a Trieste: Caroline Murat, Contessa di Lipona, 6 giugno-15 agosto, 1815* in *Archeografo Triestino*, 1924, Terza Serie, XIII

POLOVTZOV, ALEKSANDR ALEKSANDROVICH [ed.], *Correspondance diplomatique* (St Petersburg, 1901). (Vol. CXII of *Imperatorskoe Russkoe Istoricheskoe Obschestvo Sbornik*)

PONS (DE L'HÉRAULT), ANDRÉ, *Souvenirs et anecdotes de l'Ile de'Elbe* (Paris, 1897)

POTOCKA, COUNTESS ANNA TYSZKIEWICZ, *Mémoires* (Paris, 1897)

POUGET, BARON FRANÇOIS-RENÉ CAILLOUX (*dit*), *Souvenirs de guerre* (Paris, 1895)

POUMIÉS DE LA SIBOUTIE, *Recollections of a Parisian* (London, 1911)

POZZO DI BORGO, COMTE CHARLES-ANDRÉ, *Correspondance diplomatique* (Paris, 1890)

PRUSSE, LOUISE DE [PRINCESSE ANTOINE RADZIWILL], *Quarante-cinq années de ma vie* (1770 à 1815) (Paris, 1811)

RABEL, ANDRÉ, *Le maréchal Bessières, duc d'Istric* (Paris, 1903)

RAMBAUD, JACQUES, *Il tentativo di Murat contro la Sicilia nel 1810* in *Archivio storico per le province napoletane*, 1911, XXXVI, 434–50, 695–709

RAPP, COMTE JEAN, *Mémoires* (Paris, 1895)

REBOUL, FRÉDERIC, *Campagne de 1813* (Paris, 1910–12)

RÉCAMIER, JEANNE-FRANÇOISE-JULIE-ADÉLAÏDE BERNARD, *Souvenirs et Correspondance* [ed. Lenormant] (Paris, 1859)

REINHARD, MARCEL, *Avec Bonaparte en Italie* (*lettres inédutes de son aide de camp, Joseph Sulkowski*) (Paris, 1946)

REMACLE, COMTE L., *Bonaparte et les Bourbons. Relations secrètes des agents de Louis XVIII à Paris sous le Consulat* (Paris, 1899)

RÉMUSAT, CLAIRE-ELISABETH-JEANE DE, *Mémores, 1802–8* (Paris, 1880)

La Révolution française, see Gaffarel

Revue de France, see Le Brethon

Revue de Paris, see Murat-Rasponi, Montesquiou-Fezensac, Martel

Revue des Deux Mondes, see Vandal

Revue historique, see Weill, Wertheimer

Revue Napoléonienne

RICARD, JOSEPH-BARTHÉLEMY-HONORÉ-LOUIS-AMABLE DE, *Autour des Bonapartes* (Paris, 1891)

RICCIARDI, GIUSEPPE NAPOLEONE, *Relazione autentica del fazione operate in Calabria nel 1815 da re Gioacchino Murat* in *Archivio storico italiano*, 1876, Terza Serie, XXIV, 70–89

RIVIÈRE, CHARLES-FRANÇOIS, DUC DE, *Mémoires posthumes* (Paris, 1829)

ROEDERER, COMTE PIERRE-LOUIS, *Oeuvres* (Paris, 1853–9)

ROGERS, SAMUEL, *Italian Journal* (London, 1956)

——, *Recollections of the Table Talk of* (London, 1952)

ROOS, HEINRICH U. L. VON, *Ein Jahr aus meinem Leben* (St Petersburg, 1832)

ROSSELLI, JOHN, *Lord William Bentinck and the British occupation of Sicily, 1811–1814* (Cambridge, 1956)

ROUSTAM, RAZA, *Souvenirs* (Paris, 1911)

RUDÉ, GEORGE FREDERICK ELLIOTT, *The Crowd in the French Revolution* (Oxford, 1959)

S.J. ***, *Dernière campagne de l'armée franco-italienne sous les ordres d'Eugène Beauharnais en 1813 et 1814; ... la campagne des Autrichiens contre Murat, etc.* (Paris, 1817)

SAINT-CHAMANS, ALFRED-ARNAUD-ROBERT, COMTE DE, *Mémoires* (Paris, 1896)

[SAINT-ELME, IDA], *Mémoires d'une contemporaine* (Paris, 1827–9)

SAINT-HILAIRE, EMILE-MARCO DE, *Souvenirs intimes du temps de l'Empire* (Paris, 1838–9)

SAUNDERS, LLOYD CHARLES, *The Holland House Circle* (London, 1908)

SASSENAY, HENRI-ETIENNE-JOSEPH FERNAND, MARQUIS BERNARD DE, *Les derniers mois de Murat. Le guet-apens du Pizzo* (Paris, 1896)

SAVARY, ANNE-JEANNE-MARIE-RENÉ [duc de Rovigo], *Mémoires* (Paris, 1828)

SCHLITTER, HANS *Kaiser Franz I und die Napoleoniden* (Vienna, 1888)

SCHLOSSBERGER, AUGUST VON [ed.], *Briefwechsel der Königin Katharina und des Königs Jérôme von Westphalen, sowie des Kaisers Napoleon I, mit dem König Friedrich von Würtemberg* (Stuttgart, 1886–7)

SCHMIDT, CHARLES, *Le Grand-duché de Berg (1806–1813)* (Paris, 1905)

SCHOELL, MAXIMILIEN-SAMPSON-FRIEDRICH, *Recueil de pièces officielles destinées à détromper les Français etc . . .* (Paris, 1814–16)

SCHUERMANS, ALBERT, *Itinéraire général de Napoléon Ier* (Paris, 1911)

SÉGUR, PHILIPPE-PAUL, COMTE DE, *Histoire de Napoléon et de la Grande Armée pendant l'année 1812* (Paris, 1825)

SERVIÈRES, JEAN, *Les réfugiés corses à Marseille pendant la Révolution de 1793–1797* in *Société des Sciences Historiques et Naturelles de la Corse*, Bulletin, 441–4, 1922

SERUZIER, BARON THÉODORE-JEAN-JOSEPH, *Mémoires militaires* (Paris, 1823)

Sitzungsberichte der Kaiserlichen Akademie der Wissenschaften, see Cresceri

Société des Sciences Historiques et Naturelles de la Corse, see Servières

STENDHAL [MARIE-HENRI BEYLE], *Correspondance* [ed. Martineau and Litto] (Paris, 1962–8)

SUCKOW, ——, *D'Iéna à Moscou, fragments de ma vie* (Paris, 1901)

TALLEYRAND-PÉRIGORD, CHARLES-MAURICE DE [prince de Bénévente], *Correspondance inédite* (Paris, 1881)

——, *Mémoires* (Paris, 1891–2)

TATISCHEFF, SERGE, *Alexandre Ier et Napoleon, d'après leur correspondance inédite, 1801–12* (Paris, 1891)

THIÉBAULT, PAUL-CHARLES-FRANÇOIS-ADRIEN-HENRI-DIEUDONNE BARON, *Mémoires* (Paris, 1895–6)

THIERS, LOUIS-ADOLPHE, *Histoire du Consulat et de l'Empire* (Paris, 1845)

THOUMAS, CHARLES, *Les grands cavaliers du premier Empire* (Paris, 1890)

The Times, see Angervo

TRAVALI, GIUSEPPE, *Documenti su lo sbarca, la cattura e la morte di re Gioacchino Murat al Pizzo* (Palermo, 1895)

TURQUAN, JOSEPH, *La générale Junot, duchesse d'Abrantxès* (Paris, 1901)

VALENTE, ANGELA, *Gioacchino Murat e l'Italia meridionale* (Turin, 1941)

VANDAL, ALBERT, *L'avènement de Bonaparte* (Paris, 1903)

——, *Napoléon et Alexandre I* (Paris, 1891)

——, *Le Roi et la Reine de Naples* in *Revue des Deux Mondes*, 1910, LV, 481–514, 757–88; LVI, 42–75

VANEL, JEAN, *Les Origines de la Famille Murat* (Rabastens, 1971)

VAUBLANC, COMTE VINCENT-MARIE VIENNOT DE, *Mémoires* (Paris, 1857)

VIEL CASTEL, HORACE DE, *Mémoires* (Paris, 1883)

VIGÉE LE BRUN, MARIE-LOUISE-ELISABETH, *Souvenirs* (Paris, 1869)

VIGNOLLE, COMTE MARTIN DE, *Précis historique des opérations militaires de l'armée d'Italie en 1813 et 1814* (Paris, 1817)

VILLÈLE, JOSEPH, COMTE DE, *Mémoires et correspondance* (Paris, 1889–90)

VILLEMAIN, ABEL-FRANÇOIS, *Souvenirs contemporains d'histoire et de littérature* (Paris, 1854)

WEBSTER, SIR CHARLES KINGSLEY, *British diplomacy, 1813–1815* (London, 1921)

——, *The Congress of Vienna* (London, 1963)

WEIL, MAURICE-HENRI, *Les Bonapartes Jérôme et Caroline à Florence* in *Revue des Etudes Napoléoniennes*, 1919, VIII (2)

——, *Les Dessous du Congrès de Vienne* (Paris, 1917)

——, *Joachim Murat, roi de Naples; la dernière année du règne* (Paris, 1909–10)

——, *Le Prince Eugène et Murat, 1813–1814* (Paris, 1902–3)

WEILL, GEORGES, *Les lettres d'Achille Murat* in *Revue historique*, 1906, XCII, 71–90

WELLINGTON, ARTHUR WELLESLEY, DUKE OF, *Dispatches* [ed. Gurwood] (London, 1844–7)

——, *Supplementary despatches* [ed. 2nd Duke of Wellington] (London, 1858–72)

WELSCHINGER, HENRI, *Le duc d'Enghien* (Paris, 1913)

WERTHEIMER, EDUARD, *Un projet de divorce entre Louis Bonaparte et la reine Hortense* in *Revue Historique*, 1896, LXI, 62–7.

——, *Die Verbannten des Ersten Kaiserreichs* (Leipzig, 1897)

WILSON, SIR ROBERT THOMAS, *Narrative of events during the invasion of Russia by Napoleon Bonaparte and the Retreat of the French Army* (London, 1860)

——, *Private diary of travels, personal services and public events . . . in the campaigns of 1812, 1813, 1814, etc.* (London, 1861)

ZIVY, HENRY, *Le 13 vendémiaire an IV* (Paris, 1898)

ZUCCHI, CARLO, *Memorie* (Milan, 1861)

Index